Echoes from a Distant Frontier

Women's Diaries and Letters of the South
Carol Bleser, Series Editor

A Woman Doctor's Civil War: Esther Hill Hawks' Diary
Edited by Gerald Schwartz

A Rebel Came Home: The Diary and Letters of Floride Clemson, 1863–1866
Edited by Ernest McPherson Lander, Jr., and Charles M. McGee, Jr.

The Shattered Dream: The Day Book of Margaret Sloan, 1900–1902
Edited by Harold Woodell

The Letters of a Victorian Madwoman
Edited by John S. Hughes

A Confederate Nurse: The Diary of Ada W. Bacot, 1860–1863
Edited by Jean V. Berlin

A Plantation Mistress on the Eve of the Civil War:
The Diary of Keziah Goodwyn Hopkins Brevard, 1860–1861
Edited by John Hammond Moore

Lucy Breckinridge of Grove Hill: The Journal of a Virginia Girl, 1862–1864
Edited by Mary D. Robertson

George Washington's Beautiful Nelly:
The Letters of Eleanor Parke Curtis Lewis to Elizabeth Bordley Gibson, 1794–1851
Edited by Patricia Brady

A Confederate Lady Comes of Age:
The Journal of Pauline DeCaradeuc Heyward, 1863–1888
Edited by Mary D. Robertson

A Northern Woman in the Plantation South:
Letters of Tryphena Blanche Holder Fox, 1856–1876
Edited by Wilma King

Best Companions: Letters of Eliza Middleton Fisher and Her Mother,
Mary Hering Middleton, from Charleston, Philadelphia, and Newport, 1839–1846
Edited by Eliza Cope Harrison

Stateside Soldier: Life in the Women's Army Corps, 1944–1945
Aileen Kilgore Henderson

From the Pen of a She-Rebel: The Civil War Diary of Emilie Riley McKinley
Edited by Gordon A. Cotton

Between North and South: The Letters of Emily Wharton Sinkler, 1842–1865
Edited by Anne Sinkler Whaley LeClercq

A Southern Woman of Letters: The Correspondence of Augusta Jane Evans Wilson
Edited by Rebecca Grant Sexton

Southern Women at Vassar: The Poppenheim Family Letters, 1882–1916
Edited by Joan Marie Johnson

Live Your Own Life: The Family Papers of Mary Bayard Clarke, 1854–1886
Edited by Terrell Armistead Crow and Mary Moulton Barden

The Roman Years of a South Carolina Artist: Caroline Carson's Letters Home, 1872–1892
Edited with an Introduction by William H. Pease and Jane H. Pease

Walking by Faith: The Diary of Angelina Grimké, 1828–1835
Edited by Charles Wilbanks

Stories from the Land: Oral Histories of Upcountry Southern Farm Women
Edited by Melissa Walker

Echoes from a Distant Frontier:
The Brown Sisters' Correspondence from Antebellum Florida
Edited by James M. Denham and Keith L. Huneycutt

Echoes from a Distant Frontier

The Brown Sisters' Correspondence from Antebellum Florida

Edited by
James M. Denham
and Keith L. Huneycutt

University of South Carolina Press

© 2004 University of South Carolina

Published in Columbia, South Carolina, by the
University of South Carolina Press

Manufactured in the United States of America

08 07 06 05 04 ˆ 5 4 3 2 1

Library of Congress Cataloging-in-Publication Data

Aldrich, Corinna Brown, 1812–1854.
  Echoes from a distant frontier : the Brown sisters' correspondence from antebel-
lum Florida / edited by James M. Denham and Keith L. Huneycutt.
    p. cm. — (Women's diaries and letters of the South)
Correspondence of Corinna Elizabeth Brown Aldrich and Ellen Maria Brown
Anderson.
Includes bibliographical references and index.
  ISBN 1-57003-536-9 (cloth : alk. paper)
  1. Aldrich, Corinna Brown, 1812–1854—Correspondence. 2. Anderson, Ellen
Brown, 1814–1862—Correspondence. 3. Women pioneers—Florida—Corre-
spondence. 4. Sisters—Florida—Correspondence. 5. Frontier and pioneer life—
Florida. 6. Florida—Social life and customs—19th century. 7. Florida—
Biography. 8. Brown family—Correspondence. I. Anderson, Ellen Brown,
1814–1862. II. Denham, James M. III. Huneycutt, Keith L., 1956– IV. Title. V.
Series.
  F315.A43 2004
  975.9'04'092—dc22

                                                          2003026101

This book is dedicated to Mannevillette Sullivan, Jane and Raymond Gill, and Elizabeth Traynor, worthy legacies of the Brown-Anderson Family

Contents

List of Maps and Illustrations / ix
Series Editor's Preface / xi
Acknowledgments / xiii
Introduction / xvii
Editorial Procedures and Policies / xxxi

Chapter One
"Our Pilgrimage Is at an End": South to Mandarin,
East Florida, 1830–1835 / 1

Chapter Two
"Our Indian War": 1836–1837 / 18

Chapter Three
"As Noble a Heart As Ever Throbbed": Dr. Edward Aldrich / 51

Chapter Four
"The Ladies of Llangollen": A New Home / 76

Chapter Five
"Log-House, Pine Tree and Cracker": Newnansville, Alachua County / 102

Chapter Six
"Everything Is Hubbub Here": The War Continues / 128

Chapter Seven
"What Restless Creatures We Are": Further Peregrinations / 151

Chapter Eight
"Going and Coming": Back to St. Augustine / 185

Chapter Nine
"I Live on Hope": Pensacola / 208

Chapter Ten
"We Are Nearing Our Desired Haven": Key West / 229

Chapter Eleven
"I See I Am Fiz-z-z-zing Now": Summer and Fall in Key West / 257

Chapter Twelve
"The Uncertainty of Our Lives": After Key West / 281

Epilogue / 297
Bibliography / 303
Index / 317

Maps and Illustrations

Maps
Antebellum Florida and South Georgia, circa 1850 / xviii
Upper East Florida, circa 1835 / 11
Lt. James W. Anderson's Seminole War, circa 1839–42 / 130

Illustrations
Villette Anderson / xix
Portsmouth, New Hampshire / xx
Elizabeth Dearing Brown / xxi
Mannevillette Elihu Dearing Brown / 2
Corinna Brown / 3
Ellen Maria Brown / 3
George Long Brown / 4
Delia (Dorothy) Dearing Hall / 4
Adelaide Mary Brown / 6
Notice to builders / 13
David Levy Yulee / 22
Osceola / 33
Coacoochee (Wild Cat) / 33
"Picolata Stages" / 46
"Inland Conveyance" / 46
Picolata, Florida Territory / 47
St. Augustine / 48
View of Fort Marion and St. Augustine / 48
Medical notice of Dr. Edward Aldrich / 52
Robert Raymond Reid / 56
Mary Martha Reid / 56
Thomas Douglas / 70
Osceola / 77
Fort Harlee / 103
Square number twelve / 107
Lt. James Willoughby Anderson / 107

Fort King, circa 1839 / 138

Judge Isaac Bronson / 159

St. Augustine Plaza, circa 1840s / 159

Corinna Brown Aldrich, circa 1840s / 171

Law notice, Louis Aldrich and William A. Forward partnership / 171

"The election" / 174

Notice for *Stephen and Frances* packet / 180

Medical notices of Dr. E. S. Aldrich / 183

View of Buffalo, New York, circa 1848 / 191

Fort Gratiot, Michigan, circa 1840s / 201

Medical notice of Dr. E. S. Aldrich / 204

Virginia Anderson / 211

Bird's-eye view of Key West, circa 1855 / 230

Joseph Lancaster / 231

Utica city plan, 1849 / 233

Baggs Square, Utica, New York, circa 1850 / 233

George Long Brown, circa 1850 / 286

M. E. D. Brown, circa 1860 / 289

West Point quarters of Edward Willoughby Anderson / 291

Edward Willoughby Anderson / 295

Elizabeth Felicia Masi Anderson / 298

Georgia Anderson / 298

Villette Anderson / 299

M. E. D. Brown, circa 1890s / 302

Series Editor's Preface

Echoes from a Distant Frontier: The Brown Sisters' Correspondence from Antebellum Florida is the twenty-first volume in what had been the Women's Diaries and Letters of the Nineteenth-Century South series. This series has been redefined and is now titled Women's Diaries and Letters of the South, enabling us to include some remarkably fine works from the twentieth century. This series includes a number of never-before-published diaries, some collections of unpublished correspondence, and a few reprints of published diaries—a potpourri of nineteenth-century and, now, twentieth-century southern women's writings.

The series enables women to speak for themselves, providing readers with a rarely opened window into southern society before, during, and after the American Civil War and into the twentieth century. The significance of these letters and journals lies not only in the personal revelations and the writing talent of these women authors but also in the range and versatility of the documents' contents. Taken together, these publications will tell us much about the heyday and the fall of the Cotton Kingdom, the mature years of the "peculiar institution," the war years, the adjustment of the South to a new social order following the defeat of the Confederacy, and the New South of the twentieth century. Through these writings the reader will also be presented with first-hand accounts of everyday life and social events, courtships and marriages, family life and travels, religion and education, and the life-and-death matters that made up the ordinary and extraordinary world of the American South.

Rarely is a collection of women's antebellum letters from Florida found, especially one from isolated East Florida dating from the time when the Second Seminole War (1835–42) raged out of control. *Echoes from a Distant Frontier* is just such a find. In 1835 the attractive Brown sisters, Ellen and Corinna —then in their early twenties, made their way to the Florida territory from Portsmouth, New Hampshire, to seek their fortunes in this largely undocumented region of the South. Over the next twenty years their experiences as pioneers were recorded in a series of letters to their brother Mannevillette, a renowned lithographer, who lived abroad when not at home in Utica, New

York. The well-educated sisters wrote him lively letters about life on the southern frontier including their observations on the tragic Indian conflict, politics, marriage, religion, and romance. Although these young women did not grow wealthy on the rough frontier, they did marry young, up-and-coming, southern men and settled down in Florida. Seemingly, Ellen and Corinna adjusted fully to southern values and institutions, including slavery. While they did not live in Florida's plantation belt, they owned slaves and in their writings home they sounded much like southern-born slaveholders. Indeed Ellen, after she returned North before the Civil War, not only defended slavery and southern secession but also advised her only child, a West Point cadet, to leave the academy and join the Confederacy, which he did.

Echoes from a Distant Frontier contrasts strongly with the two previous publications in this series, which are based on the nineteenth-century writings of two Charlestonian women who left the Palmetto State and the South over the heated issues of slavery and secession: Angelina Grimké became one of the North's best-known abolitionists; Caroline Petigru Carson left South Carolina when the war came in 1861 and eventually became an expatriate artist in Rome. Neither Grimké nor Carson ever returned home.

Editors James M. Denham and Keith L. Huneycutt, through the expertly edited letters of Ellen and Corinna in *Echoes from a Distant Frontier,* provide us with a fascinating glimpse into a world seldom chronicled in our existing literature.

CAROL BLESER

Acknowledgments

The editors wish to acknowledge the kind assistance of numerous librarians, archivists, and descendants of Ellen and Corinna Brown. Principally among these is Miss Mannevillette Sullivan, the great-granddaughter of Ellen Brown Anderson. The editors' relationship with Miss Mannevillette Sullivan began in 1994, when James M. Denham came across the complete Anderson-Brown correspondence collection while visiting the United States Military Academy at West Point on a military history fellowship. At that time Alan Aimone, director of special collections, encouraged Denham to contact Miss Sullivan, who, only a year or so before, had sent the collection to the U.S. Military Academy library with the intention of bequeathing it. Since that time Miss Sullivan, her cousin Jane Gill, and Jane's husband Raymond Gill have provided the editors with permission to publish all of their family's correspondence that has been recovered. They have also offered advice and provided family genealogy and photographs taken of paintings of many of the correspondents. The editors also wish to acknowledge the assistance of another family member, Elizabeth Traynor, who kindly shared additional letters, diaries, and other materials with the editors. Without these people's constant support, advice, and cooperative spirit this book could never have been written.

During both the initial and the final stages of this book the editors benefited from advice and consultation from various professionals. First, James M. Denham attended the documentary editing seminar put on by the National Historic Publications and Records Commission (NHPRC). Sometimes known as "Camp Edit," the seminar is hosted by the Wisconsin Historical Society on the campus of the University of Wisconsin for scholars working on historical editing projects of various kinds and offers both theoretical and practical instruction by professionals in the field. Denham would especially like to thank Michael Stevens of the Wisconsin Historical Society and the scholars who shared their insights and offered advice on this project: Beth Luey and Diana W. Hadley, Arizona State University; and Beverly Wilson Palmer, Pomona College, Claremont, California. The capable secretarial staff of the Florida Southern College English department, namely Elizabeth Partington and Sheila Hughes, executed several drafts of the first transcriptions, thus providing the editors with the first rough version of the letters on disk. Peter Krafft, director of cartography at Florida State University, prepared the beautiful maps for this work. We also gratefully acknowledge the assistance of Carol Bleser, professor emerita of history at Clemson University and editor of the Women's Diaries and Letters of the South publication series at the University of South Carolina Press. She provided useful insights in the selection of letters for our book. We are proud to number *Echoes from a Distant Frontier* among the titles in her series.

The editors also wish to thank Samuel Proctor, professor emeritus at the University of Florida, for sharing correspondence that helped shed light on the collection's brief stay at the university library. Other persons assisted the editors in various ways. David Coles, employed at the Florida Archives in the 1980s and 1990s (now history professor at Longwood College in Farmville, Virginia), first informed James M. Denham of the existence of the letters. The editors also wish to thank Florida Southern College, which provided extended financial support to both editors for travel and other expenses in the pursuance of this project. Especially helpful was a sabbatical leave for Keith L. Huneycutt during the spring semester 2001.

Others to whom we are indebted for their contributions and assistance are, in alphabetical order: Richard Aust, Oneida County Historical Society, Utica, New York; Joseph Barth, United States Military Academy; Barbara Brookes, Utica Public Library; Craig Buettinger, Jacksonville University; Paul Camp, University of South Florida; Bruce Chappell, P. K. Yonge Library, University of Florida; Suzanne Christoff, United States Military Academy; Patricia Coate, Columbia, South Carolina; Jim Cusick, P. K. Yonge Library, University of Florida; Edward Dacey, United States Military Academy; Mary Flekke, Nora Gailbraith, and Sara Fletcher Harding, Florida Southern College; Darren Harper, Bryan-Lang Library, Woodbine, Georgia; Mark Harvey, Michigan State Archives; Frank Hodges and Jose Garcia, Florida Southern College; Claudia Jew, Mariners Museum, Newport News, Virginia; Joe Knetsch, Florida Bureau of Land Archives, Tallahassee; Peter Krafft, Florida State University; Al La Bruna, Theodore Roosevelt Inaugural National Historic Site, Buffalo, New York; Frank Laumer, Dade City, Florida; Susan Lintelmann, United States Military Academy; Vicky Luffman, Florida Southern College; Randall MacDonald, Florida Southern College; Kevin Marken, Oneida County Historical Society, Utica, New York; Richard Matthews, University of Tampa; Joan Morris, Florida State Archives; Ken Nelson, Lakeland, Florida; Jody Norman, Florida State Archives; Kitty Oelker, Florida Southern College; Andrew Pearson, director of the Florida Southern College Library; Dan

Roberts, Oneida County Historical Society, Utica, New York; Thomas L. Reuschling, president of Florida Southern College; Kathleen Salsbury, Munson-Proctor Art Institute, Utica, New York; Taryn Rodriguez-Boette, St. Augustine Historical Society; Beth Roper, Florida Southern College; Frank N. and Irene Schubert, Washington, D.C.; Leslie Sheffield, Florida State Archives; David Smolen, New Hampshire Historical Society, Concord, New Hampshire; G. Dekle Taylor, Jacksonville, Florida; Charles Tingley, St. Augustine Historical Society; Jim Vearil, Jacksonville, Florida; Jo Ann Vranken, New York State Historical Society, Cooperstown, New York; June Weltman, Mandarin Historical Society; Jean Whitehead, Florida Southern College; Dick Williams, Oneida County Historical Society, Utica, New York; and Bertram Wyatt-Brown, University of Florida.

LAKELAND, FLORIDA

Introduction

On June 5, 1882, Villette Anderson wrote her uncle Mannevillette Elihu Dearing Brown that while alone in her Washington, D.C., apartment, she had found a "bag of letters that Mother told me when I was a child to read when I grew up. They are mostly my father's letters. And there are some of mother's. I always lugged them around with me, but they were in such a confusion. But last night," she wrote, "I sorted them by date and I found them not at all gloomy, but a very interesting history." When M. E. D. Brown read this letter in his art studio in Utica, New York, he would have thought of his niece, born thirty-six years earlier and named for him. He would have remembered his sister Ellen Anderson—left alone on the Florida frontier in 1847 with tiny Villette and two other children—struggling to survive after her husband had been killed in the Mexican War. He would have then carefully filed the letter away with the hundreds of others he had received from Ellen, from his sister Corinna and her husband Dr. Edward Aldrich, from his brother George and his wife Matilda, and from other extended family members who resided on the Florida frontier in the 1830s through 1850s. While M. E. D. Brown did not visit Florida until many years after his siblings left the state, these letters, carefully saved and added to those between Villette's mother, Ellen Brown Anderson, and aunt, Corinna Brown Aldrich, during the 1830s and 1840s form the basis of this work. And yes, together they make "a very interesting history."

Portsmouth, New Hampshire–born Ellen Maria Brown (1814–62) and Lt. James Willoughby Anderson (1812–47), a native of Norfolk, Virginia, were married in St. Augustine, Florida, in 1840. A West Point graduate and member of the U.S. Army, Anderson had begun his service in the Second Seminole War (1835–42) the year before. After meeting at a frontier outpost where Ellen's brother-in-law was employed as an army surgeon, James and Ellen fell in love, married, and shared a life together until James's death in the Mexican War in August 1847. Widowed with three children, Ellen remained in Florida until she left the state for St. Mary's, Georgia, in 1850, moving to Bridgeport, Connecticut, in 1850 and then New York City in 1851, where she remained for the rest of her days. She lived not only by her own efforts but also by the charity

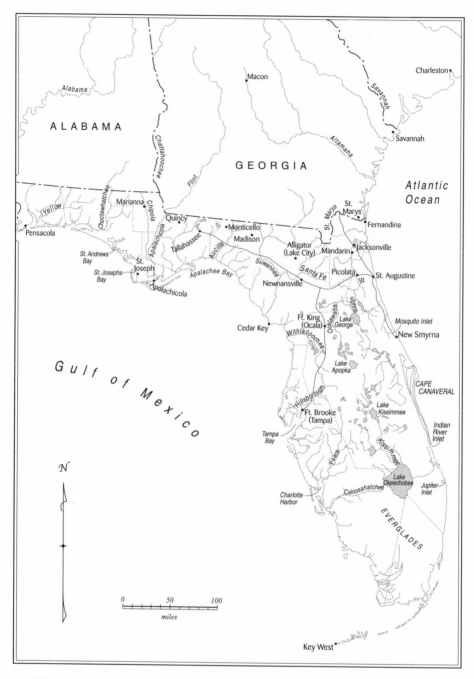

Antebellum Florida and South Georgia, circa 1850. Map by Peter Krafft.

Villette Anderson, painting by M. E. D. Brown, circa 1863. Courtesy of Mannevillette Sullivan.

of her sister Corinna and brother-in-law Dr. Edward Aldrich; her brother George, who operated a store in Newnansville, Florida; and her artist brother M. E. D. Brown.

Ellen, Corinna, Mannevillette, George, and Charles Brown were the children of Elihu and Elizabeth Brown of Portsmouth, New Hampshire.[1] When Capt. Elihu Dearing Brown (1777–1819) married Elizabeth Dearing Brown (1785–1832) in 1806, he was already well known in New England maritime circles. A ship designer, owner, and master, Brown invested his energy and savings in numerous ships fitted out as privateers against the British during the War of 1812. Commanding a number of privateer vessels himself, Brown earned both fame and fortune as the captain of the *Fox,* which netted many British seizures and thousands of dollars to Brown, his crew, and investors. Even after the Peace of Ghent (1814), Brown continued his privateering—this time sailing in the service of the Argentine revolt against Spain. While commanding the privateer *Constitution,* commissioned out of Buenos Aires, Brown and his crew were captured by the Spanish when their ship ran aground off

1. Elizabeth Dearing was born in 1785 and married Elihu Dearing Brown on January 6, 1806, in Portsmouth. See Rosemary Courtney, "M. E. D. Brown (1810–1896): American Lithographer and Painter," *American Art Journal* 12 (autumn 1980): 66.

Portsmouth, New Hampshire. Illustration from J. F. W. des Barres's The Atlantic Neptune *(London, 1777); copy from the New Hampshire Historical Society.*

the coast of Africa. Taken back to Spain as a prisoner of war, Brown died of consumption in Cadiz on September 20, 1819.[2]

After the death of her husband, Elizabeth—comfortably situated on account of her husband's estate—still found it difficult to maintain her Portsmouth household on South Street. Even so, the Brown children—Henry Alexander

---

2. Brown's death was reported in the *Portsmouth New Hampshire Gazette,* November 9, 1819. For an excellent treatment of Elihu D. Brown and his privateering exploits, see Richard E. Winslow, *"Wealth and Honor": Portsmouth during the Golden Age of Privateering, 1775–1815* (Portsmouth, N.H.: The Portsmouth Marine Society, 1988), 131–39, 150–63, 184–201, 244. See also William G. Saltonstall, *Ports of Piscataqua: Soundings in the Maritime History of Portsmouth, N.H.* (Cambridge: Harvard University Press, 1941), 158–65; Raymond A. Brighton, *They Came to Fish: A Brief Look at Portsmouth's 350 Years of History* (Portsmouth, N.H.: Portsmouth 350 Inc., 1973); Courtney, "M. E. D. Brown," 66–77; and James L. Garvin, *Historic Portsmouth* (Somersworth: New Hampshire Publishing Company, 1974). According to an oral interview with Miss Mannevillette Sullivan by James M. Denham, Belleville, Illinois, July 12, 1995, family tradition asserts that Mannevillette Elihu Dearing Brown was named for a village on the French coast that his father frequented during his privateering days. No doubt George Long Brown was named for his father's fellow ship captain and business associate George Long; see Winslow, *"Wealth and Honour,"* 134, 151. Charles Burroughs was named for Rev. Charles Burroughs, rector of Saint John's Church in Portsmouth, which the family attended. For other information on family members, especially M. E. D. Brown, see John J. Walsh, *Vignettes of Old Utica* (Utica, N.Y.: Utica Public Library, 1982); George C. Groce and David H. Wallace, The New York Historical Society's Dictionary of Artists in America, 1564–1860 (New Haven: Yale University Press, 1957), 87; *Utica Daily Press,* September 2, 1896; *Utica Morning Herald,* September 2, 1896; and "M. E. D. Brown," in Peter Hastings Falk, ed., *Who Was Who in American Art, 1564–1975: 400 Years of Artists in America* (Madison, Conn.: Sound View Press, 1999), 1:469.

Elizabeth Dearing Brown of Portsmouth, New Hampshire, circa 1820s, painting from memory by M. E. D. Brown. Courtesy of Mannevillette Sullivan and Jane and Raymond Gill.

(1807–25), Adelaide Mary (1808–33), Mannevillette Elihu Dearing (1810–96), Corinna Elizabeth (1812–54), Ellen Maria (1814–62), Charles Burroughs (1816–40), and George Long (1817–57)—were raised by their mother and three unmarried aunts.[3] After their mother's death in 1832 Ellen, Corinna, Charles, and eventually George Brown decided to leave Portsmouth and migrate to the Florida Territory. Staying behind was Mannevillette, who was beginning a career as a lithographer, locating variously in Boston, Philadelphia, and New York.[4]

3. Courtney, "M. E. D. Brown," 66; Portsmouth, New Hampshire, *City Directory* (1827), 3.

4. M. E. D. Brown entered the American lithography industry in its infancy. Brown enjoyed moderate success as a lithographer. In 1833 in Philadelphia he employed twenty-one-year-old Nathaniel Currier, who along with James Merritt Ives created the most distinguished lithography firm in the United States. See Walton H. Rawls, *The Great Book of Currier and Ives' America* (New York: Abbeville Press, 1979), 32; Bryan F. LeBeau, *Currier & Ives: America Imagined* (Washington, D.C.: Smithsonian Institution Press, 2001), 17; and Harry T. Peters, *Currier and Ives: Printmakers to the American People* (Garden City, N.Y.: Doubleday, Doran & Co., 1942), 5.

The other Brown siblings' decision to sell the family home in Portsmouth and relocate to the new Florida frontier was based not only on an adventurous spirit but also on the marriage of their Aunt Delia Dearing to a well-to-do settler in East Florida, Dr. James Hall, who owned a large estate near the community of Mandarin on the east bank of the St. Johns River below Jacksonville.[5] Thus in November 1835 Ellen, Corinna, and Charles began their new lives in Florida. Dr. Hall provided them with adjoining acreage, and soon the three siblings were experimenting with crops, including citrus, mulberry trees for silk culture, and cotton. Though first living under the same roof with the Halls, they soon began construction of their own house nearby.

During most of their residence in Florida the Brown sisters inhabited one of America's most isolated frontiers. When the Brown siblings arrived in the territory in 1835, Florida contained only slightly more than seventy thousand persons, about one half of them black slaves. As they traveled about the territory by land and by boat, Ellen and Corinna continually commented on what was strange and new to their eyes. They were struck by the territory's diversity of landscape and by the character and distribution of its population. Most of the territory's inhabitants were concentrated in Middle Florida between the Apalachicola and Suwannee Rivers (where the sisters never lived). There plantation agriculture similar to that which emerged in the black belt of Alabama and Mississippi prevailed. But in East Florida, where the sisters mostly lived, population remained extremely sparse until after the Second Seminole War (1835–42). Within only a few years after that conflict, however, settlers attracted by a federal land give-away scheme pushed south rapidly. According to Larry Rivers, filling this void "were more and more cotton planters, some from Middle Florida, others from southern cotton states." With this new influx into Alachua, Marion, and Orange Counties, slave-based agriculture came to dominate in the decade preceding the Civil War. The sisters and their brother George were there to witness this transformation firsthand.[6]

5. *Portsmouth (New Hampshire) Journal of Literature and Politics, Rockingham Gazette and State Herald,* June 14, 1833.

6. On the various aspects of the Florida frontier and its evolution, see Larry Eugene Rivers, *Slavery in Florida: Territorial Days to Emancipation* (Gainesville: University Press of Florida, 2000), 65–66; Canter Brown Jr., *Florida's Peace River Frontier* (Orlando: University of Central Florida Press, 1991); Canter Brown Jr., *Ossian Bingley Hart: Florida's Loyalist Reconstruction Governor* (Baton Rouge: Louisiana State University Press, 1997), 21–37; Sidney Walter Martin, *Florida during Territorial Days* (Athens: University of Georgia Press, 1944); James M. Denham, *"A Rogue's Paradise": Crime and Punishment in Antebellum Florida, 1821–1861* (Tuscaloosa: University of Alabama Press, 1997), x, 3–5, 61–66; James M. Denham and Canter Brown Jr., *Cracker Times and Pioneer Lives: The Florida Reminiscences*

As migrants seeking both economic opportunities and escape from a harsh winter climate, the Browns were among many New Englanders who traveled to Florida in the antebellum era. Newcomers engaged in commerce, teaching, journalism, and a host of other pursuits. Some, such as Ralph Waldo Emerson and John Tappen of Massachusetts, stayed only temporarily. Others, such as Charles Hutchinson of Connecticut and Daniel Ladd of Maine, relocated permanently. The influx of New Englanders continued into the late nineteenth century. Perhaps Florida's most famous migrant after the Civil War was Harriet Beecher Stowe, who settled only a mile or so from the Browns' original Mandarin homestead. Even though they were raised in a comfortable New England household, Corinna and Ellen adapted well to Florida's harsh frontier conditions.[7]

During much of the time that the Brown siblings in Florida were writing to their brother M. E. D. Brown, the aspiring artist was on the move. Before

---

of George Gillett Keen and Sarah Pamela Williams (Columbia: University of South Carolina Press, 2000); and Daniel L. Schafer, "U.S. Territory and State," in *The New History of Florida,* ed. Michael Gannon (Gainesville: University Press of Florida, 1996), 207–30. On the development of the Middle Florida plantation belt, see Clifton Paisley, *The Red Hills of Florida, 1528–1865* (Tuscaloosa: University of Alabama Press, 1989); and Edward E. Baptist, *Creating an Old South: Middle Florida's Plantation Frontier before the Civil War* (Chapel Hill: University of North Carolina Press, 2002). Other works that examine Florida as an integral part of the southern frontier are Joan E. Cashin, *A Family Venture: Men and Women on the Southern Frontier* (New York: Oxford University Press, 1991); John Solomon Otto, *Southern Frontiers, 1607–1860: The Agricultural Evolution of the Colonial and Antebellum South* (Westport, Conn.: Greenwood Press, 1989); and Malcolm J. Rohrbough, *The Trans-Appalachian Frontier: People, Societies, and Institutions, 1775–1850* (Belmont, Calif.: Wadsworth, 1990), 197–218.

7. For other works that discuss migration patterns of northerners into nineteenth-century Florida, see Anne E. Rowe, *The Idea of Florida in the American Literary Imagination* (Baton Rouge: Louisiana State Universtiy Press, 1986), 5; John S. Tappen to Benjamin French, December 13, 1841, Dorothy Dodd Room, State Library of Florida, Tallahassee; James T. Campbell, "The Charles Hutchinson Letters from Territorial Tallahassee, 1839–1843," *Apalachee* 4 (1950–56): 13; Jerrell H. Shofner, *Daniel Ladd, Merchant Prince of Frontier Florida* (Gainesville: University Presses of Florida, 1978); Norma B. Cuthbert, "Yankee Preacher-Teacher in Florida, 1838," *Huntington Library Quarterly* 7 (1944): 95–104; Douglas McMurtrie, "The Beginnings of Printing in Florida," *Florida Historical Quarterly* 23 (October 1944): 63–96; James Owen Knauss, *Florida Territorial Journalism* (Deland: Florida State Historical Society, 1927); John T. Foster Jr., and Sarah Whitmer Foster, *Beechers, Stowes, and Yankee Strangers: The Transformation of Florida* (Gainesville: University Press of Florida, 1999); and Fletcher M. Green, *The Role of the Yankee in the Old South* (Athens: University of Georgia Press, 1972).

settling permanently in Utica, New York, Brown traveled widely while studying in European art centers such as Paris, Rouen, Florence, Venice, and Rome
from 1838 to 1848. From 1835 to 1851 when they left Florida, Ellen and
Corinna too moved frequently, living in such places as Mandarin, St. Augustine, Newnansville, Fort King (Ocala), Pensacola, and Key West. After 1851
their brother George Brown, a Newnansville merchant and farmer, continued
to write to his brother and sisters. George married Matilda Stewart of nearby
Liberty Bluff plantation in 1851. The couple lived together in Newnansville,
where Matilda gave birth to three children: Adelaide (1852–75), Ellen (1856–
59), and George Jr. (1858–70). George Sr. died in 1857, but Matilda and her
children remained in Florida until after the Civil War. Even after the war
Matilda and her family continued to correspond with Mannevillette and with
Ellen's children from their homes in Newnansville, Gainesville, and Ocala and
during a brief sojourn in Tennessee. Most of the letters M. E. D. Brown sent
his siblings in Florida have not survived, but he carefully saved the letters they
wrote to him. While all four siblings kept Mannevillette constantly informed
of their progress and experiences in Florida, the letters from Ellen and Corinna
were the most numerous and informative. These provide the primary focus of
this study.

The Brown sisters were not pampered plantation women raised in comfort.
Corinna and Ellen Brown were vibrant, young, northern-born women thrust
into a dangerous and, to them, alien environment. Though they were determined to make their own way in the world, both women married southern
men and adjusted easily to southern institutions. Their values and prejudices
were typical of well-to-do, conservative northerners who migrated south. Their
education, cosmopolitan upbringing, and good breeding failed to shield them
from stereotypical attitudes on race and social class. Such attitudes are evident
in their condescension toward Indians and Florida's more humble folk, whom
they referred to disparagingly as "crackers"—and who formed the majority of
Florida's white antebellum population. For example, not long after she arrived
in Florida, Ellen described the "country folks" as "made of clay, indeed the idea
of having a likeness taken is too ridiculous to mention. . . . They are the most
squalid miserable creatures in the world."[8]

The sisters came in contact with the institution of slavery from the first
moment they arrived at their aunt's farm in Mandarin. While they never lived
in Florida's plantation belt, they did witness slavery in towns and on the crude

---

8. Ellen Brown to Mannevillette Brown, January 31, 1837, Anderson-Brown Papers,
United States Military Academy, West Point, New York (hereafter USMA).

frontier. Both Dr. Aldrich and George Brown owned a few slaves. While Dr. Aldrich's constant movement from place to place makes it difficult to trace his ownership of slaves with any degree of certainty, George Brown's ownership of slaves is easier to document. Always with a keen eye toward business, George began acquiring slaves from the moment he established himself as a merchant and farmer in Alachua County. In 1850 George owned five slaves (two men, one woman, and two children). At his death in 1857 this total had grown to seven. Once the sisters were married, slaves assisted them in their house-keeping and child-raising duties. Ellen and Corinna apparently found little offensive in slavery. Their writings betray no sense of squeamishness about the institution. On the contrary, Corinna often expressed exasperation with those house servants under her supervision. For example, soon after setting up her new house in Newnansville, Corinna complained to Mannevillette that "your sister has a house to keep and servants to <u>drive</u> that requires more time and patience to keep in order than a New England Hotel. I declare I would not give a Yankee waiting maid for any four negro servants without the cowhide. I sometimes think to spare my lungs & nerves," she continued, "I will take up [the] weapon of a broomstick if not the unladylike one of a cowhide. The argument or a threat they don't understand & nothing has as yet produced anything but a <u>grin.</u>"[9] Such comments, while hurtful to modern ears, might well have been spoken by a southern-born slaveholder. Thus on the whole the sisters shared the mainstream opinion of southerners and northerners that blacks were inferior and that the institution of slavery in the hands of paternalistic whites was beneficial to both races. Abolitionists and like-minded Yankee politicians such as John Quincy Adams (whom Corinna called a "ninny") were considered misguided fools.

Conditioned to mainstream southern attitudes on race and politics after spending their adult lives in Florida, Ellen and Corinna readily accepted the values of their adopted home. Particularly adamant in this regard, Ellen quarreled repeatedly with Mannevillette in the days leading up to the Civil War—even as she resided in New York City—over such matters as slavery, the South's right to secede from the Union, and which side (North or South) was most at fault in the breakup of the Union.

Ellen and Corinna Brown were not only skilled writers but also keen observers of their surroundings. This skill of observation is particularly the case with Ellen, who poured out her heart to Mannevillette over the frailties of

---

9. Corinna Aldrich to Mannevillette Brown, January 26, 1840, Anderson-Brown Papers, USMA.

human nature and the seemingly antagonistic natures of men and women. Both women continually expressed their opinions on romance, marriage, the subordinate status of women, and religion. Baptized in the Episcopal Church in Portsmouth, the sisters attended services in Jacksonville, St. Augustine, Pensacola, and Key West when they could. The sisters' religious faith was of the sort practiced among devout and pious New Englanders. With a faith that was more intellectual than emotional, the sisters continually derided and poked fun at the style of worship they encountered on the southern frontier. Still, continual references to God in their writings make clear a deep religious faith, especially in Corinna. The ever-present specter of the death of loved ones gave the sisters an opportunity to reflect on their religious beliefs. Nevertheless, the sisters refused to take part in what Corinna referred to as "distracted meetings," which were common in that time and place. On one occasion she wrote to her brother that she had attended a camp meeting, and "they tried very hard to convert me—but I have too sincere a respect for religion ever to become a fanatic."[10] The sisters' comments and observations on religion and other matters reflect the well-informed, thoughtful attitudes of northern women thrust into conditions of the most challenging sort.

Ellen and Corinna Brown lived in a little-documented area of frontier East Florida during the years of the Second Seminole War (1835–42) and its immediate aftermath. Both women experienced the terror and witnessed the bloodshed of this tragic conflict, and these frightful images no doubt confirmed their image of the Seminoles as ruthless savages. As pioneer settlers on the frontier's edge and as wives of men who took active roles in the war, the sisters shared the danger and heartbreak of the other men and women in their primitive surroundings. The family's letters add useful information and intriguing observations to supplement the scarce surviving records of the area. Most important, however, Corinna and Ellen provide an image of a world rarely glimpsed in available literature. While existing scholarship on the lives of plantation mistresses has become increasingly available, the lives of less privileged women have remained more obscure.[11] Both as well-educated New England women

---

10. Corinna Aldrich to Mannevillette Brown, June 3, 1838, Anderson-Brown Papers, USMA.

11. For experiences of southern women, see Cashin, *Family Venture;* Drew Gilpin Faust, *Mothers of Invention: Women of the Slaveholding South in the American Civil War* (Chapel Hill: University of North Carolina Press, 1999); Bertram Wyatt-Brown, *Southern Honor: Ethics and Behavior in the Old South* (New York: Oxford University Press, 1982); Catherine Clinton, *The Plantation Mistress: Woman's World in the Old South* (New York: Pantheon Books, 1982); George C. Rable, *Civil Wars: Women and the Crisis of Southern*

struggling to survive on America's southernmost frontier and as the wives of southern-born men, the sisters offer valuable new insights on their own circumstances and on a largely undocumented region of the South.

Well-educated, politically astute women married to men engaged in military, political, and economic affairs, Ellen and Corinna interacted with and commented on the families of many of the leading lights in East Florida, such as David Levy Yulee, Joseph Smith, Robert Raymond Reid, Isaac Bronson, Charles Downing, Joseph Hernandez, Samuel Burrett, John L. Doggett, Gad Humphreys, Ossian Hart, Thomas Douglas, Joseph Lancaster, and Benjamin

---

Nationalism (Champaign: University of Illinois Press, 1989); Elizabeth Fox-Genovese, *Within the Plantation Household: Black and White Women of the Old South* (Chapel Hill: University of North Carolina Press, 1988); Margaret Ripley Wolfe, *Daughters of Canaan: A Saga of Southern Women* (Lexington: University of Kentucky Press, 1995); Sally G. McMillan, *Southern Women: Black and White in the Old South* (Arlington Heights, Ill.: Harlan Davidson, 1992); and Carol Bleser, ed., *In Joy and Sorrow: Women, Family, and Marriage in the Victorian South* (New York: Oxford University Press, 1991). Works that explore women in Florida are James M. Denham, "Cracker Women and Their Familes in Nineteenth-Century Florida," in *Florida's Heritage of Diversity: Essays in the Honor of Samuel Proctor,* ed. Mark I. Greenberg, William W. Rogers Jr., and Canter Brown Jr. (Tallahassee: Sentry Press, 1997), 15–28; Canter Brown Jr., *Women on the Tampa Bay Frontier* (Tampa, Fla.: Tampa Bay History Center, 1997); and Tracy J. Revels, "Grander in Her Daughters: Florida's Women during the Civil War," *Florida Historical Quarterly* 78 (winter 1999): 261–82. Recently some letter collections and memoirs have appeared that shed light on southern women. Two works that focus on a northern-born woman who married into a southern family are Wilma King, ed., *A Northern Woman in the Plantation South: Letters of Tryphena Blanche Holder Fox, 1856–1876* (Columbia: University of South Carolina Press, 1997); and Anne Sinkler Whaley LeClercq, ed., *Between North and South: The Letters of Emily Wharton Sinkler, 1842–1865* (Columbia: University of South Carolina Press, 2001). Conversely, for the letters of a southern woman who married into a northern family, see Eliza Cope Harrison, ed., *Best Companions: The Letters of Eliza Middleton Fisher and Her Mother, Mary Hering Middleton, from Charleston, Philadelphia, and Newport, 1839–1846* (Columbia: University of South Carolina Press, 2001). Other works are Joan E. Cashin, *Our Common Affairs: Texts from Women in the Old South* (Baltimore: Johns Hopkins University Press, 1996); Carol Bleser, ed., *Tokens of Affection: The Letters of a Planter's Daughter in the Old South* (Athens: University of Georgia Press, 1996); and Augusta Jane Evans, *Beulah* (1859; reprint, edited with an introduction by Elizabeth Fox-Genovese, Baton Rouge: Louisiana State University Press, 1992). Two collections that focus on Florida women are Denham and Brown, *Cracker Times and Pioneer Lives;* and Arch Fredric Blakey, Ann Smith Lainhart, and Winston Bryant Stephens Jr., eds., *Rose Cottage Chronicles: Civil War Letters of the Bryant-Stephens Families of North Florida* (Gainesville: University Press of Florida, 1998).

D. Wright. Their comments on military leaders such as Winfield Scott, Thomas Jesup, William Worth, and Seminole leaders Osceola and Coacoochee, and on national political leaders such as John Quincy Adams, Martin Van Buren, Henry Clay, and James K. Polk indicate that they were well informed about the military and political issues of the day.

At first glance it might seem that women, unable to vote, would have been uninterested in and unconcerned with politics. But as historians such as Elizabeth Varon have shown, this was often not the case with well-to-do or well-educated, curious women such as Ellen and Corinna.[12] It is clear from the letters that the sisters kept abreast of local and national politics by reading state and national newspapers and by interacting with Florida's male and female elite settlers. Among Ellen and Corinna's small circle of friends, politics was a daily subject of conversation. This avid interest in politics was no doubt enhanced by the important bearing politics had on their husbands. Dr. Aldrich's livelihood relied to a large extent on federal governmental reimbursement from his service as a surgeon in the military, and later he sought federal appointment to various posts. The women too understood the direct bearing that politics had on military policy. Ellen and her husband jointly speculated on how certain presidential candidates might affect his own regular army service. From their writings it is clear that the sisters were ardent followers of the Whig Party. For instance, they frequently made disparaging comments against Martin Van Buren and James K. Polk while lauding their favorite American statesman, Henry Clay. But personal friendship with Democratic politicians—such as David Levy Yulee—often altered this partisanship. Like most antebellum men and women, the sisters viewed political campaigns as prized American rituals and exciting respites from their daily routines. The sisters made frequent comments on political elections, and these comments peaked during the elections of 1840 and 1844.

The women were avid readers and aspiring authors. The letters discuss their optimistic plans for publishing works of fiction and essays but often bemoan the circumstances that thwarted most of their attempts. Nevertheless, despite sometimes being hurriedly composed, the letters display Ellen's and Corinna's literary skills: detailed descriptions, exciting narratives, and perceptive character sketches join numerous biblical and literary allusions, including references to the works of writers such as Dickens, Trollope, Martineau,

---

12. Elizabeth R. Varon comments and expands on this new scholarship in *"We Mean to Be Counted": White Women and Politics in Antebellum Virginia* (Chapel Hill: University of North Carolina Press, 1998), 3–9, 71–72.

Byron, and Shakespeare, to enrich the letters. Foreign words and phrases also appear frequently.

⨌

Housed at the United States Military Academy (USMA) Library at West Point, New York, the Anderson-Brown collection contains approximately 850 letters spanning the dates 1831 to 1899. In 1992 Miss Mannevillette Sullivan bequeathed the collection to the USMA, from which her great-grandfather James Willoughby Anderson graduated.

The letters remained in Miss Sullivan's family home in Washington, D.C., until approximately 1975, when a series of unfortunate circumstances resulted in the unauthorized sale of the letters to collectors in Gainesville, Florida. When Miss Sullivan learned of the whereabouts of the collection, she purchased it back at great effort and personal sacrifice.[13] From 1976 to 1986, when she had reacquired most of her family's letters, the collection was circulated widely in the Gainesville area among potential buyers and even was stored temporarily in the vault of the P. K. Yonge Library at the University of Florida. Efforts to sell the entire collection to that institution eventually proved unsuccessful. While the letters were at the University of Florida, Professor E. Ashby Hammond used them in his study of medicine in nineteenth-century Florida.[14] Unfortunately, during this time and after, parts of the collection were arranged in numerous ways, exhibited to collectors, photocopied, and partially transcribed. No doubt some were sold off during this time also. For a time some transcriptions were exhibited in an antiques/relics store in McIntosh, Florida. In the 1980s, long before this project took shape, James M. Denham discovered these transcriptions while passing through McIntosh on a research trip to Gainesville. The proprietor allowed him to take notes for use in his Ph.D. dissertation. Notes from these transcriptions; some letters appearing in an article published in 1928 by Miss Sullivan's father, Francis P. Sullivan; and some citations of letters cited in Professor Hammond's study make it apparent that Miss Sullivan did not recover all of the letters.[15] Miss Sullivan also purchased photocopies of originals sold before she could reacquire her collection. After recovering as much of her family's correspondence as she could, she made the decision to lend and eventually bequeath it to West Point.[16]

---

13. Mannevillette Sullivan, oral interview by editors, Belleville, Illinois, July 12, 1995.

14. E. Ashby Hammond, *The Medical Profession in 19th Century Florida: A Biographical Register* (Gainesville: George A. Smathers Library, University of Florida, 1996).

15. Francis P. Sullivan, ed., "Letters of a West Pointer, 1860–1861," *American Historical Review* 33 (April 1928): 599–617.

16. Mannevillette Sullivan, oral interview by editors, Belleville, Illinois, July 12, 1995.

Editorial Procedures and Policies

Throughout the project the goal of the editors has been to make these letters accessible to both general readers and scholars alike. The letters are organized into chronological chapters with brief introductions and editorial bridges in italics. Although some of the extant letters are not immediately germane to the scope of the book and are not reproduced, many of these do provide important information crucial to a fuller understanding of the correspondents' lives and are mentioned in editorial bridges, which also provide a vital narrative link between letters whenever different correspondents from different locations are included or events in the interim need explanation. Notes have been provided to offer historical context, to clarify obscure phraseology, to translate foreign phrases, to identify biblical and literary allusions, and to identify persons, locations, or events mentioned in the letters. Though kept to a minimum, they also provide readers with suggestions for further reading.

The editors have employed an editorial style conducive to readability. Obvious slips of the pen have been silently corrected. Extraneous marginalia are treated as postscript, and superscript is lowered to normal height. Paragraph indentations are sometimes added when an obvious change of subject occurs. In a few cases, as an aid to the reader, minor punctuation, mainly commas and periods, is silently added. The editors have attempted to transcribe the punctuation as closely as possible to the original without sacrificing clarity. Often the correspondents wrote with great haste to complete letters before the mail's departure or during brief interludes during frustratingly busy schedules. As a consequence the punctuation often is nonstandard yet generally clear. The writers often used short dashes in place of commas or periods and often used slightly longer dashes for periods. Within the same letters dashes might also be used as in modern standard punctuation—to set off nonrestrictive elements or for emphasis; Corinna's punctuation at first seems especially confusing, but it becomes understandable with familiarity. The editors have chosen to retain these dashes except at points where an end-stop period is called for by an uppercase letter beginning the next sentence. When a proper noun follows one

Chapter One

"Our Pilgrimage Is at an End"
South to Mandarin, East Florida, 1830–1835

On August 10, 1831, in Portsmouth, New Hampshire, Elizabeth Dearing Brown wrote to her son Mannevillette Elihu Dearing Brown, a twenty-one-year-old lithographer. Brown had been working in Boston since 1827 but was at that moment in New York City.[1] His mother was anxious to learn of his prospects. Since losing her husband in 1819 Elizabeth Brown had supported her six children. The family remained in their house on Portsmouth's South Street, and funds from her husband's maritime enterprises were substantial at first but in time became less so. Elizabeth Brown's unmarried sisters, Delia, Ann, and Mary, lent emotional support and provided what financial support they could.

Mannevillette was Mrs. Brown's oldest living son, but in 1831 her five other children, rapidly reaching adulthood, also occupied her attention. Her oldest daughter was Adelaide (twenty-three), followed by Corinna (nineteen) and Ellen (seventeen). Charles (fifteen) was her second-oldest son, and George (fourteen) was her youngest. Mannevillette and Charles corresponded with their mother regularly. Mrs. Brown was apparently a strong matriarch, freely advising her sons on many subjects. She thanked them for writing even while chastising them for bad spelling and admonishing them to use a dictionary.[2]

That winter Corinna and Ellen remained at their Portsmouth home while caring for their ailing mother. As spring approached, the sisters heard some interesting news from their Aunt Delia (Dorothy) in St. Augustine, Florida. Aunt Delia, Corinna wrote Mannevillette, had "<u>converted</u>. She had been to St.

1. Courtney, "M. E. D. Brown," 66.
2. Elizabeth Brown to Mannevillette and Charles Brown, December 8, 1831; Elizabeth Brown to Charles Brown, February 2, 1832; Elizabeth Brown to Mannevillette Brown, June 1832, Anderson-Brown Papers, U.S. Military Academy, West Point, New York (hereafter cited as USMA).

Mannevillette Elihu Dearing Brown, self-portrait, as a young man during his years in Europe. Courtesy of Mannevillette Sullivan and Jane and Raymond Gill.

Augustine with two Methodist ministers, one of whom she rode with, & the other rode at her side; but, these did not convert her, at least so she says; but a lady, residing in the same house with her at St. Augustine. She has written us a long letter about the matter, but I would not read it, because I knew I should only laugh, and be perhaps ten fold more a child of Satan than I am now for I know her style. I suspect she will write to you of Charlie, that is, if she does not return . . . immediately."[3] By spring of 1832 Mrs. Brown had begun to suffer from an undisclosed illness. Her condition steadily declined until she finally passed away in October. Mrs. Brown left no will, and letters suggest that she was seldom lucid for the six months before her death.

In 1833 Mannevillette continued his successful work in Philadelphia and Charles attended writing school, but the future was less certain for the Brown daughters. By the first of the year their deceased mother's debts had been liquidated by the selling of their part ownership in "the store"; each family member had some cash and Aunt Mary paid board, so Corinna felt that they should be able to get by until summer. Throughout that spring the Brown siblings considered their options. Mannevillette suggested that Corinna, Ellen, Adelaide,

3. Corinna Brown to Mannevillette Brown, March 28, 1832, Anderson-Brown Papers, USMA.

Corinna Brown about the time she came to Florida and before her marriage to Dr. Edward S. Aldrich, painting by M. E. D. Brown. Courtesy of Mannevillette Sullivan and Jane and Raymond Gill.

Ellen Maria Brown about the time she came to Florida and before her marriage to Lt. James Willoughby Anderson, painting by M. E. D. Brown. Courtesy of Mannevillette Sullivan and Jane and Raymond Gill.

*George Long Brown as a
young man about the time he
came to Florida, painting by
M. E. D. Brown. Courtesy of
Mannevillette Sullivan and
Jane and Raymond Gill.*

*Delia (Dorothy) Dearing
Hall, miniature, watercolor
on ivory. Courtesy of Elizabeth Traynor.*

and George join him and Charles in Philadelphia, leaving Aunt Mary behind in the Portsmouth house to take in boarders. Some tension among the siblings about the settlement of the estate was evident. Aunt Mary spoke of finding work in Philadelphia.[4]

Although settlement of Mrs. Brown's estate would be a problem for some time, various developments were combining to move the family from Portsmouth. Their mother's death and also their Aunt Delia's marriage on April 24 to seventy-three-year-old Dr. James Hall, a well-to-do resident of East Florida and native of Keene, New Hampshire, prompted the move.[5] Delia Dearing's presence in St. Augustine had become a matter of some comment in that far-away locale. Sometime before her marriage to Hall she had opened a millenary

4. Corinna Brown to Mannevillette Brown, March 21, 23; April 8, 1832, Anderson-Brown Papers, USMA.

5. *St. Augustine Florida Herald,* August 15, 1833; *Portsmouth (New Hampshire) Journal of Literature and Politics, Rockingham Gazette and State Herald,* June 15, 1833. Hall, a veteran of the Battle of Yorktown, first obtained Florida land in 1790 when Spanish governor Juan Quesada granted him 775 acres on Julington Creek, which flows into the St. Johns River near present-day Jacksonville. Hall expanded his holdings in 1804 when he married the recently widowed Eleanor Prichard. Expelled from East Florida in 1810 by Spanish authorities for his part in the Patriot War (1810–15), Hall was stripped of his lands. Returning in 1813, he appeared before the Spanish governor and was "pardoned" but left East Florida again due to the hostility of the Spanish settlers toward "revolutionists." After biding his time in Camden County, Georgia, Hall returned in 1818 when he petitioned Governor José Coppinger for two five-hundred-acre tracts near his old homestead. Hall returned to Florida near the time of its transfer to the United States. Hall and his wife assumed a prosperous lifestyle, raising cattle, cutting timber, and growing crops. Among the first farmers to develop citrus groves, Hall, for several years by that time a widower, was one of the most substantial citizens in East Florida when he married Dorothy Dearing (Delia) in 1833. See various land records and affidavits in the James Hall Papers, box 60, P. K. Yonge Library of Florida History, University of Florida, Gainesville. See also Hammond, *Medical Profession in 19th Century Florida,* 233–35; Mary M. Dupree and G. Dekle Taylor, M.D., "Dr. James Hall, 1760–1837," *Journal of Florida Medical Association* 61 (August 1974): 626–31; and Webster Merritt, *A Century of Medicine in Jacksonville and Duval County* (Gainesville: University of Florida Press, 1949), 1–4. For the Patriot War and the society of East Florida during this period, see Rembert W. Patrick, *Florida Fiasco: Rampant Rebels on the Georgia-Florida Border* (Athens: University of Georgia Press, 1954); William S. Coker and Susan R. Parker, "The Second Spanish Period in the Two Floridas," in *The New History of Florida,* ed. Michael Gannon (Gainesville: University Press of Florida, 1996), 157–66; Schafer, "U.S. Territory and State," 214–17; Charlton W. Tebeau, *A History of Florida* (Miami, Fla.: University of Miami Press, 1971), 89–114; and Brown, *Ossian Bingley Hart,* 6–17.

Adelaide Mary Brown, pencil drawing by M. E. D. Brown. Courtesy of Elizabeth Traynor.

shop in St. Augustine and, according to a local newspaper applauding her efforts, had "found business brisk and had sold her merchandise at a profit of 50 percent. Moreover she had enjoyed fine wealth and a great many acquaintances and friends."[6] On her marriage to Hall, Delia left St. Augustine and joined her husband at his large plantation near Mandarin, on the St. Johns River below Jacksonville. Delia's mercantile success and of course her marriage to Dr. Hall no doubt made East Florida an attractive future destination for the siblings. But their enthusiasm was dampened when news reached Portsmouth that Adelaide (the first sister to visit the Halls in Mandarin) had died while on a visit there on October 10.[7]

The next year (1834) proved to be an exciting one for the Browns. While Corinna and Ellen were busy at work writing a novel they hoped to submit for publication, Aunt Ann visited the Halls in Mandarin. By February the sisters in Portsmouth learned that she had decided to stay in Florida. "Dr. Hall," Corinna wrote Mannevillette, "has given her an acre of land & orange trees for

6. "Enterprise of a Yankee Lady, " *Portsmouth Journal of Literature and Politics, Rockingham Gazette and State Herald,* quoted in *St. Augustine Florida Herald,* August 15, 1833.

7. *Portsmouth Journal of Literature and Politics, Rockingham Gazette and State Herald,* November 16, 1833.

a grove, she is going to plant it; in 5 years it will be worth a thousand dollars—at least this is the last news."[8]

On March 23 Corinna explained that they had sent the book to Philadelphia, and she discussed details of plot, characters, grammar, and spelling. Perhaps wary of the negative image held in those days of "scribbling women," Corinna insisted that Mannevillette not reveal their involvement in the project. "[D]on't, any how, or any way, let anybody know we had a hand in it," she insisted. "It would disgrace us, even if we were to get the prize, I would not own it. Don't let Pomeroy[9] know it."

One of the first specific indications that the sisters were interested in a journey to Florida comes in Corinna's letter of August 14. Corinna told Mannevillette that her doctor had recommended a trip to Florida, hoping the climate might improve her health. Thus she, Ellen, and Aunt Mary planned to visit Delia. Yet the summer and fall found the sisters not in Florida but rather in Philadelphia. Pomeroy was there, and the sisters considered moving there on a permanent basis. Although the Browns were kept busy by friends and social events, even attending a ball in February and taking horseback-riding lessons in May, Corinna and Ellen were not content there, as Ellen revealed in her letter to Mannevillette in February and as did Corinna in several letters. On March 3, Corinna wrote Mannevillette that her real wish was to join Aunt Delia in East Florida.[10] Corinna had only come to Philadelphia, she explained, to gratify Pomeroy, but soon the engagement was broken off due to his "libertine" behavior. On July 4, Corinna confided to Mannevillette that she had had some good experiences in Philadelphia and had gained knowledge of the ways of the world but that she was eager to get on with her life.[11] The sisters returned

8. Corinna Brown to Mannevillette Brown, February 21 and 28, 1834, Anderson-Brown Papers, USMA.

9. Pomeroy was her fiancé.

10. When American authorities organized the Florida Territory, they merged both Spanish provinces, East and West Florida, into one. Nevertheless, the habit of reference and the organization of the territory into separate judicial districts resulted in the region east of the Suwannee River being referred to continuously as East Florida. The reference also served to distinguish the region from Middle Florida, a region with denser settlement and markedly different social and economic characteristics. For a general portrait of territorial Florida during these years, see Sidney Walter Martin, *Florida during Territorial Days;* Denham, *"A Rogue's Paradise;"* Schafer, "U.S. Territory and State," 207–30; Dorothy Dodd, *Florida Becomes a State* (Tallahassee: Florida Centennial Commission, 1945), 1–26; and Tebeau, *History of Florida,* 151–58.

11. Corinna Brown to Mannevillette Brown, March 3; April 9; June 23; July 4, 1835, Anderson-Brown Papers, USMA.

to Portsmouth, but like their brother Charles, they were eager to relocate to Florida. By August 4, Charles had already made arrangements for his own journey. Corinna, Ellen, and Aunt Mary also prepared to leave. Dr. Hall intended to assist them.

In the meantime Mannevillette moved to Geneva, New York. In the next several years until his decision to travel to Europe, he lived variously in Ithaca and Utica. His choice of Utica was a natural one given the town's increasing prosperity and its growing reputation in central New York as an art center. Several of the town's leading business and political leaders quickly recognized his talents, and he formed important relationships that would advance his career for many years to come, notably with Thomas R. Walker and Roscoe Conkling.[12]

At the time the Browns migrated to Mandarin, located on the east bank of the St. Johns River only a few miles south of Jacksonville, East Florida contained approximately twenty thousand inhabitants. Most of the American settlers, the majority of whom had arrived in the territory since the transfer in 1821, lived clustered around the St. Johns River in the area between St. Augustine and Jacksonville. A fairly substantial number of Creoles also lived in St. Augustine, the ancient capital of Spanish East Florida, dominated by the Castillo de San Marcos, renamed Fort Marion by the Americans. By the late 1820s settlers from Georgia entered the new territory, and by 1824 Alachua County, just west of St. Johns and Duval Counties, was formed. A further boon to settlement occurred in 1826 when the United States established a land office in Newnansville (known previously as Dell's and near present-day Gainesville). The isolated village was soon connected by a road running approximately one hundred miles inland from St. Augustine. As more and more settlers pushed south to occupy the new lands, they confronted Indians determined to hold their ground. Conflict between individual settlers and Seminole, Creek, and Mikasuki populations with their African and African-American vassals resulted; by 1835 the region was ripe for war. Unknown to the Browns, tension between the Seminoles and American authorities was at the breaking point. Three years earlier under the Treaty of Payne's Landing, a select group of Seminole leaders had agreed to investigate lands in the West for the purpose of relocating there. Despite subsequent pacts made in the Arkansas Territory by a delegation of chiefs agreeing in substance to migrate west, many Seminoles

12. M. M. Bagg, *Memorial History of Utica, New York from its Settlement to the Present Time* (Syracuse, N.Y.: D. Mason & Company Publishers, 1892), 184–86; T. Wood Clarke, *Utica for a Century and a Half* (Utica, N.Y.: Widtman Press, 1952), 35–36.

in Florida, along with their Creek and black allies, already plotted to resist. Thus, when the Browns moved to the St. Johns River community of Mandarin, the surrounding frontier was about to erupt in war. Residents of Duval County began preparing for the possibility of conflict with the Indians as local authorities constructed Fort Eaton on the eastern shore of the St. Johns about four miles from Mandarin.[13]

The sisters' first letter posted from Florida follows.

[Corinna Brown to Mannevillette Brown]

Mandarin [to Geneva, New York]
November 25, 1835

My dear brother,

I am happy to inform you our pilgrimage is at an end. We arrived in Mandarin yesterday morning, after a journey of four weeks. We left Portsmouth Saturday Oct 25th, just at sunset, had a cracking breeze round Cape Cod; (The waves, as the sailors say ran mountains high) and arrived in N.Y. on Tuesday. We remained there until the 28th, then set sail & in two days were off Cape Hatteras. Then our star set—we were becalmed for ten days—Then a breeze ahead blew up & we beat down to Charleston. Just as we were near enough to put in for a harbour it blew a gale. We went into Charleston & there remained two days. I was not sorry however for this breeze, as it gave us an opportunity to see the city of Charleston, which we should not otherwise have had. It is an antique looking place, and will make you feel sad in spite of yourself. Every thing looks dull & gloomy; the dampness of the atmosphere effects every thing, particularly the paint, and makes new dwellings look in a few months like

---

13. On Mandarin and the surrounding community on the eve of the Second Seminole War, see Brown, *Ossian Bingley Hart,* 31–34; Mary B. Graff, *Mandarin on the St. Johns* (Gainesville: University of Florida Press, 1953), 16–33; John K. Mahon, *History of the Second Seminole War, 1835–1842,* rev. ed. (Gainesville: University Presses of Florida, 1985), 1–86; Denham and Brown, eds., *Cracker Times and Pioneer Lives,* xiii–xix, 1–25, 99–108; Daniel L. Schafer, *Anna Kingsley* (St. Augustine, Fla.: St. Augustine Historical Society, 1994); J. Leitch Wright, *Creeks and Seminoles: The Destruction and Regeneration of the Muscogulge People* (Lincoln: University of Nebraska Press, 1986), 17–44; Francis Prucha, *The Sword of the Republic: The United States Army on the Frontier, 1783–1846* (New York: Macmillan, 1969), 269–73; Brown, *Florida's Peace River Frontier,* 34–46; James W. Covington, *The Seminoles of Florida* (Gainesville: University Press of Florida, 1993), 50–71; and John K. Mahon and Brent R. Weisman, "Florida's Seminoles and Miccosukee Peoples," in *The New History of Florida,* ed. Michael Gannon (Gainesville: University Press of Florida, 1996), 190–93.

those that have been built 50 years at the north. Then they are all built in the <u>Spanish style</u>, surrounded by high walls forming a court inside, or what we call a garden. These are tastefully ornamented with flowers. Roses were in full bloom, and to my New England optics looked lovely beyond description. However these sweets are all concealed from passers by unless one gets a peep now & then through some lattice, or half closed gait [*sic*]. The "pride of India" trees are growing in all the streets like the linden trees in Chesnut St.—Phil. & I think in summer must make a delightful walk shade. They were injured by the severe frost last winter, and of course are not flourishing now. But to go on with our voyage, we were 2 <u>days</u> from Charleston to ~~Jacksonville~~ the St. John's river. Then had to <u>beat</u> over the bar, and then to crown all, were <u>becalmed</u> & could not get up to Jacksonville for two days. The sail up the river, however, was pleasant & would have been delightful if we had had a good wind. The banks are much more diversified than I expected, & the river itself is like a succession of beautiful lakes; at Jacksonville 'tis not more than half a mile wide, & at Mandarin 10 miles above, 'tis more than 5 miles; & thus it constantly varies! 'Tis sweet indeed. Jacksonville is not much of a place. Perhaps 50 buildings or more & plenty of pigs & children. The dwellings are like the Pharisees' platters, besides being but half finished.[14] There are some decent people, some invalids from the north, whom we found very agreeable, but generally speaking they are as rough as their houses. Mandarin is still a less place; but 'tis said it will yet be the brightest spot on the St. John's. Every one thinks the rail road will strike here, & if it does, it will make a city of it in a little time. I hope it will but at any rate it will benefit the place as it must strike near here. Charles & Aunt Mary intend to buy a lot of land adjoining the Dr's & put up a house. Charles is going to cultivate oranges and mulberry trees. The Dr. says he cannot but succeed if he is industrious. I want M. to sell the old house in P. She owns all but our part & it will bring $1000 now. And then build a pretty house here which she can do for $600 & furnish it prettily and conclude to remain here. The climate is <u>delightful</u> and living is cheap. You cannot board here for less than $4 or $5 per week, but if you have a house you can provide for a family for $2 per week— there's the difference. 'Tis lovely, dear, <u>very</u>.

Aunt Delia's house is in the midst of the pines, built in cottage style—two stories, but small. Still I think we shall be contented. If I had you & George with us I should be happy—you must take good care of your health dear, and write often. I had a letter from W to day. I don't think he will be here before next fall. He has gone into partnership with his brother in law who is an eminent

14. See Matt. 23:35.

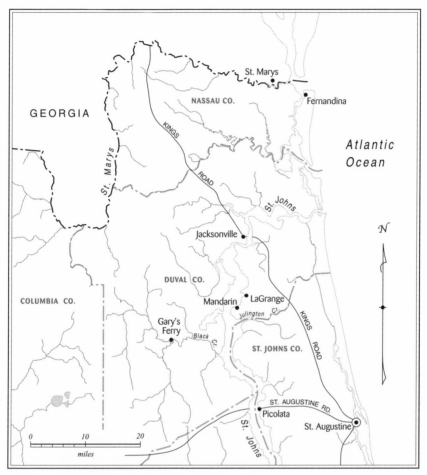

Upper East Florida, circa 1835. Map by Peter Krafft.

physician in Mobile & I doubt not he will do well. He thinks so himself. I am
writing at random dear, & in haste. The mail goes to day & if I do not finish this
before it leaves I shall not be able to send it for a week. You must excuse errors
& what I leave unsaid this time & will remember next. I have scarcely got settled
yet either in mind or body, but hope to in a day or two. E & I are going to St.
Augustine next week with the Dr. En passant.[15] The Dr. is a fine old man, I like
him very much. He is rather older than I expected, but I like him better. When
I return I will tell you all about our visit. Write to me soon, dear & tell me if
you do not think my ideas about selling the old house in P[ortsmouth] are good

15. French: "in passing."

& if you for your part would be willing provided she should conclude to do so. I think it would be best, but I will write to you on this matter again dear when I have more time—now I must hasten. We are all well & send much love to you. Aunt D[elia] would be happy to see you in Mandarin. Aunt D says we may consider this our home as long as we are contented but I would not advise you dear to come here for more than a visit at present. The loss of the groves has made the people poor, but in two or three years they will bear and by that time the rail road will be here, and then it will be the place to make money, but I should love to see you dear, if you can come for a visit.[16] I must say farewell. I will write again by next mail if I do not go to St. Augustine, but if I do I will write by the next <u>after</u>. Direct to Mandarin St. John's river East Florida care of Dr. James Hall. I long to hear from you.

Yours affectionately,
Corine

[Ellen Brown to Mannevillette Brown]

Mandarin [to Geneva, New York]
December 6, 1835

My dear Mann,

I have written you two letters and burnt them both, because I thought it sinful almost to put your patience to the test of deciphering my hyroglyphicks [*sic*] and finding for your trouble that they expressed nothing but nonsense. However don't expect because I send this that it will contain aught better than it [confers]. I have given up the hope of doing better and this is indeed a disparing [*sic*] effort. I have been here a fortnight and am by no means in love with the place. It is too new. The climate is not miraculous nor inconceivable, nevertheless it is most decidedly a warm climate. To be more explicit—we find a fire a very comfortable and comforting friend and sleep under a couple of blankets and a quilt with as much ease as ever, not to mention the occasional addition of a cloak. But we are not chilled through by the opening of a door, can at noon day stand out doors without bonnet or shawl, provided you feel indifferent to tan, and never dream of such a thing as having our teeth chatter. Our noses get red, but never (as yet) blue—Which is pretty much all I have to say concerning the weather except that we feel the dampness of the rains very

---

16. On February 8, 1835, the surrounding area suffered a devastating freeze. See Graff, *Mandarin on the St. Johns,* 16–17; and T. Frederick Davis, "Early Orange Culture in Florida and the Epochal Cold of 1835," *Florida Historical Quarterly* 15 (April 1937): 235–39.

Notice to Builders.

I have for sale at my landing on the *Julington Creek*, St. John's River, from fifty to one hundred thousand Bricks, at eight dollars per thousand, they are one size smaller than the Charleston and Savannah Bricks, as for the quality, they are equal to them if not superior. I am prepared to furnish those that wish to purchase, one hundred thousand every thirty days if required, or I will get them ready as otherwise ordered, by giving due notice.

N. B. The Julington Creek is fifteen miles above Jacksonville, and has a safe harbor, and any vessel that sails up the St. John's, can load from a plank at my landing.

REUBEN LORING

St. Augustine. May 27th, 1835   8—tf..

Notice to builders. At the time the Brown siblings joined their Aunt Delia in Upper East Florida, migration into the region was advancing swiftly. Much of this growth halted quickly, however, as a result of the outbreak of the Second Seminole War. St. Augustine Florida Herald, *January 13, 1836.*

much on account of the exceeding careless manner in which the houses are built.

I will endeavor to give you some idea of Aunt Delia's mansion, as I suppose that of course to be the one you are most interested in, and because, besides I have been in but one other. "Vel"[17] then your aunt's domicil is two stories two rooms on a floor and two [shed] rooms which are [apartments] on the lower floor with slanting roof. All the rooms are small. The largest about the size of our smallest parlour at home. This latter apartment is plaster; in all the rest the clap-boards are as visible on the inside as the out. The only difference being the additional ornament of beams on the inside. One of the chambers is finished also after a fashion and these two rooms have very Christian furniture. Dark now; when I get a light I'll tell you more about it. "Vell" now, all the houses

---

17. This is Ellen's rendition of a German pronunciation of "well."

here even the littlest have a piazza and all the two story ones a balcony above the home. Aunt D's is furnished with these likewise. But there is nothing outside of the house to give the idea of a cottage paradise. The fence is a Virginia rail fence and the pines grow close up to it, in front, & on one side there is a pasture and on the other a dead orange grove. Have you got an idea? The soil here is all sand. The pines are little, lean, and miserable, growing at sufficient distance to admit the grass to grow all over the ground; there is no underwood— excepting in the hammock lands. This makes pine barren. If the ground bears anything else but pines and grass, it is hammock land and the only land worth cultivating. The roads are cut through these pine barrens and when they are straight and especially when they terminate towards the river, the effect is exceedingly pretty. The new roads are the most curious articles. Oh the stumps! and over them you go, you may avoid a good many, but it is impossible to avoid all. There is very little cleared land except where the settlements are. The nearest to Aunt Delia's is Mandarin four miles off. The place where she lives has no name.

You see I am writing down (higgledepiddlede?) just what comes into my head. My intention is to give you an idea of the place. I have no doubt that it is improving fast and, that property will be valuable here by and by when the rail road is built. All the talk here is about the Indians and all the world is going up to "Alachua"[18] to fight them. You see the time has come for them to go, and they arnt willing. What you don't understand in this letter I will endeavour to explain in my next. I should like to see you but I cannot in my conscience ask you to come here with any other idea than that of making a visit. But I do want to see you. All the folks send love. Floridians call themselves "crackar"[19] Why!

18. Ellen is referring here to Alachua County; "Alachua" in the context Ellen is using here refers to the large, sparsely settled region west of the St. Johns.

19. This term, "cracker," refers to those settlers recently arrived from neighboring states, mainly yeoman farmers and herdsmen. Drawn to Florida by the fertility and availability of public land, particularly in East Florida where wild hogs and cattle were in abundance, they grew staples such as corn for subsistence. Hunting and fishing supplemented their diets, but many of this group also herded cattle and hogs on the open range. Sometimes referred to as "plain folk," crackers were also disparagingly referred to as "poor whites," especially by northerners. The precise origin of the term is controversial, but it originates from one or a combination of sources: 1) the cracking of whips by those who herded cattle or pigs in the open range; 2) the habit of rural southern people of cracking corn to make bread; or 3) the propensity of rural southern folk to boast or "crack." The roots of the phrase can even be traced to many of the native southerners' Scotch-Irish antecedents. See Grady McWhiney, *Cracker Culture: Celtic Ways in the Old South* (Tuscaloosa:

I don't know. Tomorrow all the malicious muster at Jacksonville to go and fight the Indians. Hurra for the romantic? Good bye.

.... I'll do better next ... Ell

[Corinna Brown to Mannevillette Brown]

Mandarin [to Geneva, New York]
Dec. 22, 1835

My dear Manne,

I have just received your kind letter of the 18th inst.[20] I am exceedingly happy to hear from you dear, and also to learn you are so happily situated. Your description of the Dutchman and his tribe reminds me of a crew from the same quarter I once met with. Your comparisons are quite unique. You ask me to tell you of our voyage to this land &c. I think ere this you must be well acquainted with all the facts relating thereto. I have written you three documents before since my arrival, and Ellen has written you one, I trust you have received them all. I wrote to you on the 20th of Oct. from Portsmouth; did not you receive it? I have had one letter from George since we arrived. I have written him two or three. I feel anxious about the little rogue—you must make him write to you often.

Charles is well & seems to be very happy. He says if you will send him the paper on silk you mention he would like much to have it. Aunt Mary intends to put up a house on a lot back of Dr. Hall's: the houses will be within call of each other. This I like. I believe I mentioned these affairs in my last. Ann, Mary, & Ch. will purchase the lot together for $300—or $100 each. There will be 20 ackres, it has been planted & is worth $50 per acre, but the Dr. will consider them. I think it a very pretty spot & doubt not it will be the best thing they can do. They will have a comfortable home from the time they put up their house, and will probably in four or five years be rich. In short they like the idea & so do I. You ask me to tell you about Dr. Hall. Aunt D. & him. Dr. Hall is a fine old gentleman, liberal as a prince although he is spare in body.... He says but little but what he does say is to the purpose. I like him very much. Aunt D is just the same as ever, so is Ann, excepting that they are both a little thinner.

University of Alabama Press, 1988); Frank L. Owsley, *Plain Folk in the Old South* (Baton Rouge: Louisiana State University Press, 1949); James M. Denham, "The Florida Cracker Before the Civil War as Seen through Travelers' Accounts," *Florida Historical Quarterly* 72 (April 1994): 455–57; Denham, "Cracker Women and Their Families," 15–28; and Denham and Brown, *Cracker Times and Pioneer Lives,* xiii–xix.

20. This is an abbreviated form of *instant,* meaning "of this month."

M looks just as she did when you left home, Nab[21] is fat as a bear—and I am about so, so, neither fat nor lean—but very well. I have not had better health for a year. James Kincaid is here—he has the rheumatism, but is better—also one Mr. Adams belonging to Portsmouth. I fancy you don't know him—he is a nice young man. The rest of the good folks of this region are gone to fight the Indians—'tis said there are 350 volunteers from Florida besides the regular troops—so you see the Indians are not likely to conquer. However . . . 'tis most probable they will not attempt to fight. 150 of them have already been into the camps on friendly terms, and more are daily adding to the number. There was some alarm that the negroes should rise & fight with the Indians, but this fear has subsided & peace & good order reigns.[22] You would have been amused could you have been here last week, and have seen the poor frightened devils scudding through the woods, trembling at shadows & shrinking at stumps. One of the <u>guards</u> actually fired at an <u>oak stump</u>—it made much fun. You must not scold me dear, for the manner in which I write. I am hurrying for the mail. It only leaves once a week. It goes tomorrow morning & I have to finish this. . . . Mr. [J. B.] Danforth is expected here every day. He is one of the Directors of the rail road.[23] I want to see him. We have not been to St. Augustine yet,

21. Ellen.

22. Fear that black slaves might join the Seminoles against the whites predominated among many of the white settlers of territorial Florida. Indeed, the large numbers of blacks among the Seminoles, themselves the progeny of escaped slaves; the prominent role of blacks in Seminole leadership councils; plus the polyglot nature of the tribe lent credence to the belief that war against the Seminoles might provide the opportunity for slave revolt. In addition to links already cited on the Seminoles, see Kenneth W. Porter, *The Negro on the American Frontier* (New York: Arno Press, 1971); Kenneth W. Porter, *The Black Seminoles: History of Freedom Seeking People,* rev. and ed. Alcione M. Amos and Thomas P. Senter (Gainesville: University Press of Florida, 1996); George Klos, "Blacks and the Seminole Removal Debate, 1821–1835," in *The African American Heritage of Florida,* ed. David R. Colburn and Jane L. Landers (Gainesville: University Press of Florida, 1995), 128–56; Jane Landers, "Free and Slave," in *The New History of Florida,* ed. Michael Gannon (Gainesville: University Press of Florida, 1996), 167–82; Jane Landers, *Black Society in Spanish Florida* (Urbana: University of Illinois Press, 1999); Mahon and Weisman, "Florida's Seminoles and Miccosukee Peoples," 193–99; Canter Brown, "The Florida Crisis of 1826–1827 and the Second Seminole War," *Florida Historical Quarterly* 73 (April 1995): 419–42; Rivers, *Slavery in Florida;* and Daniel L. Schafer, "'A Class of People Neither Freemen nor Slaves': From Spanish to American Race Relations in Florida, 1821–1861," *Journal of Social History* 26 (spring 1993): 587–609.

23. The East Florida Railroad Company was a Boston, Massachusetts, company chartered by Florida's legislative council in 1835 and by the U.S. Congress in 1837. Its purpose

but shall go soon. We are not going until the volunteers come back here! About the lectures on painting, Manne, keep up a good heart—go ahead. They will gain for you more laurels than you are aware of. We amuse ourselves here by reading & brushing up on French—roaming through the pine barrens— digging in Indian mounds &c. We have discovered no curiosities as yet. Mr. Adams picked up a piece of an earthen pot! You must write to me often dear, very often. I will do the same. All send much love & wish to see you as much as I do. I hope if not before, you come next fall. Deo Volante.[24] . . .

Farewell a while dearest. God bless you. Yours in love ever

Corinna

---

was to build a railroad linking the Atlantic and the Gulf of Mexico. Along with Danforth, its other directors were Samuel L. Lewis, John Henshaw, and Stephan White. Because of the destruction, dislocation, and economic hard times brought on by the Second Seminole War, the company—like the locally chartered Florida Peninsula and Jacksonville Railroad Company—was unsuccessful and eventually disbanded. On the company, see Memorial to Congress by the President and Directors of the East Florida Railroad Company, December 14, 1835, in Clarence E. Carter, ed., *The Territorial Papers of the United States,* 26 vols. (Washington, D.C.: U.S. Government Printing Office, 1934–62), 25:212–13; *St. Augustine Florida Herald,* September 10, 17, 1835; and *Jacksonville Courier,* September 10; December 3, 1835.

24. Italian: "God willing."

Chapter Two

"Our Indian War"
1836–1837

On December 3, 1835, the *Jacksonville Courier* reported the murder of Charley Emaltha, a Seminole Indian leader friendly to the whites. No whites had been killed yet, the journal reported, but the Indians "have evinced every manifestation of determined hostility. The inhabitants are flying in every direction; while military corps are organizing and repairing to the frontier to protect the lives and property of those who are exposed to this wiley and secret foe."

On December 28, 1835, Seminoles attacked a body of 108 soldiers under the command of Maj. Francis L. Dade on the Fort King Road near the Withlacoochee River as they trekked through the frontier on their way to reinforce the isolated Indian agency at Fort King (Ocala). Dade's Massacre, the greatest Indian victory against a regular military force until Custer's defeat by the Sioux in 1876, was part of a simultaneous uprising planned by the Seminoles with their Creek and black allies. The same day that Dade's column fell, Redstick Creek leader Osceola murdered Indian agent Wiley Thompson and four other men just outside the Fort King stockade. St. Johns River plantations were also attacked. It is not likely that word of Dade's Massacre had reached Mandarin by the time Ellen wrote of the excited nature of her community. [1]

1. On Dade's Massacre and the events surrounding the opening attacks of the Seminoles that precipitated the Second Seminole War, see Frank Laumer, *Dade's Last Command* (Gainesville: University Press of Florida, 1995); Mahon, *History of the Second Seminole War,* 103–7; Covington, *Seminoles of Florida,* 79–80; Mahon and Weisman, "Florida's Seminoles and Miccosukee Peoples," 192–95; Edwin C. McReynolds, *The Seminoles* (Norman: University of Oklahoma Press, 1972), 153–55; Prucha, *Sword of the Republic,* 273–75; Rivers, *Slavery in Florida,* 201–5; Sidney Walter Martin, *Florida during Territorial Days,* 233–35; Rembert Patrick, *Aristocrat in Uniform: General Duncan L. Clinch* (Gainesville: University of Florida Press, 1963), 67–91; and James W. Silver, *Edmund Pendleton Gaines: Frontier General* (Baton Rouge: Louisiana State University Press, 1949), 167–70. It took nearly two months for a relief column under the command of Gen. Edmund P. Gaines to

[Ellen Brown to Mannevillette Brown]

St. Johns River [to Geneva, New York]
January 10th, 183[6]

My dear Manne,

I feel particularly nervous to day, as you may perceive by the handwriting, but I have been intending to write to you for a week and have put it off from day to day until today, when I thought I would commence in hopes of finishing some time before the next mail leaves. Do you hear anything your way about our Indian war? We have had one [tough] battle—sixty Americans wounded and four killed.[2] They say the affair will not end under 3 or 4 months. This is the chief subject of interest here at present, from all accounts the country is in a bad condition at the theatre of hostilities, but we see nothing of it, though we hear a great deal.[3]

We have formed a couple of very pleasant acquaintances here in the persons of two young ladies, one Miss Smith, a sister of a gentleman whom we boarded in the house with last winter, and one Miss Leaton who belongs to Amelia Island and who is visiting her aunt who resides here. Both very genteel girls. We have not been to St. Augustine yet for 3 reasons, first because it is hard getting in, 2d because it is expensive after you have got in, and 3d because it is dull in

---

survey the battlefield. In a letter to his father Lt. George McCall described the macabre scene. See George A. McCall to Father, May 1, 1836, in George A. McCall, *Letters from the Frontiers* (Philadelphia: Lippincott, 1868), 299–316. See also E. A. Hitchcock to Maj. Gen. Edmund P. Gaines, February 22, 1836, in John T. Sprague, *Origins, Progress, and Conclusion of the Florida War* (reproduction of the 1848 edition, Tampa, Fla.: University of Tampa Press, 2000), 108–9.

2. Ellen is referring here to the Battle of Withlacoochee on December 31, 1835, in which approximately 250 regulars and 500 volunteers fought the Seminoles near their stronghold on the Cove of the Withlacoochee. The attack came as Gen. Duncan Lamont Clinch's force was crossing the river, which was disastrous for Clinch's regulars because many of the volunteers under the command of Gov. Richard Keith Call never crossed the river. Recriminations between the regulars and volunteers began quickly. See Mahon, *History of the Second Seminole War,* 107–13; Covington, *Seminoles of Florida,* 81–82; McReynolds, *Seminoles,* 156; Prucha, *Sword of the Republic,* 275; Sprague, *Origins, Progress, and Conclusion of the Florida War,* 92; Patrick, *Aristocrat in Uniform,* 93–154; and Herbert J. Doherty Jr., *Richard Keith Call: Southern Unionist* (Gainesville: University of Florida Press, 1961), 96–108.

3. For newspaper coverage of the first two months of conflict in the Mandarin area, see *Jacksonville Courier,* December 10, 17, 24, 1835; January 7, 14; February 11, 1836; *St. Augustine Florida Herald,* January 6, 13, 20; February 6; March 9, 1836; and *Savannah Georgian,* January 4, 25; February 4, 1836.

there: on two accounts, one is, that the beaus great and small have all gone to the war, and the other, the people feel poor because they have lost their orange groves, and therefore, you see, there are no parties and of course no frolicks. The society here is as yours, a mixture of the poor genteel and the rich vulgar as you could imagine—the rich who belong here and own negroes and lands and the poor who have come here in hopes of getting them, all hopes, however, are deferred at present on account of the war with the Seminoles.

Jan 12th

I left off writing the other page in order to let the Doctor write a document, and immediately afterwards some company arrived which did not leave until this morning. So now I go ahead. Our visitor was Mr. Dale, one of the engineers employed upon the East Florida railroad. Young, handsome, and tall, a native of Springfield Mass., but he is gone to return, in all human probability, no more! <u>Sic transit gloria mundi</u>.[4] We see considerable company here for "a remote ville" but its kind is just as may be, good, bad and indifferent—if either prevails it is certainly the latter.

They are just commencing to survey the land for the railroad which is to be the making of Florida, and particularly of the part where it spans the river, which is a matter of more interest to speculators and landholders than to you and me except, indeed, so far as it facilitates the means of travelling and brings a far more civilized "life" my way.

Charlie goes at planting hand and heart and the Doctor predicts he will be a rich man. You don't know how striking the contrast is to be between living here and in Phila. I feel as if I was out of the world. There in the midst of a large boarding house I heard of everything as it were as soon as it happened, here I am unsure that new news be old everywhere before it reaches us. Was a new novel published; or a war threatens; or a runaway couple married; each by turn was the talk of the hour and gave place to some succeeding novelty. Here every body knows every body; and I had learnt the history of every inhabitant of the settlement, and all the advantages and disadvantages of every particular location the new railroad might, could, would, and should take and was just getting to close our discussions of both when an Aaron's serpent[5] in the shape of this Indian war swallowed up every other subject of interest. But this is novelty of the most complete and entire kind. Every day brings new reports, and each

4. Latin: "Thus passes away the glory of this world," from "Imitation of Christ," generally attributed to Thomas à Kempis (1380–1471). For further information about this work and an English translation, see Harold C. Gardiner, ed., *The Imitation of Christ* (Garden City, N.Y.: Image Books, 1955).

5. See Exod. 7:8–13.

more interesting than the last. And then there be alarms and false alarms and there be the courageous and there be some of the most dastardly pusillanimous cowards you could conceive of. And there be scouts, patrolls [*sic*], and volunteers and . . . all kinds of militia affairs, mixing up . . . ludicrous and serious in a curious manner.

You have no idea how much like children men can act. The way the superiors command, and the privates obey, and both to-gether are using Uncle Sam's surplus treasury is a caution to republicks! Corine sends her love and will write next week, likewise Ann, Mary, Charlie & the latter desire me to add that his hand has grown so clumsy that he despairs of ever being able to use a pen as he has done. I close my epistle in some dispair of its ever reaching you, for our post office affairs are in most precarious disorder. Good bye, Ellen

post Master died—post Master drunk

In the winter of 1836 Mannevillette moved to Ithaca, New York, and on February 3, Corinna wrote to him that the widening war had engulfed the surrounding area: "I suppose you see by the papers how very generous the South Carolinians have been to us. . . . There were many families upon the river above Black Creek, 15 or 20 miles from us who were turned out of their homes without money and without food, but thanks to Heaven, they are now comfortably provided for and will be until they can return to their plantations which is thought will be three months." The settlers, she continued, stayed "penned up in houses, we go no where & see nobody, save a straggling officer, a negro, or a militia man now and then—And we can get nothing done either for love or money." That summer Corinna informed Mannevillette that many predicted that the "Creeks and Seminoles . . . [might] unite. . . . I think a more bloody and ruinous war will be fought with these savages before they are subdued, than has ever, yet been witnessed on our fair land. The accounts of the Creek Indians' deeds of horror are enough to curdle our own heart's blood. They offer to be much more bloodthirsty and indiscriminate in their slaughter than the Seminoles have been, but the Lord only knows what they may do. . . . It is not generally thought they will cross the Julington, but if they should, they will have much to do, before they reach us, so we shall have time to quit. They have been so bold as to ride up to St. Augustine and yell, steal horses and ride off again. They were pursued by the city guard eighteen miles, but were not overtaken. I say Mann, what a pretty fix the country would have been in if we had gone to war with France![6] Or even should the slaves rise about this time,

---

6. At the time of Corinna's writing, the Andrew Jackson administration was embroiled with the French government over spoilation claims of Americans against the French

David Levy Yulee, a close friend of Ellen and Corinna, was a lawyer, planter, territorial delegate to Congress, and U.S. senator. Florida State Archives.

it would make a glorious work—the horrors of St. Domingo enacted over again in earnest. . . . Mr. [David] Levy[7] of St. Augustine is here to day, he is playing chess with Ell. I say this that you may know we are pretty generally

---

dating back to the Napoleonic Wars. When the French legislature refused to appropriate funds to satisfy their agreements, Jackson threatened war. The dispute was amicably settled with the help of Great Britain. See Mahon, *History of the Second Seminole War,* 117; John A. Garraty, *The American Nation: A History of the United States to 1877,* 7th ed. (New York: HarperCollins, 1991), 272–73; Arthur M. Schlesinger Jr., ed., *The Almanac of American History* (New York: Putnam, 1983), 232–33; and Henry Blumenthal, *France and the United States: Their Diplomatic Relations, 1789–1914* (New York: Norton, 1970), 38–49.

7. Already a friend to the Browns, David Levy would become one of the leading political figures in antebellum Florida. In 1836 Levy was practicing law in Judge Raymond Reid's law office in St. Augustine. David Levy was the son of Moses Elias Levy, a prosperous Jewish West Indian merchant and land speculator who held vast acreage at the time Florida became an American territory. Levy attended Harvard University and was admitted to the bar in 1832. A leading Democrat and advocate of statehood, Levy was elected to the legislative council in 1837–38 and played a leading role in the territory's constitutional convention at St. Joseph. Disinherited by his father because of disagreements

quiet. He is anxious that we should go to St. Augustine and pass the summer."[8] Indeed, the sisters and their family were in significant danger. A local newspaper reported that the Indians were well supplied with food, having captured almost five thousand head of cattle just south of Julington Creek and east of the St. Johns. These, added to the twenty thousand already in their possession, as well as substantial amounts of other provisions, ensured that the Seminoles could sustain a significant war. "They have carried away all of the corn from the plantations and stored it; and with the extra labor of colored slaves in addition to their own, they will be enabled to raise an abundance. From the best information we have," the journal continued, "their prospects are very promising."[9]

If the sisters had desired to leave their exposed position on the frontier, they could have sought protection at either the nearby village of Jacksonville just to the north or at St. Augustine approximately thirty-four miles to the southeast. The villages could be reached by the Atlantic, but the more common route was via steamboat south on the St. Johns to Picolata and then eighteen miles east to St. Augustine by stage. Jacksonville, atop the St. Johns River, was plotted and laid out in 1822, one year after Florida became an American territory. Fourteen years later when the Brown sisters arrived, Duval contained approximately thirty-eight hundred people, while the county seat contained approximately seven hundred people. The village was composed mostly of southerners relocating to the new territory, but the town also contained a significant minority of northerners seeking economic opportunity in the emerging territory. Bishop Henry Whipple, who visited Jacksonville in 1843, found "no redeeming traits in its character"; the "soil is exceedingly sandy and every step you take it seems as if you would sink beneath the sand. The houses are poorly constructed & the place is dull enough." And yet, as Whipple reported, the village's inhabitants seemed to have an exalted opinion of themselves, for, as he explained, they

---

stemming from religion and other matters, Levy added an older family surname and by 1843 would be known as David Levy Yulee. That year he was elected territorial delegate to Congress. In 1845 Yulee became one of Florida's first U.S. senators, the first Jew in U.S. history to hold that office. On David Levy Yulee see Tebeau, *History of Florida,* 131, 138, 172–73, 189–92; Schafer, "U.S. Territory and State," 215, 221–25; and Arthur W. Thompson, "David Yulee: A Study of Nineteenth-Century American Thought and Enterprise" (Ph.D. diss., Columbia University, 1954).

8. Corinna Brown to Mannevillette Brown, June 9, 1836, Anderson-Brown Papers, USMA.

9. *St. Augustine Florida Herald,* July 12, 1836.

"vainly imagine that Jacksonville is the ne plus ultra of civilization & refinement and that in them strangers can behold all that is desirable in mankind." But Jacksonville's growth and prosperity were steady. The town eventually over-shadowed St. Augustine, to the south.[10]

In the late 1830s St. Augustine prospered, largely due to the influx of military personnel and federal dollars brought in by the Second Seminole War. When Corinna and Ellen arrived, St. Johns County contained about seventeen hundred souls while the "Ancient City" boasted a few hundred. And yet St. Augustine would soon have two newspapers: the Democratic *Florida Herald* and the Whig *News*. The most recognizable landmark in St. Augustine was the Castillo de San Marcos. The town's quaint appearance charmed visitors. Capt. John Mackay thought that the city was "prettily situated [with] an appearance of comfort, cleanliness, and stability not often seen in southern towns"; another newcomer from New York wrote relatives back home that St. Augustine "resembles Montreal more than any place I have ever seen; the same narrow streets."[11] Not all of those who visited St. Augustine were as charmed by its appearance. When John Audubon visited the village seven years before Mackay arrived, he wrote to his wife that he believed St. Augustine "resembles some old French village and is doubtless the poorest village I have seen in America," and a few weeks later Audubon's impressions had changed little: "St Augustine is the poorest hole in the Creation—The living very poor and very high—was it not for the fishes in the Bay and a few thousand oranges that grow immediately around the village, the people must undoubtedly abandon it or starve for they are all too lazy to work, or they work at such price as it puts

10. Lester B. Shippee, ed., *Bishop Whipple's Southern Diary, 1843–1844* (Minneapolis: University of Minnesota Press, 1937), 39. For information on Jacksonville see Pleasant Daniel Gold, *History of Duval County, Including Early History of East Florida* (St. Augustine, Fla.: The Record Company, 1929), 99–120; T. Frederick Davis, *History of Jacksonville, Florida and Vicinity, 1513 to 1924* (St. Augustine, Fla.: Florida Historical Society, 1925), 51–86; T. Frederick Davis, *History of Early Jacksonville: Being an Authentic Record of Events from the Earliest Times to and Including the Civil War* (Jacksonville, Fla.: H. & W. B. Drew Company, 1911), 29–96; Richard A. Martin, *The City Makers* (Jacksonville, Fla.: Convention Press, 1972), 6–21; James Robertson Ward, *Old Hickory's Town: An Illustrated History of Jacksonville* (Jacksonville, Fla.: Old Hickory's Town, Inc., 1985), 115–39; and Sidney Walter Martin, *Florida during Territorial Days,* 185–89.

11. John Mackay to Eliza Mackay, April 9, 1838, box 45, Miscellaneous Manuscripts, P. K. Yonge Library, University of Florida, Gainesville; George R. Fairbanks to Samuel Fairbanks, November 5, 1842, Fairbanks Papers, box 69, folder 4, P. K. Yonge Library, University of Florida, Gainesville.

it out of the question to employ them"; of the land surrounding St. Augustine, Audubon also had little positive to say: "The Country around," he observed, "[is] nothing but bare sand Hills."[12]

With the influx of military personnel (many of them well educated and sophisticated), the town provided social opportunities for the sisters. Balls, masquerades, and parties were frequent. For example, a physician who was stationed with the military contingent in the town in 1837 was astonished to find over sixty ladies at a ball one evening in St. Augustine. "Last night," the man lamented, "I most anxiously wished that I could waltz, for no other reason" than "merely to feel and be felt by the ladies."[13] Even if the society of St. Augustine was often boisterous, the town was also one of the only places in the territory that the sisters could enjoy the kind of social and intellectual stimulation to which they were accustomed. This was so in large part because, like Jacksonville, the village was already attracting well-to-do northerners with respiratory ailments seeking respite from harsh northern winters.[14]

Despite the dangers of their position on the Florida frontier, the Browns were determined to stay in Mandarin: On February 16, Corinna wrote to Mannevillette that she hoped the old house in Portsmouth would sell soon so that they could afford to move out of Dr. Hall's house and thereby remove the tensions caused by their living there. On April 7, Corinna wrote that plans for building their own house in Mandarin were well under way. By late summer Charles, Mary, and Ann were cultivating twenty-three acres they had acquired for twenty dollars per acre.

12. John James Audubon to Lucy Audubon, November 23; December 5, 1831, in Kathryn Hall Proby, *Audubon in Florida: With Selections from the Writings of John James Audubon* (Coral Gables, Fla.: University of Miami Press, 1974), 15, 17.

13. Edward M. Coffman, *The Old Army: A Portrait of the American Army in Peacetime, 1784–1898* (New York: Oxford University Press, 1986), 106. For more on the relations between soldiers and civilians in wartime Florida, see William B. Skelton, *An American Profession of Arms: The Army Officer Corps, 1784–1861* (Lawrence: University of Kansas Press, 1992), 211, 223–24; and James M. Denham, "'Some Prefer the Seminoles': Violence and Disorder among Soldiers and Settlers in the Second Seminole War, 1835–1842," *Florida Historical Quarterly* 70 (July 1991): 38–54.

14. On St. Augustine, see Thomas Graham, *The Awakening of St. Augustine: The Anderson Family and the Oldest City, 1821–1924* (St. Augustine, Fla.: St. Augustine Historical Society, 1978), 1–83; Shippee, *Bishop Whipple's Southern Diary,* 16–28; John Hammond Moore, ed., "A South Carolina Lawyer Visits St. Augustine—1837," *Florida Historical Quarterly* 43 (April 1965): 361–78; and Sidney Walter Martin, *Florida during Territorial Days,* 181–85.

[Corinna Brown to Mannevillette Brown]

Mandarin [to Ithaca, New York]
May 25, 1836

My dear Mann,

I am sorry to inform you, that your suspicions respecting the Indians over-coming Florida seem about to be realized. Alarms of their being near are frequently <u>false</u>, and <u>some true</u>, still Dr. Hall says he apprehends no danger from them on his plantation. Neither do I immediately, but unless measures are taken to defend the town, I know no reason why we should be more exempt from danger than others. I shall merely state facts to you, and then you will know as much about the matter as I do, and can draw your own conclusions. Gen. [Winfield] Scott[15] has disbanded all the militia, and retired with five U.S. companies within the walls of St. Augustine—there crouched behind a strong Fort.[16] Nobody is no doubt safe while the whole river lies open to the attacks of the savages without one solitary soldier to defend it.

For several weeks Indian raids have been discovered about the plantations near here. It seems they have been in pursuance of a Mr. [George S.] Mott, a rich man whom they had sworn to kill. He has been a trader among them, and used to whip them. Last week he returned from New York—said he believed they would kill him if they have a chance, that he would go to his plantation and if he could not stay there, he would return and help fight them. Night before last he went, and began to put out some small trees. Just at sunset which

15. Born in Virginia in 1786, Scott received a commission as captain in the regular army in 1808. Scott served with distinction in the War of 1812 and went on to become one of the most important American military figures in the first half of the nineteenth century. Intelligent, enigmatic, and confident, the future "Fuss and Feathers," was a master of traditional military tactics but could never adjust to the style of warfare necessary to subdue the Seminoles. His career suffered for his lack of success in Florida, but only briefly. Scott won acclaim in the Mexican War, and though too old to take field command he served the Union after resigning his commission in 1862. See Thomas W. Cutrer, "Winfield Scott," in *The United States and Mexico at War: Nineteenth-Century Expansionism and Conflict,* ed. Donald S. Frazier (New York: Macmillan, 1998), 380–82; Timothy D. Johnson, *Winfield Scott: The Quest for Military Glory* (Lawrence: University of Kansas Press, 1998); and John S. D. Eisenhower, *Agent of Destiny: The Life and Times of General Winfield Scott* (New York: Free Press, 1997).

16. This policy caused anger and frustration among settlers. See Governor Call to the Secretary of War, April 28, 1836, in Carter, *Territorial Papers,* 25:279–81; Mahon, *History of the Second Seminole War,* 160–67; and Prucha, *Sword of the Republic,* 280–81. For raids around the Mandarin area in the spring of 1836, see Brown, *Ossian Bingley Hart,* 34.

it appears is a favorite hour of attack with the Indians, he was placing a tree, and one of his negros putting the earth round it. They fired and shot him dead. The negros ran. The Indians then scalped Mott, went into his house, took what they pleased, set fire to it, and cleared into the woods. This was on the bank of Julington Creek, a branch of the St. John's, directly opposite the settlement of Mandarin, six miles from Dr. Hall's. The brave men at the settlement or village—heard their rifles & war whoop, saw the house on fire, knew they were Indians, and did not attempt to pursue them—but ran hither and thither like mad people. Of course, if we do not have a guard they will be emboldened to do the like again. They are trying to get up a volunteer corps today, but whether they will succeed or not I can't say. 'Tis bad for the natives to leave their crops, now in excellent condition, and promising, if taken care of, abundant harvest. Besides in most instances these are their sole dependence, and they may as well defend themselves from famine as the sword. They have also petitioned to Scott for a guard, but I think it doubtful if they get one. 'Tis thought the reason they did not do any mischief here before, was because they were determined to kill Mott and did not wish to raise any alarm, until they had accomplished their purpose.[17] But whether this be true or false time only can decide. If they attack another plantation as near us, I shall get frightened but at present we are all as quiet as possible, and go on fulfilling our dull routine of duty much as if nothing had occurred. One reason why we do is if they come on this settlement, they will destroy plantations higher up the river first, and we shall get the alarm in time to clear out by water; (minus our goods and chattels, however, which I should not relish at all!) But I am in hopes we shall get a guard, and I don't believe we shall have to quit here—aunts Anne, Mary, Dolly [Delia], Charlie & Dr. swear they won't be "driven" off, and I think they are right—they would lose their crops, and, leave their groves to be destroyed and their house pillaged, if not burnt. Of course, we shall not put up a house at present so 'tis no matter about the request I made of you in my last.

The old house will be disposed of I suppose before you get this (I shall sign for you as [attorney in fact]). Dr. has bought hard lumber & it must be paid for—the surplus cash will be deposited in the savings bank in P— until we can

17. St. Augustine and Jacksonville newspapers that would provide more details of Mott's murder have not survived. Nevertheless, subsequent issues of the *St. Augustine Florida Herald* beginning on August 17 announce the settlement of his estate. Mott's murder is discussed in the *Tallahassee Floridian,* August 6, 1836; and *Savannah Georgian,* May 23, 1836. Five days later the *Georgian* reported that people in the Mandarin area had, before Mott's murder, felt themselves secure but now "are leaving their places."

build which will probably be next autumn or winter—'tis said we shall be in no possible danger after October, enough troops will then be in the country to subdue the devils. They want Nab & I to go to Jacksonville, but we laugh at them. I deem no part of the Territory less liable to attack than another, and again I would almost as lief [18] encounter the Indians as the Jacksonville mob. It is the nastyest [*sic*] dirtyest [*sic*] place I ever was in & such a hole I guess as you never saw. What is the reason I do not hear from you, dear, your last was March 25—Do write & let us know what you are about—Nab & I are stupid as Jackasses. Nothing to do but eat, drink, & sleep or rather be coddled in our juices. . . . This is a lovely climate, however, only hot in the middle of the day, good breeze from 3 o'clock P.M. to ten A.M. The fun we have is laughing at the crackers when there is false alarm of Indians!—hurrah for old southenders. This leaves all well & in good spirits, I will write again soon. If there is danger, we shall get off—so don't be alarmed. We shall put our cowardly legs in requisition quicker! C[harles]'s orange trees grow nice—much love from all.

Yours ever

Corinna

[Corinna Brown to Mannevillette Brown]

Mandarin [to Ithaca, New York]

May 27th, 1836

My dear brother,

I wrote to you yesterday concerning the Indians. Today I have received your kind letter of the 23rd ult [19] hasten to answer it by the same mail. We had another, (I believe false) alarm last night—an old man & his daughter—one third indian and two thirds negros in blood—came to Mandarin and stated that at their house, situated on the main or king's road eight miles from here, and thirty from Augustine, that just at sunset their dogs began to howl. They at first supposed it was at wolves—but from their manner afterwards supposed it must be at Indians. They waited until the moon was down and then stole off—the dogs ceased not their barking. This morning a dozen men rode out to the place—there are no other houses within six miles of it. They discovered a shoe track, but <u>no mocasin</u>. They traced it round the house into the woods to where a horse had been tied; there the man, indian or devil, jumpt on and rode off.—'Tis possible it might have been an Indian spy—they are crafty enough to steal shoes & of course to put them on, they know they are traced, but the Dr.

---

18. "As lief" is an archaic phrase meaning "prefer to."

19. This is an abbreviated form of Latin *ultimo*, meaning "of last month."

says it is more probable it was a white Indian after stealing cattle. The Dr. says the excitement is evidently kept up to induce [Gen. Winfield] Scott to send a guard for this place and he thinks 'tis well—for although it is not probable the Indians will come on this neck of land, still 'tis possible they may, and we ought to be able to defend it in case they <u>should</u>. I have just read the petition to Scott for 30 men. I am in hopes he will grant it. 'Tis a very well written article.

—Now to your letter, dear, I am very glad you have ordered the mulberry trees, silk worms, &c. I expect to make money by them yet—they thrive well here and if the Indians <u>should</u> come, they will not disturb the trees I am told, they never have. But our house as I before informed you we are advised not to build, until next winter, so the request I made about the loan, I retract, as we shall not want any furniture for a year at least. I thank you for it dear as much as if I had received it. As for our domestic matters of which I spoke—I am happy to say all is <u>harmony</u>. Aunt D has an attack of inflamatory rheumatism, slight but all the rest are well. You ask how much land we have?—about 30 acres, that is as much as C. can cultivate alone, and leave room for his groves in the bargain. We plant mulberry trees ten feet apart. They gave $20 per acre for their land. I am sorry you did not get that you speak of, but I have come to the conclusion that almost "what-ever is, is right."[20] Nevertheless I would not let a like chance slip again if I had one, because that land must soon increase in value. New York is a flourishing state. I hope you will get the situation as surveyor. I believe you will from what you say. We shall all do well yet, I doubt not; perseverance and industry never go unrewarded. You would laugh to see M, A. & C. They are regular farmers with their dairy, poultry yard, potato patch, corn field &c. Their log kitchen looks curious, but it answers very well to cook in & they sleep here now and will until they get their other house up, which I am in hopes will be early next winter. Nab & I have nothing to do but eat, drink, & snooze, but I look to <u>brighter</u> years.

I have 40 cocoons that will hatch in a few days. They are all pure white. I am glad you have sent me some eggs. I want more than I have to begin with. I fed them on the native mulberry until a few days of their spinning, then a man gave me some leaves of the worms [Multicanlis]. The cocoons look full & well. If the Indians make us run I will take them with me, confound the scamps, how much trouble they make, but I don't blame them. It must be rare fun for them. You would die a laughing to see the crackers (as they call the natives) they are so frightened. Dr. went to Mandarin yesterday—he says he never saw such a set of crazy, foolish devils in his life. I write in haste for mail. I don't

20. From Alexander Pope's philosophical poem *Essay on Man* (1733), epistle 1, line 294.

know as I shall get it to Mandarin in season, if not it will be mailed at Jacksonville. I shall write to you often while this excitement lasts which I suppose will be all summer—but if we get a guard there will be no cause for it. After October there can be no danger. I don't think our yankee courage will fail us however. But if I do get frightened, you may depend I shall run, but not until I do, for my legs are <u>weakly</u>, and I want them to last me as long as possible . . . Corinna

[Corinna Brown to Mannevillette Brown]

Mandarin [to Ithaca, New York]
June 16, 1836

My dear Manne,

Enclosed I send you the deed of that bothering old South [Estate]. I am thankful to get it off my hands anyhow; had the business been left with me, I would have had it advantageously settled long ago—N'importe,[21] we must make the best of it now. I am glad it is to be sold. I wish you to go before a Justice Peace . . . I do not presume to tell you what to do, but I think you may not deem it necessary to do more than sign it—After you have done your duty, I wish you to forward it to George <u>immediately</u> and request him to do the same. I have just had a letter from him. He approves of selling it at any price, if we do not intend to return to P[ortsmouth] and I am sure we do not, as we do not wish to starve just now; better be tomahawked; and then our orange trees grow finely; George will go down to P. for Mary and settle the business—do not fail to forward it immediately. I have left some blanks to be filled up by George or Mr. Larkin. I have written to the latter in hope he will get more for the house. There's something like 30 or 40 dollars due the [major] now and two drafts to the amount of 100 and odd dollars for boards purchased for the new house &c. It is necessary to dispose of it to discharge these debts. Possibly we may be able to build in the fall . . . at any rate we shall begin next winter if ever. Don't let those New Yorkers forget to send me the <u>Mulberry trees</u>. I depend much on them. People say they are going to be the wealth of this country—and I do not know why they should not be <u>ours</u>—at any rate I'll try it. I suppose you are off or ready to go on your expedition by this time. Well, sign the deed and after <u>that</u>, you will have a glorious time. I should like well to go if I were you.

I suppose you hear all about the Indians now. They are kicking up such a row all over the South, government begins to take notice of it. I learn by the papers Gen. Jackson is much displeased with [Winfield] Scott. I am glad he's

---

21. French: "no matter."

awake at last. They have all been asleep in Washington and Scott has been playing tag with the Indians instead of fighting them, the while. I declare I have no patience when I think of the abominable and unnecessary delay of this war. It might have been brought to a close this spring with but little blood shed, had Scott had liberality of soul enough & have sacrificed his own feelings for the publick good and united with [Gen. Edmund Pendleton] Gaines.[22] But now in my humble opinion the U.S. have to lose more than man for man before the matter will be ended.[23] It is feared the Creeks will join the Seminoles. If they should, they will make havoc, I reckon. The Creeks are blood thirsty and the Seminoles brave—at least they have proved themselves of late. 100 well-mounted were seen around St. Augustine day before yesterday—They were pursued by the volunteer corps, but were not overtaken. The regulars did not think it necessary to <u>follow</u> <u>them</u>! The Indians call Scott and his troops the <u>gophers</u> because of their slow movement. The [Tallahassee] Floridian says they have been travelling for their health. They cut them, and <u>good</u>. The Seminoles seem to be round the place more for plunder than ambuscades, now, although I wouldn't have you think I suppose they would be gentle with either you or me, were we to come in their way—but their object seems to be to get horses & negros now. They have taken many within a week. In the fall most of them will be [situated], and furthermore, they will be in <u>complete</u> <u>readiness</u> for the winter campaign. They are making a very large crop themselves. They have <u>lots</u> of negros, and they will help themselves where they please to the white man's crops. 'Tis feared they will be even more troublesome next month & August than they have been because then will be harvest, but I am in hopes ere

22. Edmund Pendleton Gaines, a native of Virginia, joined the army in 1799, was a veteran of the War of 1812, and participated in Andrew Jackson's invasion of Spanish Florida in 1818. Gaines was known for his petulant personality and white mane of hair; his enemies referred to him as "Granny Gaines." Passed over for command in favor of Winfield Scott and Zachary Taylor, Gaines saw his career stagnate during the 1830s and 1840s. He owned a large plantation near present-day Gainesville (a town named for him). See Silver, *Edmund Pendleton Gaines;* and David J. Coles, "Edmund Pendleton Gaines," in *The United States and Mexico at War: Nineteenth-Century Expansionism and Conflict,* ed. Donald S. Frazier (New York: Macmillan, 1998), 172.

23. On the controversy between Scott and Gaines and its overall ramifications on the campaign against the Seminoles, see Mahon, *History of the Second Seminole War,* 135–67; McReynolds, *Seminoles,* 162–65; Mahon and Weisman, "Florida's Seminoles and Miccosukee Peoples," 193–95; Johnson, *Winfield Scott,* 116–17; Eisenhower, *Agent of Destiny,* 149–61; Silver, *Edmund Pendleton Gaines,* 176–90; and Patrick, *Aristocrat in Uniform,* 123–28.

then we will have <u>soldiers</u> in the field—I see several companies are already on their way.—somehow I can't get frightened although most of the southerners are half crazy. When I hear the dogs howl in the night then I am skittish and <u>then</u> there is the <u>least</u> cause for alarm. The Indians in former times never have been in this neck and therefore it is presumed they will not come now, but if they should, they won't come without giving us warning very well. They say it will take 5,000 to subdue the Creeks—and there are 5 or 6,000 of them—Scott could not quell 1,000 Seminoles with 2,000 men. <u>Great</u> <u>General</u>! His talent for tactics is quite bewildering! —

Dr. is much better—but we have all (but Ell & Charles) got the enfluenza, even the negros are sick with it. I feel as if I were made of sand, brains and all— heighho! . . . Corinna

[Corinna Brown to Mannevillette Brown]

Mandarin, [to Ithaca, New York]
July 12th, 1836

Well my dear,

I am glad to hear from you at last. I did not know but you had cut & quit with the rest of my correspondents. As for the Indians, the opinion whether we are to apprehend danger from them in this quarter is as fitful as the sunshine & showers of April—today a trumpet is raging, tomorrow a dead calm. For myself I feel very quiet but am ready to run if necessary. God grant it may not be; I do not believe it will. We have had no recent alarms. It is supposed all the scamps are gathered together to join in the green corn dance—a religious festival they never fail to observe when the corn is in the milk, before they eat of it. They have a black drink prepared (a sort of vomit) which they drink in purification before taking of the first fruits. Those who can take the largest draught without retching are entitled to great credit. 'Tis said Powell's Indian name is singahola and not Osceola & that it was given him because of his manly potations! be this as it may, he <u>is</u> a <u>guerrier</u>[24] & has well earned the laurels of war.[25] There was a report a few days since that he had been assassinated, but I

---

24. French: "warrior."

25. On the origins and notoriety of Billy Powell, or Osceola, as the Black Drink Singer and the ritual of consuming the Black Drink brewed from holly during the annual Busk, or Green Corn Dance, see Patricia R. Wickman, *Osceola's Legacy* (Tuscaloosa: University of Alabama Press, 1991), 31; Wright, *Creeks and Seminoles,* 22–33, 26–28, 249–55; and Mahon, *History of the Second Seminole War,* 14. According to James W. Covington, Osceola's name derived from "Asi-yaholo from *asi* (Black Drink) and *yaholo* (singer)—a reference to

Osceola. Florida State Archives.

Coacoochee, (Wild Cat)

Coacoochee (Wild Cat). Florida State Archives.

do not think it is correct.—There is to be much bloodshed yet ere he is laid low.—Gov [Richard Keith] Call is about to make a summer campaign now to destroy their crops, which are very large, but it is by many thought a mad scheme; they think it will fail and will reap disgrace instead of renown.[26] He has but 1000 men—Heaven grant it may do well. If this war is ever brought to a close, this country will become a green land. Plenty will smile on it—notwithstanding its desolate appearance now. Every thing we have attempted is flourishing, our corn is full in the ear, potatoes are sprouting, orange trees are shooting out although so newly planted—& etc, all but the house & perhaps 'tis well that is not growing, for we can do without it until the war is over, then there will be strangers in the land and we shall want a home.

In respect to the one hundred dollars you so kindly proffer (I <u>know</u> I should get it if I asked, dear) accept our poor thanks, as we do not want it at present, but we shall want it next spring I think. The trees I do want—a mulberry grove will be a fortune to us, if all else should fail, but we have no reason to doubt for God has prospered all our efforts and in spite of Indians we are glad of the move we made in coming out here. You say you think we lose some of your letters—I know I do, your last was 5th March, this is 12th June, but I am glad to get even half of them, you must also lose many of mine I write to you very often—this week since I sent you a letter enclosing the deed of the house for you to sign. [I] could not sign it without a <u>legal</u> permission—I hope you will get it in safety—if it has not come to hand look for it—you ought to have it.

---

the song of the attendant who offered the black drink to the participants at the Green Corn Ceremony" (*Seminoles of Florida,* 9). See Mark F. Boyd, "Asi-yaholo or Osceola," *Florida Historical Quarterly* 33 (January–April 1955): 249–305; and Brown, *Florida's Peace River Frontier,* 36–41.

26. At the time of Dade's massacre, Richard Keith Call, a native of Kentucky, was serving as general of the Florida Militia. By March 1836 President Andrew Jackson, Call's friend and mentor, had augmented his command, appointed Call territorial governor, and ordered Call to join regular forces under Gen. Duncan Lamont Clinch in pursuit of the Seminoles. Call had extensive military experience under Jackson in his campaign against the Creeks and during the First Seminole War, but his success against the Seminoles was limited, causing a breach between the two. At the time Corinna wrote, Gen. Winfield Scott had ceased operations against the Seminoles during the summer months. Call vehemently protested and got himself appointed head of military operations in Florida. His summer campaign was unsuccessful, and Jackson relieved him in November. See Tebeau, *History of Florida,* 160–63; Mahon, *History of the Second Seminole War,* 101–2, 162–89; and Doherty, *Richard Keith Call,* 93–117.

We shall not build until the war is over—a man has promised if he lives to put it up in two months then. The silk cultivator we <u>have</u> <u>not</u> <u>received</u>. The reason of my letters being sometimes mailed at Jacksonville is, I miss the Mandarin mail sometimes, & forward it by driver to J. S. J. Burrets[27] of whom we wot[28] has gone to Cuba. I believe he is <u>bad</u>, but he has reputation here, he is rich & money you know "opens every heart & every door even to the veriest wretch that ere disgraced humanity." He says his wife gets drunk!—I hear from other sources he has broken her heart & come well nigh breaking her head—'tis well however to think the best we may of "human kind"—he treats me very politely. Every one is coaxing Ell & I to go into St. Augustine. I wish to see the city as well as a little civilization once more. I think I shall go in for a few days but shall not afford to stay long.

We have a grand thunder storm just now. I would you could witness one of these same, they are truly sublime. I supposed I should be very much terrified of them, but they do not disturb me at all. I rather take pleasure in them. I suppose it is because they are so frequent, we have them almost every day. Then they refresh the air & make everything so sweet—and we have such brilliant rain bows, and the birds sing so blithely after they are over, dear me, I am getting quite rural. I hope you will be able to read this—my stationary wants replenishing—<u>all</u> the foxes say they will write after this—they should have written before but my pen is always ready. They send a deal of love and are all well. We enjoy our health very much, & do not find this climate at all oppressive. I do not think the weather generally warmer, or so warm even as the <u>dog days</u> in New Eng—but the heat is uniform. We have delightful mornings & evenings & <u>cool</u> <u>nights</u>, always.—I want you & George to move out here, but

---

27. Corinna is referring to Samuel L. Burritt, a twenty-six-year-old native of Connecticut. A prominent landowner, attorney, and Whig politician, Burritt served in the house of representatives of the territorial legislative council (1836 and 1839). He also served in the U.S. Senate in 1847 and 1848. Burritt's wife cannot be identified, but two years later he would marry Louisa Douglas, the daughter of Thomas Douglas, U.S. district attorney. Corinna and Ellen visited him and his family often. His homestead, one of the earliest established in Jacksonville, was near the northeast corner of Bay and Market Streets: "One of the most pretentious in town. There were large grounds, with stables, servants' quarters, and Mr. Burritt's law offices. The vacant lots on the river front, also Burritt property, abounding in shrubbery and shade trees, gave beautiful surroundings" (Davis, *History of Early Jacksonville,* 107). Also U.S. Manuscript Census, Population (1850), for Duval County, Florida, p. 94 and John B. Phelps, comp., *The People of Lawmaking in Florida, 1822–1993* (Tallahassee: Florida House of Representatives, 1993), 15.

28. Archaic English: "know."

not until the war is <u>over</u> & we get a house. I would give a world to see you— Dr. has recovered, but all old age must affect sickness—all join in love & good wishes. . . . Corinna

Aunt Mary & them tell me to send love again & they will write a P.S. next time. At least they want you to come & see what fine <u>crackers</u> they have become.

[Ellen and Corinna Brown to Mannevillette Brown][29]

Mandarin, [to Ithaca, New York]
July 19th, 1836

My dear Mann,

I suppose by the time you receive this you will have heard from some other source of the destruction of two more plantations up the St. Johns. The people had just begun to recover from the panic occasioned by the murder of Mott and now they are again flying. This happened, three days since fifteen miles from us. The plantations were owned by Dr. [William Hayne] Simmons[30] of Charleston and Col. [Miller] Hallows[31] an Englishman, who has been a col. under Boliver, the former an old bachelor and the latter very handsome and hastily married, both very much liked, especially the first. They were residing together, but on the morning of the attack, Dr. S. had left the house for a few minutes when it was besieged by six or seven of the red rascals, of course the

---

29. Corinna's portion of this letter is mostly illegible, so the editors have omitted it.

30. William Simmons was a native of Charleston and graduate of the University of Pennsylvania Medical School. Migrating to St. Augustine soon after the transfer of flags, Simmons took an active role in East Florida's social and cultural affairs. In 1822 he published *Notices of East Florida: With an Account of the Seminole Nation of Indians By a Recent Traveler in the Province* (Charleston: A. E. Miller, 1822). An excellent biographical sketch of Simmons is by George Buker in a facsimile edition of *Notices* published by the University of Florida Press in 1973; see xi–xliii. Ironically, Simmons had advocated humane treatment of the Indians against the white "invaders." In 1824 Simmons joined John Lee Williams in selecting Tallahassee as the site of the new territorial capital. Simmons remained a leading figure in St. Johns County until his death in 1870. In 1837 he was appointed registrar of the federal land office. See also Graham, *Awakening of St. Augustine,* 56; Proclamation of Governor DuVal, March 4, 1824, in Carter, *Territorial Papers,* 22:854–55, 25:442; and Hammond, *Medical Profession in 19th Century Florida,* 563–65.

31. Miller Hallowes was a prominent landowner in St. Johns County. His name appeared on a petition to Congress protesting Florida statehood. See Memorial to Congress by the Citizens of East Florida, February 5, 1838, in Carter, *Territorial Papers,* 25:469–74; see also 463.

Col. could not make [a] stand against so many so he followed his friend. They escaped in a boat. Col. H. was dangerously wounded, but the Dr. had one or two shots at them, whether effective or not I am unable to inform you. Both their dwelling houses, with their cotton houses, containing very valuable crops of cotton, were entirely destroyed.[32] Dr. Hall still continues to think our situation a safe one, although we are deserted by almost all in our neighborhood, only two remaining, one man who sleeps at our house and one woman, whose husband is a volunteer in the army with him about.

If he were present however I doubt if it would make any difference. They say every time he goes away she buries her crockery, and every time he comes back he makes her dig it up. He belongs to a company of men who volunteer to be stationed at Mandarin and protect the neighborhood, but no sooner are they mustered into the service, than the best part of them are sent off and we are worse off with the remainder than we were before, when each man could do his best at his own home. These fellows [Indians] know as soon as a place is deserted and never attack unless they are sure of escape. Could they but ever be surprised and cut off you should have far less to fear than now when with them to dare is to do. Is it not outrageous in the government to bring this war upon these people and then leave them so unprotected? I think you must be somewhat sick of indian affairs, yet when I am writing of them I think I have so much to tell that I am never ready to quit.

Ann tells me to give her love to you and tell you that she is quite black now and she thinks by the time the indians come she shall be so nearly of their own color as to be just ready to run off with them. The fact is our folks hate to think of danger, they have fine crops of corn and potatoes in the ground and don't want to leave them. If, however, any mischief is done on this side of Julington creek (three miles from us) it will be time for us to think seriously of it. Heretofore in all these troubles with their successes they have never passed that place; because, so say the learned in these matters, if they do they can easily be cut off either by soldiers stationed at Mandarin or St. Augustine. Why this should be the case does not appear so evident to me seeing they have proved themselves capable of slipping by any quantity of troops in any situation. Nevertheless, they may not like to venture it, and in their hesitancy may be our safety. I don't a bit care for Jacksonville, but I should like to go into St. Augustine and enjoy myself and avoid questions. My pride and my curiosity is all that would be concerned in my flight were it to take place.

---

32. The attack was described in the *Tallahassee Floridian,* August 6, 1836, and the *Savannah Georgian,* July 26, 1836.

Think of your charming sisters remaining eight months in the country—forty miles from town. To me it is quite terrifying! Suppose I give you a description of all our acquaintances; that is, those in whom we take an interest, not the crackers, it would take a Hogarth to describe them.[33] Why then, our large circle of friends and acquaintances consists of three lawyers—Two of them invalids who reside alternately at Jacksonville or St. Augustine, and the other squire a very sensible, homely little person who resides at St. Augustine. These three we are very well acquainted with although we do not see them very often, because when we do see them it is either when we visit Jacksonville where they are very polite to us (for be it known to you we are almost if not entirely the only decent women out of St. Augustine.) There be one Miss Critchton,[34] second rate, here! with all the notions about Aristocracy your second rate people always have understood. Second rate in my opinion made up from private observations. And I hear of another damsel who is from all accounts a paragon of beauty and intelligence. She is found at present in St. Augustine and the others have gone to St. Mary's, from whence they came, to reside during the trouble leaving us the clear field, lack a day![35] . . . We don't however trouble each other with the frequency or length of our visits. Jacksonville is a little miserable village, (although an incorporated city—a city government being rendered necessary or at least more convenient on account of Florida's being a territory) and both that and St. A—expensive. As for Mandarin it is just what you might imagine a place twelve miles from a village and forty from town in a flat sandy country, and such a flat, sandy country! would be Home. I give you an idea. . . . Your [humble] servant

Ellen M. B.

33. William Hogarth (1697–1764) was a British artist famous for his engravings, noted for their realistic and sometimes unpleasant details satirizing immoral behavior.

34. This could refer to the daughter of A. W. Critchton (U.S. Manuscript Census, Population [1840], for Duval County, Florida, p. 141). Critchton served as justice of the peace and represented Duval County in the 1838 constitutional convention in St. Joseph; see Secretary of War to David Levy, February 19, 1840, in Carter, *Territorial Papers,* 26:64, 89. Ellen may also be referring to one of the daughters of John W. Crichton listed on a plat map dividing up land at the mouth of Julington Creek among Crichton's heirs. The daughters were Eliza M., Eleanor A., Mary M., Letitia, and Louisa; see Crichton Document (1841), Jacksonville Historical Society, Jacksonville University Library, Jacksonville, Florida.

35. Aphetized form of *Alack-a-day,* originally "shame or reproach to the day"; in later usage an expression of mere surprise (J. A. Simpson and E. S. C. Weiner, eds., *The Oxford English Dictionary,* 2d ed., 20 vols. New York: Clarendon Press, 1989 [hereafter cited as *OED*]).

[Ellen and Corinna Brown to Mannevillette Brown]

Mandarin [to Ithaca, New York]

August 1, 1836

Mon frere,[36]

We have duly received the authorized contract accompanied by a small paper of mulberry tree seeds. At present there is so much confusion and uncertainty here about every thing that one knows not this week but that before another elapses whether his house and his land may be laid waste and himself either dead or destitute, and under such circumstances you may well think one feels little spirit for improvement. You wish to know something of the state of Charlie's and Ann's and Mary's affairs. I am amused at your notions of things here at the present. I am convinced of one thing that in all matters whatsoever, except music, its own peculiar province, the ear can never judge without the assistance of the eye. Nevertheless I will speak unto your ear and you may get as good an idea as you can. Mary, Ann, and Charlie together bought 23 acres at 20$ an acre. This you see swallows their capital. We sold the old house to buy a new one. On that they have set out an orange grove which you know must grow, and planted a patch of sweet potatoes which next winter they will eat, perhaps you don't know that they don't live in Aunt Delia's house but have stuck up a shanty to hold them until the war is at an end. Their land is good for Florida.

Your idea of slaves and negroes is dramatically opposite to truth. You may hire a slave at 10$ a month and he will more than pay for himself—a free negro won't work at all either for love or money. Reflect a moment and you will easily envision why this is the case. These are uneducated men of the lowest order of intellect and with their ambition necessarily confined to their grade. Though never so rich they would still be what and where they are. And indeed they have no idea of wealth. All their pride consists in their exemption from the obligation from doing a task (a negro's day's work which is not so large as a white man's at the north) a day, and all their enjoyment in eating, playing on a fiddle and dancing and shouting, and for their amusement they have plenty of time and excepting the first opportunity. All this and a great deal more, I will not tire you with, necessarily follows from their situation in society, and until that is changed will continue so. They have no master to make them work and they will only do enough to keep them from hunger and clothe them. White negroes are out of the question and on this too, I could enlarge but must draw

---

36. French: "my brother."

to a close for Mary and Ann have promised a Post Scriptum. Perhaps you are glad of it. Charles, who by the way is a great favorite with the darkies, he being an exceedingly reasonable master, is to have a free black boy, that is he has the possession of him. Of pigs, horses and oxen for the same reason as negroes, they have three cows and plenty of hens and chickens and now I believe I have answered pretty nearly all of your queries so good by. El (just let me hint the necessity of burning this without delay.) Pride.

[Ann Dearing, Mary Dearing, and Corinna Brown to Mannevillette Brown]

Mandarin, [to Ithaca, New York]
August 8th, 1836

Dear Man, you complain of my not writing. The only reason I can give is the want of something that would amuse you and compensate for the postage. I have been roused up a little by the Indians making the whole river act so much like fools. Some are so foolish now that they make their wives go to bed with their shoes on. In drilling the soldiers, they have turned out all the widowers and bachelors in the territory. One or two in particular I must mention. The first is a . . . with as much yellow wiskers[37] as would fill a bushel, behind them you see a pair of white eyes and a mouth so . . . you would think you [were] looking into a stage stable too. He is 27 years old and has had 2 wives & thinks he should like another. There is another that likes Mary very much because she is so familiar. That is not all for there is one . . . at Jacksonville that is in fact after Mary and another after me. What a devil of a time there will be after the war. I will write you the truth in full next time. Yours affectionately, Ann

Dear Man, now Ann has [written] all the lies she can muster up at present and now I will try to tell the truth and give you a description of our dwelling; we have got in the first place a log house and live just like crackers as they call the lower class of people here. We have ducks and fowls and turkeys coming into every door, and Charles has planted a good patch of corn and another of sweet potatoes and that I think will keep us well this winter. They grow well and promise a good chance. Charles and Ann and me live together and the girls live with D. till we get our new house. We live in the midst of the woods. I do not see anyone for a month except the . . . once a month. We shall be like Orangatangs if the war does not end soon. I have got the tooth ache so I can scarcely write . . . [Mary]

37. Archaic spelling for *whiskers*.

P.S. I think, my dear Manne, you cannot but be satisfied this time—you have four signatures. I have just received yours of July 12th. I am glad you have got the deed. The limbs of the law in your place are fools, send that document along as soon as you can—G. Wants it—As for the rest of your letter—Pshaw—don't try to tell me you are in love!—What I have to say <u>seriously</u> (for before I was quizzling) is this—if the lady is what you say she is I wish you success. I think your chances good for the present. There is no difficulty in winning affection (<u>from young ladies</u>!) in retaining it lies the charm! Of one thing be sure,—don't vex her—for spirit is commendable where the occasion calls for it—but prove her amiable. 'Tis a paramount virtue. I know <u>you</u> are good natured—have tolerance however, in love matters, it is of but little avail. We only profit by <u>experience.</u> The Indians are still raising the devil. Sometimes I get half frightened out of my wits but I rally them again. You are mistaken in thinking we should have warning from our neighbors. The only warning if they cross the Julington without being discovered at the time will be their <u>yells</u> round the house! Still 'tis not thought they will dare to come—and if they do they may be discovered in time for us to take flight. I deem not one part of . . . may be safer than another—if we run we know not where to stop—so have we have to stick by, and save our property if we can. The folks want Ell and I to go to St. Marys and stay a month or six weeks. If it were not so expensive, I would for the <u>respectability</u> of the matter! But think we can't spend $50 for fun just now. If I yet think—I am philosophical you see—it must be my nature and if I lose one leg and they burn up my hands, which by the way I have scarred up a little in making fires! I can jump with the left leg into the St. Johns! My love to you dear, good bye, Corrine

[Corinna Brown to Mannevillette Brown]

Mandarin [to Ithaca, New York]
August 30th, 1836

You ask my dear in yours of the 1st if we have mosquitoes in this land. I wish you could see me! My feet, hands, arms, and neck are covered completely with their bites. Sometimes my face looks like a currant pudding! As for the abominable tough tales in circulation respecting the Seminoles—all I can say is turn a deaf ear to them—some are true but more false—a man for instance merely for the pittance of 8 or 10 dollars for carrying an express will go into St. Augustine or some settlement, and cry "Indians near," and in two days set the whole territory by the ears. For my part I am sick of their lies! Major [Benjamin Kendrick] Pearse [Pierce] a son of the ex-Governor of New Hampshire arrived in Florida last week with 300 regulars under his command—he went immediately to Picolata took a train of baggage wagons to Fort Drane—left

200 men there & took one hundred and went out on a scout towards the Indian nation—(Fort Drane is on the borders of their land, 'tis said they are now building a new town there for the accommodation of their families this winter—Daring devils!) He met with a party of from 300 to 500 Indians, fought them killed 10 or 12 and wounded others, but could not ascertain the number, as they carry their wounded off the field immediately (the whites you know leave theirs until after the battle is over)—They think it a great disgrace to be scalped, and if they can avoid it never leave any of their dead behind them— But if they are scalped they never go near them afterwards but leave them for the crows and buzzards to pick.

—To return to Major Pearse again, (old Sir William Braddock like) he drove the Indians into a hammock—which is a spot of rich land where the trees and shrubbery grow thick enough to form a dense forest. These hammocks vary from one to five miles in extent—and when cleared and cultivated are very fertile. All the rest of Florida is swamps or lagoons—and open Pine barren—poor ground with one tree to an acre, like the Irishman's apple orchard. The hammocks of course are the only hiding places they have. But Major Pearse again returned & took a reinforcement of 200 men and again followed on their trail into the hammock, 'tis thought he will whip them well— hurrah for yankees![38]

—The Creek war [in Alabama] it appears is over—Gen. [Thomas Sidney] Jessup [Jesup][39] with 1000 [Tennesseans] and 600 friendly Creeks will be here

38. Benjamin Kendrick Pierce was a native of New Hampshire who joined the U.S. Army in 1812. On August 21, 1836, he was brevetted for distinguished service "in the affair at Fort Drane." He died on April 1, 1850. See Francis B. Heitman, *Historical Register and Dictionary of the United States Army,* 2 vols. (1903; reprint, Urbana: University of Illinois Press, 1965), 1:791. Major Pierce was very popular among the settlers. For his brief but sharp campaign, which began on August 15, see Mahon, *History of the Second Seminole War,* 177–78; *St. Augustine Florida Herald,* August 24; September 22; October 27, 1836; *Tallahassee Floridian,* September 10, 1836; and Governor Call to the President, October 22, 1836, in Carter, *Territorial Papers,* 25:335–36.

39. A native of Virginia, Thomas Sidney Jesup entered the army in 1808. Serving with distinction in the War of 1812, Jesup was appointed quartermaster in 1818, remaining at the head of that service for the next forty-two years. Jesup took command in Florida in December 1836 and was relieved on May 15, 1838. He served with distinction in the Mexican War and died in 1860. See James M. Denham, "Thomas S. Jesup," in *The United States and Mexico at War: Nineteenth-Century Expansionism and Conflict,* ed. Donald S. Frazier (New York: Macmillan, 1998), 211; and Chester L. Kieffer, *Maligned General: The Biography of Thomas Sidney Jesup* (San Rafael, Calif.: Presidio Press, 1979), 153–212.

the 18th of next month and march as soon as possible after that time. 'Tis thought the war will be over before Christmas. I hope it will. If so we shall get a house up this winter—and that I am about as anxious for as I can [be and] for the war to be over. You ask how many orange trees we have—E & I have 150 from 3 to 7 years old engaged. C & D are to have them in September or October for $30 the lot—set out and warranted. If the fellow sticks to his bargain 'tis a good one. C, M & A have now about 200 small ones—but they will buy more by & by—'Tis too early to transplant them yet. They have had as many as 50 die from the drought. We shall have much rain next month—then will be good time. I am glad you are likely to get that situation (or whatever you call it) as draughtsman—it will be an intellectual improvement as well as a pecuniary advantage. I meant by "potatoes sprouting" (you perceive I answer your epistles regularly)—I meant that we are not eating sweet potatoes—our Irishmen were finished long ago—planted in Feb & cut in May they wont keep here . . . obliged to cut them as they are dug. The sweet potatoes we are eating now are the mother potatoes called; from these, the slips or tops are cut and planted in rows like vines—these winter potatoes are now growing finely but will not be fit to dig before the last of next month. M, D & C. Will have probably 100 or 150 bushels—so you see we shant starve this year—as for the account of society in your place 'tis worse than this—they don't let the negroes come to table here!—as for the lame duck you mention let her go!

By the way, I have unpleasant news to relate—I have not heard from my honourable friend Dr Walker since January—the last letter I received from him was so friendly written. I would not but hope the Indian difficulties prevented my hearing from him, but I can think so no longer—and have sent him a dismission! I doubt not 'tis what he wanted—but I would rather do it than he should. Alas! affection! Byron said rightly 'tis but a phantom. How ever I trust any one again—verily I would not confide even in a saint—yet I cannot believe all are bad—I have an internal consciousness of rectitude that convinces me our human nature is not altogether . . . degraded—not wholly destitute of principle and honour—honour alas he professed to be an honourable man—a poor substitute these words for deeds! But he was not to blame perhaps. I disclosed a great crime to him—I told him I had NO-MONEY! . . . [Y]ou know what Pom's fault was: "Our [Castle] was poor"—what a pretty set of vagabond fortune hunters it has been my lot to meet with. Tell a man any thing but that you are poor and he will be your friend—but disclose that fatal truth and he will shun you as a pestilence. Beware of it, boy—I warn you from experience. I wish another personification of purity would come to me with their soft [soap]—nothing would satisfy me but slapping their chops!—not with a pudding stick either. But let them go—I always had more opinion of empty pockets than broken hearts—& if I had acted upon it I should have been wiser—n'im-porte[40] the Lord take a liking to them—and may they meet with a better friend than your sister!

I have an item to mention of more importance—Nab & I are writing a book—I think it will be pretty good! We shall have it done about the first of Nov. But how shall we get it to you and what will you do with it? We can send it to NY. Is there any one I can direct it to who will forward it to you? If we send it—you must get it published if you can get any one to buy it—better try the Harpers. Let them submit it to a committee if they choose but on no account give up our names! It will be a sort of take off and would make us liable to severe remarks—but I have no doubt it will sell if published, still I would not risk any thing for it. If I could sell the copy right for any thing—I would, because if it had a run—we could make our fortunes! If it does not do well, I shall write another & try some thing else. But more of this by and by—don't mention it until you get it—after you read it—Do what you think best with it—but swear not to say who wrote it—for we have hit up two or three I am afraid will know their pictures as it is. If you send to us—direct to care of Dr. J. Hall at Jacksonville—we shall get it just as directly—every body knows him or send to Augustine in care of D[avid] Levy Esq. and we shall get it or send to the Dr. directed to Mandarin. It will be forwarded from St. Augustine. No difficulty—all well & send love. I will write again anon—Yours affection-ately

Corin

[Corinna Brown to Mannevillette Brown]

Mandarin, [to Utica, New York]
Nov. 2nd , 1836

Alas, my dear Manne how fleetly old time wings his way. I have been a year in the wilderness; a year; can you believe it? When I reflect upon the many anx-ious, weary, sad hours I have passed in Florida it seems indeed a year, an age! Yet when I take a careless survey of this vanished year, or contrast it with the happy eventful year preceding it, I can scarcely convince myself that I have wasted so much of life!—But a truce to the blues. Your kind favour of the 30th ult reminds me how remiss I have been of late in writing both to you & George. But I have a good excuse for my brevity as well as for my silence.—When Aunt Mary was first sick I would not write lest I should alarm you unnecessarily;

---

40. French: "no matter."

then she was too ill for me to write—and since she has been convalescent, she has required so much <u>attention</u> that both I & El have been fully occupied. I had only time to scratch a few lines when I sent the deed. I intended to write again the next mail, but was prevented by Mary & the Dr.'s both having an ill turn. They tell me these attacks are common after the fever in this country; be that as it may, I think Aunt Mary still is in a very critical situation. During her fever she was delirious almost all the time so that we did not dare to leave her night or day—she was ill three weeks, then sick & better alternately for 3 or 4 weeks—now she is able to go about the house, but she neither gains flesh or strength—she has her senses but her mind is very weak and her feet & face swell <u>very badly.</u> These symptoms alarm me, she appears very much as Mother did and I fear is hastening from us in the same way. I may be mistaken but I speak as I think. We can but hope better things.

You speak about our <u>book</u>, alackaday, we were going on gloriously when Aunt M was taken ill, but have done nothing since. If Aunt Mary gets better, as I trust in Heaven she will, we may finish it so as to send it on in the spring, if possible.—As for our house we shall not attempt to put it up as yet. In the first place M being the biggest proprietress is not fit to undertake it—and in the next the war is not over, and there is nobody to build it. I am in hopes this latter difficulty however will soon be obviated—if not it will be no use to build. Our trees i.e. one hundred and fifty from 3 to 9 years old are set out—we are not to pay for them unless they live and then only at the rate of [two bits!, two levis!, two nine pences!] a price cheap enough! Besides these we have 50 Aunt Hall warrants to E & I and M, A, and C have about 200—if they grow we will have plenty by & by.

One item of good news I have to tell. Dr. is likely to get one Spanish claim of 10,000 & another . . . of 9,000 he will get the first & perhaps the second. They are attachments given him by the Spanish governor for property destroyed and confiscated during the Patroit war. I am glad your business continues good. Our harvest is very good, better than we could have expected for the first year. We have corn & potatoes plenty. Oh! I long for this tedious war to be over—I have no doubt then things would have a different aspect—there would be more people in the country, more provisions & more cheerful faces, now everybody looks dull and cheerless, everything looks neglected. It would give a new impulse to business. I am sure "poor little me" . . . would be affected by it, although I don't believe there is a more contented spirit in the land, or one more willing to take the world as it goes than that same <u>me</u>. You speak of snow, 'tis chilling to be sure! Still, I should feel sad if I did not think I should once again hear Sleigh bells jingle!—We have a hanging day today, bleak, cold, drizzling, driving rain, enough to chill even a lighter heart than mine; but we

Picolata Stages.

HAVING Commenced running twice a
n week, persons can depend on them
to arrive in St. Augustine on Monday afternoon and leave at 10 o'clock Tuesday morning, and will leave Picolata at 9 o'clock the
day following, the Steamboat arrival which
will be on Wednesday evening. Each passen-
ger is allowed 50 lb. baggage, all over $1 per
hundred.   J. P. LEVY.
Dec. 12.

*"Picolata Stages" (above) and "Inland Conveyance" (below). Regularized travel in terri-
torial Florida, while difficult and arduous, was well established by the 1830s. The Brown
sisters often traveled by stage and steamboat to and from such places as Jacksonville, Mandarin, Picolata, and St. Augustine.* St. Augustine Florida Herald, *January 13, 1836.*

INLAND CONVEYANCE
To St. Augustine, E. F.

THE improvements made in the mach
nery of the fine steam packet FLOR-
DA, Capt. Hubbard, will enable her to
form with ease a trip every week, and s
will regularly in line with the Steam pack
Wm. Seabrook, from Charleston, leav
Savannah every Monday afternoon:
Arriving at Darien every Tuesday mornir
   "   St. Mary's every Tuesday evening
   "   Jacksonville every Wednesday mo
           ning,
   "   Picolata every Wednesday evennin
Returning
Leave Picolata every Thursday afternoon.
   "   Jacksonville, every Thursday night,
   "   St. Marys every Friday,
   "   Darien every Friday night or Satur
         day morning,
Arrives at Savannah every Saturday after
         noon.
   Stages in readiness at Picolata for S
Augustine, 18 *miles;* for further particular
apply to   R. & W. KING & CO
   Savannah, Nov. 18, 1335.

Picolata was an important stop on the St. Johns River. It linked the river with St. Augustine, directly to the east. It also served as a military post during the Second Seminole War. Florida State Archives.

have this comfort, perhaps after this storm is over, we shall not see any but summer weather again until Christmas, and possibly not then.

En passant,[41] E. and I have not yet been to St. Augustine. We are determined <u>Deo Volante</u> to go before January, however, and we comfort ourselves with that! <u>babies</u> aren't we dear? N'importe when how the wind whistles! . . . .
Corinna

[Ellen Brown to Mannevillette Brown]

Mandarin [to Utica, New York]
Feb 4th, 1837

My dear Mann,

. . . I shall direct this to Utica, as you desired, although it is past the time when you said you would be in Albany. I shall send this by Jacksonville mail, which starts three days before the Mandarin, and by the latter will write to Albany. So you see I comply with your requests in all particulars. As for the Indian affairs, they are all uncertainty. I will send you some of our newspapers by which you will perceive, that there is an opinion prevailing that the war will

41. French: "in passing, by the way."

St. Augustine. Library of Congress. (image split)

View of Fort Marion and City of St. Augustine, Florida. St. Augustine Historical Society.

soon be brought to a close. Whether it will or no, is a matter concerning which the wisest can but conjecture. I hope it will; for then Aunt Molly[42] will put up the house and we shall get on quite smart. In addition to an orange grove; they have set out a peach orchard, a plumb grove, and fig trees etc. In two or three years, we shall have a sweet place here. It is small, but what there is of it is made good use of, which I take to be quite as well as to have a great unwieldy plantation which one is unable to cultivate.

I am glad to hear you have had a pleasant year. I think to lay up pleasant recollections is quite as good as to lay up money. Is it not the best use you can make of time, to enjoy it? For my part nothing grieves me so much as to think I have wasted my time, (which is certainly to have committed the greatest of follies,) but I cannot think that time wasted which has left a lasting impression of pleasure upon memory. We are sure of the enjoyment we have had, besides pleasures of a social kind are very apt to improve the heart: which is quite as good (and oftentimes more needful) as to improve the head. I hope you are convinced. Indeed I don't intend to write you a homily, but I am a natural Joseph Surface for sentiments and I fancy you crying out with Sir Peter Teazle "Oh d—— your sentiments."[43]

Well then let us talk about something else. Corine and I have been into St. Augustine, where Corine still remains. The folks were very polite to us, and we behaved as well as we knew how, whereupon I suppose there was a mutual good impression, certainly there was on my part, and you know these things are almost always mutual: Happiness reflects happiness does it not? I know I am writing . . . you a most miserable affair, but I am fidgety and my eyes plague me, perhaps I'll do better next time. The mulberry trees have not arrived, they will do just as well when ever they do come. Their having been delayed is not a matter of importance.

I like your idea of introductions, manners etc. A man should choose what society it pleases him to move in and conform his manner to it. A man's manners are his cast, and in our land, where a gentleman is a <u>rara avis in terris</u>,[44] good manners will often do for a man what money is supposed always to do. My dear Man, I am inclined to think American Society generally is very

---

42. Mary.

43. Joseph Surface and Sir Peter Teazle are characters in Richard Sheridan's *School for Scandal* (1777).

44. Latin: "A bird rarely seen on earth." The complete phrase is *rara avis in terris, nigvogue simillima cygno:* "a bird rarely seen on the earth, and very like a black swan" (Juvenal [ca. 55–ca. 138], satire 6, line 165).

deficient in polish: but this is high treason. The weather here is very delightful at present. I saw some little white flowers in bloom two or three days since. The Jessamine blooms here this month, so also does a flower which Charley is of opinion is the American azalea. The blossom is something like our northern honey-suckle, but it grows in bushes.

You say Corine and I (I presume I am included) must come and see you, verily, my good fellow, it would be the delight of our souls, but wither is the needful to come from? It is the patent of nobility here to take a journey to the north during the summer. Why don't you get married and give us a chance to make you a visit? faith, it would be of no use, for we have not the wherewithal to pay our passage. Peradventure we will get some prizes by and by. Peradventure one of us might come. I would resign in favour of Corine with all my heart and assist her with all my might. The glorification of a journey would be a gratifycation [*sic*] to me. Half price is cheap you know. I don't know as I would get married if I were you, for perhaps you might get a cross, silly, good for nothing wife, that would be worse than none. Anne says she cannot promise to come and see you, but she will come and feel of you one of these days. I say ditto. Aunt Hall says she hopes you will not wait until she has to put her specs on to look at you, before you come and see her. We have had a letter from George [in Philadelphia] and are afraid he is sick, write and ask him, tell him to take a trip to Florida, if his lungs are affected; the journey would be of great service to him, besides the advantage of avoiding the spring weather, which you know is most to be dreaded by invalids. Good bye,

Ellen

Chapter Three

"As Noble a Heart As Ever Throbbed"

Dr. Edward Aldrich

In the spring of 1837 Corinna, Ellen, and Charles Brown along with their Aunt Ann remained with Delia on the Hall plantation in Mandarin. As the Seminole War raged around them they had few opportunities to explore their new environs. Even so, they did have the chance to meet many of the soldiers on the move throughout their area. One such chance meeting found Corinna in the presence of a young surgeon attached to a volunteer regiment. The relationship that soon matured into romance brought dramatic change for Corinna and her family. Dr Edward S. Aldrich had graduated from the Medical College of South Carolina in 1833 at the age of twenty-three. In 1836, one year after establishing a medical practice in Isaiah Hart's home in Jacksonville, Aldrich joined the First Regiment of Volunteers in Jacksonville on May 13.[1] While Corinna's thoughts increasingly focused on this army surgeon, Ellen resisted the idea of matrimony. Expressing her determination to maintain her independence, she declared, "What a confounded shame it is, that, because a poor devil is a woman, she can neither get a chance to improve her mind nor get money. Get married is all the advice to her: but I won't get married. Those that are worth having are poor, and I'll be blest if I['ll] buy an opportunity to repent."[2] Corinna, however, began to take a different point of view. Below she reveals the nature of their relationship with Dr. Aldrich.

[Corinna Brown to Mannevillette Brown]

Mandarin [to Utica, New York]
May 30, 1837

---

1. Florida Militia Muster Rolls, Seminole Indian Wars, Florida Department of Military Affairs, St. Augustine, Fla., no. 67, vol . 1, pp. 52–53, 58–59; Hammond, *Medical Profession in 19th Century Florida,* 5–10.

2. Ellen Brown to Mannevillette Brown, January 31, 1837, Anderson-Brown Papers, USMA.

MEDICAL NOTICE.
DR. EDWARD ALDRICH,
A GRADUATE OF THE MEDICAL COLLEGE OF SOUTH CAROLINA,
Having chosen a permanent location at Jacksonville, Duval County,
OFFERS HIS SERVICES IN THE PRACTICE OF
MEDICINE, SURGERY & OBSTETRICS.
☞ DR. ALDRICH may be found at Mr. I. D. Hart's, and will be ready at all hours to attend to calls.
Dec. 16, 1835.   42tf

Medical notice of Dr. Edward Aldrich. Jacksonville Courier, *December 24, 1835.*

My Dear brother,

. . . I told you I did not intend to marry. But I have suffered myself unknowingly to be led from flower to flower accepting attentions that served but courtesy until I am completely sick of the path I inclined to pursue. I can see <u>now</u> the honourable course. . . . Dr. Edward S. Aldrich of St. Mary's, Georgia at present Surgeon General of East Florida, a gentleman of birth and education, not wealthy but independent, of a wealthy and highly respectable family, has asked me to marry him. He has been educated at north, is young and small of stature . . . but of good reputation in his profession as you may judge from the present station and has as noble a heart as ever throbbed—a whole souled Southerner, generous, proud, and independent—keeps his servant and drives his gig, etc. He says he has been soiled—that I doubt not. He says he has sown his wild oats—this I doubt not either—If I marry him—but if not he goes to Europe forthwith, he says and to the devil afterwards. He wished to take your sis for better or worse and was rejected. A burnt child dreads the fire—But he again pled his own cause and has nearly won it. He says he does not want money but me. I told him I had no heart to give. He said if no one else had it he was willing to take my hand without one, provided I gave that willingly. I reflected upon my present <u>dependent</u> situation and promised him an answer in a month. If favorable, I shall be married as soon as I can get ready. He offered to write you. But I preferred to write myself. He tells me I may live wherever I please. If I should decline selecting a place he will probably fix upon St. Mary's, the present residence of his father's, or Charleston S.C.—But of this hereafter have you anything to say? I have, I think, placed the picture in its true light; if the shadows fall not where they should—be candid.

. . . What are your prospects for business my dear? Favourable I hope—for I want some money—not much—but E and I are completely out of coppers— I should like for you to send us ten dollars if you can spare it—we do not want but little at present and we are in hopes we shall get some prize money ere long—but if not, if I get married I shall call on you for little more. My wardrobe is in horrible order—but as Ell says I should like a few fineries—for the family credit. But ten dollars will do for now if you will oblige us that much my darling. If I marry I shall take Ellen with me wherever I locate myself.

And now to a third part of my epistle. My head is as full as an egg and very like an addled one[3] Mary has not yet received her money for the house. . . . If you mail her the amount or part of it you will confer a great favour—she really wants it I know. I believe I shall have to get married!! The trees we have never received—the seeds came by mail—we are all in good health and spirits—the war is hoped to be over—but I doubt it very much—part of the troops are to be disbanded tomorrow but I fear they will have to be mustered again— though I sincerely hope not. If I am married this summer I shall come & see you—but if not until fall will you come to the wedding? . . . yours affectionately, Corinna

P.S. Do not hesitate to discuss all the contents of this epistle freely—I told Dr. A I would not answer until I had written to you—But you may as well say yes, dear Manne—for 'tis but a lottery after all & any horses will have a tight squeeze to break out of the little opening I have left that's flat—still I may speak freely—C —

[Corinna Brown to Mannevillette Brown]

Mandarin [to Utica, New York]
June 6, 1837

My dear Manne,

. . . What in the deuce did you tell me to write to Albany three months ago for? All that time it seems I have been edifying head quarters at Washington

---

3. An addled egg is spoiled; an addled brain is confused or useless.

with long accounts of journeys, histories of friends and enemies, of flirtations, of speculations upon matrimony, of business, &c. & c. I am as mad as a dog—I suppose I have written six or eight—all gone to Albany sans one that I sent to Ithaca with directions to have it forwarded to Albany in case you had left there. The last letters were of some importance. I wish you had received them—but you did not—and now it matters not—as the principal theme of the last will be "knocked in the head I think"—Still if you can, send to Albany & get what you can—those sent last week, and the week before are probably there. I should rather you would and after you have read them burn them. By the way, you ought to burn all our letters, my darling, as they generally treat local matters and should edify you only.[4]

In respect to our visiting you this Summer—I can only say it would delight us exceedingly to come—but I think the pull upon your pockets would be rather a stretcher. You say you may send for us in about a month. You are best acquainted with your own finances. If they will admit of our coming—it would please us both. but I beseech you on no account to run the risk of insolving yourself. The trip would be expensive, although we should not care to stay north more than five or six weeks. From here to N.Y. it would cost us $25 (twenty five) each—the expense after that I know nothing about—but now for speculation. We have the expectation of $150 prize money—from Phil. If we get that—(as we may, our chances are pretty good—) it will defray our expenses there and back again. Then say what will be the expense from N.Y. to U— and what board is? Don't hesitate to speak candidly, dear—If I did not believe you would, I would not write at all about it. Indeed you cannot refuse to as it is a mere matter of pleasure with us—and by not speaking plainly you would defeat us in the main object of our journey—enjoyment—It amounts to this. If we do not get the 150, I do not myself think it would be wise or prudent for us to start—we will wait for you to come and see us which I think you better do in the Fall—say about first of October. I have no doubt (I have spent three months in St. Augustine & two in Jacksonville) and I have no doubt I say that you would make a "very pretty penny" by passing next winter in East Florida. Your quondam friend Rev. David Brown[5] (with whom I passed last

---

4. Fortunately, Mannevillette did not comply with Corinna's wishes, though it is unclear what the women did with his letters of these years. If they did not dispose of them, which seems doubtful given their closeness to him, the hot, humid climate would have made saving them difficult, and the women's continual movement would have made losing them more likely.

5. Family correspondence implies that Mannevillette may have known David Brown in Boston. Before coming to Jacksonville, Rev. David Brown served briefly as pastor of a

winter) says you could have as much as you could do, one winter, at least—I think so too. I also think after you had glorified yourself in St. Augustine, you might play the same game over again in Jacksonville. Think of this—If you come you must bring frames for your pictures—on these you could make your profit—at any rate—you can think of it as a <u>dernier ressort</u>.[6] I don't want to encourage you too much, or make you give up a certainty, for an uncertainty— but it is my opinion and others that you would do well. You can say you come for your health if you like and daub all the faster! That is a la Northerner! I gave you a long description of St A. in one of my Albany letters. 'Tis a dull gloomy—quiet looking place; still I have no doubt you would spend as happy a winter there as you ever passed in your life. The Society is good & <u>ladies gay</u>—dancing, riding, & sailing, amusements. Your expenses would probably be greater than at the North—board is seven dollars per week—fire—washing —&c. extra—rents high. But still I think you would clear your expenses thrice over. Then you could pass as much time with us as you pleased.

I hope in God—We shall get up a house this fall. If you go down to New York—just please see <u>why those Mulberry trees did not come</u>. . . . your sis Corin.

---

church in Lockport, New York. Arriving in St. Augustine in 1833, Brown soon thereafter became the second minister of what would later become the congregation of the St. Johns Episcopal Church. The first service of the church was held in 1829. The congregation was formally incorporated by the legislative council in 1839. Other congregants within the circle of the Browns' friends were Samuel L. Burritt, John and Maria Doggett, and the families of Judge Thomas Douglas, Dr. A. S. Baldwin, and Joseph B. and Eliza Lancaster. Brown remained at St. Johns in Jacksonville until 1843, leaving for the North that year. Serving for many more years as a minister in the North, he died in 1875 in Lambertville, New Jersey. See Davis, *History of Early Jacksonville,* 81–84; Gold, *History of Duval County,* 110; Joseph D. Cushman Jr., *A Goodly Heritage: The Episcopal Church in Florida, 1821–1892* (Gainesville: University of Florida Press, 1965), 15–20; Edgar Legare Pennington, "The Episcopal Church in Florida, 1763–1892," *Historical Magazine of the Protestant Episcopal Church* 7 (March 1938): 27–28; George R. Fairbanks, "Early Churchmen in Florida," in *Historical Papers and Journal of Semi-Centennial of the Church in Florida, 1888* (Jacksonville, Fla.: Church Publishing Co., 1889), 9–11; James J. Daniel, "Historical Sketch of the Church in Florida," in *Historical Papers and Journal of Semi-Centennial of the Church in Florida, 1888* (Jacksonville, Fla.: Church Publishing Co., 1889), 32–33; and James Owen Knauss, *Territorial Florida Journalism* (Deland: Florida Historical Society, 1923), 57–58.

6. French: "a last resource or resort."

Robert Raymond Reid, judge of the Eastern Judicial District from 1832 to 1840, when he became governor. His daughters Rosalie and Janet as well as his wife Mary Martha frequently entertained Ellen and Corinna at their St. Augustine home. Florida State Archives.

Mary Martha Reid. Florida State Archives.

[Corinna Brown to Mannevillette Brown]

Mandarin [to Utica, New York]

July 5th, 1837

Another glorious fourth I have passed in the Pine Barren. Well 'tis in some measure my own fault—that's grand consolation. Where did you pass the happy day dear? And how? I had a basket of West Indian fruit (olives, apples, oranges, &c.) sent me & Aunt Molly raised some cake & mince pies in her log cabin—And there we made jolly together but wished for you & George. By the way have you received my letters of late? & if so, what do you think of my flirtation with Dr. Aldrich? I think, I shall have to tye the knot—honour bids us do it and utility favours the match—besides he is noble hearted—but—but —

I can never treat him as I do now—but that warmth of attachment I have felt for another—I doubt if I can ever feel again. Yet it is folly to talk thus. I must marry him. Will you come to the wedding? I shall put it off until the Spring if I can. E & I have given up the idea of coming North this summer—and accepted an invite from the daughters of Hon. [Robert R.] Judge Reid to pass the Summer in St. Augustine.[7] [Col. Thomas] Jessup [Jesup] has made his head quarters there & it will be very gay. 'Tis said the Indians are not going to fight—but I think they are—however every precaution is taken to defend the inhabitants if they should. About George—have you heard from him? Poor thing, I wish I could assist him.

As for those impudent Editors of the Chronicle—they awarded me the prize and payed me what? Ten dollars instead of one hundred. I sent them a letter—under my assumed name. I am sure they have swindled me—because

---

7. A native of Augusta, Georgia; graduate of South Carolina College; and member of Congress (1819–23), Robert Raymond Reid moved to Florida in 1832 when he was appointed judge of the Eastern Judicial District. A leading Democrat and proponent of statehood, Reid chaired the constitutional convention in 1838. Serving as judge until 1839 when he was appointed governor by President Martin Van Buren, Reid moved his wife Mary Martha and two daughters Rosalie and Janet to Tallahassee. Reid was a thoughtful, introspective man with an affection for biblical study and the classics, and he and his two daughters died in 1841 during the yellow fever epidemic in Tallahassee. See "Diary of Robert Raymond Reid, 1833, 1835" (unpublished manuscript, WPA Historical Records Survey, 1939–40, Jacksonville, Florida); Stephen F. Miller, *The Bench and the Bar of Georgia,* 2 vols. (Philadelphia: Lippincott, 1858), 2:204–26; Walter W. Manley, E. Canter Brown Jr., and Eric W. Rise, *The Supreme Court of Florida and Its Predecessor Courts, 1821–1917* (Gainesville: University Press of Florida, 1997), 61–66; Paisley, *Red Hills of Florida,* 85, 100, 102, 104–5; and Denham, *Rogue's Paradise,* 28.

if the tale was not worth one hundred dollars, it was not the prize tale & ought not to have been published as such—I <u>jawed</u> them well. And I will give them more [of the] <u>same</u> if they will give me a chance—good they don't know who they are fighting with. I will have my fun, if I cant get my pay. I know the trash is not worth one hundred dollars—but that is not the thing—they promised to pay that for the best offered—& if that was the best I ought to have it. Don't let on that I am the author of "The Grumble Family"—for the world I would not have it known. Is it ill or well received? Have the other papers copied it?

What think you of coming out here dear next Winter? By the way, in one letter I requested you to send me ten dollars. I believe the letter was directed to Albany—And in the same—I asked you if convenient to send Aunt Mary that balance you owe her—thirty dollars. She would not ask for this, but her Portsmouth business is not yet [completed &] she is out cashed. . . . Dr. & Aunt Hall are gone to Charleston—Dr. is quite sick—he thinks the voyage will benefit him—'Tis strange he should seek for the fountain of youth out of Florida—he has got part of his claim from [the] Government—they have granted him eleven hundred dollars and moreover entre nous[8] is going to die—but neither of these events will benefit you or I![9] Aunt Mary's health is poor—but I am in hopes she will recruit when cool weather comes again—'tis monstrous hot—all send love again.

Dearest, Good bye,

Yours ever,

Corinna

P.S. Send me the <u>L'argent</u>[10] I ask for, if you can conveniently—there are a few articles I want—but very few—but I don't want to get in debt for them—ten will supply me—I will write again soon & more fully until when I go to St. A next week for a short visit. Dear adieu. C—

<u>Burn these letters</u>—

---

8. French: "between us."

9. Dr. Hall's will provided that upon his death "all debts and funeral expenses should be paid out of my . . . goods and estate." It also provided that "all the rest of residence of my said goods and estate both real and personal of whatever name or articles and whatever I intend shall remain to the use and to the benefit of my kind and well beloved wife, Dorothy, for and during her natural life after death to pass . . . to any issue of mine begotten by me." Hall's will provided that Dorothy make payments to the trustees of Hall's granddaughter in one-thousand-dollar installments until his estate was liquidated. See Will of Dr. James Hall, September 20, 1834, Duval County, Florida; copy in James Hall Papers, box 60, P. K. Yonge Library of Florida History, University of Florida, Gainesville.

10. French: "money."

P.S. my dear brother, since this was written, I have received another visit from Dr. Aldrich—he is going to Charleston to remain about six weeks—and will claim your sister's hand on his return!—Heighho! there is often a ship between to post by, but 'tis not likely there will be one this time. I will write you more fully and until then adieu. C—

[Ellen Brown to Mannevillette Brown]

La Grange[11] [Mandarin to Utica, New York]
July 9th, 183[7]

As for knowing women better than I do; whether or no I know them in individual cases, permit me to tell you, you have never been on the spot to judge with regard to a general knowledge of them, being a woman myself, I very humbly opine that I ought to know them better than any man has a right to think he does. Won't you allow me to be a better judge of the motives of a [woman] than yourself?

So much for your ability to determine and now for your opinion that "marriage is the ultimatum—the great aim of women," you must pardon my prolixity but I cannot suffer a brother of mine to entertain this absurd, and, as it appears to me, derogatory opinion without at least letting him hear my dissenting voice. That sometimes it may be an object I grant; that when it is so, as it must of necessity be with those who "stand the least chance," "it is natural they should complain the [same]" I grant also, as you very pertinently observe, "men do the same in all their different pursuits." If you would use the word men in its most general sense—all mankind you would express my opinion equally well. But that you should think getting married is an aim, nay the ultimate object of all women, shows that you have not well considered. You must suppose it an object very difficult to accomplish; of course you would not suppose a very probable, certainly possible occurrence an ultimate object of half the world. And yet it appears to me that to suppose it a very probable and certainly possible occurrence would be most natural, most compatible with general experience. Besides let me tell you that opportunities are much more plentiful than your sex are aware of; if every man that gets rejected tacitly or verbally should let it be known, I think the tables would be a little turned. You are as anxious to get married as we are. I do not accuse you of making it the business of your life. Upon your own ground; that [the] bad are only bad on some points and upon my own that what's held a fault by one person may not be so by

---

11. La Grange (the Hall plantation) is now known as Plummer's Cove. A historical marker for the Hall estate stands between Beauclerc Point and Mandarin.

another, added to the usual influence of property, station, and friends—the number of those who have nothing to recommend them must be very small. Can you suppose women are willing to marry anything upon any terms? . . . Then to marry well is this "ultimatum." What is it to marry well? Upon joining answers to this question depends the interest of morals, often the peace of familys—but I need not go on. That can scarcely be the object with half the world which is at its outset so indefinite. I candidly believe the chief thing which caused this opinion to prevail, as I believe it does, among your sex, is this: although the objects of men and women are in general ultimately the same, . . . you do not see either their aims or their means of fulfilling them. Marriage being their only publick act it strikes you as being their only act of interest. Strange that you should not reflect that it is, and by your accusing too, often, very often the means instead of the end; else why ever say that women marry for money, for station, for revenge, or any of the objects reported unworthy? You cannot make inconsistencies agree. [Ellen]

[Corinna Brown to Mannevillette Brown]

Mandarin [to Utica, New York]
August 2nd, 1837

My dear brother,

Your kind favour of the 8th ult containing the gratifying intelligence that you have all our letters save one—came to hand by the last mail—what <u>one</u> did you lose? It was not probably of much consequence—as you reply to all matters I recollect discussing excepting my visit to St. Augustine—, which . . . was a merry one. Rev. D[avid] Brown is coming north this Summer—he will probably see you if you go to Albany. I believe he wishes you well—at any rate be polite to him, dear—for he has been very, <u>very</u> polite, and friendly to your sis. I wrote you, mon cher, ere I received the document, that E. and I had given up the idea of coming north, & had accepted an invite from the daughters [Rosalie and Janet] of Judge Reid Supreme Judge of the territory[12] (him!) to pass the summer in St. Augustine. Ellen is already there—she has been gone a fortnight—I did not feel like going when she left—but have since received a second invitation—which, <u>Deo volante</u>, I shall [accept at] the earliest opportunity.

My dear—In respect to my communications concerning Dr. A. I can only say I have behaved <u>very childishly</u>. Indeed you must think me a very <u>visionary</u>

---

12. As judge of the Eastern Judicial District of Florida, Robert R. Reid also sat on the Territorial Court of Appeals, which met each year in Tallahassee. See Denham, *Rogue's Paradise*, 25.

maid but then—there are extenuating circumstances. I have been so unfortunate in my previous <u>five hundred</u> engagements—that in truth—although my
reason told me I ought—my heart would not let me trust in Dr. A's professions
—and <u>I sent him away sorrowful</u> for no other reason.—However, fate ordered
that we should meet again—and he vows no if I told him to be off—he won't
go!—I told him I had written you word I had rejected him. It affected him
very much—he said he would come on and see you about it. I told him he
should not—I would write you. He is at present in Charleston. I have just
received a letter from him—He is off on <u>Furlough</u>. He expected to return in
Sept. & then I agreed to go to Charleston with him to resign—but—an express
steamboat is gone to C— with orders for his worship to return <u>immediately</u> to
Florida—his regiment is ordered to the Field. To resign under such circumstances would savor of cowardice—of course he cannot. He will be so mad—
and I am so glad—I am not ready to quit the sisterhood yet. I shall write him
a letter and tease him.—

And now dearest to other parts of your letter. For the manner in which you
have treated our overtures about coming north—<u>I sincerely thank you</u>. It's
frank—kind—brotherly—dear—and will <u>add</u>, if any thing can, to the confidence I already have in you. But in justice to myself I must say it was not <u>pleas-
ure</u> induced me to make the proposals I did. At the time, I was not aware of
the universal depression—I thought my own pecuniary concerns would be different—and worse than all <u>I wanted to get rid of Dr. A</u>. and out of the way of
the hints and innuendo I knew I must be daily subjected to for <u>not bettering
my situation</u> when I had an opportunity &c. But Pope says whatever [is] is
right[13] every day's experience makes me more a convert to his opinion. Had
fortune favoured me I should not have been engaged to Dr. Aldrich—which
event may add much to my future happiness—and as therein the <u>womenfolks</u>
say, would have very much injured my valued friend. Be that as it may—I have
not much faith in [broken] hearts—although I am not a heretick in all matters
of Love[14] as things are, so let them remain. I would not alter them if I could
<u>now</u>. —

The draft you propose to send will be very gratefully received—for we are
out cashed—the last three dollars in possession I gave E when she went in
town. The fact is we should not have been so badly off—but we have been unfortunate. We bought some orange trees—the drought killed them. We have

13. This is the last line of book 1 of English poet Alexander Pope's *Essay on Man* (1731).
14. The phrase "heretics in love" appears in English poet John Donne's "The Indifferent" (1633).

some more—we hope to be more successful—then our first visit to St. A. was expensive—we had to board—of course as we knew nobody . . . about a fortnight—it cost us over $50—Generally our expenses are <u>very</u> little—we <u>visit now wherever we go</u>. Charles has a tolerable crop—and if God sees fit to send us a little rain he will do as well as he can expect.—The money for the old house. . . . you misunderstood George. I had a letter in the last mail however with the final settlement and shall have about $100 all by accounts which would but barely do it only half . . . is in notes and mortgages on the house— as for George—he merits assistance. I hope he will succeed. I wish it was in my power to assist him—but it is not—at present—I hope for better days— Manne—I can't help thinking I was born to a better lot than this. I do believe I could fill a higher station—and not prove an unfaithful stuard[15] I tremble at the prospect of prosperity. The few gleams of sunshine in my life have been followed by such black clouds—the least ray now seems but the sure precursor of the storm. But a truce to the blues. I promised not to have them for six weeks— and but two are gone—your encouraging prospects give me the greatest pleasure. In deed I have no doubt of your success. Be frugal—not mean—God knows how much I detest all sorts of meanness—But don't misunderstand your sister dear—whenever she says be <u>frugal and go to Europe</u> of all things. I wish you to do that. It will be the <u>sure</u> stepping stone to Fortune and <u>Fame</u>!

. . . It is rumoured that Thomas Jessup is to be superseded by [Alexander] Macomb—the Floridians are getting up a petition to have Jessup remain. <u>I think</u> it very impolitic to remove him. I have no other news to relate—I will write again shortly. My going to St. A. will depend on Dr. A's <u>movements</u> somewhat—Dr. Hall's health is much improved by his trip—all well and send a deal of love. The trees I forgot to mention they did not come. A bill of laden or rather a letter . . . came saying they were shipped to C— but no last name. . . . Don't attempt to send more. We can get them very cheap here now—also the seeds sent by mail are not worth postage. We all thank you for the [care] you have taken in sending them and regret we were not more fortunate— <u>n'importe</u>—we have <u>some</u> <u>trees</u> and they grow very rapidly. . . . [Corinna]

[Corinna Brown to Mannevillette Brown]

La Grange [to Utica, New York]
September 4, 1837

My dear brother,

Your last kind favour enclosing the bank note was duly and gratefully received. It came in [the] nick of time. Albeit I am not yet married I have

---

15. Archaic spelling of *steward*.

promised if the troops are not ordered to the fields before the first of October—
to give <u>myself away on that day</u>, Dr. A. says if I do not consent he will resign,
and I am unwilling he should do so. It would savour of cowardice—though
he has not one drop of such base blood in his veins. But I have other notions
for wishing him to retain his commission, it is both lucrative and honourable—
he wanted to see your last letter—but of course I told him I could not let him.
If you choose you can write <u>part of your next</u> so that he can see it. I wish you
knew him—Manne, he grows more in favour with me every day—indeed if
devoted love and unwearied attentions can ensure affection—he cannot fail to
gain mine—so far he has left <u>nothing undone</u>. I have just received many beautiful presents from him via Charleston from where he has just returned.

As for the tale I spoke of it was published in the Chronicle—(I forget the
date)—Sometime in June I think. . . . for my sake do not breathe to any one that
I am the author. I have a motive for keeping it secret, I will explain hereafter—
<u>be sure you do not tell the author</u>. I do not think any one will enquire, but they
<u>might</u>—the Philadelphia Saturday Chronicle is the name of the paper. I write
in great haste . . . and now if I do not hasten I shall miss the mail.

Ellen is still in St. Augustine where she has been for the last six weeks. I
wrote for her to come home to day. I want to see her & I cannot at present ful-
fil my promise of joining her there. I am happy to hear such good tidings from
you, dear as your last contains. Heaven grant you may continue to prosper. I
have just written to George to P— lest he should return there! Do you know
whether he intends to remain at Pittsburg? I feel anxious about him. I hope to
hear from him by next mail—You must not look <u>glum</u> because of the haste in
which this is written, dear, my excuse is honest. You ask me if it is hot—no—
not now—it has been a sort of a hot place here, I tell you for a month past—
but now the weather is delightful—we seldom have hot nights, even in July &
August—but never in the other months—which renders the heat during the
middle of the day less oppressive. Now, however, the weather is <u>altogether fine</u>.

I have heard that Osceola says he does not intend to fight any more—he is
at the camp of the Regulars with [fifteen hundred] warriors—they are peaceable, <u>but will not give up their arms</u>. The Secretary of War has advised that no
active measure be taken to remove them until after the first of <u>November</u>. If
these orders are obeyed, they probably about that time will be ready to try
another shooting match with the palefaces. The object of the wise rulers is to
give them opp'y to go peaceably <u>if they will</u>—I <u>hope</u> they may be so inclined.
All well & send love—dear—I will write again soon, until then, a'dieu—

Your sister, Corine

Corinna Brown and Dr. Edward Aldrich were married at the Halls' La Grange plantation on September 28, 1837. The Second Seminole War was in its second inconclusive year. Within one month of Corinna and Edward's marriage, Gen. Thomas Jesup, after a series of frustrating negotiations with Osceola, Cao Hadjo, Coacoochee (Wild Cat), King Phillip, and others, ordered Osceola and some of his fellow tribesmen seized under a flag of truce. The seizure came on October 22 only a few miles from St. Augustine.

Gen. Joseph Hernandez thereupon marched Osceola and his fellow captives to the Castillo de San Marcos (Fort Marion). Within days of their capture Coacoochee, John Horse, and others made a dramatic escape and inaugurated a new phase of the war after joining their comrades Arpeika (Sam Jones) and Halpatter Tustenuggee (Alligator) in the lower part of the peninsula. But Osceola remained in custody some weeks until he was shipped to Fort Moultrie in Charleston harbor, where he died of malaria on January 31, 1838.[16]

With Edward still attached to the army, Corinna and Ellen remained with the Halls in Mandarin. By the beginning of the year Edward began exploring opportunities in Georgia, finally selecting Macon. Ellen remained with the Halls while Charles and aunts Mary and Ann built their own homestead adjacent to that of the Halls.

[Corinna Aldrich to Mannevillette Brown]

Jacksonville [to Utica, New York]
Oct[ober] 9th, 1837

Dear Brother,

Every day since the eventful 28th I have wished to write you, but every day has brought along its many seemingly important cares to steal away the hours that should have been devoted to you.———Thus you perceive, dear, I am unchanged in nature, although changed in name. Can you believe that I am married, Manne! I assure you I can scarcely realize it, notwithstanding the new scenes, new faces, and new names continually presented to remind me of it. I

---

16. An account of Osceola's capture is contained in the *Tallahassee Floridian,* November 1, 1837. On the seizure of Osceola, see also Mahon, *History of the Second Seminole War,* 211–18; Covington, *Seminoles of Florida,* 92–93; Wickman, *Osceola's Legacy,* 43–46; Porter, *Black Seminoles,* 85–86; McReynolds, *Seminoles,* 193–95; Kieffer, *Maligned General,* 184–90; Prucha, *Sword of the Republic,* 287–90; and Sidney Walter Martin, *Florida during Territorial Days,* 235–36. On this phase of the war in the Mandarin area, see *Tallahassee Floridian,* August 12; September 30, 1837; and *St. Augustine Florida Herald,* January 7, 14, 21; March 22; August 12, 1837.

always supposed, however, that being married would work a great change in me—in my habits, thoughts, feelings, &c. but I do not find it yet, that the Leopard has changed his spots, and perhaps this is the strongest and best reason why I do not feel altogether so matronly, dignified, self-conceited, and pompously important as most young ladies feel privileged to upon the occasion! Nevertheless, one thing is certain, dear, I am happier than I have been for years. I have found a kind, affectionate, and faithful friend in Dr. Aldrich—one with whom as a companion, I would ask no higher Heaven <u>than</u> <u>to</u> <u>live</u> <u>always</u>.— . . . Dear I believe as far as we are concerned that love will only add with life. And my faith is fixed on this, our dispositions are alike, (excepting his is rather the best.) <u>and</u> <u>we</u> <u>love</u> <u>each</u> <u>other</u>!

I have taken it for granted that you have received the newspaper we sent you last week, but though that informed you of the fact, it did not of the particulars of the <u>wedding</u>!—Know then, that we gave out many invitations at St. Mary's, St. Augustine, Jacksonville, &c. intending to make merry if possible. All were accepted, and we in readiness; but alas! the elements would not be propitious—I almost thought another deluge would destroy the earth, until about the <u>trying</u> hour, then it cleared off—& where were our friends—a hundred miles apart! One old county Judge made his appearance & him we converted into a priest! (not without some opposition on my part, however, I assure you!) It seemed that he had anticipated the heavens and prepared a sort of epithalamium (is it right?) <u>N'importe</u>, he got as far as "in the words of the immortal Poet"—hem, hem, hem, & there alas he stopt—looked in his hat— searched his pocket book, alias saddle bags, found his scrap of paper—and closed the ceremony by <u>reading</u> <u>what</u> the immortal poet said! We then eat cake, drank wine, &c., wished earnestly for you and George—Danced until midnight and ended the happy day by getting <u>Aunt</u> <u>&</u> <u>Dr.</u> <u>Hall</u> as jovial as champaign would make them.—The next day we came to Jacksonville. Since then I have received visits of many of those whom the weather prevented from being present at La Grange—among them Dr. Aldrich's father & sister[17] spent

17. Edward's father was Whipple Aldrich. A native of Rhode Island, Aldrich migrated to St. Marys in the early 1810s. Aldrich held property in Camden County, Georgia, and Duval County, Florida. He was fifty-five years old when Edward and Corinna were married. Like his son, Whipple Aldrich was a physician, but he earned most of his income from a mercantile establishment in St. Marys, Georgia. He also owned eight slaves. He died in 1852. See U.S. Manuscript Census, Slave (1850), for Camden County, Georgia; Larry Durbin, comp., *Camden County, Georgia, Cemeteries* (Jacksonville, Fla.: Southern Genealogist's Exchange Society, Inc., 1993), 1; and *Georgia Genealogical Magazine* 32 (April 1969): 2187, 2191.

a few days with us. I esteem them very highly and have promised to return their visit at St. Mary's in the next boat—probably in a few days;—Nell & Aunt Ann are with me now. Charles left this morning—I hear G is coming on immediately. I wish you were with him. It is very uncertain, however, how long we may remain here—probably but a few months, still during that time, or after, wherever else we may be, it will delight me, dear, to have a visit from you. Were the Dr. here, he would join me in the request—but he is absent—I will only add I shall be proud to introduce him to you as a brother, and I have no hesitancy in saying am sure you will love him as one. He already regards you, and often expresses a wish to see you—and trusting the time is not distant when that wish shall be gratified both for him & thee & me—I'll bid thee, dearest, for a little while farewell.—still your sister, Corinna

[Ellen Brown to Mannevillette Brown]

Mandarin [to Utica, New York]
Nov. 12, 1837

My Dear Mann,

Our sister being "wooed, and married, and or, Kissed and carried away," I take it into my great head that an epistle from the maid of the pine barrens might not be unacceptable. You can't imagine how the weddings flourish in this part of the world. Notwithstanding the pleanty [*sic*], however, I have not taken a ticket. To speak practically—the great lottery is being drawn in which I have no immediate interest either in prizes or ranks. ahem! [eras!] as I used to say. Corine has married a very clever little chap, and they are to my thinking monstrously in love with each other. Said gent is well off, not rich,—good looking, not splendid, and altogether a gentleman, which latter clause cannot be applyed to all the professional characters, and little great men of this region of war. I write with a steel pen, and occasionally drop my ink, don't mistake the blots I have licked with my tongue, for tears I have shed with mine eyes; for though I consider myself a widow yet my sentiments are somewhat after the fashion of the fat landlord in the play: "My wife, God bless her, has gone to Heaven. She is happy, I'm contented." Which being interpreted means that I consider her getting married a God blessed thing. She is in St. Augustine at present, when the war is over or rather when this campaign is closed he will, if the war is not over, resign and he and his <u>cara sposa</u>[18] will travel one or two months in west Florida, after which, in the spring they intend to go to the north and take a look at the world in that direction, after which, they intend to fix

18. Italian: "dear bride."

upon a place of residence most probably in Florida, most certainly in the South, after which I have promised to go and take up my abode with them. . . .

I am glad to hear you speak of going to Europe. I want you to go. I should like to myself. How I regret that my name is not Nickolas instead of Ellen. I'd go to the world's end if I was a boy. A rolling stone gathers no moss, but a fig[19] for the moss says I—so long as one rolls. My Dear Man, most of the maxims and generally received opinions of society, the greatest sceptic, if he is not obstinate, will find to be true and sensible; but there is this to be considered, in every possible course of life one must make a choice of evils. Can't you branch upon this idea?

Corine has written you word that she is going to take me with her. It is all very well for her to think so, but as for my throwing myself upon the bounty of a stranger, however generous he may be, especially after he has taken one member of the family without a pin in her pocket, I hope you have not such a mean opinion of your sister as to think that her pride or her generosity would suffer her to entertain the idea for an instant. I know human nature like a book, so long as a person is independent matters may go splendidly, but if you take away that idea verily one's happiness is a house built on sand. I know that I stand not independent but if I must be an incumbrance, it shall be to those to whom fate and my birth have made me one. If ever it shall please God to permit me to earn my living by the sweat of my eye brows as the frenchman called it, I shall take the curse of Adam upon me with a great deal of pleasure. Don't suppose that I am out of sorts in making these remarks—I merely express them because they passed into my head, my thoughts always run away with my tongue and my pen. You will hardly guess from my staunch way of writing that I am one of the merriest crickets that sings in the pine-barrens but it is nevertheless a fact, precious little do I suffer the ills of life to fret me. Did it never occur to you that most of peoples troubles arise from doubt? A firm decided character is most likely to be a happy one. At least so thinks your sister. I want very much to come to the north next spring. After Corine has gone (it does not enter into her plans to take me with her on that jaunt) people will say: Why don't Nabby go? Cant you and I patch up an expedition? If you can advance the needful, I can advance the person, but as the needful is not always forthcoming you need not think too much about it, for I assure you I shall not. All send love. Good bye. Ell

---

19. An obscene gesture made by thrusting one's thumb between the index and middle fingers and raising the fist in defiance.

[Corinna Aldrich to Mannevillette Brown]

La Grange [to Utica, New York]
December 4th, 1837

My dear brother,

Your kind epistle of the 24th Oct. I received but two days since—& be assured I should have replied to it earlier. A new name has not altered my character, dear—I am still your <u>fond</u> <u>sister</u>. I wrote to you from Jacksonville about the first of October—which document I trust you have ere this received—Immediately after that I went to St. Mary's to visit Dr. A's relatives—We remained there ten days which time passed very delightfully. They are an amiable family and treated me with every kindness and attention—The <u>old</u> <u>Dr.</u> Aldrich I like almost as much as his son!—He is a <u>gentleman</u>—about 50 years of age and full of good humour. He has a second wife—kind-hearted—but like many others troubled with <u>simplicity!</u>[20] Edward's oldest sister Letitia is an amiable and accomplished young lady of <u>sweet sixteen</u>—She is goodness itself, but <u>not</u> <u>pretty</u>—I wish you knew them all. I hope you will ere long—In your letter to Edward—I thank you in his name. He is off to fight Indians—but if I have an opportunity I will send it to him. I know he will be delighted to receive it—and will reply to it <u>sur-le-champ.</u>[21] He would have written to you— but on our return from Georgia—he was ordered to St. Augustine—and a week after that—to be in readiness to take the field. He had not time even to write to his father and left me to make his apologies all round. The Army left St. A on the 20th ult—but Ell & I remained in the city until Tuesday last—and should have staid longer but for Aunt Ann's being taken very ill—I am sorry to say she has had a severe billious fever, and still continues very low. There is however a favourable change in her this morning—and I humbly trust in a few there will be a perceptible change for the better—I have a deal to write you about, dear, but my time is so much occupied with poor Ann—you must excuse me until she is better.

Do you hear from George? I feel anxious about him.— We have not heard from him since the 22nd of Sept. Then he said he should sail for Florida on the 18th of October. I shall try to write to Portsmouth today to ascertain if he has left there—he may be sick—I cannot forbear to speak of the weather. Dearest

---

20. Aldrich's first wife and Edward's and Letitia's mother was Letitia Sherman Aldrich. She died in 1831. In 1834 Aldrich married Jane S. Johnson. See Durbin, *Camden County, Georgia, Cemeteries,* 1; and *Georgia Genealogical Magazine* 32 (April 1969): 2191.

21. French: "immediately."

it is such as one would imagine for Paradise—just air enough to stir the leaves
—and that so soft and balmy—it seems as if one could not breathe it and be
sick. . . . Give my love to your friend Mrs. [Sarah] Walker[22] soon as I have leisure
to take a little pain—or rather to be a little careful in my penmanship—I will with
pleasure endite her a Post Scriptum. . . . Dearest your affectionate sister [Corinna]

[Ellen A. Brown to Mannevillette Brown]

Mandarin [to Utica, New York]
Friday Dec. 21st, 1837

My Dear Manne,

We have just received two letters from you, or rather Corinna has. You
must not forget your promise to write to me. I like the idea of yours and the
reasons you give for it. However I promise you I will prove a good correspondent so far as regards . . . punctuality. I have no lines, steel pen, bad ink, and the
fidgets. You asked me to give you some account of our views and prospects, if
I understand you right. For myself it is most probable that I shall remain for
the next year in status quo—that is to say, just here in Mandarin, in the course
of that time it is most probable Corinne and the Dr. will be settled somewhere
or other should that be the case I have promised to go and live with them. The
Dr is at present with the army but we expect him home every day. The regiment to which he belongs is discharged, but as he is a staff officer and very fas-
tidious in every thing we do not expect to see him until the last gun fired. It is
thought it will very speedily be brought to a close, but this is an opinion never
to be relied upon until it is proven by the fact. The best news we have is that
the Indians are starving. If it be that and that alone will bring them to terms.
Parson Brown has taken our little Jacksonville Courier under the shadow of
his wing.[23] In which shadow it will probably come out of the shade. I have
promised to drop a penful of ink for him occasionally. I have always been
threatened with authorship you know should any unequivocal symptoms of the
disease present themselves I will gratify the very natural curiosity you would

22. The wife of Thomas R. Walker, one of Utica's leading lawyers, business leaders,
and art patrons.

23. The *Jacksonville Courier* was founded in 1834. The journal was published by L. Currier & Company and edited by Rev. David Brown, persons already known to the Browns.
Mannevillette had worked with Nathaniel Currier some years earlier in Boston and Philadelphia. One source notes that Brown was "one of the most genial and unselfish men that
ever graced a paper" (quoted in Gold, *History of Duval County,* 111; and Knauss, *Territorial Florida Journalism,* 34–35, 57–58).

Thomas Douglas served as U.S. district attorney for the Eastern Judicial District of Florida from 1826 to 1845. He and his wife Hanna often entertained Ellen and Corinna at their home in St. Augustine. He and his family attended the St. Johns Episcopal Church in Jacksonville with Ellen and Corinna. Florida Supreme Court.

probably feel on the subject. The old Dr. is quite sick. Aunt Ann is recovering. Aunt Mary, Corinne, Charles, Deal,[24] and myself in good health. . . . [Ellen]

. . . At the time I wrote I might have felt a passing qualm but I assure you my general health is excellent. Amanda (aunt M's apprentice girl) says of late—there has been such a feeling of pulses and looking at tongues that the hens even have held up their bills and put up their claws! But I trust the worst is over. Aunt Ann is daily improving—and the old Dr. quite recovered. He however has had another ill turn—but this is to be expected in old age—I have been out nursing (at Charles's place) since my return from St. Augustine—Mary is now so far convalescent—that I presume I shall have to come and get the good samaritan past this side of the branch. . . . I flatter myself that I am a tolerable nurse & I hope if you get sick (which God forbid) you will give me a trial—I hope ere long to have a <u>house</u>—then Nab promises to live with me. . . . ever your fond sis,

Corinna

24. "Deal" is a shortened version of "Delia."

I spent last evening <u>tete a tete</u>[25] with Mr. [Samuel L.] Burritt—we had all sorts of talk and he tried to convince me that he is not the bad man the world has represented him. He has a fine mind and is either a better man than he is thought or a very exceedingly cunning one. He is engaged to a very sweet girl of St. Augustine, one Miss Louisa Douglas.[26] He . . . wants polishing. So much for him. I should like to get acquainted with you. Can you understand that feeling? I don't know what manner of man you are. I hope I shall have the pleasure of your acquaintance one of these days. Don't get married nor tangled in love scrapes until I know you. You must not forget that you are to go to Europe I have this idea very much at heart.—if I had money I would go with [you] and I think I could be at least so troublesome that you could scarce object. But this is all over as I used to say in times past. Good bye. Ever Yours Ell

[Corinna Aldrich to Mannevillette Brown]

Jacksonville, [to Utica, New York]
Jan. 17th, 1838

Dear Brother,

So this is but the second time I have written the date of the New Year—I trust it is not too late to return your kind congratulations and wishes—that every blessing may attend you is the earnest and honest prayer of your sister. My dear, the reason I have not written to you of late is other than formerly— is simply and sincerely, it has not been in my power. I have not thought less often of you.

On my return from St. Augustine, as I told you, I found Aunt Ann very ill . . . three weeks we were all occupied with her. Just as she began to get convalescent, the old Dr. was taken sick; and as I suppose you have ere this been informed took his departure for a better world.[27] On the evening after his burial,

25. French: "in private conversation."

26. Louisa Douglas was the twenty-two-year-old daughter of Thomas and Hanna Sanford Douglas. Douglas was district attorney of the Eastern Judicial District of Florida. Natives of Connecticut, the Douglas family migrated to Florida in 1826 from Indiana. Both Louisa and her sister were educated in Connecticut. Louisa and Samuel L. Burritt were married in Philadelphia in September 1838. See U.S. Manuscript Census, Population (1850), for Duval County, Florida, p. 94; *St. Augustine Florida Herald,* September 29, 1838; Thomas Douglas, *Autobiography of Thomas Douglas, Late Judge of the Supreme Court of Florida* (New York: Calkins and Stiles, 1856), 34, 90–91; and Manley, Brown, and Rise, *Supreme Court of Florida,* 123–27.

27. Hall died on Christmas Day. His grave is in a section known as Plummer's Cove near Mandarin. See Lucy Ames Edwards, comp., *Grave Markers of Duval County* (Jacksonville, Fla.: Privately published, 1955), 51; and Merritt, *Century of Medicine,* 9.

Dr. Aldrich returned unexpectedly from the campaign and in a few days, he returned once more to this hateful place—our stay dear, however is made endurable by the prospect of a speedy move. Edward is much engaged with settling his business here—as in the course of a couple of weeks he will take up his bed and walk.[28] Intending to locate in some more agreeable vicinity if possible—but at any rate, to change, if it is for the <u>worse</u>, that however, cannot be—He desired to be most affectionately remembered to you—and further requested me to thank you for the friendly letter and say he would with pleasure reply to it by this mail if possible—if not, certainly by the next.

The crackers will not let him alone—he has said repeatedly to them that he could not and would not attend to practice—but the poor devils get sick or injured & call for him—and humanity bids him go—notwithstanding he neglects his own business—spends his time, and hopes for no reward—save the blessing of a quiet conscience. He is now gone to see a couple of poor wretches —one thrown from a horse while racing and almost killed—the other fell through the wharf and broke his arm—the former has been a patient nine days—he is in <u>hopes</u> he will recover—besides these he has two or three other critical cases—taken by favor—I tell you all this dear, that you may know if he does not write immediately, <u>it</u> <u>is</u> <u>not</u> <u>from</u> <u>neglect.</u>

Rev. David Brown & lady are staying here. He has the charge of the Jacksonville Courier at present. He extends his compliments to you—and begged me to request you to write some articles for him—on whatever topic you please—whether it be your profession—your travels—the signs of the times; <u>not</u> politics, or what you will. I fancy you have other fish to fry! Nevertheless I have told you—I promised to write for him but somehow I can't find time to answer the demands of my private correspondence & business—to write public documents. Ell favoured him with an address for the New Year—but it was thought too severe—and only part of it was published. I believe she sent you a paper. I expect Ell here today—I hope she will come. She has been staying with Aunt H—she is very lonely now. . . . Rev. B preached a fine funeral sermon for the old Dr. on the 7th . . . I shall suffer the time of E's absence, which will be some weeks, with them—Then I will, <u>Deo Volante</u>, write often—Also if I ever get settled I promise to be a faithful writer—but at present—the home of today may be a strange & distant place to-morrow—and I cannot compose my thoughts as I could and write when matters about me are more improved— Do you hear from George often and do you really know <u>how</u> he is? I feel very

28. See John 5:8.

anxious about him—He is young—out of business and I badly fear out of health—but I know of nothing to be done. I urged him to come here—he declined. . . .

Corinna

[Ellen Brown to Mannevillette Brown]

Florida [Mandarin] to Utica
February 17, 1838

My Dear Mann,

The mails are very bad as you say and what is worse my chance of sending an epistle to the office after it is written is very "dubious" as the crackers say. By the way, do you know that the folks in this part of the country are called crackers as the new Englanders are called yankees. . . . I am very much obliged for the X. US.[29] You mention having sent me one before—unless you allude to one you sent Corine about the time of her marriage, I grieve to say it has not been received. I mention it because if the conveyance is unsafe we will not use it. Concerning my coming to the north I am afraid the trip will be too expensive to you—as for myself the whole of my possessions in the cash line amounts to the 10 you sent me. I should like to come . . . but I consider your pockets. I have seen so little of you since I have grown up to be a thinking animal that I have no idea of your way of viewing things as this may also be the case with you. I will just mention that I am one of the most simple straight-forward persons alive; there is never but one meaning and that the most obvious one to anything I say. I told you I wanted to go north and so I did and do but upon reflection viz. that it would cost you upward of a hundred I considered that I had done wrong and was sorry that I had mentioned it, nevertheless I am very much gratified by your free and liberal offer to bear charges. I hope it will please Heaven that we shall shake hands with each other one of these days, and have a good long chat about all matters past, present, and to come.

I don't believe any one has written you word the poor old Dr. is dead. He died last Christmas day. I think it must be so from your not mentioning it. I intended to write you word but probably forgot it, by mistaking the intention for the act. I would take more pains with my chronography but the more I spare my eyes the better Christian I think myself. They are the greatest affliction of my life especially as I am now situated where I have nothing to entertain

---

29. This is probably a ten-dollar bank note or a draft on a bank in New York branch of the Second Bank of the United States. There was no U.S. paper money issued at this time.

myself with but books pen and ink and am obliged to refrain almost altogether from using them. I would run about the woods if this was not the most uninteresting country under the canopy of Heaven. I sicken over the self denial I am obliged to practice. One thing however I have contrived to do but by no means so well as I would have done it under other circumstances. I have written an article for a new magazine that is to be forthcoming in March. To be published by Parson Brown and called the Florida magazine,[30] I will send you a copy as soon as it is in print. I wrote it for the [Jacksonville] Courier but he begged it for the magazine which I take to be something of a compliment although it may not be so but merely taken to fill up the book.

That you might get your epistles one at a time and so hear the oftener, I suppose Corine would write oftener but her time is taken up in driving about [so] that she is not aware how the weeks slip away. She was very sorry and quite surprised that you complained of her and thought her letters must miscarry; may be that is the case. Good bye—Ellen

[p. s.] All the folks send love not excepting myself who as St. Paul would say am the least of the apostles.[31] It is a mighty cold uncomfortable day.

[Corinna Brown Aldrich to Mannevillette Brown]

Jacksonville [to Utica, N.Y.]
Feb 21st, 1838

My dear brother,

Your kind favour of the 21st ult arrived in due time at La Grange. But was not immediately received by me owing to my absence in St. Augustine, else I should have replied to it earlier. Indeed I should have written at any rate—had it been in <u>my</u> <u>power</u>. You laugh at me because I make want of time an excuse for negligence, you think. But my dear, you ought not. I do assure you I am not unmindful of you. I think of you as often—and as fondly as ever. Because I love another, is it any reason I should not love you? No, dear one, the heart does not contract, it expands with new affection.—I will tell you why I have not written oftener of late.—I have never felt settled since I have been married.— Constantly anticipating a removal to some <u>better</u> <u>land</u> and all the time on . . . through this again. The mail leaves but once a week—and I think I wont write to have my letter a week old—and when the time comes <u>to write</u>

---

30. The prospectus for the *Florida Magazine* appeared in the *St. Augustine Florida Herald and Southern Democrat,* August 8, 1839. The journal was never actually published.

31. See 1 Cor. 15:9.

I have generally been so situated that I could not write. Are you convinced dear of my <u>innocence</u>? If not I will tell you more—'Tis often <u>Edward's fault</u>, scold him—he spends one half of his time in teazing me. He promises better manners when he gets located elsewhere in business! But I think unless he begins soon to reform he will forget how to improve. Old habits you know are hard to break! I wish you were here that I might give you an oral description of our day's maneuvers. I am afraid I should not do justice on paper—n'importe—Time is fleet—I think we shall see you next Summer—then you will have an opportunity to judge for yourself.

In the mean time, dear, I will write as often as possible. Why does not that lazy Ell do duty better—she has only been with me one week for the last month—excepting a few days we spent at La Grange last week. She would have remained here with us—but <u>Judge</u> [John L.] Doggett[32] with whom we sojourn could not accommodate her with a room—Besides we do not want her to stay here! It is miserable—uncomfortable—dirty, sandy (2 feet thick in some places)—no society—no anything—E & I would not remain but for E's business—We intend to quit in the course of ten days, if possible. It is uncertain whether I shall go to Macon or not. I would like to do so—but E. is afraid the journey would be too tedious. . . . [Corinna]

32. One of the leading citizens of Jacksonville, John L. Doggett migrated to Florida from Massachusetts in 1822 with his wife Maria Fairbanks. Together they had four children: Aristides, John L. Jr., Maria C., and Simeon T. In 1824 Florida's legislative council granted Doggett the right to operate a ferry crossing the St. Johns River. One year earlier he received the contract from the county to build the first Duval County Courthouse. A leading Duval County Democrat, he represented his county in the legislative council in 1824–27. In 1827 he served as the body's president. Doggett served as judge of the Duval County Court during the 1830s. On March 6, 1840, Gov. Robert Reid appointed him examiner of the Jacksonville Branch of the Bank of the Southern Life Insurance & Trust Company. By 1843 he was serving as acting collector for the Port of Jacksonville. Doggett died at his residence in Jacksonville on January 8, 1844. See U.S. Manuscript Census, Population (1840), Duval County, Florida, p. 94; Gold, *History of Duval County*, 104–5; Phelps, *People of Lawmaking*, 28; *Jacksonville Courier*, January 1, 1835; Carter, *Territorial Papers*, 25:477, 26:34, 673; and *St. Augustine Florida Herald and Southern Democrat*, January 16, 1844.

Chapter Four

"The Ladies of Llangollen"

A New Home

During the winter of 1838 Edward pondered whether or not he would remain in the army. But as he explained to his brother-in-law, he had definitely ruled out Jacksonville as a place to settle permanently: "[O]f all places . . . Jacksonville would be the very last spot in Florida I should select . . . with a society made up, of the refuse of the veriest scum of the States! I was first induced to visit Jacksonville on account of a planting interest of ours situated on the river, four miles above this place. While . . . there the war commenced, and ever since I have remained, attached to the army. God knows," he continued, "I thought, ere this we should have been victorious; but our [operations] have been so badly conducted, and ineffectual, that I must either resign, or decide to spend a lifetime attached to an impotent army, engaged in an unglorious war—an anomaly in the annals of American warfare—an army that gets whipped every time it gets a fight. It has one good quality, however, it won't stay whipped." [1]

Edward ultimately decided on Macon, Georgia, as a place to establish a medical practice. Between March 25 and October 22, Corinna's letters to Mannevillette in Utica were addressed from Edward's office in Macon on Commerce Row.[2] One letter of particular interest reveals Corinna's memory of seeing Osceola:

As for the Florida War, it never will be ended. I have just received a Jacksonville paper which tells of Indian depredations within fifteen or twenty miles of that place. It is shameful that such things should be. As for Osceola or Powell, I believe I told you I had seen his worship. If they have represented him as you describe, they have indeed done him injustice. I never saw a more finely formed man—graceful in every limb & motion—an oval face—the cheek bones

---

1. Edward S. Aldrich to Mannevillette Brown, February 14, 1838, Anderson-Brown Papers, USMA.

2. *Macon (Georgia) Southern Post,* April 21, 1838.

Osceola. After a series of failed negotiations Gen. Joseph Hernandez, acting on the orders of Thomas Jesup, seized Osceola under a flag of truce on October 21, 1837. Corinna witnessed Osceola and the other prisoners marching through the streets of St. Augustine. After being incarcerated in Fort Marion, Osceola was transported to Charleston, where he died of malaria on January 30, 1838. Florida State Archives.

not very high—Fine features and mildness & sweetness of expression very unusual with those of his race. I saw many of them while in St. A. As for their dress it is very like our Northern Indians. When I saw Powell, he wore a sort of tunic of blue cloth and ornamented with coloured fringe and beads—very flashy moccasins made of skin & ornamented with beads—he tied a blue cotton handkerchief round his head—in the top placed two bunches of feathers —white & black ostrich—given him by Mrs. [Rebecca] Downing of St. A[3] altogether in spite of his savage aristocracy—his valour—his heroism—his misfortunes—in spite of the thousand humbugs fancy tried to gather, I could not convince myself that he was more than a pityful dirty Indian. I did pity him; but that was all. . . .[4]

Corinna despised Macon. Even so, her brother George was planning to move there and Edward hoped to find him a position there. Corinna stayed with

3. Rebecca Downing, a native of Virginia, was the wife of Charles Downing, who served as Florida's territorial delegate to Congress (1837–41). After her husband's death in 1841 she moved to Jacksonville. See U.S. Manuscript Census, Population (1850), Duval County, Florida, p. 92.

4. Corinna Aldrich to Mannevillette Brown, April 29, 1838, Anderson-Brown Papers, USMA.

various families whenever Edward was traveling.[5] Meanwhile, in March, Corinna left her sister at the Aldrich family home in St. Marys, Georgia, where Ellen wrote the following letter.

[Ellen Brown to Mannevillette Brown]

Saint Marys [Georgia to Utica, New York]
March 31, 1838

<u>Mon cher frere,</u>[6]

It is an age since I have written a french word or indeed any kind of a word seeing as how I am making a visit in Dr. Aldrich's family as you may perceive by date. I received an epistle from you forwarded from Mandarin. You complain of me and not without cause. But indeed you should not have cause if I were not so terribly afflicted in a visionary way to wit. I am attacked now and then with such violent inflammation of the eyes as to render it a matter of great difficulty for me to write. I hate to mention this thing because it seems as if every one must be tired of hearing of it, but it is nevertheless just so. I wrote you just before I left La Grange in Feb. I think (indeed it appears to me I have written you two or three letters since the date you mention. I am certain that I have written to you mentioning the receipt of the money and also about the death of the poor old Dr. Perhaps you have received them since you wrote— March 2). In my last I promised to write regularly and should have done so if I had been able but I could not for the cause above mentioned.

Corine and the Dr. were going to Macon in Georgia and I agreed to accompany them as far as St. Mary's where I have remained since (about a fortnight); they have gone on their journey and will be gone probably a month. I have an invitation to stay untill they return, don't know whether I shall do so or not. You say you are said to be engaged all the time. You are somewhat like your sister. Indeed all the sentiments of your letter are so similar to my own as to surprise me with one exception, you say that ladies think that if a gent looks at her twice he is or wishes to be engaged. I am a woman, I know that you gents have a way of looking and a way of acting too, that you don't care your neighbors should notice and when you alter your minds, or worse, the damsel alters hers you would have it believed it was all nothing. Don't talk to me. I know all about these things. One thing I believe, the more one roves about the less one is likely to be pleased and the heart that it seems has often loved has not only

---

5. Corinna Aldrich to Mannevillette Brown, July 31; August 13; October 10, 1838, Anderson-Brown Papers, USMA.

6. French: "my dear brother."

never loved but is never likely to love; those kind of characters marry for interest for ambition for accident or live unmarried. I wonder how people that have any opportunity of knowing human nature can be enthusiastic on any subject under heaven. We are such betwixt and between half good, half bad, indifferent sort of creatures with just sense enough to make trouble for ourselves deserving after all more charity than censure. How can a person expect to find a being one could love? I hate to be obliged to bring my imagination down to the level of humanity and I am certain I could never invest any one with the rainbow coloured mantle of my dreams but I should instantly be reminded of the fable of the Ass and the Lion's skin.[7] I believe I can write the history of most flirtation in one short sentence—To love for moments to be disgusted for years.

I have just received a letter from Charles. All the folks live. George is on his way to Pittsburgh. We are a bad set of correspondents—because we keep flying about so, but it certainly is a pleasure to me to write and a far greater one to receive letters so you must . . . pick up your old idea of writing to me every week and I will make you the same promise to be fulfilled as far forth as is in my power. Good bye,

Yours Ell.

[P.S.] This is a very pleasant family but the most curious place you can imagine. The wonder to me is how it comes to be a place at all. There is no commerce no business, no lions.[8] The only male unmarried thing of a marriageable age is the school master and he is engaged. No balls no parties no rides no nothing at all except going to meeting 7,000 people absolutely in a state of somnambulism.

[Ellen Brown to Mannevillette Brown]

Mandarin [to Utica, New York]
April 30, [1838]

My Dear Mann,

You perceive that I am again established at home, that is if I have any home. I left Georgia exactly one week since (Corine has concluded to remain in

---

7. In Aesop's fables the story is as follows: "An ass put on a lion's skin and passed for a lion with everyone. Men all ran from him, and so did the animals. But when the wind blew, the skin was carried away, and there the ass stood, exposed. Then everyone ran up and fell to beating him with sticks and clubs" (translated by Lloyd W. Daly in *Aesop without Morals: The Famous Fables, and a Life of Aesop Newly Translated and Edited* [New York: Thomas Yoselof, 1961], 215–16). In *Brewer's Dictionary of Phrase and Fable* (New York: Harper & Brothers, 1953) the ass is said to have exposed himself "when he began to bray."

8. Ellen could mean lion as in "one who is strong, courageous, or fiercely brave" since her next sentence refers to the lack of interesting men in St. Marys; she also might mean

Macon as I presume she has informed you). I received a letter from you while there and answered it. I should have written you again from there had it been possible but my sight is so bad that I write now with the utmost difficulty and this is the first day that I have felt as if I could attempt it at all for the last three or four weeks.

Aunt Mary has got the frame of her new house erected for which Heaven be praised! All the folks are well. The war is status quo. George has gone to Pittsburgh. Do you intend to pay us a visit before your departure for Europe? I hope so. How long do you intend to be gone? O dear Mann I am terribly in the low lands. It seems to me the most terrible affliction that could befall me to have the nerves of my eyes so weak. Here I am weeks and weeks in utter solitude and can employ myself in no manner whatever. I can neither read, write, nor sew. My spirits are utterly broken. . . . I should have made a delightful visit in Georgia if the "varmints" would only let me alone but upon me Mann the way the old young ladies go on (while I have my senses I'll stand clear of women older than myself who happen to have the wish without the ability to get married). Some of the old "varmints" abuse me and persecute me and say all manner of evil against me falsely. I certainly wish to have a good opinion of my own sex . . . particularly Mrs. Aldrich our Brother-in-law's mother and her sister and a friend of theirs Mrs. Delony.[9] But for the major part of my acquaintance both there and in other places the most I get from them is envy, hatred, malice, and all-uncharitableness. . . . My dear Mann, don't marry an envious woman. Also have thou nothing to do with homely women. I'd rather encounter the spoilt child air of a beauty a hundred times over, than the low ill concealed envy with the disposition to pick and fret that is so apt to lurk in the heart of a homely would be belle—for these be such animals. Now with your sex I believe the core is different. I think the homely are generally decidedly preferable to the handsome. Your sex are spoilt by flattery. I believe I'll quit the subject. I feel such a disposition to abuse all the world. Is it not a singular world, My Dear Mann, so full of selfishness, littleness, meanness, malice, envy? All picking and pulling at one another. Lying, deceaving,[10] cheating to the very uttermost of each one's own particular ability. Each one wishing to reduce all

---

"things of note, celebrity, or curiosity (in a town, etc.); especially in plural, to see, or show, the lions" (*OED*). Both usages were common in the early nineteenth century.

9. Mrs. Delony and Miss Delony were listed among passengers on the steamboat *Florida,* arriving in Savannah from Black Creek (*Savannah Georgian,* December 8, 1839).

10. Archaic spelling for *deceiving.*

others to the level of their own inferiority. I can lay my hand upon my heart and swear this disposition is not in me. I could almost swear for many of my acquaintance and there are others for whom I can swear that it is in them as I have proved in a way so disagreeable as to make me sicken over the race. I'd rather be a cow, a horse, a pig, a potato, anything rather than a woman if all women must bear the character some deserve. I hate to be ranked with such cattle in every way[11] — Ell — — — — —

[Ellen Brown to Mannevillette Brown]

La Grange [to Utica, New York]
May 9th, 1838

My Dear Manne,

 . . . Many thanks for the needful—it amounts to a small fortune here in the wilderness. Aunt Mary says you may pay her when it is convenient for you. She is in no special need of the money at present. She has not made her arrangements for going north yet, but intends doing so forthwith. You shall hear of her whereabouts from me and from herself also. She wants to see you very much. So also does Aunt Ann. They say you must certainly come here and make them a visit before you go to Europe. They would walk a hundred miles to see you. They and Charles . . . are erecting a very pretty house which will be finished by midsummer. Charles attends altogether to his little plantation. He will have a beautiful place here in the course of a year or two. It is christened (now all places must have a name you know among us southerners) Llangollen. What think you of that? You know Charlie would die if it had not a sounding title, so we fetched upon that. We, rather I, said in play, that inasmuch as it was a sort of refuge for old maids it ought so to be called.[12] Charles liked the name for its euphony. George I have not heard from since I came from St. Marys.

11. Mannevillette subsequently informed Corinna of Ellen's difficulties with some of the "damsels of St. M[arys]," to which Corinna pointed out to him on June 9, 1838, that it was "nonsensical for her to give the malicious remarks of an envious old maid a thought. Dr. Aldrich's family and all those worth caring for, love her very much, and speak of her in the highest terms."

12. The original Llangollen is in Wales. Ellen's phrase "old maids" alludes to the famous "Ladies of Llangollen," Lady Eleanor Butler (1739–1829) and Miss Sarah Ponsonby (1755–1831). They lived together in their home, Plas Newydd, from 1779 to 1829. "There they lived in complete isolation . . . and neither left the cottage for a single night until their deaths. Their devotion to each other and their eccentric behavior gave them wide notoriety" (Sir Leslie Stephen and Sir Sidney Lee, eds., *The Dictionary of National Biography* (1917; reprint, Oxford: Oxford University Press, 1970), 3:501.

While I was there Corinne received an epistle from him announcing his immediate departure from Portsmouth for Pittsburgh where I presume the youth now is. Corinna and Dr. Aldrich have taken up their residence in Macon. I have promised to go and live with them when they go to housekeeping, probably next winter.

You ask me if you can come south in September. Why bless your soul if it is health you are thinking of you can come any day out of the 365 you please. You may think how much need you have to fear a sickly season when I tell you that your letter occasioned me to ask when it occurred—I did not know. The climate of this place is particularly healthy, neither is the heat so very great as a northerner might imagine. I have felt <u>more</u> <u>warm</u> <u>weather</u>, but certainly not <u>warmer</u> weather here than elsewhere. But I won't fill my paper with a description of the climate. September is exactly the right time for you to come because Corinna promises us a visit at that time and you could meet her here which would be very pleasant. You must come to the South anyhow before you go to Europe. You know you must see a little of your own land if it is but just to swear by when abroad. I am glad you are going and if you don't study hard and make yourself a marvelous great painter, I'll knock you with a light-wood knot. There be no stores in Florida. Mann if I only had four or five thousand cash in my pocket what a grand chance this would be for me. <u>Nolens Volens</u>[13] I would saddle myself on to you.

I have not read the books you mention although I saw them in Jacksonville. I do not read any at present on account of my eyes. There are no bookstores here—people send to Charleston for their books. I have never been at loss for something to read since I have been here, only for something to read with. I borrow books of my beaux when they have any that I desire. When they do not, I read those in the house. Reading and writing are to me like room to a tiger. They render me over all the ills of life victorious. But I must give them up. They tell me electricity would be likely to restore my eyes—when I have an opportunity I intend to try it. At present I bathe them in cold water and take exercise. For the latter I walked to Mandarin the day before yesterday and on my return walked on ahead of Aunts Mary and Hall, who were taking exercise with me, and it being just at that misty hour between twilight and moonlight I missed my way and when they arrived at home they missed me. It is no joke to be lost in the pine barren. The perfect level of the ground, the sameness of the trees, the absence of any other object by which to direct inexperienced steps. Also the innumerable, interminable cattle tracks which tempt you to go in

13. Latin: "willing or unwilling."

every direction render them as puzzling as a labyrinth. But I had sense enough to stick to the road so I insisted that I was not lost although when they found me I neither knew where I was nor which way to go. But the way I frightened the folks and the way they ran and hollowed and blared the tin trumpet, and the way I was tired after having walked about 12 miles between the hours of 4 and 10 made about as sweet a row as you could imagine.

As to my coming to the north it would be a mighty expensive business I opine and you want all your old coppers now for your European expedition. Besides I would by no means come if it would prevent your coming to the south. You say you will bring me anything I want from the north. You are a right dear fellow—bring me a side saddle and bridle i.e. if you know how to select an easy ladies' saddle. If not, you must not waste your money for it is impossible for a woman to ride well with an uncomfortable saddle or a poor bridle. I don't know the price of these things; if they are expensive do not get them at all. I speak firmly because you might take it into your head to buy me something equally expensive but not so valuable. Remember I prefer your interests to my whims and I think you have been quite generous enough already so don't let my asking influence you if such was not your intention. . . . P.S. If you can't come and see me before you go to Europe, I'll take the first fellow I can get and come after you. . . . Good bye Ellen.

[Ellen A. Brown to Mannevillette Brown]

La Grange [to Utica, New York]
May 22, 1838

My Dear Manne,

. . . if you only had some dear sweet acquaintances here I might tell you the news for in a little tittle tattle busy body community like . . . this, there is always plenty of scandal afloat you know. But inasmuch as it could not possibly interest you to know that major [John] Mackay was married last week or Dr. E. K. White challenged,[14] or any other on-dit[15] that makes up the daily talk, you must take such an epistle as I can spin and weave from my own word gatherer.

---

14. E. K. White practiced medicine in Alachua and St. Johns Counties during the 1830s and 1840s. He also served under Edward Aldrich as assistant surgeon in the First Florida Volunteers. In 1838 he represented Alachua County in the state constitutional convention at St. Joseph. In 1840 White became judge of the Alachua County Court. See Carter, *Territorial Papers*, 26:60; Florida Militia Muster Rolls, Seminole Indian Wars, Florida Department of Military Affairs, St. Augustine, Fla., no. 67, vol . 1, pp. 43–46; and Hammond, *Medical Profession in 19th Century Florida*, 678.

15. French: "hearsay, rumor."

Imprimis.[16] My health is better than when I last wrote and consequently my eyes and consequently my spirit . . . the new house which is being built is in good health. Also, Miss Mary and Miss Ann, and Mrs. Hall, and Master Charlie are in good health. I had a letter from Corinna of the same date of your last. She says you are going to Macon. So you oughter. We have not heard from George lately, so I can send you no news from that quarter. Aunt Molly has not started upon her travels yet. . . . I never send you news of the war because I presume you hear as correctly and quickly as I do by way of newspapers. For example, I heard last night that General Taylor had taken four hundred Indians. Now if this be the first intelligence you have of it let me know and I will mend my manners in this subject. I am entirely out of the way of the excitement of the war if indeed it creates any. I bathe in cold water, I swim in the river, I eat bread and butter—I write letters which read as the writer did talk, [show] and shutter. When do you propose to leave Utica? Do you go from thence to ny City? There be two acquaintances of mine in that place. One Mr. Emory Rider of the firm of Rider and Young, Forwarding and Commission store N. 95 Beaver St. He is a Florida man and might be of service to you in case you wished to send yourself to Florida direct—He is well spoken of. You can introduce yourself to him or not as your intent or fancy may direct. Blue eyes, dark hair, pleasant expressions, remarkably fine teeth (wherewith he will immediately smile.) About five feet ten, stout. So you can pick him out. Married, so you can [look] after his wife. When Aunt Molly goes, if she goes to ny you will or can hear of her whereabouts from this same gentleman, for and because she will call upon him immediately. You see I am spinning a letter. My other acquaintance is a navy officer stationed at the yard. His present rank I don't know. He used to be a passed Middy and a good man. But I think it very likely that you care very little about it.

Do you know I think sometimes when I read your letters that you don't know what to say to me. You know the usual advice is to write as one would talk? This cannot be followed exactly, yet I think as nearly as I can, I do it, not strategically but from laziness. Just as association brings one thought after another—down they go upon the paper. And just so I talk, thinking aloud. I am going to the grand city of Jacksonville tomorrow and shall have my letter mailed there. Do you know it takes a month for an answer to arrive from any letter which you and I may write to each other. How long does it take for you to get a letter from Macon? It is Sunday and there is a meeting at Mandarin where all the folks have gone except your [obedient servant]

Ellen M. Brown

16. Latin: "first."

[Ellen Brown to Mannevillette Brown]

Jacksonville [to Utica, New York]
May 30th, 1838

My Dear Mannevillette,

Our good Aunt Molly leaves this day for ny in the schooner <u>Ajax</u>. From thence she goes to Portsmouth direct. She will probably arrive in ny about a fortnight from now. That is to say, about the time you receive this same epistle, my duck, she will stay there a week or more. . . . She will remain in Portsmouth about a month and from thence return to Florida the most direct way she can. She will write to you when she arrives in both places. Alas it would give her great pleasure to see you while there and moreover you might possibly return together but all that you can settle in your own heads.

I have sent my compliments to you to day by way of one Dr. [E. K.] White. Knowest thou such a person? He says he knows you, and shall see you in Utica. He is no great of a man according to my measurement, but for all that and all that he always makes me a polite bow, and has promised to speak of me in the handsomest manner. The poor fellow has rendered himself very unpopular in this community, where everyone is so over-good that having no sins of their own to attend to they must . . . set about seeing that their neighbors repent, by falling in love with a married lady. The sin that doth most easily beset the Floridians is envy, [which is] of course the greatest of faults—envy. The fault which in itself includes all others is that of being charming. Now the lady in question is a picture to look upon and a lady in her manners, what further she is I know not, but this I know that these two things are what will subject her to severe remarks of themselves. For my part I think White showed a good deal of taste in falling in love with her, but no kind of wisdom in letting it be known. And she poor thing I can't give her credit for either taste or judgement. It is certain that she did not know this world most especially the world of Florida or she never would have suffered him to pay her so much attention. I wonder if you take an interest in all these things.[17] I am writing where I cannot see although I be seated in the office of the Hon? Judge Doggett. . . .

All the folks here are in good health. Parson Brown says you must not go to Europe; it will spoil your taste. I told him you are coming to Florida and he must talk to you himself that for my part I had always persuaded you to go supposing it absolutely necessary to your becoming great in your profession, but he

17. In July 1839 White married Susan Kellogg of Canaan, New York. See *St. Augustine Florida Herald and Southern Democrat,* July 25, 1839.

is of an entirely different opinion. He thinks you should study here, establish your taste, etc., and then go. He says [Dorman?] has never been in Europe but for all that he is one of the best living artists. What do you think of all this? He says you must come and see him when you come here. He also told me some stories of artists of his acquaintance, one who he says was ruined by going to Europe. I write these things for writing's sake not that I think they will influence you [in] any great [way.] Nevertheless as they were said by a man of good judgement and one who takes an interest in these things . . . it is as well to have them suggested to you. . . . Ellen Brown

[Ellen Brown to Mannevillette Brown]

La Grange [to Utica, New York]
June 9th, 1838

My Dear Mann,

I wrote to you from Jacksonville announcing the departure of our good aunt Molly for N.Y. from whence you will hear from her I presume. . . . How long before we shall see your pretty face in Florida? I think you can get business here if such is your fancy. We have not heard from George this long time, nor from Corinna, or from you. I believe you are all asleep. Perhaps you are getting in love. Have a care my Dear Mann, you know the old couplet: "Love is like a dizzyness. 'Cause it will not let a Man about his business." Now your business is to write me an epistle forthwith and if thou dost it not, I shall forthwith indict you for a love affair, firstly for the cause shown in the couplet and secondly for the suspicion which ariseth in my mind from your epistle this last received but one. Now a female flirt might get the character from the number of beaux who chose to fall in love with her, but a he male flirt must get it from the number of damsels he falls in love with. Whereupon you may see how this same flirting is in our sex power and in yours the want of it. Hurrah!

There be a great many little folks, in this little Florida world, who have suddenly become big folks by dint of our big Florida wars—which make ambition virtue! Ahem!—and that is one of the whys why I think you might get some phizes[18] to paint if you are so disposed. I asked one or two persons incidentally, and they said ay, without doubt. Maybe however you don't care nothing at all about it no how and so there endeth the matter.

The new house is getting on fast. Aunt Ann, Charlie, and Aunt Hall are well. Mann how queerly our folks scatter round the world, now here, now

---

18. "Colloquial abbreviation of phiznomy, physiognomy," meaning "face, countenance; expression or aspect of face" (*OED*).

there, two or three in one place and one in two or three places. I wonder where the family [trunk] will next branch! Real Americans, always going. I think we are as fair an example of the roving propensity of our Country as could be cited, out of the Far West. The community here is made almost altogether of original vagrants. Here is the bankrupt, the broken in character, the wildcards, the fag ends of society. Here stops the pedlar, here comes the poor scholar. Here the juggler becomes a man of business. The petty rascal of another place, a pillar of the church. All sorts of little folks too little to be thought of by aught but the census in the great cities here meet, grow up according to their several abilities and fill their stations high as well as those they left behind them. 'Tis curious to look upon these things as I see them and then reflect what a man of talent lies crushed beneath the immovable weight of circumstances. If these thrown off . . . from the general mass of society . . . without education can bring so much stature to every walk of life, what might we not expect could society be so regulated that every mind should be educated and every talent allowed its proper sphere for action.

I left this rather unfinished with intention of throwing [it] in my fire but, My Dear Mann, what curious speculations arise in the mind just carrying the idea out. This letter has lain unfinished since the 9th day for I was so disheartened at not receiving any letters that I concluded nobody cared whether I wrote to them or not. But now that I have received one from you I shall go on in my old way concluding that you are very glad to receive one although there be nothing in it beyond a few of my precious thoughts. I could not help laughing at your questions about my fat, the originating cause of my complaints is weakness of constitution however I am in very good care. Meat I eat very little of— very little—cold water I use a great deal. Exercise I take a great deal of and the blues make you mean blue-stocking blues are not . . . natural to me. I am not like the French cadet who when someone remarked that he was serious replied "no I am billious," but vise versa you tell me I am melancholick and I reply no I am not billious. Your remarks on our gen. nature are good not by any means such as I should think one would be ashamed to express[. A]t any rate they perfectly agree with my own notions, on the subject, but as for your opinion of the women I must set you to rights. . . . [Ellen]

[Ellen Brown to Mannevillette Brown]

La Grange [to Utica, New York]
July 14th, 1838

And My Dear Mann,

You do not know how to spell. Also my Brother you cannot imagine how sincerely I can sympathize with you in this misfortune; every word that you write on this painful subject expresses exactly my own condition. We have this consolation, between ourselves, that neither will be likely to discover the other's deficiencies, or, in case of such discovery both will be charitable. This is all the solace I can offer you; for myself I hold a booktionary in one hand, ever, while a pen is in the other, and yet behold how I am flouted by all people respectably trained in this subject, and worst of all, right or wrong in the particular instance, I never dare lift up my voice in self defense. I remember on one occasion when I was challenged and the dictionary was referred to, the lady disputed it—claimed it must be an old fashioned one so impossible was it for her to believe that I and the standard could agree. I often look up a word and write it wrong after all. & apostrophise in the words of Eloisa: "Oh write it not my hand. The 'word' appears already written—Blot it out my tears!"[19] Want of eyes grates upon me pretty much as want of time does upon you, I suspect. I hope you enjoyed your ride. I hope also to accompany you myself one of these days. Riding a <u>cheval</u>[20] is the exercise and amusement most of which I am, above all others, fond; as for "promenade" by which I understand you to mean a sort of saunter, it is the right way to go through the streets of an inhabited town, but in the open country give me fast riding any gait you please. . . . 15th —. . . . Time would not be gained by directing my epistles to Jacksonville. I sometimes have yours mailed there when too late for the mail here; because the mail goes from there twice, from here but once, a week; in that way I gain two or three days, and sometimes can be put in there and go on with the same mail that started from here the day before. Jacksonville is twelve miles below, Mandarin four above us—with the difference that in going to J—it is necessary to cross a ferry, so the difference, you see, is considerable. Am I right in directing your letter to Oneida County? . . . The floors are being laid to the new house so that will be ready for your reception all in good time. Do those Utica ladies ride well? I don't mean well for ladies, but well. I must give you an idea of the way people are . . . in this part of the world.

I challenge the world to produce a similar instance. At a cracker wedding the other evening when it came the bride's turn to respond instead of the usual "I will" lo and behold she ejaculated "I won't." The justice supposing there must be some misunderstanding on her part repeated but she again astonished the company with "I won't. I told you I would not before" and took her seat— determined not to obey! I pray the example spread.

19. Compare to Alexander Pope's "Eloisa to Abelard" (1717), lines 13–14: "O write it not, my hand—the name appears / Already written—wash it out, my tears!"
20. French: "on horseback."

Your northern unenlightened imaginations cannot imagine the innumerable quantity of mosquitoes which swarm and swarm throughout the air wherever you go at this time in this place. . . . I have never seen the like before but have been told by persons whose veracity was to be relyed upon that they in some places equal the description given of the plague of Egypt laying sometimes upon the ground in such quantities as to cover a man's foot, when pressed into them like light sand or soil. This species does not sting. Did they, they would render life intolerable. They are called blind mosquitos. They sometimes oblige people to quit their houses. These things are told to me as facts whether they be so or not, and from what I have seen this past week I am inclined to believe the possibility of it; anyhow the fact is universally credited here. Yours Ellen

The final few months of 1838 were busy for the extended family. By that time Mary had returned to Florida. Meanwhile, Mannevillette had set out for Paris to study art, apparently during November. In order to help finance his trip overseas Brown made arrangements with Thomas and Sarah Walker, a prominent couple from Utica. Arriving on December 3, 1838, after a sixteen-day voyage, Mannevillette described his journey and his sight-seeing tour of Paris. Mannevillette partially financed his stay in Europe by copying masterworks for the Walkers and other American customers.[21]

Later that fall Ellen wrote Mannevillette that after falling out with Aunt Delia she left La Grange and moved in at Llangollen, the house Charles and Mary had built. "I suppose you perceive that I direct my epistles nowadays at Llangollen instead of, as formerly, La Grange. The fact and truth of the matter," she wrote, "was that Mrs. Hall treated me after such a fashion as I would not put up with; so I quit her quarters and took up my abode for the present, with Mol [Mary] and Vance [Ann] and Charles. I shall make an effort in the spring to find some way of taking care of myself; inasmuch as I do not contribute anything to the general establishment here; I feel as if I should find my own fodder."[22]

21. Ellen Brown to Mannevillette Brown, October 8, 1838; Sarah Walker to Mannevillette Brown, November 14, 1838; Mannevillette Brown to Ellen Brown and Corinna Aldrich, December 16, 1838, Anderson-Brown Papers, USMA. For a brief account of Mannevillette's business affairs in Europe, see Rosemary Courtney, "M. E. D. Brown," 72–74; Courtney's article (p. 72) gives January 1839 as the date of Mannevillette's departure, which Mrs. Walker's letter places two months earlier.

22. Ellen Brown to Mannevillette Brown, October 14, 1838, Anderson-Brown Papers, USMA.

Also that fall Corinna anxiously awaited her brother George's arrival in Macon. Edward, she wrote, had "done his best to get him a situation" in Macon "at a salary of fifteen hundred dollars per year. They will await G's arrival. E. will befriend him to the last. He is very anxious to meet him."[23] But these plans never materialized. Indeed, the Aldriches did not remain in Macon much longer. George had decided to try his luck in Charleston instead; and Corinna abandoned Macon and joined Ellen in Mandarin. By late November the entire family (except for George) was back in Florida: Edward was in Tallahassee, and Charles, Ann, and Mary were still working on their little plantation.[24] Corinna's next missive follows.

[Corinna Aldrich to Mannevillette Brown]

[Mandarin to Paris]

Sunday P.M. Dec 30th 1838——

I do not believe, mon cher ami, that the strange sights you have seen, and the <u>voulez vous, play trait</u>[25] dinning in your ears, have quite knocked old Florida out of your brain—but I dare say—it seems an uncouth place in recollection, and its concerns of but little interest—further than they concern those you left behind you—Know then, my dear, that the Seminoles still reign triumphant—they go to & fro in the land without molestation—and our valiant soldiers sit quiet & make their pipes in peace, or at any rate give no signs of other than amicable feelings towards their savage foes.—I feel particularly voluble on this theme, since but for our milk sop generals—I should have now been on my way to Tallahasee [*sic*]—not that I wish to be away from Llangollen—except to be with Edward. He has promised to make ready for Ell's & my reception as early as possible—We shall take the Georgia route—Drunken drivers & runaway horses versus straggling Indians—You perceive I have had a taste of the former—on my journey from Macon. I hope Edward will not be inconvenienced by the latter on his journey—I cannot but feel anxious about him—although I should not have been afraid to have accompanied him.—I wish I knew what you are about, and how you get along in your <u>parly-vous francois</u>[26] suppose it would be proper in me to mend my pen—that my writing may be legible & you not be like goose Haven forget your native tongue!—

23. Corinna Aldrich to Mannevillette Brown, October 14, 1838, Anderson-Brown Papers, USMA.

24. Corinna Aldrich to Mannevillette Brown, October 14, 22; November 30, 1838, Anderson-Brown Papers, USMA.

25. Corinna's phrase is not decipherable.

26. Corinna playfully means "your French speaking."

While in Savannah—I was at a fashionable party—a thing came into the drawing room so completely starched and padded—with his [chin mowed] and his hands jammed into a pair of white kids tighter than his boots or the straps of his pants—I said to a lady—that must be from Paris—It can't belong here—she replied—ah yes. . . . the thing asked me to dance—& he only remarked about five or six times—"Ah Madame there's no place like home."—and then he looked so placid. I could not trouble him with a reply—I thought I should like to know something of Paris, but I was afraid to inquire—I thought it a pity such sops should go abroad—and give us a national stigma—returning with all they got on their backs—Ell says she is afraid I shall make her letter ashamed—there is danger as I am encroaching on her limits—and Mary & Ell are chattering as fast as frenchmen around me—I saw Dr. [Abel Seymour] & Mrs. [Eliza Scott] Baldwin[27] in Jacksonville—called on them & met them at a party—they promised to come up to see us—told me you were well and in good spirits—which was the best news they had to tell or I to listen to—I shall write again soon—a long letter—when you return my dear I trust you will find me under my own roof—and our good friends around us—Do write often & tell us of all you see & hear—E & I hope to go to Europe yet—God bless you[.]

ever your fond sister
Corinna

[Ellen Brown and Corinna Aldrich to Mannevillette Brown]

[Llangollen to Paris]
February 17th 1839

My Dear Manne,

It seems about impossible for my letters to reach you, and I don't know as it is of any consequence if they do not, for after I have told you that we are all well

---

27. Born in Oswego, New York, Abel Seymour Baldwin received a medical degree from Little Geneva (now Hobart) College in 1838. Migrating to Florida with his new wife Eliza, Baldwin established a medical practice in Jacksonville, involving himself in most of the business and philanthropic affairs of the new town. He was elected to the Florida House of Representatives in 1852 and to the Florida Senate in 1858, 1860, and 1861. Baldwin opposed the secession of Florida from the Union but was commissioned chief surgeon of East Florida and placed in command of the General Confederate Hospital in Lake City. In 1873 he was the driving force behind the establishment of the Florida Medical Association. He died in 1898. See Hammond, *Medical Profession in 19th Century Florida*, 36–39; Davis, *History of Early Jacksonville*, 76–78; and Merritt, *Century of Medicine*, 10–16.

and unaltered in condition save so much of change as is the inevitable effect of time, I seem to have written all that can be of interest to you in your far distant abode. I mean all of interest that I can relate. Behold! I cannot so much as tell you who are the candidates for the next Presidency, of your world of acquaintances, I know not even their names. It follows of course that mine epistles must be the entire and original creations of my very ignorant head.

. . . Corinna is still staying with us. Edward has moved to Middle Florida. She expects him to come for her in about a month. They are not going to Tallahassee but to Madison County in the vicinity of that city. As I write from the theater of a war I suppose I ought to speak of that; all I can say is that I heard an officer in active service remark that if a man should live for three generations he might stand a chance of seeing its termination. George has gone to seek business in Philadelphia. We have not heard from him since his departure from Charleston on that errand. Corinna and Charles have gone to ride <u>a cheval</u>. Mrs. Hall lives in solitary magnificence at her plantation La Grange. I suppose you are aware (I can't remember if I have informed you of it) that I have removed myself from her premises, and now reside at Mr. Charles Brown's place Llangollen. You ought to visit the bona fide Llangollen in Wales. If there be any truth in travelers' descriptions, (of which, by the way, you ought by this time to be a judge) there is some of the richest landscape on the earth. Not on that account, however have we given the name to our little spot of land in the flat [woods of] Florida but because this is a sort of old maids' hall. I suppose of course you have read or heard of the ladies of Llangollen.— — — —

If you have or have not heard of the bona fide ladies of Llangollen—I doubt not you will be glad to hear of, or from, the pseudo ladies of Llangollen and as mine sis has dropt her pen, to go out, and <u>drop corn</u> . . . I will pick up the quill and finish out this piece of work. She informed you I had gone to ride. I had a pleasant trot, which is probably as much as you care to hear of that. I really wish my dear, that I had something of interest to relate, but there is nothing new. Why do you not tell us of your whereabouts? I long to hear from you and know how you get on in your <u>Parly Francois</u>. Really, Manne, I have almost forgotten all I knew when I left the north. My brains have been occupied with worldly matters of material nature. I have had but little time for study. I do hope, however, in the course of this year to get settled and then Ell & I are determined to brush up our knowledge boxes. We have not given out the idea of your going to Paris yet. Edward says he will take us by & by if the gods do prosper him. Ell is going to Middle Florida with me next month, <u>Deo Volente</u>. Manne how long do you propose to be absent?—one year or two ? Do tell us when you write that we may know when to expect you. How much it would delight us to hear of your coming & yet alas how changed you will find us all.

What a pity old time will not pass us by. He is so neighbourly he will take us all by the hand, faster than we can help I assure you, however, and trust you will not run out of remembrances dear. Write to us often. How is the climate with you? We have lovely weather. All send lots of love. God bless you.

The peregrinations of the family continued into 1839. By March, for some unknown reason but perhaps to be closer to her husband, Corinna left Mandarin and began boarding at Mineral (or Suwannee) Springs on the east bank of the Suwannee River in Columbia County. In a letter to Mannevillete in Paris she noted the hostility toward northerners: "This end of the union—between the Indians and the Abolitionists, the southerners will have plenty to do—Else for ought— . . . They would assist the John Bulls. They are so inveterate against the Northerners." Also, of her primitive surroundings, she wrote: "The village post office is kept in a kind of store adjoining my rooms. Consequently, my ears are constantly assailed by inquiries for letters, oaths, and curses at disappointment, badly read extracts from the different newspapers, cracker remarks, chicken fights, horse races, betting, bullying, country politics, horse laughs, etc. is it not delightful? & for me too—who loves refinement as I do I live on the hope that I may not degenerate. I expect by Fall to get a log cabin of my own. (We have no lumber, no saw mill. No house carpenters here.) Then I will have no society, save that beneath our own roof."[28] Finally, a month later, she offered her impressions on Florida's plight: "It is frightful to reflect upon the history of poor Florida. Preyed upon as she always has been & still bleeding at every pore, without one hope of promised relief. It is indeed to be lamented, that this cruel & senseless war cannot be terminated. In a very few years Florida might become the garden spot of our beloved country. Italy does not boast a more Edenlike climate and its facilities of improvement I am told are unlimited."[29] That same year Corinna's friend Rev. David Brown offered his own appraisal of the dreadful surroundings in war-torn Duval County. Somewhat less optimistic of the county's future prospects, Brown shared Corinna's melancholy view of the present: "The evils attendant upon war," he wrote his superiors, "are seriously felt by our community and at present are in no degree mitigated by the prospect of the future, which is gloomy in the extreme."[30]

28. Corinna Aldrich to Mannevillette Brown, March 31, 1839, transcription of letter in possession of the editors.

29. Corinna Aldrich to Mannevillette Brown, May 4, 1838, Anderson-Brown Papers, USMA.

30. Rev. David Brown as quoted in Pennington, "Church of Florida," 34.

[Ellen Brown to Mannevillette Brown]

[Llangollen to Paris]
May 22, 1839

My Dear Manne,

I have just received a letter from you dated Thurs. 18th Feb. It must have come by the direct route I think. Three months seems to me very short time for a letter to travel so far. I suppose by this time that you have heard how our sister Corinna has gone to Suwannee River East Florida to live where you must direct your letters to her. George has at length obtained a situation in Philadelphia with a salary of five hundred dollars a year. Charles is still having corn and digging 'taters at Llangollen. You need not grieve yourself so "very very very" much about the affair with Aunt Hall as you call it. I feel inclined to be loquacious on this subject, but force myself to be silent. One thing, however, I might as well remark. I go and see her very often and consider it my duty so to do.

Concerning the money, you probably have received a letter before informing you that we drew from Mr. Walker's hands two hundred and twenty five dollars which money shall be repaid agreeably to promise in November. Aunts Mary and Ann are in good health and send their love to you. Aunt Hall is also well and I suppose would send her love also if I had said anything to her on the subject of my writing. Aunt Mary says I should tell you that she anticipates a great deal of delight in having you return and tell about the pleasures of travelling which she considers much like the pilgrim's progress.[31] Your letters are very interesting. As for poor Rome, all the idea I have of it is, that it is a heap of rubbish which fanciful folks try to make something out of. I am sorry to say it is out of my power to give you any information on the subject whatever, beyond what I am sure you must be as well acquainted with as I am. If anything cometh into my head be sure I mention it.

Aunts Ann and Mary intend to raise silk worms. This will probably be the prevailing business of the community. A great many persons have already entered into it, but the thing is but just started. It is without doubt the proper business for E. Florida. Charles wrote George word where you were and that you would like to hear from him. I shall write him agreeably to your request, although I advise you not to expect much from that quarter. His income is small and his debts are large. We are just eating ripe plums and black berries, both wild and inferior. This would be a splendid country for fruit if it was

---

31. Christian, the main character of John Bunyon's moral allegory *The Pilgrim's Progress* (part 1, 1678; part 2, 1684), undertook a journey during which he encountered the temptations and obstacles facing a typical Christian hoping to reach salvation.

properly attended. Charles intends to plant his land entirely in valuable trees. He of course is hindered from doing any great deal by want of capital, but all that industry and perseverance can do, he does and will accomplish. Wild grapes are here in the greatest abundance and I have seen some tropical plants under cultivation. You probably in the course of your peregrinations may meet with some seeds of rare fruits or other plants which it would not put you to any inconvenience to bring home, anything of the kind which strikes your fancy as either good curious, or you might as well "tote." This is the misused word for the verb "to bring" in all its moods and tenses, among the crackers, and cracker is, as I suppose you very well know the epithet applied to Georgians and Floridians, as Yankee is to New Englanders. It was a surprise to hear you would not stay in Europe another week if it were not for your profession. I think you must have left your heart somewhere in ny state. Rouse up your genius, and exalt your mind. Your organ of locality has been suffered to grow too large. Invigorate your bump of comparison.[32]

I have not seen the letter you wrote to Corinna but suppose I shall when next I see her. She mentions having received letters from you by way of Macon. I wish very much it was in my power to make my missives as interesting as your letters. You tell me all letters from home are very interesting and I believe you and . . . [you] think I ought to write to you more often and I make good resolutions every day to that effect. I write as often as I may. . . . With regard to the paper I use I should mention that I am obliged to use such as I can get. . . . [Ellen]

[Charles Brown to Mannevillette Brown]

[Llangollen to Paris]
May 25th, 1839

My Dearest Brother

On reading your letter of the 18th of Feb, I unhappily perceived that you labor under a great mistake. I intended only to draw $250 from Mrs. Walker, but George deceived and mortified me a third time by stating that there was fifty six dollars more in Portsmouth than there really was and I was forced to draw last Feb. from Mrs. Walker the whole three hundred which I shall

---

32. Ellen speaks the language of phrenology, which she refers specifically to in her letter of June 21. Phrenology was a popular pseudoscience founded by the German physician Franz Joseph Gall (1758–1828). Phrenologists claimed to be able to determine the qualities of a person's brain, disposition, and character by examining the person's head. See *Encyclopaedia Britannica*, 11th ed., s.v. "phrenology."

endeavor to procure for you and placed as per ordered at your disposal in the Fall (Sept). Ellen was against my drawing it but I supposed you had left the amount with Mrs. Walker and it was best to draw it, it was my own mistake. This makes me the more bound to see it paid up at the given time, though I should not have drawn this balance had not George deceived me. I should not have thought of building had he been honest with me and told me he had spent the money; he not only committed this fault but foolishly told me he was ready to meet my drafts, when he had not a dollar to fund. I instantly drew the drafts to the amount he ought to have held and the mortifying results you too well know, but thanks be to God and your noble assistance, I have been able to pay all up. George has got into business with $500 a year, has banished all amusements, and I hope will become a steady youth. He wrote me a long confessional letter and begged forgiveness from the heart, which was, of course, granted. His employers are Ingraham & Martin Philadelphia, Penn.

Our <u>palace</u> is the largest in the neighborhood of log houses. We are to give it the first christening this afternoon, by holding a meeting sermon by the rev. Mr. [Samuel F.] Halliday[33] have thus far a very pretty crop and should the season continue, I shall have an abundance of good things of the land. Ellen has written all the news and as I am proverbial for short letters you must not think strange of it if this is a specimen. We are all enjoying good health and <u>Deo Volente</u> may continue as the fractious nature of our Aunt Dolly is somewhat cooled down. All is harmony. These little differences must be expected in families dear Man, though I intend to practice patience and gentleness for our stay here is short and we should all be prepared for the mansions above.

How would you like to call me 'Medice Docte'! if the title pleases you, you are at perfect liberty to do so, as I have a full degree though rather premature I was wanted in the army and passed by a conclave of Doctors about six months since. Yet shall continue my studys [*sic*] and get a regular diploma from college.

I have wrote this in a great hurry my dear Man, it was to correct any misrepresentations (that word has almost choked me) so farewell forgive all bad spelling and mistakes, and believe me to remain your

faithful brother
Charles D. Brown, M.D.

[Corinna Aldrich to Mannevillette Brown]

Mineral Springs, Columbia County, East Florida [to Paris]
June 9th, 1839

33. On February 26, 1840, Gov. Robert Raymond Reid nominated Halliday to serve as justice of the peace in Duval County (Carter, *Territorial Papers,* 26:89).

. . . I will not repeat the dull tale of our removal hither—further than to say Edward's business continues excellent, and should success attend him for a few years to come—we'll quit the wilderness & join the busy world again with light hearts and full pockets. Edward would have gone for Ell, ere this, but for an unfortunate kick from a horse, which broke two of his ribs, & disabled him from taking so long a ride—he is now, however, much better, and waits the issue of the late treaty with the Seminoles. Gen. [Alexander] Macomb[34] has concluded a peace with them for the summer.[35] They, to remain in the Territory undisturbed south of Peas' Creek; and the regulars to stay quiet & acknowledge themselves whipt! So much for our gallant Army! It is said that at first the red men refused to treat on any terms, but the Gen. told them if they did not, he should send the Florida volunteers down upon them—that the regulars would ride from the field any how—wherefore they came to terms immediately! It is feared, eventually, that there will still be war in the land, and I think myself we have every reason to fear it—for, the same causes that first gave rise to hostilities still exist—and will those who have lost relatives, friends, and home, at the hands of these savages suffer them now to rest in peace on the land still [soa]king with the blood of their murdered? Not so—I replied, they assert in the publick prints that they will not submit to such treaty—that the Indians shall quit the territory or die, & thus the matter stands. I have no doubt <u>for a few weeks</u> there will be peace, & in that time I intend to get Ellen here. . . . I write very badly, dear, but the reason is I have loaned my table & left my desk at home & consequently am obliged to write in the parlour in the midst of chattering tongues & noisy visitors, in the shape of three or four little scamps of from ten to twelve—that interesting age, you, no doubt, remember in our own

34. Alexander Macomb was born in the Michigan Territory and enlisted in the army in 1799. Achieving the rank of general in the War of 1812, he was breveted a major general after the Battle of Plattsburgh, New York. He was named commander in chief of the army in 1828 and served in this position until his death in 1841. See Heitman, *Historical Register,* 1:680.

35. For more on this peace proposal, the temporary "truce," and its controversial nature, see Mahon, *History of the Second Seminole War,* 256–63; Prucha, *Sword of the Republic,* 296; Covington, *Seminoles of Florida,* 97–98; and Brown, *Florida's Peace River Frontier,* 54–55. See also The Commanding General to Officer Commanding Fort King, April 11, 1839, in Carter, *Territorial Papers,* 25:604–5; The Secretary of War to Zachary Taylor, June 4, 1839, in Carter, *Territorial Papers,* 25:614–15; *St. Augustine Florida Herald and Southern Democrat,* August 8, 15, 29, 1839; *St. Augustine News,* May 18, 25; June 1, 8, 15; July 27; August 3, 1839; and *Tallahassee Floridian,* June 8, 15, 22, 1839.

case! Mrs. Webb[36] the lady of this manshin [*sic*] desires her love to you—& says you must come to Florida on your return. She wants a <u>family picture</u> taken. I am afraid it might be like the vicar of Wakefield's.[37] Nevertheless, I believe she would have it taken! And such a group they'll make! I have lately been reading Fisks Travels in Italy—I am very much pleased with his style indeed he is very full & clear. I took much interest in his description of Florence in particular—knowing that you were there or had been there. . . . E's visiting a patient but sends his love.—C.

[Ellen Brown to Mannevillette Brown]

[Mandarin] Florida [to Paris]
June 21, 1839

My Dear Mann,

I have just received a letter you dated 16th of April. Your letters appear to arrive regularly in three months from Florence. This is swift traveling. Your letters are very interesting. I wish I could make my answers as much so. I have not heard from George since I last wrote you. I advise you to write to him. He is in Philadelphia. I have told him to write you. Corine is still at Suwannee Springs E. F. her health is much improved. Master Charles is budding trees. Miss Mary is churning butter. Now I suppose at this your mouth waters at the recollections of a New England dairy. Put away such thoughts from your mind <u>mon cher frere</u>, this is the land w[h]ere a good cow gives a pint of milk! It will give you a better idea of the place to be informed that we have ripe corn at this date but it is early for it. There seems to be a prospect of cessation of hostilities with the indians, but, my friend, they have whipped us—not we them. Gen. Macomb has been sent on by government to buy peace and has succeeded on condition of letting them do as they would have done had we never meddled with them, retain their lands. I do not know the particulars of the transactions. It is said they are to remain south of Peas creek. I believe that stream emptys into Charlotte harbor in the gulph of Mexico. I don't know where that is either. It is my opinion they will find that selling of peace so profitable that there will be more to buy in a few months. . . . Your letters have somewhat abated my desire to visit Europe, nevertheless the strong thirst of change is in me—the wish to see for myself.

36. Corinna was probably at the residence of John F. Webb, who served as justice of the peace for Columbia County. See Carter, *Territorial Papers*, 26:88, 259.

37. Corinna seems to refer to the first chapter of Oliver Goldsmith's domestic novel *The Vicar of Wakefield* (1766), in which the vicar describes his large family.

Art thou a phrenologist? Thou oughtest to be or at least to make up your mind as to the truth or nonsense of the science for your profession's sake. I am getting to be a professor or believer. Although unlike most believers I am not satisfied with the development of mine own cranium. So far from it seeming to me ridiculous the reasonableness of the thing is for me the strongest argument in its favour. I said I was not satisfied with mine own cranium. I don't mean that my vanity is hurt. But I seem to have developments to which there is nothing correspondent in my character for example I have a large organ of adhesiveness yet form no strong attachments. It was speaking of my love of change which put phrenology into my head just this minit.[38] Perhaps what Pomeroy used to say of me is true. There is consistency in inconsistency. Would a phrenologist allow that one might adhere to a love of change? May not one have a pet fancy as well as fancy a pet—Love traveling as well as love a monkey? Eh?

I did not tell you what Aunt Ann is doing—she is sewing. She sends her love to you Mrs. Hall as well. She has a very sweet lady boarding with her at present therefore she is not living a la solitaire at plantation La Grange. They talk of building a silk factory on a lot of land immediately adjoining ours. Should it be done it will increase the value of ours a hundred fold by making that town which is now country. I wish some good luck would happen to our family. Fortune seems forever floating around us but we get only a sprinkling of its wealth. I don't know as we get that even. We have a fine crop of corn this season. Does good fortune have anything to do with that? Charles is great [on] planting. He is very fond of horticulture. His success in grafting is quite a wonder to the ignoramuses. He has an apple graft growing on a rose bush. Should it bear fruit we will give you fresh apples and fresh oranges at the same time when you come home. We will have a new edition of Italy here one of these days. New and improved in some respects, for we have chimnies and fires in them. . . . We shall not have you speak of your constant disappointment. This I think would not happen to me for my ideas are all brought down to the lowest possible minimum of expectations. Still I would travel if I could. . . .

Ever yours Ellen

[Ellen Brown to Mannevillette Brown]

East Florida [Mandarin to Paris]
July 23, 1839

---

38. Archaic spelling of *minute*.

My Dear Mann

I am expecting Corinna here every day. Do you get her letters? She writes to you very often, but the mails are miserably bad in her part of the world—worse than they are here. I have requested George to write to you; for myself, I know nothing of his affairs, not so much, I presume, as you do. It appears to me he must be cashless. This is the season of peaches and watermelons, with us, and we have an abundance of them. People here eat half a watermelon at a time. Have you been accustomed to eating them that way? In New Hampshire you remember they are reckoned injurious, the contrary is the case here.

Our Indian war remains in status quo. Gen. Macomb has been making a treaty with the red folks which they as us have laughed at. As it is show, I will give you, as near as I can remember it, the reply of the Indians as it was rendered by the interpreter, and related by the interpreter, and related by an eyewitness. I am sorry I cannot give you Macomb's speech first as the effect of the answers is considerably heightened by it, but also my memory has not been able to retain both. So here goes for the answer. "Old Boss, we berry glad to hear you come so far to speak good tinge; we 'fraud we give you much trouble, we want so much whiskey." Charles will make a fine crop of corn this year, he has not done so well any season he has been here as this. Corine and Edward are about leaving Suwannee Springs with the intention at present of locating at Newnansville: another squatting place in the territory. The especial reason of his not remaining at Suwannee I know not, but <u>reckon</u> one motive may be a madcap cousin of his who has been practicing there for a year or two past and who gave up practicing upon E's settling there with the intention of studying law. I opine E. thinks he would resume the practice, were the field again open, inasmuch as he gave up the practice when he was sick and has now recovered.

The grand difficulty in this country is that there are no decent houses to live in and this gives people a discontented feeling which I am inclined to think they would not feel could they live orderly. This however will soon be remedied as they are erecting steam mills all over the country. Hitherto they have been obliged to live in log houses entirely (with a very poor exception in favour in Jacksonville where there has been a mill for some time past), except indeed they hit upon the super-refinement of a clapboard one. Now if you have never seen the identical article to which I allude, your imagination probably reverts to all manner of wooden houses in New England and elsewhere and you ask, what more do people want? If 'les extremes' do not absolutely 'se touchent' in this instance, certain it is that clapboard stands at both ends of the list. Clapboards here are split out rough ends nailed together perpendicularly and make the most unsubstantial houses you can imagine. I knew a tree to fall on one and beat it right down to the ground, cupboard, crockery and all. A family would be more safe in the crust of a pumpkin, and about as well sheltered from the weather in a hen coup. My dear Mann I sometimes think you will consider my letters very trashy and uninteresting, and so you must consider them, but what am I to do. Every thing around you is matter of interest to me, you cannot walk a yard in the street, you cannot sit an hour in the house but, it seems to me, you must see something describable which it would please me to have a description of, but such is not the case with me, all that is describable about me I have at different times sent you an account of, and for aught else, I go no where and see nobody except the methodist circuit minister who preaches at aunt Hall's once in three weeks and the next day at Mandarin, whereunto he generally contrives to make me follow. The same is a little ill looking piece of humanity as I ever happened to be acquainted with but withal a good christian, which is the highest praise. I think I have told you that the Presbyterian parson preaches at our house once a fortnight. This is done because there are no other houses in the neighborhood large enough to have preaching in them. All the folks are in good health. Aunt Ann and Aunt Mary are making a pie. They send their love to you. Aunt Mary says she is cultivating some figs and a lot of other good things for you and wants to know when you are coming home to look at them. She thinks if you don't make haste she will be too old to see you. Good bye.

Ever yours

Ellen

Chapter Five

"Log-House, Pine Tree and Cracker"

Newnansville, Alachua County

In the fall of 1839, after exploring his options in Macon, Georgia, and Hamilton County, Florida, Dr. Edward Aldrich decided to move Corinna and his extended family to Newnansville, Florida.[1] Edward's decision to move to Newnansville was based in large part on his reenlistment in the army as surgeon. As the center of the army's war against the Seminoles, the Alachua County seat offered easy access to several forts in the area: Fort Gilliland, within the village itself, Fort Harlee on the St. Augustine Road about ten miles to the east, and Fort Clarke, ten miles directly south of Newnansville on the other side of the San Felasco Hammock. Attached to the two military units in the area, Edward also planned to establish a medical practice in Newnansville. In 1839 Alachua County contained roughly twenty-three hundred people, about one fourth of them slaves. Newnansville was the largest inland town in East Florida. Situated just south of the Santa Fe River about fifty miles from the Georgia-Florida boundary, the town had the region's only superior court by 1828. In 1842 a federal land office was established. The Second Seminole War, beginning its fifth year in 1840, brought temporary prosperity. Federal dollars flowed in, and the town swelled with perhaps as many as two thousand pioneers flooding in from devastated farms. Yet even if the frontier village offered promise as the nexus of military and commercial activity, it was still

---

1. For more on Newnansville, see Susan Yelton, "Newnansville: A Lost Florida Settlement," *Florida Historical Quarterly* 53 (January 1975): 319–31; Rebecca Phillips, "A Diary of Jesse Talbot Bernard: Newnansville and Tallahassee," *Florida Historical Quarterly* 18 (October 1939): 115–26; Jacob Rhett Motte, *Journey in the Wilderness: An Army Surgeon's Account of Life in Camp and Field during the Creek and Seminole Wars, 1836–1838,* ed. James F. Sunderman (Gainesville: University of Florida Press, 1953), 90–92; and Mary Lois Forrester, comp., *Lest We Forget: A Town, Newnansville, Florida* (Alachua, Fla.: Privately published, 1999).

Fort Harlee. Florida State Archives.

exposed to Indian attacks despite the close proximity of numerous forts. Only a year earlier, for example, an army surgeon visiting Fort Harlee found the "country . . . literally alive with red-skins. . . . The whole country is in a state of direful consternation. I met wagons and carts flying in every direction, the inhabitants universally abandoning their fields of corn throughout the fertile region of the Alachua."[2]

And yet other dangers also presented themselves. That summer the sisters, their aunts, and Charles suffered from deadly fevers. Corinna, Ellen, and Charles became extremely ill and nearly died. In December, Mary and Ann became so ill that Edward and Corinna rushed to Mandarin, but Mary died before they arrived on Christmas Day.[3] Soon plans were under way to leave Mandarin for Newnansville. Aunt Ann, convalescing, was staying with Aunt Hall and would join them in Newnansville when she fully recovered. Only Aunt Hall would remain. As Corinna explained to Mannevillette two months

2. Samuel Forry to J. W. Phelps, April 12, 1838, "Letters of Samuel Forry, Surgeon U.S. Army, 1837–1838," *Florida Historical Quarterly* 7 (July 1928): 102–3.

3. Corinna Aldrich and Ellen Brown to Mannevillette Brown, December 14, 1839, Anderson-Brown Papers, USMA.

before Mary's death, Ellen too had decided to move to Newnansville. Edward and Charles, Corinna added, "are about to try the mercantile business. E. is to give his name and capital, and Charles to attend to business. I suspect they will do well. The opening is fine for a small business and they can increase by and by. The head quarters of the army are to be here this Winter, and it will of course bring much into town. It is said there will be an army of twenty thousand there by the last of next month."[4] Thus in October the family set out for their new home. As Corinna explained to Mannevillette, Edward "came for us with an escort of mounted riflemen from the regular Army. We made quite a trail with our barouche in which were seated Nell, Edward and myself, our servants on horseback, our baggage wagon, and guard of cavalry. Nevertheless I was very glad to reach Newnansville, with all its stumps, its numerous log cabins and vegetable gardens. I said to myself, 'There's rest and safety here.'"[5]

Upon his arrival in Newnansville, Edward Aldrich began taking an active part in his new community. In January he presided at a dinner held in honor of newly appointed governor Robert R. Reid when the former judge visited Newnansville on his way from St. Augustine to Tallahassee. Edward joined James Pindarvis, Bennet M. Dell, Joseph S. Sanchez, John L. Doggett, David Levy, and many other of the region's leaders in honoring the territory's new governor. As the presiding officer, Edward offered the first toast: "<u>Florida</u>: Though misfortune should render her a wilderness; with warm hearts to defend, and a wise Governor to direct, we feel that she yet must rejoice, and blossom as the rose." Charles Brown also attended the gathering. Taking his own opportunity to express his faith in the newly appointed governor's ability, he later offered a toast to "<u>The Ladies of Newnansville</u>: Bright and beautiful stars; enchanting us with their loveliness."[6]

For the sisters as well as their neighbors the Indian war continued to consume their energies. Providing Mannevillette with her own observations, Corinna declared, "I do not believe seriously that the 'Florida War' will be ended, in our generation! None of the officers think so either. In fact, they are all preparing for themselves at different Posts, comfortable houses, etc. & are bringing out their families. The posts you know are every 20 miles square all over the eastern portion of Florida. There is to be a sort of campaign in Middle

4. Corinna Aldrich to Mannevillette Brown, September 29, 1839, Anderson-Brown Papers, USMA.

5. Corinna as quoted in Forrester, *Lest We Forget*, 32.

6. *St. Augustine Florida Herald and Southern Democrat*, January 16, 1840.

Florida, but it is not thought Gen. [Zachary] Taylor will accomplish much. When they get there the red men will be among the missing."[7]

In the same letter Ellen offered her own appraisal of the state of affairs. Most to the point was her none-too-flattering description of her new village: "Here are we in an inland city containing about 15 hundred inhabitants or more . . . [in] cracker [houses] built of logs and surrounded by the dull monotonous uninteresting pine barren. I cannot for my life match yours with an equally particular description, for after I have written log-house, pine tree and cracker the only addition I can summon to memory is pig and dog. You mix up these ingredients in any and every possible way, add a little of some proportion of alcohol and the result will always be Newnansville." Corinna noted that she came in contact with a "few sprinklings of officers through the town but they make very little variety. To say nothing of their being to a man sick of Florida and its unmanaged and unmanageable war." Ellen thought better of describing these folks in detail because she lacked the time and space and "because they are my friends and . . . I could not do them justice. Oh Florida, Oh Frumpery, Oh Manners! It is malicious to speak the truth of one's friends."[8]

While his sisters regaled Mannevillette with their impressions of their new surroundings, George Brown was trying his luck (without much success) in Philadelphia. After losing his job George hinted that if something did not turn up soon, he would join his siblings in Florida.[9] As the year progressed Mannevillette continued his studies in Europe. Moving from Paris to Rouen, he kept his family in Florida abreast of his movements while detailing the sights and people he encountered. From Rouen, Mannevillette traveled to Florence, where he worked at the private gallery of the grand duke copying paintings by Van Dyke. Later Mannevillette accompanied a group of other painters on an excursion to Rome.[10] For the next ten years Mannevillette studied, worked, socialized, and visited European art centers.

Meanwhile, in January 1840 the Second Seminole War was beginning its fifth bloody and inconclusive year. In May of that year Gen. Zachary Taylor relinquished his overall command of U.S. troops in Florida to Gen. Walker K.

7. Corinna Aldrich and Ellen Brown to Mannevillette Brown, December 14, 1839, Anderson-Brown Papers, USMA.

8. Ibid.

9. George Brown to Mannevillette Brown, November 11, 1839, Anderson-Brown Papers, USMA.

10. Mannevillette Brown to Corinna Aldrich, October 24, 1839, Anderson-Brown Papers, USMA.

Armistead. Although most of their hiding places were south of Alachua County, the Seminoles were still able to continue their raiding operations. One of the most dramatic of these occurred in May 1840 when Wild Cat (Coacoochee) ambushed a caravan carrying a troupe of actors on its way from Picolata to a performance in St. Augustine. Even so, time was running out for the Seminoles. A series of retaliatory raids against the isolated Seminole villages effectively removed the Seminole threat from the immediate area.

By 1840 General Taylor had divided Alachua and other counties north of the Withlacoochee River into twenty mile squares. Forts were constructed in the middle of each square. Soldiers built roads linking the squares, and patrols scoured the perimeter of each square for Indians.[11] Newnansville fell within square number twelve, under the command of Maj. De Lafayette Wilcox[12] of the Second Infantry.

Sometime shortly before September 1839[13] Ellen met a young lieutenant attached to Wilcox's command at the newly constructed Post no. 12. James Willoughby Anderson, who would soon command that post, was the oldest child of William and Jane Willoughby Anderson of Norfolk, Virginia.[14] Graduating

11. Mahon and Weisman, "Florida's Seminole and Miccosukee Peoples," 196–97; Tebeau, *History of Florida,* 166–68; Prucha, *Sword of the Republic,* 295–300; Mahon, *History of the Second Seminole War,* 249–51; Sprague, *Origin, Progress, and Conclusion of the Florida War,* 220–46; K. Jack Bauer, *Zachary Taylor: Soldier, Planter, Statesman of the Old Southwest* (Baton Rouge: Louisiana State University Press, 1985), 90–95.

12. De Lafayette Wilcox was born in Connecticut and joined the army in 1812. He was appointed brevet major in 1832 and died in 1842. See Heitman, *Historical Register,* 1:1034.

13. The earliest extant correspondence between James and Ellen is a letter from James dated September 21, 1839, written at Black Creek. This rather formal letter expresses James's concern for Ellen's spiritual well-being. The letter is in the possession of Ms. Elizabeth Traynor.

14. James Willoughby Anderson had two brothers and one sister. William Anderson, his youngest brother, died in Norfolk on December 27, 1837, at the age of twenty (*Army and Navy Chronicle,* January 11, 1838, p. 32). Benjamin Franklin Anderson joined the U.S. Navy in 1831, serving on the *Ontario.* After a brief stint at the Norfolk Naval School in May 1838 he resigned on June 23, 1838. Anderson's sister was Virginia Anderson. Family genealogy on the Andersons was supplied to the editors by Miss Mannevillette Sullivan. See also George W. Cullum, *Biographical Register of the Officers of the United States Military Academy, West Point,* 2 vols. (New York: D. Van Nostrand, 1868), 1:563–64; Heitman, *Historical Register,* 1:164; Edward W. Callahan, ed., *List of Officers of the Navy and Marine Corps from 1775 to 1900* (New York: L. R. Hamersly and Company, 1901), 24; and *Army and Navy Chronicle,* August 24, 1837, p.126; May 10, 1838, p. 304; and June 28, 1838, p. 416.

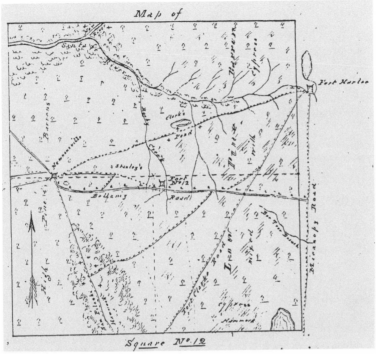

Square number twelve showing Bellamy Road, Fort Clarke Road, Santa Fe River, Fort No. 12, Hammock, and Newnansville. National Archives map; copy, St. Augustine Historical Society.

Lt. James Willoughby Anderson, daguerreotype taken just after the siege of Vera Cruz, Mexico, 1846. Courtesy Mannevillette Sullivan, Jane and Raymond Gill, and Elizabeth Traynor.

thirty-fifth in his class at the United States Military Academy at West Point in 1833, Anderson served briefly in Maine and the Michigan and Wisconsin Territories before arriving in Florida with the Second Infantry late in 1837.[15] In December 1839 Maj. Bennet Riley of the Fourth Infantry was promoted to lieutenant colonel and given command of the Second Infantry. Gaining a reputation as an aggressive and skilled commander, Anderson soon formed a strong professional and personal relationship with Riley. Assuming his new command in the spring of 1840, Riley made Post no. 12 the headquarters of the Second Infantry.[16] In late May, Anderson and his troops evacuated their post and were ordered to Fort King (Ocala), the site of the previous Indian agency and the place where Osceola and his men had killed Wiley Thompson and others in December 1835.[17]

Ellen's relationship with James had a profound effect on her letter-writing habits. Few of her letters written during these years survive. Her letters to Europe may have been lost; more likely, however, her letters were directed primarily to James, who became the focal point of her life. When she was with him she apparently had little or no time for correspondence; when they were apart her correspondence was with him. Likewise, Ellen became the center of James's life, as his letters bear witness. Like Ellen, James was a talented writer. Unfortunately, James did not save Ellen's letters to him as long as he was stationed near her. But James's letters to Ellen provide us with his innermost feelings and offer valuable insights into early nineteenth-century courtship rituals in difficult circumstances. From his letters we may also infer the seriousness of their relationship.

[James W. Anderson to Ellen Brown]

No. 12 E. F. [to Newnansville]
March 7, 1840

---

15. *Army and Navy Chronicle,* September 14, 1837, pp. 169, 184; March 28, 1839, pp. 207–8; December 26, 1839. Anderson's roommate at West Point was Francis H. Smith, who recalled an incident when Anderson was nearly dismissed from the academy for sneaking off the campus to Benny Havens's tavern in Highland Falls. Sylvanus Thayer had actually dismissed the youth, but several of Anderson's well-placed fellow cadets interceded with the Jackson administration for relief. As the story goes, Anderson met with the president and the order for dismissal was countermanded. See Thomas Fleming, *West Point: The Men and the Times of the United States Military Academy* (New York: William Morrow & Company, 1969), 70–71.

16. *Army and Navy Chronicle,* December 12, 1839, p. 382; April 30, 1840, p. 287.

17. Ibid., May 28, 1840, p. 348; *St. Augustine News,* May 15, 1840.

Dear Ellen

I send by the bearer a few books (among them Alciphron)[18] which may possibly amuse you or your sister a moment or two. I often think of your promise to give me a few lessons in the art of reading poetry in order that I may have the pleasure of reading to you: but when I am with you, it always escapes me—make me useful to you—make me worthy of you—Give me the means of contributing as much as possible to your happiness.

Your tears make me feel very guilty. Whenever you shed tears, it always not only gives me pain from the fact that I believe you suffer, but also because that suffering appears to me to arise from some discovery of my unworthiness. I would give much for a correct knowledge of myself; for then I might correct or counteract, but I profess no self-knowledge and have been swayed in a great measure by my impulses—too much, I admit, for my own good—but I will put an end to my egotism for I am always more puzzled, to speak the truth, in speaking of myself than of a third person.

It would be a sore grievance to me, should anything alienate your affections from me, nor will I look to such a picture. I am jealous of "Every [smile] that you bestow upon me" & am not willing to become "Mine own Enemy"—

I was in hopes to see you tomorrow & so promised & will yet, if I can possibly. . . . In conclusion, I will add a request which is, that, should there ever be anything in my notes to cause you the least uneasiness tear them into a thousand tatters and cast them forth upon the winds for though the knowledge of such an act on your part would surely be a bitter dose for me, yet would I prefer it rather than that you should suffer in silence—

Yours truly,

A

[J. W. Anderson to Ellen Brown]

No. 12 E. F. [to Newnansville]
March 17, 1840

Dear Ellen,

I send you a work on phrenology, with which I think you will be interested. . . . The Secretary of War says "that the troops in Florida must be relieved" & I anticipate our removal about as much as I do the end of the war.

---

18. Alciphron, a Greek rhetorician, "was probably a contemporary of Lucian (2nd century a.d.). He was the author of a collection of fictitious letters, of which 124 (118 complete and 6 fragments) have been published; they are written in the purest Attic dialect and are considered models of style" (*Encyclopaedia Britannica,* 11th ed., s.v. "Alciphron"). An English translation was published in 1791—this is probably the text that James sent to the Brown sisters.

I am all alone—no one to talk to—none to listen—& am about to bury myself mind & body in some outdoor occupation for the benefit of Uncle Sam—Don't pity me, unless you come & see me—then you may; but then I should not need your pity—

"Far from thee my spirits languish

"Near thee I can know no rest

"Thus forever gloom or anguish

"Shades my soul or [wings] my breast.

is the first verse of the poetry in your album—or is it not original? I wrote it not—

Ever Yours,

A

[Corinna Aldrich to Mannevillette Brown]

Newnansville [to Rome, Italy]

March 22, 1840

My very dear brother . . . how varied our life has been, and must I add, how sad. No, M. doubtless the bitter has been mingled with the sweet in our life as in others' but probably not any larger proportion of the former than for the rest of mankind. And yet I hate to think of the years that are gone. I cannot brook to look back. I believe I am a little blue today, the fact is, I am unwell—and the Dr's away to fight his country's battles—he has departed—or rather to heal the wounds of those who have turned their ploughshares into rifles and their pruning hooks into spurs. Not to talk in enigmas, however, Col. [David] Twiggs[19] of the regular army with 250 troops—joined by . . . of the volunteer corps with 120 men—and ten <u>blood hounds</u>, have departed on an expedition for the south guided by an Indian prisoner—who promises most faithfully to lead these gallant heros to where the red men are planting corn—somewhere it is said on the Oclawaha. They set off in excellent spirits. Edward not excepted, in the full belief that if they do not terminate the war, they will certainly find Indians—for myself I believe it will be a complete farce. The dogs, I have seen; and have no faith in them—they may track an Indian—as they are said to have been raised in the West Indies to hunt runaway Negroes—but they look not

---

19. A native of Augusta, Georgia, David E. Twiggs (1790–1862) served in the Creek War (1813–14) and participated in Andrew Jackson's invasion of Florida in 1818. See Jeane T. Heidler and David S. Heidler, "David E. Twiggs," in *The United States and Mexico at War: Nineteenth-Century Expansionism and Conflict,* ed. Donald S. Frazier (New York: Macmillan, 1998), 441–42. See also Heitman, *Historical Register,* 2:976.

remarkably ferocious to me. I have seen many dogs that looked more so. Nevertheless, in the dogs they put their strong hold—and in their guns their strength. I can scarcely say I hope they may not be disappointed for if they meet, many must die—and in such fighting Edward is in as much danger of being picked off as any among them. I put my trust in the God of battle—his will must be mine.

We hear of Indian murders every day—last week two men from this place were fired on about 15 miles from here—by fifteen of the wild devils. One escaped—the other Mr. Mcbraigh, a very fine man—was murdered & scalped by them. It seems they were riding along in conversation—in the open pine barren—wholly unconscious of danger—as the Indians generally attack from the hammock, where the underbrush affords a safe retreat—but lately they have become emboldened by success—and no spot is now safe a mile from town—as I said the gents were fired on by 15 Indians, yet strange to tell, so poorly do they aim, that but one ball took effect[. T]hat struck Mcbraigh's horse—he immediately threw his rider, who took to the woods but was pursued and tomahawked—they cleft his skull & took off a small scalp. Mr. McNeil escaped—strange to tell—neither of these men were armed[20] think of Bulwar's opinion that hell could not be a place of eternal punishment—unless the tortures were changed because men would become <u>used to it</u>.[21] Does it not seem verified here—daily men here are fired on—in every place, and at all hours of the day, and yet they will continue to rush unarmed into the face of danger—I am right glad that I shall not soon be called upon to try the dreadful woods again.

Edward and I returned three weeks since bringing Aunt Ann with us. I couldn't bear to leave her there alone since poor Aunt Mary's death. She seems very happy with us—and is in good health. Aunt Delia would not quit her plantation—she intends boarding at Jacksonville, however, so she can overlook it. Charly has a man on his place to take care of it. He is gone to Savannah for

20. On March 26, 1840, the *St. Augustine Florida Herald and Southern Democrat* reported that Reverend Mr. McRae in company with Reverend Mr. McVeil and a small boy were fired upon by Indians within five miles of Micanopy. Mr. McRae was killed, and Mr. McVeil received four ball holes through his clothes and one in his horse but made his escape to Fort Walker. The boy got into Micanopy. See also *St. Augustine News,* April 3, 1840.

21. This is probably a reference to Edward Bulwer-Lytton (1803–73), a member of the English Parliament and a prominent writer. His best-known work is the historical novel *The Last Days of Pompeii* (1834).

goods—I expect him home tonight. I heard from George last week—he has no business yet—but was in expectation of a situation.

You observe that money matters look badly in our country—indeed they have done so—but the prospect seems to be brightening a little. Edward has not yet obtained his government claims—but all the officers say he will get paid. Much is due him, and I sincerely hope he may receive it in season to assist his friends as well as minister to his own comforts—five thousand dollars will be due him in May—but whether he will get it before another session of Congress is doubtful—he will try hard for it—he has already sent on a part of his accounts—the others he cannot arrange until his return—which some say will be in six weeks—some three & some two—I think four—should he be disappointed in making their collections dear, I am sorry to say he will not be able to assist you, beyond your need. It would not be well to draw on him for more than about one hundred dollars at first—or until you hear from me again. I have not had opp'y to consult him in the matter—but then I know the state of his business so well—that I know he could not conveniently raise more than that at a time—with out some sacrifice but should it be necessary dear—he would make any—I merely speak this candidly dear—because my first offer was so free for you to draw largely. . . .

Ell is seated on the sofa with her beau . . . he is a Lieut. of the 2nd Infantry—about 30 years of age—will probably be a captain—He appears to be a clever fellow & gentlemanly man—but I am not in love with him! He is rather tall—but ugly as a rail fence. You must come home and take a peep at him. He commands the Post at No. 12. I believe he is of good family—a native of Virginia—I do not know that they intend marrying soon. . . .

I would give much to see you . . . I want you to tell me if I am not changed. People tell me I look the same. I do not feel the same.———Perhaps I might if I were to return to the enlightened part of the world again—but I am sure I degenerate every day I remain in the interior of Florida. I hope Col. Twiggs may rout the Indians & terminate the war. Then I shall expect to take up my duds & depart—as well as the rest of the good folks—but all of this is fantasy—if I do not quit Newnansville until the war is ended, I fear I shall have to remain here a long time———I am much interested in your descriptions mon cher—they are very vivid. . . . Do you know that I have a very large lot of chickens. I have 35 chickens & seven hens sitting. Don't you think I will have plenty of poultry?—by the way, do you have hens in Italy like ours? We are obliged to raise them, because we have no market at present—no country produce to depend on. We have a fine garden—we had radishes, lettuce, turnips, & green peas—already—We have every variety of vegetable planted and all seem to thrive, the soil is very rich. Our flower garden is principally in the woods. Wild flowers are plentiful but I don't pay much attention to ornamental matters here. We are living in a rented house—it is much larger and more pleasantly located than ours—besides Edward wished to occupy our house as an office and hospital—which he does—he will get rent for it as a dispensary & hospital while he is in the army from Uncle Sam—and use it as a private office also—you see this is the way we do things here—but 'tis all right—both must be had - - - - Well, darling I have been all round to enquire who has a message to send—all say send my love—Mr. Anderson not excepted—As for Ell you can't expect much of her—all she can do is entertain Mr. Adonis[22] she promises to write you soon. . . . Corinne

[Corinna Aldrich to Mannevillette Brown]

Newnansville [to Rome]

April 5, 1840

. . . The soldiers returned from the campaign a few days since[23] were not gone as long as expected. I believe I wrote you last week that they would be gone six weeks—but as usual they got out of <u>provisions</u>! They killed two Indians—E. brought home a scalp & three heads from some graves he opened near Lake Eipopka[24] of a man, one woman very large & one little papoose with all the hair on—it looks like a mummy—he says the graves were made on the surface of the ground with strips of bark like a canoe. The body is placed in with the knees drawn up to the chin & the hands bound across so as to take up the least length or space—then tightly bound up with linen bandages. It is then covered with bark so as to effectively prevent the rain from penetrating—the bodies are thus preserved much longer from decay—their beads, jewels, cups, rifle, etc. is buried with them—generally all they possess—but I suspect either the possessions of these were small—or some previous grab[25] had visited their silent dwellings—as I only found some beads—a pair of earrings & a tin cup, buried with the little girl.

He describes the country about the Adawahair [Oklawaha] as being very beautiful—high hills, large lakes—oak hammocks & immense wild orange

---

22. Corinna ironically compares James to Adonis, the exceedingly handsome youth of Greek mythology with whom Aphrodite fell hopelessly in love.

23. See "Twiggs Expedition," *St. Augustine Florida Herald and Southern Democrat,* April 9, 1840.

24. The contemporary spelling of this lake was "Ahopopka." It is now known as Apopka.

25. This could be a noun meaning "thief."

groves—deer—turkies & c. in the greatest possible abundance—It must be an Eden indeed—I wish the war was over that I might take a peep at it. . . . E. says he means to go down there to live by & by. In the centre of Lake Eipopka (which is some 25 or 30 miles in circumference) is a beautiful Island—where the Seminoles are now <u>planting</u>—our <u>armies</u> had no boats & not time or sense to make a <u>raft</u> & could not pursue them—they have come back to go again, <u>start better</u>! The two they shot had just maneuvered their light canoe to return to the island having been on shore to attend to their corn, which they had ventured to plant on this side. They must be a set of dare devils. They came on one trail; the Indians escaped but lost their packs—from which E. got about 20 lbs. of <u>count a</u> [coontie] or Indian arrowroot—it is quite equal to the West India— It grows very abundantly south—& forms a principle article of their food—the name of the Lake Eipopka means potatoes—so called from the abundance of small granulated roots much resembling the Irish Potato & used by them instead. . . . Ellen is gone to <u>preaching</u> as the natives call it—with her <u>dear</u>— Charles & Ed too—Aunt Ann is asleep—Aunt Hall is in Jacksonville—she has rented out her plantation—she has a beau—but whether she intends to venture her head again in the noose of matrimony I don't know. . . . your fond sis Corinna

[Corinna Aldrich to Mannevillette Brown]

Newnansville [to Paris]
May 23, 1840

My very dear brother,

. . . [W]e have been in daily expectation of a visit from George and instead of reporting that he was coming I wished to say <u>he is here</u>. He arrived night before last. He looks princely and seems in better spirits than when he was with us in Macon. He has come to Florida for the purpose of entering business with Charles. I have hope that with their united efforts they will do well. Their prospects are fair and they are both steady, industrious and persevering. I omitted to mention that Aunt Hall is also paying us a visit at this time. . . . Your letters are very interesting, apart from the pleasure of hearing from an absent brother, and I should regret losing one. I believe they come very directly now, in spite of war times.

Our Indian difficulties instead of decreasing seem multiplied. The expedition which Edward went out on proved but a luckless job. The Indians have since had ample revenge, sneaking about in small parties and still pursuing the trail of our retiring militia. They have done much damage, burning plantations and murdering the unwary, driving off cattle, cutting up hogs and frightening negroes. Some of their depredations have been committed in our vicinity, but the principle is Micanopy about 20 miles south of us, retreat from there being easier to their hammocks and everglades.[26] We are safe in town, but it is considered dangerous to ride out any distance without an escort. The militia are all out of service, whether they will be called in again is uncertain. It is said Uncle Sam is bankrupt and I should think so from their inability to pay the demands of those employed by them. Edward has not yet received his dues, but all the officers tell him to hold on, he must be paid, only they wish to delay. He is to be again appointed as surgeon of the Post No. 12. Col. [Bennet] Riley[27] has established his headquarters there. He is a fat, good natured, old fellow. I like him much. He has now gone south to join Col. Twiggs on a second expedition to the Waccasassa.

Ell had a letter yesterday from Mr. Anderson (who is adjutant), he did not anticipate much success—a small party of 18 went out from Micanopy last week, came on a body of 40 Indians and were, of course, defeated. Only ten men returned to the post, thus it ever is, they either go in such numbers as to frighten even the crows from their roosts or so few as to insure destruction. They should go in scattered parties of 100 or 150 men each, so I think, Gen. Taylor has left Florida & turned over the command to Gen. [Walker Keith] Armisted[28] who is no better than a clever old lady, yielding to anybody's opinion & turned from his purpose by every breath. For me, I am sick of it, I tell Edward & Charles & George, they must hasten & collect all the pennies they can

26. On May 15, 1840, the *St. Augustine Florida Herald and Southern Democrat* reported that Alexander Saunders, John Austin, and John K. Miller were killed near Newnansville. On April 30, John M. Stanley's residence was burned, his plantation destroyed, his hogs killed, and eight hundred bushels of corn stolen. Another newspaper reported that Austin was killed while returning to Newnansville after transporting merchandise for Mr. Brown to Post no. 12. See *Jacksonville East Florida Advocate,* May 12, 1840, and March 24, 1840, the latter quoted in *Army and Navy Chronicle,* April 23, 1840, p. 269.

27. Bennet Riley, a native of Maryland, entered the army in 1813. While in Florida he attained the rank of colonel. Riley fought in the Mexican War and eventually achieved the rank of general. He died in 1853. See Heitman, *Historical Register,* 2:831.

28. Walker Keith Armistead, a native of Virginia, was reputed to have fought in the Battle of Fallen Timbers (1794) as a boy. Among the first cadets to be admitted to the U.S. Military Academy at West Point, Armistead graduated in 1803. He served on the Niagara River and the Chesapeake during the War of 1812. Over the next twenty or so years Armistead served in the Washington and Boston areas. He served two stints in Florida before taking overall command on May 5, 1840. Relieved slightly more than one year later, he died in 1845 in Upperville, Virginia. See Mahon, *History of the Second Seminole War,* 274–75, 287; Cullum, *Biographical Register,* 1:91; and Heitman, *Historical Register,* 1:169.

and let us return to civilized life again. We have this comfort however, we are all well & doing well. I wish you would be here for a little while. They all look natural, Aunt M & Aunt Ann are but very little altered. Undoubtedly we are all a little older but all look as they used to, at least, I think so. Poor Aunt Mary altered more than either of them, but she is in Heaven.

I have been interrupted in my letter by the arrival of Lieut. Hoffman and others from No.12. I suppose they will dine with us. We have plenty of gentleman company, but few ladies, owing to the times, ladies are not privileged to travel. Mrs. [Arabella Israel] Col. Riley[29] & Mrs. [Mary] Lieut. [Henry] Wessells[30] have consented, however, to brave the war and pay us a visit next week. I often think what a contrast living in Florida would form to your present abode, egad, it forms a contrast to <u>all</u> other abodes I have tried or read of. It is really new. I hope you will have a chance to try it for a little while. My Negro woman has just brought me a saucer of blackberries. I wish I could hand them to you. I don't believe you have tasted any lately. You say you live abstemiously. . . . Don't study <u>too hard</u>. 'Tis said a man who works himself to death will be buried beneath the gallows, but I don't know what fate awaits those who study themselves into another world. This much I know, they gain nothing here, so my darling take my advice, rest yourself. I have two old fashioned paintings, one of the laughing, the other the crying phylosopher (I can't spell to day). The faces are of old men with lengthy beard, the tears of one still shine on his shriveled cheek while the other is all wrinkled into smiles and his little rotten teeth are quite conspicuous from his grinning. They are some family paintings of Mr. Anderson's, he is a Virginian, his family of English decent.

By the way, again you must come home this fall. Ell will be married then, if not before, <u>Deo Volante</u>, so "haste to the wedding"—Are we to have a war with John Bull? If so, we may quit here—If not, we shall probably remain here for the next year. Edward says he will not end his days here, unless his end is near. Ell & Aunt Ann are battling about Mr. Anderson's beauty. I must say he is a beauty! He is tall as a poplar tree, bright red whiskers & fierce looks. . . . Your sis C.

29. Bennet Riley and Arabella Israel of Philadelphia were married in 1836. See *Army and Navy Chronicle,* January 8, 1836, p. 16.

30. A native of Connecticut, Henry Walton Wessells entered West Point in 1829, the same year that Anderson did. Upon graduation both were assigned to the Second Infantry in 1833. Wessells later served in the Mexican War and then on the Union side in the Civil War. He remained in the U.S. Army until 1871 and died in 1889. See Heitman, *Historical Register,* 1:1019; and Cullum, *Biographical Register,* 1:560.

[James W. Anderson to Ellen Brown]

Fort King[31] [to Newnansville]
May 28, 1840

Dear Ell:

When I left No.12 I little thought that so many important things would be brought about ere my return & I rested in perfect confidence that I should be so happy as to remain near you, during the summer. I hope, however, that the change which affects me most, viz my removal from No.12 will not take place immediately. New generals bring new plans & I am so old a veteran in this war that I consider myself at perfect liberty to speculate upon all their acts & to grumble as much as I please. . . . Although on the eve of a march, considered the most important from this post, I do not feel any confidence of meeting with Indians, and being now broken up entirely in my arrangements for the summer, I should feel, as I did before I met you, did I not know that there was one who felt solicitous for my welfare. This post is a good one & I should be comfortable here were it where I would have it. Next winter we will be on the full jump in the Everglades. I presume from what I hear, No. 10, 11, & 12 will be abandoned in a month or so, also much of the other posts in the vicinity of the settlements, all of which also are garrisoned, will be garrisoned by the militia.

Remember me to the Doctor & tell him that he must prepare for very important changes in the military world around him. My love to Mrs. A and say to her that I miss her nice cake very much. Soldiers' fare is our portion, hard bread & [old] meats, with a sour orange occasionally. You must excuse my scrawls, Ellen, I write so much & the weather is so excessively warm, that my fingers are cramped & my head is a blaze. . . . Think of me sometimes, I believe I should be a mighty reckless fellow were it not for you. I hope to be at No 12 by the end of June, perhaps earlier. How long I shall remain there, I am unable to say, perhaps a month, perhaps two. As the orders are not yet issued, there is of course, some uncertainty about it. Col R & myself agree very well in this field; if any thing, better than when out of it too & I think it a doubtful matter which would break down first, although you considered me so fatigued when I stopped at your house after our return from visiting the different posts. Do not stop to criticize or I shall be ruined in your estimation.

Yours, Anderson

31. Fort King (Ocala), established as headquarters of the Indian Agency in the early 1830s near the north boundary of the Seminole reservation boundary as laid out by the Treaty of Moultrie Creek, 1823, was approximately fifty miles south of Newnansville. For more on Ocala, see Eloise Robinson Ott, "Ocala Prior to 1868," *Florida Historical Quarterly* 6 (October 1927): 85–110.

[James W. Anderson to Ellen Brown]

No. 12 E. F. [to Newnansville]

July 2, 1840

. . . Tell Charles that Mr Cole came here to day after the Sutlership of the Rgt. He rec.d the same answer as Charles did—Twiggs & [William Shelby] Harney's[32] recommendation to back him. Verily I did not know there were so many sutlers in Florida. . . . I intended to have gotten you to select something for the jackets—but I fear I shall have barely time to bid you good bye & tell you to be a good girl until I return. Make them of the cotton; if anything, it is better for the woods, the Piny Woods, the barren Piny Woods—Woes me! I shall cry my eyes out at Fort King from very spite that Twiggs has at length an opportunity to gain at his having succeeded in breaking up No. 12—my No. 12—My beautiful little post so near the pretty little city too—What shall I do? What shall I do?

July 3rd

Your brother is here—so is the Express—the order has not come—but the Col. has decided to go on Monday—No news—Cole has succeeded I hear, this morning in getting the sutlership of Fort King—I was in hopes Charles would get it; but Twiggs & Harney have too much rank for me.

Ever yours

W

[Corinna Aldrich to Mannevillette Brown]

Newnansville [to Paris]

July 5, 1840

My very dear brother,

Your two last favors of March 15 and April 11th came to hand by last mail. I had been anxiously looking for a letter for some weeks dear, and assure you they afforded me no little pleasure. I believe I have not written you since the week after George's arrival. Charles & Edward have since both been quite sick with intermittent fever, both, however, are convalescent, and eat their rations with excellent appetite. George continues very well and seems much more contented than I had expected. They are doing a safe but moderate business. The Post at No. 12 for which C. has been sutler is abandoned. The square system is about to be abolished—it is considered a failure and instead of Posts at 20

---

32. William Shelby Harney was a native of Georgia and entered the army in 1818. See Mahon, *History of the Second Seminole War,* 283–84; and Heitman, *Historical Register,* 2:502.

square miles distance as heretofore, they, i.e. Gen. Armistead intends to establish a line of posts across the peninsula, so as to confine the Indians to the southern portions (they might as will restrain the falls of Niagara). Lieut. Anderson left yesterday for Fort King where he is to be stationed for the present—It's about 50 miles from here. The attempt is now making in Congress to raise two new Battalions of Infantry, the officers to be taken from the Capts.& Lieuts. of the present infantry with brevet ranks of Cols, Majors & Capts—they are to serve during the war, the soldiers then to be discharged & the officers to return to their respective stations only to retain their brevet ranks. Lieut A. in case the bill is passed will receive the brevet of Capt. and immediately go on recruiting service to raise a company, which will be in a month in which case for aught I know Ell will go with him, but of this hereafter.

You say you shall not probably return before the summer after this. If so, we shall probably greet you elsewhere and God grant we may. I am tired of the woods. Edward says he shall either go to Charleston or Savannah to reside in a year from this—if he does as well the ensuing year as the last—and I have no doubt he will, if his health is spared. Should we remain here or wherever we may be, you will be a most welcome guest. As for your profession, doubtless you could get something to do here, a few would like to see their own phizes but you would do well, more than well in Charleston, or Savannah & I sincerely hope we may be there at housekeeping to greet you. Perhaps you might make up your mind to abide with us longer. Charleston is a pretty, pleasant & agreeable city. Since they have begun to import too, they are daily increasing in wealth and influence. We must hope for the best & trust in Him who ever guides us right. We had a stupid 4th. The whites took no notice of the day (except we had a roast pig) but the Negroes made amends. It seems to me the boot was on the wrong leg! Hurrah for the abolitionists. Edward has received a part of his claims on Uncle Sam—he will sue for the rest—I hope you understood about the draft. Edward did not pay it to Corning & Co. because it was not exactly convenient then and they had forwarded the amount to you but if you repeat the draft, E. will pay it. He wrote them word that your draft on him would be at any time acceptable. They must still retain a balance . . . in your favour. Charlie sends his best love—George ditto. [They] say they are digging, hope soon to be able to stick up their shingle in a better place.

The Florida war is turned into a political engine and the Lord knows which way it will work. At present they have plenty of steam on. 'Tis thought Harrison will be elected—if he is not, I know not what will become of the country. If he is, all will be well. Aunt Hall has returned to Jacksonville, I believe she has gone to Charleston to buy a nigger. She had a man—he did not suit her, and I bought him, and have hired him out at $125 per month. He will keep me in pin money. He is an old Jackass—Edward & Charles offered to hire him for her, but no, she would sell him, doubtless she expects to get a beau in Charleston. She is quite a belle, you would laugh to hear her talk, she thinks herself a perfect fancy, "grace in all her steps, Heaven in her eye, in every gesture dignity & love"[33] the way she flaunts & flounders about—is a caution to all parties! Ell, Ed, & I had some idea of visiting Charleston this month, but on account of the heat I think best to defer it until Sept. E's eye remains the same—she has undoubtedly returned. Aunt Ann is getting to look finely, she Ell & Ed also write in much love to you. By the way, your description of the Carnival reminds me of St. Augustine—only I suppose this is on a smaller scale but men in women's cloths seem the order of the day! Do you have fruit? We have plenty of peaches & melons, also all kinds of vegetables are coming in about big enough to gather. . . .

Ever your fond sis, Corinna

[James W. Anderson to Ellen Brown]

Pilatka [Palatka][34] E. F. [to Newnansville]
July 24 1840

Dear Ell—

As I sat, last evening, writing up the proceedings of the Court Martial[35] I heard the sound of paddles and going to the wharf, I had the satisfaction of finding a steamer putting in from the creek & on boarding her, I had the still greater satisfaction of finding a bundle of papers directed by you to this place. I was of course not at all curious until I reached my room, where upon searching the packet—I found what do you suppose. Why, I found that you had defrauded the mail. Now, as you knew that I would not resist in sharing in the fraud by opening and reading your billet as soon as I saw it, I think that the matter might be considered as resting with yourself. But alas! I am too

---

33. John Milton, *Paradise Lost,* book 8, line 488.

34. By the summer of 1840 Gen. Walker Keith Armistead had relocated the main supply depot from Garey's Ferry to Palatka on the west bank of the St. Johns River. See Mahon, *History of the Second Seminole War,* 279.

35. On July 17, 1840, the *St. Augustine News* reported that "A Court Martial is now in session in Palatka, for the trial of soldiers and mutinous conduct at that post a short time since. Col. Riley President, Lt. Col. Whistler, Maj. Wilcox, Caps Bonneville, Barnum, Hawkins, and Lt. Anderson" (*St. Augustine News* as quoted in *Army and Navy Chronicle,* July 30, 1840, p. 74).

willing to share in such frauds. Consequently I am as guilty as yourself & as it is perhaps not the first pleasure I have stolen from Uncle Sam: why, my conscience is not very much oppressed. It gives me much pleasure to know that you are in good health. I am all the time wishing myself back to No 12—poor No 12—I was the first to raise it up & the last to abandon it. It is a green spot in the oasis of my existence. . . . Do you wish to be astonished?—since I last wrote I have seen Mrs. so & so, Rosa Reed,[36] the misses so & so of St. Augustine—the famed St. Augustine. Last Saturday morning one of the members of the court was sick & the court adjourned over until Monday. I immediately mounted Dick, crossed the river & put off through the woods for St. Augustine. I got lost, never having been on the East side of the St. Johns & did not get into the town until sundown. I started off as I was, in my round jacket, & visited several ladies, whom I have treated very shabbily by forgetting their names. Among others I visited [were] those at the house where Rosa Reed is staying—of course I cannot give any opinions of the ladies as I cannot remember their names—The lady of the Sea Wall Gentleman (Your particular friend) is one of them that I refer to. Rosa spured[37] some questions about you—or rather gave me several hints—that she had heard something—I told the truth. That I was well acquainted with Miss Ellen & that I thought very highly of her—after visiting there I went the same evening to the house where the 3 misses somebodies are (I forget their names) quite lively, plenty to say & the gentleman I went with was so wrapped up in one of them that he served me the same tonick [*sic*] that I have served others viz—kept me at the house until ½ past 12 a.m. The next morning, being Sunday, I heard the ugly chime of the Catholic bells, but could not go to church, as I was to leave at 11 o'clock to return here. I intended to go through the fort & to look at the Sea Wall, neither of which did I accomplish, but left the place in ignorance whether there was anything to be seen but a few low houses with narrow lanes between them, a few officers of the Army, & a few young ladies. . . .

I have been & am yet very busy here. Since the moving of the 9th of this month I have been a busy clerk, having written between 4 & 500 full pages. The

36. This is Ellen's friend Rosalie Reid, the twenty-one-year-old daughter of Judge Robert Reid, who became governor in December 1839. Rosalie Reid eventually married Charles Black and bore a child, Rebecca. Both Rosalie and her baby died in July 1840 at her plantation Blackwood, near Tallahassee. See *St. Augustine Florida Herald and Southern Democrat,* July 30, 1841.

37. This usage of *spur* as a verb is an obsolete variant of *speer,* "an inquiry, questioning, or interrogation" (*OED*).

court has disposed of the mutineers at this post & a number of other prisoners amounting to about 30. I am tired & sick of my writing that is not for you. Tell Charlie I will pay attention to his request. I thank you for saying that you will not go away without me & remain assured I shall be with you as soon as possible. I do not intend resigning my company exactly. I have no right to be in command of one, as I am the staff officer of the Regiment. Col. [Bennet] Riley thinks that I am active & permits me to retain the command as he knows that I do not wish to lose it & as he also thinks a little more experience will be of service to Lt. Hoffman ere he has the command of it. I think you misunderstand my motives—Ell sometimes—I am perfectly willing to tell you all & every thing in which I am concerned if you wished me so to do. Yet such things as relate to the military are rather incomprehensible sometimes to the best of us—or rather inexplicable. Some of my duties again are not pleasant & I avoid speaking of them. Do not fear to tire me. Your remarks in your last only have the effect of making me renew my request that you might write without restraint. I have a good mind to get lost tomorrow on my way to Fort King & find myself at Newnansville. What say you, would it not be a good idea?—if it were not that these red skins are rather hostile at this time I would certainly do it, as it is, if I meet with Mr. Coacoochee, he might insist upon having a one handed duel, which would not be very pleasant; besides the escort that brought me here, was fired upon on their return to Fort King & as I love you so well, no wish to lose my life I will be as cautious as circumstances will admit of. . . . Do I get peaches & watermelons?—Yes Maria,[38] occasionally—but they do not taste so well as those of Newnansville.—I send you some kisses but they are not so good as those in Newnansville. Good night & God bless you. Ever Yours A———

[Corinna Brown to Mannevillette Brown]

Newnansville [to Paris]
August 2, 1840

. . . I do rejoice with you that you at last received a little of the needful. . . . I suspect one great reason why you have not received funds before is the disordered state of our money matters. The sub-treasury bill is passed but whether it will bring relief seems to be an unanswered question still. I hope it may do all the good its advocates warrant, but much I doubt it. The Florida War you mentioned has turned out to be but an electioneering inquiry & will not be

---

38. Ellen's middle name.

prosecuted with any vigor while Martin Van Burin [*sic*] (or <u>Deo Volante</u> until Harrison) takes the Presidential chair in 1841.

————You ask what would be your prospects here in painting for a few months. My dear, I am unable to say. Possibly you might get ½ doz. portraits here at $50 = fifty dollars. I doubt if you would more—and about the same number in Jacksonville, you might get 75 dollars each. I say what I think is pretty certain. I don't want to mislead you. Edward says if you return this fall you will find us here, and if you will spend a while with us, he will do all in his power for you and when you have made your visit out, he will accompany you to St. Marys where he thinks you could do as well as in Jacksonville and if he does not go with you, will give you letters to Savannah & Charleston. In those places you could do as you please. Should you not return until next summer you will most probably find us in Charleston or Savannah, but there is no saying positively in these uncertain times. I wish wherever we may be that you may be able to pay us a long visit & meet with success in your profession. But you would not be contented long here in the wild, wild, woods. No amusements, nothing to interest but solitude. No news but Indian murders and thefts. After you get <u>naturalized</u> you would do better but it takes time for that. George begins to look and act more contentedly but they all look forward to a move by & by as well as myself. Ellen will be married in Sept. or Oct.—<u>Deo Volente</u>—to Lieut. Anderson of the 2nd Infantry . . . a fine man but rather <u>homely</u>, that however is no matter for a soldier. We did not go north as anticipated, but intend to accompany Ell & Anderson as far as Charleston in the fall. It is uncertain whether he will be stationed here in the fall or where—probably here—for this war is not to end this year. Aunt Hall has been to Charleston and bought a negro man—$650. She is in Jacksonville—I heard from her last evening Charlie has also gone to C to purchase goods. His stock is not large, the market will not admit a very extensive stock. . . .

Your description of Rome, indeed all your descriptions are very good. The Holy week must have been full of interesting novelties to you. I should think such scenes would serve to aid and inspire your fancy. Particularly any original design, the <u>pilgrims</u> <u>stuffing</u> themselves was not bad—Poor things their mentality could not be concealed. You speak of getting to Naples in a month that on your way home! My yes, I wish I was with you. It would be better fun I am thinking than prowling the pine barren, but then one must know all kinds of life, fully to appreciate all & I don't despair of going to Rome yet—Some of these days I mean to sell a couple of "niggers" & start off. We are afraid Uncle Sam will so overrun [us] with sub-treasury notes, that it will be like continental money—take one hundred dollars to get a pair of shoes etc! But I <u>hope</u> not.

I think Van Burin's [*sic*] reign is short, he has commenced his system of monarchy too soon—to call for a standing army of 200,000 men at first is rather too glaring.

Aunt Ann is in fine health, so are we all, but Edward's. He is about but not well. I think he is too much exposed, his business calls him out at all hours of the night & day and that won't do for this climate. You must be careful if you would be well. Did I tell you the square system has been abandoned & the forts stationed in a line across the peninsula?—well that won't do—owing to the great rains the roads are almost impassable from one to the other, what next! 'Tis an ill wind that blows nobody good. They have been obliged to raise two thousand volunteers, which will bring many into this country though they will not be permitted to bring the war to a close, owing to the strong opposition of the goodies at the north who think the dear barbarous seminoles should not be driven from their homes—'tis needless to add, this is useless and unreasonable philanthropy now. We have news of murders of the most aggravated character every day. I have no particular ones to relate, thank Heaven, all our travelers have been so far spared. The Theatre of the war seems to be south of us. . . . We have rain, rain, rain and I fear shall have sickness. God bless you dear.

Your fond sister Corinna

[James W. Anderson to Ellen Brown]

Fort King [to Newnansville]
August 17, 1840

Dear Ell—

. . . Mrs. Riley asked not a word as to where I have been. I presume however that she thought it would not be agreeable or she would have done so. The Colonel's wishes are laws with her—suppose I add "as they should be?" Not pretending to say that all husbands' moods or wishes should be laws to their wives, as I myself will admit that I have seen some husbands whose wishes were anything but reasonable. However even a Soldier is not bound to obey any order against law or reason—such is in his contract—Of the Marriage Contract there are many interpretations: but that only is the true one wherein the parties concerned are made happy who enter into it. . . .

Ever yours, Willoughby

[Corinna Aldrich to Mannevillette Brown]

Newnansville [to Paris]
August 30, 1840

My dear Brother

Little did I think when I last wrote you and spoke of the departure of our beloved Charles for Charleston that my next epistle must contain the mournful intelligence of his journey to the Land of Spirits. Yet so it is. We received last evening letters from Savannah bringing the sad news of his early and sudden death.[39] He was on his return home and was attacked with alas yellow fever—his friends who were with him persuaded him to stop in Savannah and have medical aid, to which he reluctantly consented to, so little was he aware of the fatal disease with which he was afflicted. We are informed by those who watched by him to the last, the best of medical aid and every possible assistance that mortal hands could render, was kindly proffered but availed him not. He was seized with black vomit two days after his arrival and expired without a struggle, Friday evening August 23. It is a consolation to know that though in a land of strangers, those were found who kindly ministered to his departing spirit and that he calmly fell asleep in Jesus. But alas, alas, what can soften death, little were we prepared for the dreadful stroke, it has overwhelmed us with grief—our kind our beloved Charles—I cannot realize that he is gone. It seems as if he must return. We had none to spare from our little circle. Ah my God, forgive my lamentations, forgive the erring and wicked spirit that murmers [*sic*] when it should submit. I thought when poor Aunt Mary was taken from us that our cup of affliction was full. I did not dream the chastening rod would so soon be needed again. But the Almighty is good and doeth what seemeth to Him right. May we feel that it is so. May we acquest[40] in his great decrees and in spirit and in truth repeat the prayer, Father Thy will be done.

Your last kind favor of May 23 was duly received. I cannot refer to its contents dear. Intended today to answer it fully—it pleased me much—but alas all my thoughts are bent on our unexpected affliction. As for Charles's journey to Charleston, he was delayed in Savannah for a boat and in consequence took the overland route via Augustine—most probably he then took the seeds of that disease which did not fully develope itself until on his return several days after. He had been sick before he left as I wrote you with intermittent[41]—when first attacked he was lulled into security by the suspicion that it was merely his old complaint hanging about him. Poor fellow, God receive him.

We are all else in good health, do my dear be careful of yourself and God grant that you may be spared to return home safely to the few sad mourners

---

39. Charles and David Levy were traveling together from Charleston. A few days before his death Charles arrived in Savannah on a steamer. See *Savannah Daily Republican,* August 23, 1840. On August 25 the Savannah Board of Health listed Charles among its "Internments" and noted that he died of fever.

40. Corinna seems to mean "acquiesce."

41. Short for "an intermittent fever" (*OED*).

who are left to greet you in this vale of tears. All write in kindest and heartfelt sympathy in our mutual affliction. Ever your affectionate sister

Corinna

[Corinna Aldrich to Mannevillette Brown]

Newnansville [to Paris]
October 11, 1840

. . . I don't know what the big folks are about—but I suppose electioneering with all their might. We read in the papers of musterings and gatherings of the people in which even the ladies take part—all to march [William Henry] Harrison in and drum [Martin] Van Buren out of the Presidency—And I must say—so far as the "poor foolish women" are allowed to express their opinions —they seem to favour the right cause—Harrison forever. It is a matter worthy of remark too—that Van Buren is a widower. Don't you think it proves their consistency?——I think I should like to be in Washington the 4th of March— great will be the fun of the wigs—scarcely one I ween[42] will be on straight. If any, it will be old "Tip."

How would you like an orange! We have a few from the St. Johns—one of which I have just eaten—Would you could drop in & partake with us. Do you have any where you are?—<u>Entre nous</u>[43] they are a beautiful fruit—but give me a good Yankee apple—and scatter with the oranges—I won't cry after them— unless I "is" sick——How do you think you would content yourself among these logs & stumps—George seems to be quite busy. He is of an easy disposition, however. . . .

We received a letter from aunt Hall last mail—she has returned to her plantation, and has taken to grumbling "powerful"—Aunt Ann is going down to make her a visit shortly—and comfort her, if the thing can be accomplished, the which I doubt. It seems the man who had her place in charge—has done as man is too apt to do—taken care of himself—Aunt H. unfortunately looks for self denial in all her understrappers—not finding it, she is constantly puzzled.

Our friend Lieut. Anderson—will probably visit us in a week or so. He has applied for leave of absence—should he obtain it (which I doubt) we may go on to Charleston next month—i.e. Ed & Ell & Mr. A and myself—otherwise we shall not probably take any journey before spring—and ere then who knows what may happen—alas in this uncertain life, how little can we calculate upon the future. God grant our little flock may be spared to gather once more

42. "I ween" is an archaic expression meaning "I suppose."
43. French: "between us."

together in health and happiness—We have been greatly afflicted. May it not be in vain—May we all live as we would wish to die—ever cherishing these Christian virtues—which teach submission to the will of Heaven—that when the evil days come—we may, at least be prepared to meet them————I wish [I] had some interesting news to write you—but alas—it is dull—dull—dull—a duel was fought last week, but as you know not the parties—the particulars would be indifferent to you—the challenger proved a coward—the offense was, he got his face slapped, and it seems he deserved it. . . . ever fondly yours,

Corinna

Chapter Six

"Everything Is Hubbub Here"
The War Continues

James and Ellen were married on October 26, 1840, in Newnansville by Rev. J. T. Prevat.[1] From the beginning Ellen and James's marriage arrangements were difficult. James's military posting at Fort King precluded their living together during the first months of their marriage. Thus, for the time being Ellen remained in Newnansville with Corinna, Edward, and George until James could construct a house for them on post. The next month, taking a moment out of a busy day, James wrote Ellen of his latest military operations. He also noted that his house was nearing completion. Edward was with him and informed James that he, Corinna, and George planned to go to Charleston. James urged Ellen to accompany them:

. . . [I]f it is agreeable, or rather if you would like the trip. . . . I also wish you to ask George to get every article for us that you enumerated, every thing in fact that we shall want & have them transported to Newnansville with the first of his goods. My house as I said before, will be finished in 2 or 3 weeks, but our goods cannot reach Newnansville probably in less than 4 or 5 weeks or even six weeks from this date. You might ask him what time they will reach you & let me know. If there were any probability of my seeing you before I come to ask you to come back with me, I should not propose your going to Charleston, but as it is, if your sister goes, go with her, Ell, & by the time you return I shall have every thing ready for your accommodation & come for you. The Doctor leaves me tomorrow. His speaking of his intention has made me very homesick; otherwise I am very well.

1. See Alachua County Marriage Records, 1837–49, book 1, p. 22, microfilm copy in State Library of Florida, Tallahassee; and *Army and Navy Chronicle,* December 10, 1840, p. 384. See also copy of marriage license in Affidavit of Samuel Russell, March 9, 1852; and Affidavit of Ellen Anderson, April 2, 1852, in materials supplied to editors by Miss Mannevillette Sullivan.

To day, I have marched some 17 or 18 miles to no purpose after the run-aways—troops have been out all day, but none of us know whither they (the Indians) have gone. Everything wears a melancholy aspect & moody faces may be seen in the General's quarters & in the Soldiers tent—with the Generals, the disappointment has been very great. I have not been free from gloom; but it is because the Doctor is leaving me—So long as he remained I have felt as if there was a hope that I would not be long away from you—I cannot bear to be so longer than I have mentioned & as there is a very strong probability that we will remain here for some time to come, I want my Ellen with me—I confess my weakness—with you I am happy—without you, I am not—I once thought that if you were mine I could bear separation better—but I find that I did not think truly. Give my love to Mrs. Aldrich & Miss Dearing—Also to George—tell Mrs. Aldrich I would have tried to keep the Doctor longer, but I find that he is homesick & being in the same predicament I have a fellow feeling for him. Tell George if he can expedite matters & have our goods at Newnansville with the first of his, he will greatly oblige me. So long as General [Walker Keith] Armistead remains in Command we will remain here to a certainty. God bless you Ell, I would have written more fully & better were I not fatigued. . . . Always state in your letters the fact, should you be sick, which may God forbid, for should you conceal it, I might not be with you, when if you told me, I should, at all risks—God bless you Ell

[Willo]

[Willo][2]

Two days later James addressed his new bride once again.

[James W. Anderson to Ellen Anderson]

Fort King E. F. [to Newnansville]
November 17, 1840

Dearest Ell

I wrote to you a day or two ago by the Doctor, telling you of my prospects of remaining at this post during the winter. There is no danger of our being removed so long as General Armistead remains in command & I am hard at work at my building. . . .

Since I have returned I received your last letter to me before I joined you Ell & I read it as greedily as ever. When I first came back I thought the Colonel was inclined to treat me with coldness & I kept my distance. For the last two days, however, I have noticed a change, but for such things I care not. I shall herefrom

---

2. James W. Anderson to Ellen Anderson, November 15, 1840, Anderson-Brown Papers, USMA.

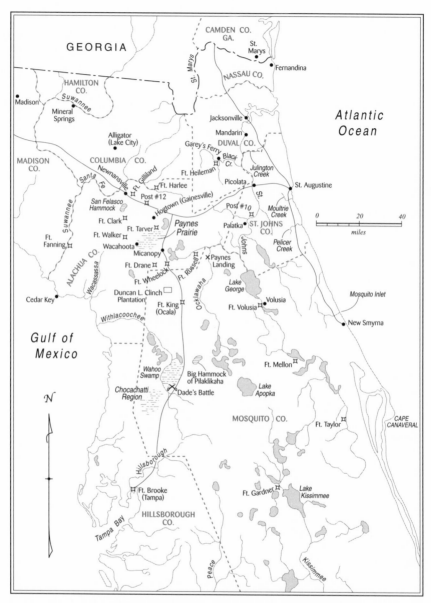

Lt. James W. Anderson's Seminole War, circa 1839–42. Map by Peter Krafft.

do my duty to the best of my ability & ask no favours of any one. I care for no such matters. My duty is governed by my conscience & my love is all yours. I anticipate much pleasure in having you with me during the winter. I think it better, Ell, my own dear, Ell, that such should be the case unless the state of your sister's health should demand your presence. I cannot at this time bear a long separation & have cursed my folly ever since the failure of the treaty that I did not overstay my leave. Now that I am here I have a great deal to do on account of the sickness of the other officers & am bound to remain. I could not get away without deserting. I cannot reconcile it to myself that I am only 50 miles from you—the distance seems at least 1000 miles. Give my love to the Doctor & tell him that we are so overrun here I am afraid he did not enjoy the force as he might have done. I wish you also to ask him whether an escort was offered him from Micanopy—I wish to know the last particularly. My love to Mrs. Aldrich & Miss Dearing & George. I suppose there can be no doubt that everything you send for reaching Newnansville by Christmas. At any rate, I shall come for you certainly by that time unless you tell me it is too early. I cannot stay long when I come perhaps two or three days. I have never had more to do than I have at the present time, indeed all sorts of duties fall on my shoulders for want of officers & so long as I continue well, I am willing but no longer. I think it better to be so employed than to have time to think much. Today, however, I have received a letter from the 2nd auditor stating that all money matters between me & the government were settled, which information has given me much satisfaction, as I had unsettled accounts of several years standing. Uncle Sam has now no chance of ever calling me a defaulter. Many an officer would give a great deal for such a document as I received to day. Good night, Ell, God bless you

Your own Willo—
until death—

[James W. Anderson to Ellen Anderson]

Fort King E. F. [to Newnansville]
November 20, 1840

Dearest Ellen,

God Bless You. I have just received your letter of the 14th, which reaching me as it does the day before I enter the field, where I shall be for the next fourteen days, has cheered me up vastly. This, however, will not interfere at all with my arrangements to have you with me as soon as our Chattels can reach you. Everything is hubbub here and I think I may also add humbug. The General has been humbugged, Capt. [John] Page[3] & the Arkansas Delegation have been

---

3. John Page, a native of Maine, joined the army in 1818. At the time Anderson was writing, Page oversaw the removal of the Seminoles from Fort Brooke (Tampa). Captain of the Eighth Infantry, Page was killed in the Battle of Palo Alto on May 8, 1846. See Heitman, *Historical Register,* 1:765.

humbugged & I suppose we shall all be humbugged during the whole winter. I keep clear of all councils either about Indians or army movements & keep myself employed in obeying orders. Troops are moving in all directions. The General is I suppose doing all he can but no results will be produced that will be of any consequence this winter. Tomorrow Col. Riley starts from here into the Chocochattee region with all the officers & men we can raise from our three posts Forts King, Russell, & Holmes, leaving behind the crippled, maimed & sick to take care of said posts. Genl. A was going to issue an order that the ladies of the 2nd. Infy should be all brought to this post from Forts Russell & Holmes, but Col. Riley suggested to him that they were not <u>subject</u> to <u>martial law</u> & that his order might be disobeyed, which suggestion has silenced the General. What think you of being subject to martial law? I certainly did not anticipate that you were entering into a contract subjecting you to it when you married me, or I should have told you of it. "I could say some things" as Dr P would say, that might not flatter my superiors but it is best to keep a civil tongue in my head unless I am ruffled willfully & as the matter does not refer to you or me, I am silent. The 8th Infy & the Genl. leave here on Monday next for Tampa. Dr. [Peter] Porcher[4] has just left my room, which bye the bye, is far too convenient for a lounge, & as he is to go to Tampa before I get back & he bids me good bye, desires to be remembered particularly to yourself, the Dr. & Mrs. A—he has amused me much by his visits, but no more of such.

I must now refer to yourself Ellen—take good care of yourself, for, as true as I live, my life depends upon you. God knows, I would be with you now & am constantly cursing my folly for coming to the confounded treaty. Every facility has been kindly extended to me by my brother officers, in order that I might bring you here & I shall come without fail, as soon as I can feel assured that our chattels, as I before said, are at N—it would be unwise for me to come before as I should certainly overstay my time, perhaps rather most probably so long as to cause the Colonel to notice it. The Colonel is my friend & I have no doubt will always be. In regard to his Lady & yourself I have something to communicate when we meet. I have taken a course which I conceive to be the proper one & I shall abide the issue. A Captain of the 8th some days ago, made remarks rather tending to the prejudice of our regiment before Mrs. Riley. An officer afterwards hinted at them at a mess table where I was sitting with

---

4. Dr. Peter Porcher, a native of Charleston, practiced medicine and owned a plantation near St. Augustine when the Second Seminole War broke out. He served as regimental surgeon in the Florida militia. See Hammond, *Medical Profession in 19th Century Florida*, 505.

perhaps a dozen others. I immediately stated that I was certain the remarks were not made before any officer of our regt. & told the gentleman that if Capt. [John W. Gunnison][5] (for such is his name & he is a Virginian too bye the bye) would repeat his remarks before me he would find one officer of the Regt. who would defend its reputation with his person, since which I have not visited the camp of that Regiment. Today while in the height of my duties I received a friendly visit from him—he was rather too friendly & as he mentioned nothing of his remarks on a former occasion, which had been commented on by me at the table & which comments had been reported to him, he of course had left an impression on my mind that he is no true son of the Old Dominion. While with me, he talked of but little but his wife & children. I did not speak of you dear, dear, wife but I thought of the risk I had run deeply. That I should have fought him under the circumstances is but too certain, had he repeated his remarks nor could I have retreated & now although I would have gained the victory on him, I feel dissatisfied with myself that I should have been so near fighting a duel.

[James W. Anderson to Ellen Anderson]

Fort King E. F. [to Newnansville]
December 1, 1840

Dearest Ell,

I reached here this evening from our scout in the Chocochattee Region where we have been running about to little purpose—not having seen an Indian since we started from Fort King.[6] We visited among other places the fields that we destroyed last summer & found that they were entirely abandoned, the Indians evidently not having visited them since we ran them off— On my arrival here Dearest, I was vexed at our ill success & fatigue, but two good sized letters from your own dear self has put me in such good humor that I could scribble all night—indeed Ell, you must not think seriously of adopting any new modes action or of affecting any material change in yourself—I

---

5. Anderson may be referring to John W. Gunnison, a native of New Hampshire and member of the topographical engineers in Florida. See Cullum, *Biographical Register,* 1:520; Heitman, *Historical Register,* 1:483; and Sprague, *Florida War,* 227.

6. On December 5, 1840, a correspondent of the *Savannah Republican* reported that "Col. Riley's command [had returned] to their respective posts, Forts King, Russell, and Holmes. They scouted to the south tow within 30 miles of Tampa and back—some of them marching 250 miles without even a sign of an Indian having been discovered" (*Savannah Republican* as quoted in *Army and Navy Chronicle,* December 1840, p. 395).

do not know how I should love you in your new character—Of this I am certain, I love you with all my heart as you are & no change in you can make me love you more—Of course it is your province to dabble in household matters & far from disliking the subject, somehow or other when you speak of it I find that it pleases me. . . . When I come for you, I shall endeavour to bring with me an ambulance, which will be the best possible conveyance for you over the rough roads. . . .

[L]ike myself Ell—you have been wounded sometimes by your best friends, to be sure, it may have been on their part unintentionally; but the effect is the same, it makes you suspicious sometimes of their motives—Of Corinna's attachment, of her love for you, you cannot doubt & the Doctor's friendship for us both I feel convinced: yet I cannot help looking upon our connexion [*sic*] with them in a worldly point of view. It may be pride, whatever it is, if I am wrong correct me. . . . But thank God—my dear Ell—you are my own wife— I was going to say that I was content—but I am not with 50 miles between us— at this distance I suppose from the length of my face sometimes I might indeed be called a <u>mourning</u>. My house is progressing—it will be finished long before I come for you. At any rate it will be sufficiently finished by the 20th—You wish to know whether there will be a campaign. By orders the Country is divided into districts & each Regiment has a district—Ours is the Ocklewaha so that we will remain operating in the country where we now are—None of our Campaigns or scouts will last over 14 days from our posts—such will be our destination during the winter. . . . your affectionate h-u-s-b-a-n-d

Willo—

[James W. Anderson to Ellen Anderson]

Fort King E. F. [to Newnansville]
December 4, 1840

Dear Ell:

Having an opportunity by a branch contractor for cattle at this post to send to Newnansville direct, I hasten to embrace it. I returned from the front on the afternoon of the 1st having been eleven days out. We visited the old fields destroyed by us last summer & went within a few miles of Tampa, but after marching through vines & bushes through mud or over sand hills saw nothing whatever of the enemy. On my return to this place I found two letters from you for which I thank you. I was tired & disappointed at having our trouble for nothing—perhaps we will have better luck next time when we go on the Oklawaha and the receipt of those two letters had a charm that restored me immediately & I sat down & wrote you a letter immediately, but as the said letter may be some days on its way, I embrace the present opportunity if it is only to say that I am delighted to find that the hateful ague & fever is not likely to trouble you any more & that I am well. Mr. [Britton] Branch[7] leaves in a few minutes, so should my letter be short you will know the reason. I have many things to say but I know not where to begin. Some things I have told you in past letters but you will probably receive this before you do them. I am at work at my house & it will be sufficiently furnished in a week or fortnight at farthest to inhabit. The colonel talks some of going to Micanopy in a week. So he told me I would have a chance to visit you, but it depends upon his getting a guide before that time arrives. We will remain scouting in the Oklawaha district this winter if Genl. A. remains in command & our command will not probably be out even over 10 days or a fortnight from our posts. As soon as our chattels arrive, drop me a line & I will be with you. I may possibly be able to stay 3 or 4 days in Newnansville but not longer. In these busy times, the Colonel cannot spare so <u>important</u> a <u>personage</u> . I had an invitation yesterday from the Col to bring you here at once to stay with Mrs. R. until my house is finished. But although the idea of having you with me was very pleasing, I declined at once. Mrs. R has complained that I did not go to her house. I called yesterday & she was very particular in her enquiries after you. She is getting very lonesome. The Col. has recovered entirely, & since the scout cooks as well as ever, buy up some chickens, Ell, as we can't do without eating yet (not have the talent) they will be useful. God bless you. I must finish as Mr. Branch is about starting I enclose this to the doctor & as I do not write to him, remember me to him & tell him the reason. Remember me to all. I am getting very homesick. In haste.

Ever Yours
Willo

P.S. Send the letter in post office at Newnansville to me. All [public] letters are not "free."

Yours truly
W

[James W. Anderson to Ellen Anderson]

Fort King E. F. [to Newnansville]
December 5, 1840

Dearest Ell—

I received your affectionate, kind & good letter . . . by the express & I do assure you there is but little chance of my tiring in reading your letters. I shall

---

7. Britton Branch of Alachua County filed an application for an Armed Occupation Act Land Grant. See Carter, *Territorial Papers,* 26:720.

also judge you by myself, & write whenever I am so inclined. I intended to have made this a long writing affair, but I am so pushed for time just at this moment I must put off much that I have to say. Let me thank you for your candour, dearest Ell, but do not say that—I fear you—every thought, feeling, mood, or act of mine is connected in some undefinable manner with your own sweet self & truly such could not be the case unless I were as confident of your love as that I loved you. Think not of it a second time, for if I said anything in my hurried letters that could clearly admit of being so construed, you have my word for it that it did not come from my heart. I will come down by Christmas provided as I said before our chattels should have arrived. . . .

It gives me also much pleasure to hear that Mrs. A will visit us at Fort King & that she is fast recovering from her sickness. I presume the governor is preparing for his exit from office by this time, that he will have to abdicate. I am as sure as can be. Genl. [Duncan Lamont] Clinch[8] is spoken of as the next governor of the territory & will no doubt get it, if he so desires. The change must be beneficial as [Gov. Robert Raymond] Read [Reid] is not fit for the present troublesome times & every body speaks so highly of Gl C.[9] . . .

Our new and elegant mansion has two rooms of the same size, both measuring 15 feet 9 inches one way & 15 feet 7 inches the other. They were intended to be 16 feet in the clear, but as you perceive, lack a few inches of it. . . . I had a good mind to head my letter "My affectionate wife" but no! I like familiar sounds best, forgive me if I have caused an unpleasant thought in my hurried writing to you. You have given me every proof that I could ask of your love &

8. Gen. Duncan Lamont Clinch, a native of North Carolina, joined the U.S. Army in 1808. He was a leading figure in the Second Seminole War. He owned a large plantation called Auld Lang Syne between Micanopy and Fort King, the grounds of which were often occupied by the troops as part of Fort Drane. Resigning from the military in September 1836, Clinch settled in St. Marys, Georgia. See Heitman, *Historical Register,* 1:311; Patrick, *Aristocrat in Uniform,* 137–79; and Mahon, *History of the Second Seminole War,* 65–66.

9. As did many others, James is confusing the spelling of Governor Reid's name with that of the militia general Leigh Read. Once William H. Harrison (Whig) defeated Martin Van Buren (Dem.) for president, most expected that Reid, under attack from the Whigs, would be sacked. They were correct. He died of yellow fever soon after his removal. See *St. Augustine Florida Herald and Southern Democrat,* July 16, 1841. President Harrison appointed Richard Keith Call governor. See Arthur W. Thompson, *Jacksonian Democracy on the Florida Frontier* (Gainesville: University of Florida Press, 1961), 71; Doherty, *Whigs of Florida,* 11; Mahon, *History of the Second Seminole War,* 295; and Sidney Walter Martin, *Florida during Territorial Days,* 254–55.

I were base to doubt it or that my happiness was not your own, as yours is &
ever will be mine. Remember me to all, God Bless you

Ever Yours Willo

[James W. Anderson to Ellen Anderson]

Fort King E. F. [to Newnansville]
December 16, 1840

You will no doubt be somewhat anxious to hear from me by the time this
reaches you, as I am in arrears considerably—indeed it is some time since I
have written or heard from you—On my part, it is entirely attributable to my
time being so much occupied that I could not even steal a moment to devote to
you my best of Wives. . . . Last Monday I was at Fort Russell, summoned to
appear before a Court of Inquiry assembled there. I went down on Sunday
rather & returned on Monday. In my absence, Private Lapenski a refugee
Polander, in whom I placed the utmost confidence, stole all the money I had in
my possession ($420), some of my clothes, & deserted & although I have offered
$100 reward for his apprehension, I have as yet heard nothing of him. I see the
benefit of being married already—had I not left some money with you, I
should have been left actually penniless. Tell the Doctor of it—he knows the
man & he might possibly meet with him in the Settlements.

By the middle of next week, I shall have all my fixture[s] at Fort King completed, but I shall await your summons as I cannot possibly remain long in
Newnansville—I am sorry but at this time it is impossible for me to be long
absent. The Colonel has been very kind to me; indeed, as he has assumed command of the post; I do as I please—provided I do my duty first & I do not
believe that I ever was accused of slighting my duty in any instance—I am jealous of my reputation in that respect as any one—for it is all that an officer has
to depend upon—I have come to the conclusion after reading your last letter
that you possess more moderation than I do & that we differ [with] . . . regard
[to] dueling. Yet it pleases me that you do not agree with me in that respect—
which very fact you may construe as an argument in your favour—that it is
morally wrong, I am convinced—Yet under certain circumstances were I not
to fight, even you, you who advocate that it would be morally wrong to do so,
would blush for me—so far, since I have been in the Army, I have escaped
without being challenger or challenged, yet I assure you, the reason has been
that I am known as one who can be provoked to combat.

You ask if there are any other ladies at the post—Mrs. Wessells & Mrs. Casey
are also here. Mrs. W I fear is not very long for this world. She looks badly &
is evidently in a delirium. Mrs. Casey is a very pleasant & agreeable lady &
strictly religious I believe. Both of the ladies arrived here within a few days

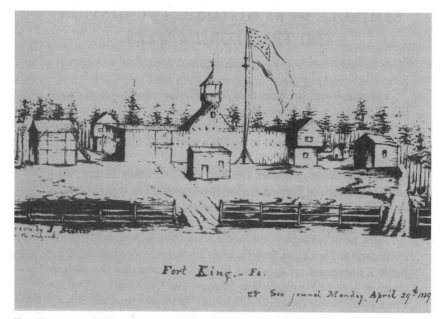

Fort King, circa 1839, as James and Ellen Anderson would have remembered it when they lived there shortly after their marriage. The editors wish to thank Frank Laumer and Richard Mathews for bringing this line drawing to their attention; the original is in the John T. Sprague Collection, Library of Congress.

past. . . . I have stated to you that the Colonel David Twiggs has been very kind to me—I find that his coldness to me on my return was caused by my getting married without telling him of it—he felt hurt, it appears. That I did not confide the matter to him as a friend I am sorry—but in some matters friends are worse than foes & besides, where you are concerned I should not consult my father. I wish to see you very much dearest & hope I shall receive my summons, at the farthest a fortnight from this time—the instant you find that the <u>things</u> are at Newnansville, let me know & I will come down with an ambulance, one waggon & an escort—at the farthest I cannot stay over 3 days—I am having your house built agreeably to your desire so you are bound to bring something to inhabit it. . . . A servant will be absolutely necessary to you here & if you prefer Amanda, we will bring her along with us—I will never trust a soldier again—confidence once abused is never regained & I would as soon have suspected a brother as Lapinski. Ever yours

Willo

[P.S.] [B]y the way—on our last scout—I found that there were a dozen Germans who sing well in our command & one evening I assembled them together. Among other songs they sang "Thou, thou who reignest in this bosom" in German (the original) it was beautiful—and under the circumstances that it was sung—its effect was thrilling—I cannot promise you much music here—We have good drummers & pipers—Good martial music, but no more—We are raising a band in New York harbour to be ready for us, as soon as—as—The Florida War is over.

[James Willoughby Anderson to Ellen Brown Anderson]

Fort King, E. F. [to Newnansville]
December 23, 1840

Dearest,

I should have written to you by the last mail, but in consequence of delaying to do so until the night before the express left, I lost my opportunity entirely; cause why, an express arrived from Tampa just as night set in & the Colonel's demand for my services was not to be refused. While Colonel [Gustavus] Loomis[10] was here, he blundered as usual upon the subject of Religion at a most unseasonable time in presence of Col. R. & states to him that his duty to his God was paramount to all others & his duty to his Country next. Col. R. replied "no—my duty to my country before all others"—& in saying so, I believe he was perfectly sincere. Now, were the question started whether my duty to you or to my country should be uppermost, I have an idea that be my decision what it might it would be somewhat unsatisfactory. I had rather the two should not be placed in opposition.

A Merry Christmas & a happy New Year to you—after all, it seems I cannot eat my Christmas pie with you & I very much fear that your summons will not be forthcoming in time for me to spend New Year's day with you. I received your letter of the 12th by the last express & in looking at the device upon the seal, I thought surely the summons had come—but on opening I was disappointed. Do not apply my railings at poor human nature so forcibly to your friends. Your friends are my friends & I believe I do them justice. I fully

---

10. A native of Vermont, Gustavus Loomis graduated from West Point in 1811 and fought in the Niagara theater during the War of 1812. Serving in Florida during the 1820s at Fort Gadsden and the Cantonment Clinch, Loomis returned again in 1837, fighting in the Battle of Okeechobee on December 25 of that year. Promoted to major of the Second Infantry on July 7, 1838, and then lieutenant of the Sixth Infantry on September 22, 1840, Loomis remained in Florida until 1842. Loomis fought in the Mexican War and returned to Florida in 1856 when hostilities between the Seminoles and the whites broke out again. Loomis served in the Union army, achieving the rank of general by war's end. See Cullum, *Biographical Register,* 1:118; and Heitman, *Historical Register,* 1:641.

appreciate their kindness to me as well as to yourself. As to Corinna I think her a pattern of a wife & think it doubtful whether you can be a better. My remarks have appeared harsh to you & you have undertaken to defend your friends. You do so warmly & I am glad to see it—but remember Ell my appreciation of your friends is in proportion to your evaluation of them. Use some other term however. You may have noticed before that I liked it not. During the treaty—two nights before the Indians bolted, Harlick Lustnugger & other Indians said to me, slapping me on the shoulder "Fliend! Fliend! You my best fliend"—& for what? Barely because I gave them whiskey. 'Tis true, we often know not our best friends.

I am now occupying my new quarters. The Colonel told me yesterday that he wished me to go for you about the 1st of next month, but I am somewhat in doubt about going until I can hear from you—as I could not remain many days in Newnansville—he goes at that time to Pilatka & on his return wishes me here to join him on a scout on the Ocklewaha. If I come to the conclusion that your brother can be back with his goods by the 10th proximo,[11] I shall come down about the 1st of the month; if not, I will abide my time as best I may, & await your summons. About transportation, I would state my dear Ell, that if I have not mentioned anything about it to you, it is because I did not give it a moment's thought—it is always at my command. I have rigged up an ambulance with four fine sorrel horses (in which the ladies ride out here every day, very imprudent by the bye at this time & I told them so) in which I intend to drive down in Stile with the Colonel's body guard. 20 horsemen, or a part of it. I shall also bring a waggon. I could bring some more but the ambulance will hold considerable & we will be as comfortable I think as you will expect or desire—if you prefer, by borrowing a side saddle, you can ride part of the way on horse back.

I have given up Dick—on the last Scout he tumbled while nearly at full speed, heels over head & I found <u>my head</u> stuck in a gopher hole. I now have a fine coal black charger as gay as a lark & handsome to behold. In my opinion he is a perfect beauty—speaking of <u>horses</u> reminds me to tell you that I was called upon two or 3 nights ago to marry a couple in my capacity as Adjt. to the Regt. but declined, not being legally authorized. I gave [Francis R.] Sanchez[12]

---

11. Latin: "in or of next month" (*OED*).

12. This was probably Francis R. Sanchez, a leading citizen of the area. He was a member of the Alachua County Commission. See Carter, *Territorial Papers,* 26:40 n. He also was a lieutenant colonel in the Alachua County volunteer regiment. See *Army and Navy Chronicle,* November 28, 1839, p. 351.

no advice to marry—nor do I think would advise any man on the subject as I do not think there are many Ellens in the world. God bless you. May we soon meet is my earnest prayer. Give my love to Mrs. A. & tell her that I think she deserves much credit in outwitting Madame [Zilphia] Stanley.[13] & that she must take care the old lady does not make it up. Remember me also to Miss D. & the Doctor. I wish them all a Merry Christmas & happy new year—& wish heartily I could spend the holliday [sic] in N— Fort King is much improved & the idea that you are coming here has reconciled me to it. . . . I wish to see an end to this warfare; yet I fear it will only be the prelude to my leaving this country. To leave Florida after all her many pleasing associations connected with it & I may go far & fare worse. This letter may be some time in coming to you in consequence of the uncertainty of Expresses. Should I not be with you write on the receipt of it—'Tis late, <u>Mon amie</u>—God bless you

Willo

In 1841 the Second Seminole War was winding down. And yet, even as the number of Indians diminished, those who remained continued to harass Florida's frontier settlers. The first three months of the year were punctuated by several violent engagements between the Seminoles and their adversaries. Also during that time, however, Walker K. Armistead initiated a series of uncoordinated peace overtures, using a combination of bribes and threats. Halleck Tustenuggee, Tiger Tail, and Coacoochee took full advantage of Armistead's disjointed peace policy and promised to emigrate, only to escape with their bands to fight again once they were resupplied.[14] Florida settlers grew dissatisfied with Armistead's policy, especially when rumors spread that Armistead was on the verge of concluding a treaty reminiscent of Macomb's 1839 pact allowing the Seminoles to stay in the lower peninsula. Public meetings were held in St. Augustine, Jacksonville, and other communities denouncing any "other arrangement other than the absolute removal of all of the Indians in Florida."[15]

13. Zilphia Stanley, a native of Georgia, was forty years old in 1840 and operated a boardinghouse in Newnansville (U.S. Manuscript Census, Population [1850] for Alachua County, Florida, p. 32).

14. Mahon, *History of the Second Seminole War,* 274–87; Covington, *Seminoles of Florida,* 99–100.

15. See "Public Meeting [Jacksonville]," *St. Augustine Florida Herald and Southern Democrat,* February 5, 1841. See also "Great Public Meeting [St. Augustine]," *St. Augustine Florida Herald and Southern Democrat,* January 8 and 29, 1841. For an overall assessment of the situation as of the middle of March, see "Tampa Bay, Gen. Armistead, Capt. Page, and the Indians," *St. Augustine Florida Herald and Southern Democrat,* March 19, 1841.

Continuing his studies in Venice, Italy, but also attending parties and enjoying the social life there, Mannevillette Brown kept his sisters abreast of his activities. The aspiring young painter supported himself by copying masterpieces for the Walkers of Utica and other customers back home. Speculating that he could earn more money in Europe making copies than by returning to America, he was uncertain how long he would stay.[16]

Meanwhile, Ellen finally joined James at Fort King that spring. Their happy union produced their first child in November 1841. Throughout the next two years Ellen and Corinna, who resided in Newnansville with Edward and her brother George, visited St. Augustine often. Their visits became even more frequent when Ellen became pregnant. Corinna kept Mannevillette informed of family matters. Her first letter of the year discusses the settlement of Charles's estate:

[Corinna Aldrich to Mannevillette Brown]

Newnansville [to Paris]
January 3, 1841

Mon cher frere: I wish you a Happy New Year! Rather late, but not the less sincere. To your last favor from Parma I have not replied, merely because, I had written immediately before its reception and news is so scarce, I often think my letters must be stale affairs at best. Some matters, however, like the following, I repeat for fear that any letter should miscarry. Edward forwarded to Corning & Co. of NY about the middle of October, a check for three hundred & forty odd dollars which was all he could get exchange for at the time. Since then he would have remitted the balance but for matter which I will explain. As a matter of course, our poor Charlie's sudden death, threw his affairs in the greatest confusion—his business being done entirely on E's capital & credit, to set matters to right has somewhat embarrassed him. He will however, eventually settle all Charlie's debts, and leave his estate on the St. John's (Llangollen) unencumbered—that estate is valued at about fifteen hundred dollars—one third of which belongs to Aunt Ann. The remaining two thirds falls to you, George, Ell & I as equal heirs. . . . I mention these things dear, because I think it right that you should know how matters stand. George has entered into partnership with E on the same terms as poor Charlie, and God grant he may be spared to enjoy whatever he may earn. He is now in Charleston

---

16. Mannevillette Brown to Corinna Aldrich and Ellen Anderson, June 8; August 13, 1841, Anderson-Brown Papers, USMA.

setting up the business and making purchases for the store. Edward says he will endeavor to send you the balance due on the four hundred, which I believe is $56 in the course of two weeks, if not before. He has wages due him for Negro hire at Fort Fanning but the road there is so difficult & dangerous, he finds but very few oppy. to collect. He will make some arrangement next week. Ellen is still with me, but expects to visit Fort King in the course of this month. In the spring she & I expect, <u>Deo Volente</u>, to go north. Mr. Anderson is high on the list for promotion & I hope will be a Capt before we go. He is of excellent family in Virginia—& I believe a kind hearted & good man & stands high as an officer. Aunt Ann is well, she & Ell are now preparing for a walk. It is quite pleasant, but unusually cold.

I suppose you know that congress is in session & that it is decided that Harrison is to be our next president. Great hopes are entertained that he will get our money matters to rights & surely it will benefit us, for when we have money & wish to send it away, we cannot do it for want of exchange. The soldiers being paid off in specie—makes specie plenty and yet we may say money is scarce. We heard from Aunt Hall last week—she was well—her orange crop has been pretty good this year. When do you think of returning home? We almost despair of seeing you, and yet we know it is best for you to stay & try to be content. I think in your last you said you were going to Venice—from thence home? I wish we may be in the U.S. to meet you—for this place called Florida does not seem a part or portion of the Union. The Indians are still at large & cutting capers & throats at pleasure. I see no hope of a termination to their game this year. Of course there is a bar to all improvement. We trust in Gen. Harrison & the new administration for an end of these things & if they fail to accomplish it, we must quit. E would leave now, but for being in contract to attend the volunteers & . . . he & G. calculate by holding on a while, to drive a profitable <u>trade</u>—by & by—& if so, I hope you may be induced to come & sojourn with us. You must excuse <u>haste</u> as it is both late (for mail) and cold. I don't know of any particular news to relate. Congress is discussing the subtreaty bill & other matters are in status quo. I have just heard of the murder of an officer's wife near here. She was passing from one post to another with a small escort & they were surprised by a large party of Indians. She . . . & 5 men killed. It seems strange that people will run such hazards. The lady was from Cincinnati & had been married but a few months, such is fate. E is looking over my shoulder and wont let me write even as well as I am disposed to. All well and write in love & good wishes for this & many coming years. God bless you— ever yours C

[James Anderson to Ellen Anderson]

Fort King [to Newnansville]

January 5, 1841

Dearest Ell—

I wrote you a few lines by the last mail including Lt. [Richard C.] Gatlin's[17] account of the tale of Mrs. [Elizabeth Fanny Taylor] Montgomery[18] know not why it is, unless it be that my mind reverted to you, that I have been so affected by her fate.[19] It appears that Lt. [Nevil] Hopson[20] was going to Wacahoota with

17. Richard C. Gatlin was a native of North Carolina. Graduating from West Point in 1832, Gatlin was a lieutenant in the Seventh Infantry and served in Florida from 1839 to 1842. Gatlin fought in the Battle of Monterey in the Mexican War. As a major in the Fifth Infantry, Gatlin resigned his commission on May 20, 1861, and joined the Confederate service. See Cullum, *Biographical Register,* 1:415; and Heitman, *Historical Register,* 1:450.

18. Alexander Montgomery was a native of Pennsylvania and graduated from West Point in 1834. Montgomery traveled to Florida in 1839 with the Seventh Infantry. Montgomery married Elizabeth Fanny Taylor only three months before she was killed on September 2, 1840, in Cincinnati. Montgomery did garrison duty at Pensacola from 1842 to 1845 and was transferred to Texas in 1845. After serving on quartermaster duty during the Mexican War, Montgomery returned to Florida in 1854, serving at Tampa Bay until 1856. Montgomery served in various administrative posts during the Civil War. See Cullum, *Biographical Register,* 1:462; Heitman, *Historical Register,* 1:719; and *Army and Navy Chronicle,* September 10, 1840, p. 175.

19. The Anderson-Brown collection contains a letter from R. C. Gatlin to "Dear Knight" written on December 20, 1840, from Micanopy and describing the attack, which took place on November 28. He explained: "Lts [Walter] Sherwood and [Nevil] Hopson and Mrs. Montgomery with an escort of eleven mounted men left this post with the view of visiting Wacahoota. They had not proceeded more than 4 miles (where Martin was shot) when they were surprised by a large body of Indians. Lt. Sherwood, Mrs. Montgomery, Sgt. Major Carrol and three privates were killed. Mrs. M. was the young bride of Lt. [Alexander] Montgomery of Infty. The bodies fell into the hands of the enemy. Mrs. M. was taken by them but killed on the ground. One soldier was found mortally wounded near her. He said to Lt. M. when he rode up — 'Lt. I fought for your wife as long as I could stand. You see that I am now dying.' The bodies have been brought to this post and interred." See Mahon, *History of the Second Seminole War,* 284–85; Sprague, *Origins, Progress, and Conclusion of the Florida War,* 249, 484; "Another Horrid Massacre," *St. Augustine Florida Herald and Southern Democrat,* January 8, 1841; *St. Augustine News,* January 1, 1841; *Savannah Daily Republican,* January 4, 5, and 9, 1841.

20. A native of Kentucky, Nevil Hopson graduated from West Point in 1837. He fought in Florida from 1839 to 1843 as a member of the Seventh Infantry. Following his service in the Mexican War he was dismissed for drunkenness. See Cullum, *Biographical Register,* 1:545; and Heitman, *Historical Register,* 1:542.

a waggon for his wife & that Lt. [Walter] Sherwood[21] & Mrs. Montgomery rode out with him, having the Sgt. Major & 11 mounted men with them—when they arrived near the point of [the] hammock where [John W.] Martin[22] of our Regt. was shot; they saw the Indians advancing & Lt. Sherwood who was the ranking officer, & in whose charge Mrs. Montgomery was placed, ordered the whole party to dismount & prepare for action, directing Mrs. M. to get into the waggon. Lt. Hopson was ordered back to Micanopy to bring a reinforcement. —Bad management & showing Lt. S' want of experience. It is a most unfortunate affair—but perhaps I may have done as he did rather than risk the imputation of cowardice. I think however I should have looked to the safety of the lady by sending her back forthwith, but Lt. S. no doubt thought her safer in the waggon than in going back. I am disgusted with these butcheries, & since that affair have kept aloof from all Florida topics. Would to God that this horrible war was ended.[23]

. . . I am tired of this roving life—Ell—and I have a living example before me of its effects on our worthy Colonel. With a naturally quick & active mind, he has been confined all his life to the Border and Camp life, without having read any work perhaps, of depth or profundity. His conversation is, of course, rough as well as his manners, being almost entirely composed of anecdotes &c. I find too, that in myself it begets a restlessness, that I can scarcely control. I return to the post, and after being there a day or two, the mechanism of writing, if I may so style it, becomes absolutely so distasteful that I find considerable effort necessary to fulfill my duties. I speak of such writing as my duties require of me—to write to you is my only consolation in my tribulation. I

21. Walter Sherwood was a native of New Jersey and graduated from West Point in 1837. Sherwood served at Fort Gibson, Indian Territory, and did recruiting service before traveling to Florida in 1840 as a member of the Seventh Infantry. He died in hand-to-hand combat near Micanopy. See Cullum, *Biographical Register,* 1:542; and Heitman, *Historical Register,* 1:882.

22. John W. Martin, a native of Virginia, was a second lieutenant in the Second Infantry. See Heitman, *Historical Register,* 1:692. On May 19, 1840, he was shot three times near Micanopy. According to an extract of a report published in the *Savannah Georgian,* Martin "received three balls, one through the abdomen, one through the arm, and one in his hand—one of his men and all the horses killed—the other two missing" (*Savannah Georgian* as quoted in *Army and Navy Chronicle,* June 4, 1840, p. 365; *St. Augustine News,* May 29, 1840).

23. Secretary of War Joel R. Poinsett ordered an investigation of this incident. See Secretary of War to Walker K. Armistead, January 10, 1841, in Carter, *Territorial Papers,* 26:238–39.

ought to fear being called a grumbler—such however is not my natural disposition & were I at your elbow, my troubles would vanish. I didn't like the idea of not spending either Christmas or New Year with you, so I determined to be most supremely miserable and effected my purpose to a greater degree, than was at all comfortable; afterwards I reflected that it would please you more if you supposed me enjoying myself & I set out to work to get out of my dumps, but it would not do. My strength was not equal to the effort. Withal however the influence has been good, as it led me into a train of serious reflections, which may leave some good results behind them.

The bridge on the Ocklawaha is completed, the party are just arriving & I suppose in 4 days we will be in, not the field, but the woods again. The Cursed Indians—I try to restrain, but it is useless. Were I in Montgomery's place, I would get to Tampa, give a great feast to all the Indians there and blow them to the Devil while they were at [the] table by springing a mine of powder under them. I will shake no Florida Indian by the hand again. That is a sign of friendship I will not extend to them as I cannot feel it.

You asked in your last, why Mrs. T. I. Smith has gone to W. A very rational answer occurs to my mind—viz that her relations are there—if you had asked, why she left her husband, I should then have been at a loss. I think she is the daughter of a baker or butcher in Washington and ran away with Smith. It was rather a romantic affair & was chronicled in the papers at the time it occurred. Give my love to Mrs. A., the Doctor, Miss D. and your brother George. Tell the Doctor to take care of his scalp and run no risks—there are yet 1000 warriors in the Territory—tell George also. Tell Mrs. A that I much fear Mrs. [Mary] Wessells will not live to see another winter. She is about but looks dreadfully. Good night. God protect and watch over you. Your own Willo

[Corinna Aldrich to Mannevillette Brown]

Newnansville [to Venice, Italy]
Jan. 24th 1841

Dear Brother,

Your favour from Venice dated 10th November came duly to hand. I am happy to be assured it left you as it found us in good health. You much lament our poor Charles's death—as I knew you must. God grant you may be spared to return to us again. There have been years of bad changes since you left - - - -

We are quite in confusion just now. Ell is preparing for a jaunt to Fort King where her old man is stationed. She expects to spend a few months there & then go North—if possible I shall go on with her in the summer, but at present all is uncertainty. From your letter we hope to see you ere then—that is—if you are not afraid to travel amongst these devilish seminoles. They have been cutting up great shines within the last week.[24] Three nights since, they burned a house within sight of <u>ours</u>! But don't be <u>alarmed</u>. They are not devils, but will not risk a single life on their side—& in that rests our security. Still had I been told when I came to Florida that I should ever witness such things. . . . But Bulwer argues that everlasting fire can be no punishment to mortals inasmuch as they would <u>get used to it</u>![25] It seems so as well as we can judge in temporal things.

To return, however, the first we knew of danger—our cook who lives in a little cabin—out of the yard came to me about 10 o'clock p. m. and told me Mr. [Edmund] Bird's house—(he is absent) was on fire—and that as it was unoccupied the Indians must have fired it.[26] In a few minutes the town was in alarm & we could distinctly hear their yells (which were answered by spies in different parts of town). Of course none dared advance upon them while their position was secured by the light of the fire. As soon as it subsided the men rode up there (it was on the outskirts of town) but they had fled. We then learned that they had tried to force open the door of a small building near—which was occupied by a man & his family—but as soon as he cocked his gun, they fled—batting down fences & etc—to get off the faster. If as we afterwards learned, they did not stop until they got ten miles from town—there they scattered in different directions—into a large hammock—or tract of oak woods & thick underbrush twenty miles in extent. Of course, as usual, our men were not strong enough to scour the hammock & so they returned & the Indians are at liberty to return if they please—or go where they can do worse. This is a shameful state of things but there seems no remedy. For myself I feel as an individual safe—but I dread to have any one leave the town even for a mile's ride—I do not think it safe—unless in large parties. On the very afternoon

24. On February 5, 1841, the *St. Augustine Florida Herald and Southern Democrat* reported Indian attacks on Newnansville, Fort Walker, and Fort Tarver. See also *St. Augustine News,* January 29, 1841; and *Savannah Daily Republican,* February 4, 1841. Later, on August 6, 1841, the *News* reported an attack on Colonel Sanchez's home and another man's house near Newnansville.

25. This is probably a reference to Edward Bulwer-Lytton, First Baron Lytton. (See note 21, p. 111.)

26. Edmund Bird was in Tallahassee representing Alachua County in the legislative council at the time of the attack. A Democrat, Bird also attended the constitutional convention two years earlier, and he served as Alachua County auctioneer. See *St. Augustine Florida Herald and Southern Democrat,* February 5, 1841; *St. Augustine News,* January 29, 1841; *Savannah Daily Republican,* February 4, 1841; Phelps, *People of Lawmaking in Florida,* 8; and Carter, *Territorial Papers,* 26:40 n. 60.

before they fired this house in the evening they shot a man[27] about 5 miles from town & it seems they followed on the heels of those who brought the body in—& while the jury was sitting over it, set fire to the building—& will be quite a memorable sight—for our house being large & in the centre of the town it was crowded with trembling neighbors. We kept watch all night. We have since however taken such precautions, as not to make it necessary to lose our rest—& what was before a source of terror, is now one of amusement! but Manne bad as it was I would not but laugh in the face and eyes of it—& so would you—had you been a witness of the faint hearts and funny <u>phizes</u>! The gents generally were brave and prepared for war—but the poor women—they chattered & made faces & came like Mother goose's beggars—some in rags, some with jogs,[28] and some in velvet gowns.

I believe this is all I have to write about dear—except to say George is returned in good health—and Aunt Ann is gone to the river to visit Aunt Hall a few weeks. I enclose to day to Baring & Co. $50 fifty dollars—being the balance on the four hundred promised excepting six dollars. I could not make it nearer—344 was sent some time since—hoping you will receive it in safety. I remain as ever your fond sis (all send lots of love—)

Corinna

[Corinna Aldrich to Mannevillette Brown]

Newnansville [to Venice]
May 30th 1841

Dear Brother, I returned from Fort King—whither Edward and I had been to pay Ellen and Mr. Anderson a visit—about two weeks since—I have been ever since ill of severe bilious fever—or I should certainly have written you before. . . . We did hope to visit the north this summer—but the Dr. has met with so much difficulty in collecting owing to the delay in paying off the troops that I am afraid the time will be procrastinated until it will be too late in the season for me to venture. I cannot go north after October, and I don't believe any payments will be made before then—however the Dr has other claims of his own on Uncle Sam that our newly elected Delegate—(who is a personal friend both of mine & of Edward's) promises to do his best to obtain.[29] Should

---

27. According to newspaper accounts, the man killed by the Indians was Henry Lindsey, a citizen of Fort Clark (*St. Augustine Florida Herald and Southern Democrat,* February 5, 1841; *Savannah Daily Republican,* February 4, 1841).

28. Variant spelling for *jougs;* "the plural form apparently refers to the construction of the collar in two hinged halves to be locked together" (*OED*).

29. Though a Whig, Edward Aldrich supported David Levy's candidacy for territorial delegate. At a dinner at Mrs. Stanley's boardinghouse near Newnansville celebrating

he be successful—you may meet me at Washington. If you go to Washington as you spoke of I will give you a letter to him. He is a fine man—one you would like much, and in whom you would find a friend. He proved himself one to poor Charley—he was with him in his 1st sickness, & waited on him like a brother. His name is David Levy. His father[, Moses Elias Levy], is a wealthy Jew—but has discarded him because he will not adhere to the Jewish creed.

If you come home dear this summer—It would not be well for you to come south until after frost—you would be sure to be sick. I shall long to see you, but I should fear your coming. I don't know but with care you might escape if you did not go into the interior—and we hope if we go no farther—to spend the warmest months on the St. John's. That is our calculation at present—to go down there in about a month & if we don't go north—George has already cleared out[. H]e would not risk another fever & I don't blame him. I have suffered dreadfully the last fortnight, and I am still quite feeble. I don't expect to get right until I can get where I can sniff the sea breeze. Ell enjoys her health finely—I never saw her look better than when I left Fort King. By the way—it is the last Post bordering on the Indian country in the Interior—but it is a large & very pretty one—I saw where Tompson & Rodgers were buried.[30] They were the Indian agents you recollect who were first shot at the very commencement of the war. We also went across the great Prairie—15 miles across.[31] It looks almost like a sea. The horizon is dimly skirted by trees—and on the farthest edge is a little settlement called Fort Tarver. It has quite a pretty effect in the distance—with its well laid out fields & neat fences.

Do you have any grain growing in Italy?—We shall soon have green corn. We have a fine garden. I hate to leave it—but I assure 'tis all I regret to leave in this place—notwithstanding I have the best (log) house in the town. I shall have a room all prepared for you in the fall & God grant you may come & occupy it, I hope to have you all with me for a little while in the fall—at least—

William Henry Harrison's inauguration as president, Aldrich offered the following toast: "*David Levy, Esq,* one of the candidates for our next Delegate to Congress—Let us begin the system of reform by voting for an honest man without regard to political prejudice" (*St. Augustine Florida Herald and Southern Democrat,* March 26, 1841; *St. Augustine News,* March 19, 1841).

30. Wiley Thompson, Erastus Rogers, and three other men were murdered by Osceola and other Seminoles just outside the Fort King stockade on December 28, 1835. Thompson headed the Indian Agency, and Rogers was sutler. The event, occurring on the same day as Dade's Massacre, triggered the Second Seminole War. See Mahon, *History of the Second Seminole War,* 103–4.

31. Payne's Prairie.

Edward has been very anxious to get a house large enough—we have at last succeeded—we have [a] good tight roof & comfortable rooms—I assure you a tight roof & a good floor is not to be found everywhere in the Interior—but don't think we have taken up our residence here for life—we only await a good opp'y to move to a better place. I think we shall have to remain here this year but I hope not much longer—I have been trying to eat some dinner—they sent me roast chicken & vegetables of many kinds with boiled ham & cabbage but I can't find a palate for any thing—I have no stomach—like the old woman Boz[32] tells about.

Edward's brother is with us at this time. Louis—he has just graduated—is about to study Law—he is a fine young man—he is here only on a visit—however. This is no place for him to study. George has some idea of spending the summer in St. Mary's with E's father—he has invited him to do so—and as there is not much prospect of business north, until another season—I think he will accept the invite. I should like you to know old Dr. A. He is a gent of the old school—one you would much esteem.

Well dear I believe I must close with a God bless you & speed your safe return. It is very warm & I am very very lazy. The Dr. has just come & fed me with some cabbage! Fine regimen for a patient.

again, adieu Corinna

32. "Boz" was the pseudonym used by Charles Dickens in his *Sketches by 'Boz,' Illustrative of Every-Day Life and Every-Day People* (1836–37), a collection of articles first published in various periodicals and also published in *The Posthumous Papers of the Pickwick Club*, a novel first issued in twenty monthly parts (1836–37).

Chapter Seven

"What Restless Creatures We Are"

Further Peregrinations

In August 1841 Corinna and Ellen, their husbands preoccupied by the war, journeyed to St. Augustine. Presumably the move was intended to distance them from hostilities in the interior. Ellen's pregnancy undoubtedly was also a primary consideration in the move.[1] In a letter fragment from St. Augustine, Corinna told Mannevillette that they hoped to remain there at least through the next spring because "it is more healthy here than in the Interior"; she also asked him to buy shoes and "Parissian finery" for her and Ellen when he returned to Paris from Venice.

By June 1841 the army in Florida had a new commander. Col. William Jenkins Worth took charge of operations against the Seminoles and devised tactics calculated to bring the war to a close. Worth understood that one way to speed the removal of the Seminoles was to find a way to encourage settlers to return to their homes, and even to establish new settlements. Along this line the *St. Augustine News* reported on July 2, 1841, that "Col. Worth . . . with a view to encourage the settlement of the country, has asked authority from Washington that rations be allowed to all such of the inhabitants as shall return to their abandoned households and also that both the pay and rations of soldiers of the Army may be allowed to all such persons as shall now step forward and make new settlements—at least for one year." Thus, Maj. De Lafayette Wilcox had "commenced a tour along the border settlements extending from the Atlantic to the gulf for the purpose of encouraging the citizens to return to their abandoned homes and also for the purpose of enrolling the names of those who may choose to avail themselves of this beneficent provision of the government." Finally, the report continued, the purpose is to "encourage the occupancy of the country by hardy, fearless pioneers, to whom protection will

---

1. Corinna Aldrich and Ellen Anderson to Mannevillette Brown, September 3, 1841, transcription in collection of James M. Denham.

be afforded by the Army, as far as practical." Worth's policy netted positive results. By October local newspapers reported seven new settlements established in areas previously unoccupied. (Worth's plan was actually a precursor to the Armed Occupation Act discussed below.)[2]

During August and September, while Ellen endured her first pregnancy in St. Augustine, James and his unit continued their operations against the Seminoles. His efforts that summer earned him a recommendation for promotion to brevet captain from Colonel Worth, who recognized his "great cleverness which resulted in the capture of a party of the enemy"; Worth's report noted that Anderson was "a young officer of high promise and merit."[3] James kept Ellen informed of camp and war news as well as he could. In his August 27 letter he explained that Chief Tiger Tail seemed to be ready to meet with Colonel Worth to discuss the Indians' removal from Tampa to western territories. He asked Ellen to urge George to forget about attempting to get the sutlership from Colonel Worth.[4]

On September 3, James proudly sent to Ellen an extract from a letter of commendation from Colonel Worth to Colonel Riley praising James for his recent actions against the Indians. Indeed, that fall the newspapers had taken notice of the young officer.[5] On September 11 the *Savannah Georgian* reported that "Anderson, McKinstry, and Davidson, young officers who have for several years, in this harassed territory, panted for the soldier's reward, and in

---

2. *St. Augustine News,* July 2, 9, 1841; April 2, 1842. For the listing and description of the settlements, see *St. Augustine News,* October 8, 1841, and *St. Augustine Florida Herald and Southern Democrat,* October 8, 1841. Likewise the *Washington National Intelligencer* reported on August 31, 1841, that Wilcox had enrolled 298 settlers to establish new settlements and reestablish old ones: "These armed settlements are chiefly in a section of the country heretofore much annoyed by Indian depredations, and may be expected to exert the happiest influence in repressing the inroads of the enemy and giving confidence to the border settlers" (*Washington National Intelligencer* as quoted in *Army and Navy Chronicle,* September 2, 1841, p. 275). On Worth's plan, also see Canter Brown Jr., *Tampa before the Civil War* (Tampa, Fla.: University of Tampa Press, 1999), 74.

3. Worth's recommendation on James's brevet captaincy was confirmed on March 6, 1843. See names of officers of the U.S. Army recommended for brevets by Brig. Gen. W. J. Worth, commanding the forces in Florida, April 25, 1842, in Sprague, *Origins, Progress, and Conclusion of the Florida War,* 554.

4. A. H. Cole was appointed sutler at Palatka (*St. Augustine Florida Herald and Southern Democrat,* September 24, 1841).

5. The letter dated August 30, 1841, was published in *Army and Navy Chronicle,* September 23, 1841, p. 300.

common with numbers of brave officers and men, have been unjustly taunted by imbecile writers, as inactive and hugging inglorious ease, have at length been blessed with an opportunity of exhibiting their attachment to country— their devotion to her cause."[6]

Because James feared that it would be some time before he and Ellen could again live together, he informed her that he was sending to her "the carpet, bureau and a few other" items "by the next opportunity." The army was still engaged in much Indian activity; for instance, Colonel Worth, he said, "has just captured an important chief near Camp Ogden named Has-pi-tar-ke and 15 of his prime warriors, 3 of which are sub-chiefs. His whole band, numbering upwards of 300, are to come in at Fort Deynand [Denaud] on the 11th."[7]

Sometime in October or November, James was transferred to Palatka, Colonel Riley's new headquarters. Ellen gave birth to their first child, Edward Willoughby Anderson, on November 11 in St. Augustine.

[James Anderson to Ellen Anderson]

Pilatka [to St. Augustine]
Saturday, December 4th [1841]

Dearest Ell,

I arrived here last night about sundown and found matters pretty much as I expected. Col Riley is absent & will probably be back much sooner than I expected—he is expected in 12 or 14 days. As soon as he arrives I shall know what quarters I am to have, at present we are all helter-skelter here. Mrs. [Arabella Israel] Riley is here with her family & Mrs. Penrose is staying with her— Lt. Penrose at present commanding the Company at this place. Whether he is to remain here I know not after the Colonel arrives. I found a Yankee Sloop here & have purchased a barrel of potatoes, a barrel of turnips, ¼ Barrel Buckwheat & ½ a barrel of Onions & if you say so, I can write on to Savannah at once and get all our groceries from that place. Let me know at any rate what you want. I intend to look over what cooking utensils I have here & let you know. What do you suppose I gave for my purchase with the Yankee—I gave $3 for potatoes, $3 for turnips, $1½ for onions, & $2½ for Buckwheat. Charles is here

6. *Savannah Georgian,* September 11, 1841; *Army and Navy Chronicle,* September 23, 1841, p. 299.

7. James Anderson to Ellen Anderson, September 3, 1841, Anderson-Brown Papers, USMA. On the seizure, see also Mahon, *History of the Second Seminole War,* 302; and Brown, *Florida's Peace River Frontier,* 57.

with my goods & Chattels; I shall send him over to Augustine before very long having no use for him at present.[8] I'll keep him out of Corinna's way perhaps, until the Doctor comes back.

It looks quite cheerful here & I am in hopes to be bettered by the change. Maj. [Joseph] Plympton has returned in good health—he is now at Fort Russell. Mrs. [Mary] Wessells was 3 days dying & insensible during the whole time.[9] Lt. W. after all was not prepared for her death & grieves much. Do you remember young Wessells who was at Fort King—It has just leaked out that he has been married 3 years without the knowledge even of his brother with whom he has been living. Mrs. Riley looks very well. I breakfasted there this morning. The Col took charge of all my property & has it locked up in a small room in his house so I suppose it is all safe—however I shall have a reckoning with Charles in a day or two. Remember me to Corinna and kiss the baby for me.

Yours,
Willo

[James Anderson to Ellen Anderson]

Pilatka [to St. Augustine]
December 5th [1841]

Dearest

I am evidently getting better at this place, having taken no medicine since I left Augustine & the weather being now quite cold. I feel very well. I would have given much to have commenced my convalescence 2 or 3 weeks ago in Augustine. I should at any rate not have been quite such a bore as I was & consequently disagreeable to every body. But it could not be helped. Even now I feel that the evil spirit hovers over me, converting many things that are pleasant into sources of discomfort & causing me to rail with bitterness at the weaknesses & faults of poor human nature. I think I am getting the better of the pain I experienced so long in my bowels. I have not had it, although I have found myself uncovered several cold mornings. Indeed I think I may safely say, I am on the mend.

I forgot Ell, that in a letter I debarred Col. Riley transferring Mr. Penrose to Co. D. by saying that I would return to D company. I do not know what the Col. will do. Penrose has applied to Washington for the transfer. I presume the

---

8. Charles was a slave.

9. On November 25, 1841, the *Army and Navy Chronicle*, p. 375, reported that Mary Wessells died at Fort King of consumption on November 16: "The death of this lovely woman . . . has created a void in the circle of her friends not easily filled."

Col. is still anxious I should remain with him by his not acting & bringing all my truck to this place—Would you believe it? Mrs. Riley's twins are both dead—they died at Fort King about the time Mrs. Wessells did. They were fine healthy children but necessarily starved to death on acct. of the condition of Mrs. Riley. Mrs. Riley is as I am told suffering great torments now—if so, she bears it like a martyr.[10] Mrs. Kinstry lost her child about the same time—as I understand the matter, the birth was premature & the child was what is called by the nurses a blue baby, having an affection of the heart.

This is the 3rd letter I have written & not a word have I had from you. I will not however think that you are unwell. I suppose <u>Mr. Ned</u> won't give you much time to do anything but attend to him. By this time, you ought to be quite strong & able to ride out occasionally. I wish I had a fine barouche[11] & fancy horses—they should be at your service. I like the atmosphere here on the river. Pilatka has been healthy during the Summer & I would not care If I were stationed here during the rest of my Florida service. I have half a mind to jump on board a steamboat & go to Savannah in order to arrange matters for our supply this winter—but as there is perhaps some doubt, some little doubt about my staying here, which will be cleared up as soon as cold returns, I shall wait a while. . . . Willo

James sent Ellen one long, final letter of the year, written December 23 and 25 and covering many topics. Of special importance was his news that he expected to "be in Augustine by the 4th or 5th of next month"; he anticipated a transfer north soon to a yet undetermined destination because the war was winding down. Meanwhile, as the year came to a close, Corinna wrote one last letter to Mannevillette updating the family's activities.

[Corinna Aldrich to Mannevillette Brown]

St. Augustine [to Paris]
December 5th, 1841

My very Dear Brother—I wrote you about three weeks since informing you that you were likely to become an uncle. It is even so. On the 12th was born a son & heir to your sister Nell . . . we calculated entirely on a gal—we are puzzled to name the boy. Ell talks of calling him for my old man. I think "Frogy"

---

10. Samuel Israel Riley died on November 15, and his twin brother, William Davenport, died two days later (*Army and Navy Chronicle,* November 25, 1841, p. 375, and December 9, 1841, p. 392).

11. A four-wheeled carriage with a seat out front for the driver, facing seats for two couples, and a calash [folding top] for the backseat.

would be a good name for him. Don't you want to peep at him—I would you could pop in this afternoon. Ell & I are keeping house by ourselves at this time—Edward & George having gone to Newnansville to settle their business & Mr. Anderson to his Post in Palatka on the St. Johns to make arrangements for our removal there. Col. Riley's head quarters are to be there & Mr. Anderson is Adjutant of the Regiment. Of course his station is at head quarters always—which makes it pleasant as 'tis always the most agreeable location. I shall remain with Ellen until Edward returns for me—that will probably be about the first of Jan. Edward & George after settling their affairs at New. are going to Middle Florida—to set up their Trades? You see I am doomed to be a citizen of the world. . . . However Ell & I do not object—we had as lief travel as sit still—especially as change is agreeable after a few months sojourn in a place like this. What restless creatures we are—Did I tell you aunt Ann is gone to N. with Edward to keep their house in my absence. . . .

One Dr. [William] Van Burin [Buren][12] is stationed at this post having been educated in France—He reminded me of some of your letters in conversation. He is a nephew of the ex-President & very agreeable & good looking & obliging notwithstanding his removal here—ousted Edward—He however intended to give up his contract—preferring the Interior for practice—He says he can make more there in a day than here in a month—besides the excitement of riding about so much to be preferred to the monotony of city practice. E. has had much encouragement to stay here—but I cannot advise him to do so—although for society &c 'tis rather to be [chosen] I am in hopes to get settled down somewhere or somehow ere you come home. . . .

Aunt Hall is still on her plantation—she sticks to her grove—& will die on it I suspect—both she & Ann are much broken—Ann the most. . . . By the way did I tell you the Dr. had bought me a new carriage, & a fine pair of horses—gave for the horses 450 dolls—this looks extravagant—but we must keep horses, & may as well keep good ones. . . . I would give you a description of Madison, the place of G & E's destination—but fear it may prove another Utopia for we seem doomed like the Jews to wander—and find an abiding place. I am in hopes, however that this time they will anchor on a surer foundation than before? & find a less <u>sickly</u> spot to inhabit—that there may not at least be that excuse to take up our bed & walk. . . .[13]

<hr>

12. William Van Buren joined the army as assistant surgeon on June 15, 1840, and resigned December 31, 1845 (William H. Powell, ed., *List of Officers of the Army of the United States from 1779–1900* [New York: L. R. Hamersly and Company, 1900], 642).

13. See Mark 2:9 and John 5:8–13.

[Ellen Anderson to James Anderson]

St. Augustine [to Palatka]
January 2, 1842

My Dear Will,

I am ashamed and sorry that you have not had a letter from me for so long, but indeed I am not without excuse. In the first place I missed the express twice and then was told there was no regular day for it. Had I known this first I would not have missed it. Do pray don't think hard of my not writing. My mind and my time have been so occupied with my infant that I found I was wearing myself out. So now I behave more sensible, or at least I intend to. I wrote you one letter which I did not send. It was full of grievances and to day I feel in so much better spirits that I have torn the other up. I went to an eggnog party last evening at Mrs. Andrews.[14] It was very pleasant. I feel quite emancipated nowadays. Every one encourages me that your health has improved but I wish to judge for myself. I count the days for you to come. You ought to be able to stay a day or two when you come. There be lots of parties. I have engaged a wet nurse to come and take care of Master Will when I choose to dissipate. As for my divine Lucy I found she was too fond of a dram, which I suspected was all the illness she suffered under. This of course destroyed my confidence in her and was the reason of my confining myself so closely to the infant, but now I have got rid of her and have one in her place who is a first rate servant. At least thus far I have had no reason to distrust her. She was very highly recommended, also. Mrs. [Hanna B.] Jenks [Jenckes][15] has a good plain cook, washer, and ironer that I can have. I wish to make enquiries about her however before I engage her. Her mistress recommends her highly, but I don't like her countenance. I should have mentioned that the woman I have with me cannot be hired out of the place. I have been requested to permit Master Will to be exhibited in a <u>tableau vivant</u>[16] Mrs. Judge [Isaac] Bronson[17] at a party

14. Mrs. Andrews was likely the wife of Christopher Andrews of St. Augustine (Carter, *Territorial Papers of the United States,* 26:138.

15. Mrs. Hanna B. Jenckes, a native of Rhode Island, was the wife of Edwin T. Jenckes, a commissioner of the Bank of the Southern Life Insurance & Trust Company (Carter, *Territorial Papers of the United States,* 26:34; U.S. Manuscript Census, Population (1850), for St. Johns County, Florida, p. 216.

16. "'Living picture'; a representation of a personage, character, scene, incident, etc., or of a well-known painting or statue, by one person or a group of persons in suitable costumes and attitudes, silent and motionless" (*OED*).

17. Sophronia Bronson and her two daughters Gertrude and Emma moved to Florida in 1840 when her husband was appointed superior judge of the Eastern Judicial District

which is to be at Mrs. Judge [Joseph] Smith's[18] next week. The idea amused me a great deal. I think you ought to be present. His hair and eyes have not changed their colour. The one being still a singular blue, the other very light.

About your enquiry for Capt. [Crogham] Ker.[19] I have Mrs. Bronson's authority for saying that Miss [Louisa] Hernandez is very much attached to him, and [it is] her opinion that there would be no difficulty in the gentleman's way on the part of any member of the family. I applyed [*sic*] to her because I see more of her and think she is better informed than Miss Smith. But I will talk to Miss S. about the Hernandezes and see what she appears to know. I had heard that Gen. [Joseph] Hernandez[20] was the difficulty in Capt. Ker's way, but cannot give my authority. Mrs. Bronson seemed quite pleased when I told her why I had enquired about the matter and begged me to say from her that

---

of Florida by President Martin Van Buren. Isaac Bronson was born in Waterbury, Connecticut, but spent most of his life in Jefferson County, New York. Bronson practiced law and was elected to Congress in 1836 as a Democrat. Bronson served as judge of the Eastern Judicial District until President James K. Polk appointed him U.S. district judge in 1846. Relocating to Palatka soon thereafter, Bronson remained in this post until his death in 1855. See Manley, Brown, and Rise, *Supreme Court of Florida,* 85–88; Denham, *"Rogue's Paradise,"* 28, 30, 34; James M. Denham, "From a Territorial to a Statehood Judiciary: Florida's Antebellum Courts and Judges," *Florida Historical Quarterly* 73 (April 1995): 451–52.

18. Frances "Fanny" Marion Kirby married Joseph Lee Smith in Hartford, Connecticut, in 1807. A Yale graduate and product of Tapping Reeves's famous Litchfield Academy, Joseph Smith was appointed superior judge of the Eastern District of Florida by President James Monroe in 1822. A man of great talents but also of great passions, Smith was continually plagued by controversy. Smith served as judge of the Eastern Judicial District until 1832 when he was replaced by Robert Raymond Reid. Practicing law in St. Augustine until his death in 1846, Smith fathered four children including future Confederate general Edmund Kirby Smith. See Manley, Brown, and Rise, *Supreme Court of Florida,* 25–30; Denham, *"Rogue's Paradise,"* 28, 30–31.

19. Crogham Ker traveled to Florida in 1836 as captain in the Louisianna Volunteers. He mustered into the U.S. Army soon thereafter as a second lieutenant of the 2nd Dragoons. He was promoted to captain in March 1840 and resigned from the army in 1851. See Heitman, *Historical Register,* 1:593.

20. Gen. Joseph Hernandez commanded the Militia of East Florida. A wealthy Creole and plantation owner, Hernandez commanded the party that captured Osceola under a flag of truce in 1837. He also served as Florida's first territorial delegate from 1823 to 1824. Hernandez ran unsuccessfully as a Whig for the Florida Territorial Senate in 1845 and thereupon moved to Cuba. He died there in 1857. See Mahon, *History of the Second Seminole War,* 99, 214–15.

Judge Isaac Bronson, his wife Sophronia, and their daughters Gertrude and Emma of New York were newcomers to Florida from New York when they first met Ellen and Corinna in 1842 in St. Augustine. St. Augustine Historical Society.

St. Augustine Plaza, circa 1840s, painting by George Harvey. Ellen and Corinna attended the Trinity Parish Episcopal Church on the right. The Catholic Parish Church is on the left. St. Augustine Historical Society.

Louisa Hernandez was unchanged. I give her words in <u>her way</u>. The damsel I find is quite in demand among the would-be-married.

Corine had a letter from Edward to day, also we had one from George last mail. They appear to be in good spirits. Edward is waiting for the paymaster, poor fellow, and the paymaster is here. However he writes that he has been able to make some collections. The paymasters will not go to Newnansville until Capt. [Samuel P.] Hintzleman [Heintzelman][21] first comes here. Such are their instructions. When he will come remains to be seen. Corine is not well at all. Lewis Aldrich [Edward's brother] paid us a visit or rather a visitation. He was very sick and vomited all night and Corine was up and attending to him and took abed in consequence. He is a dreadful stupid man, and so vain that it is quite ridiculous to think of it. My health is excellent and so is the baby's. Every one congratulates me on looking so well. I feel so if I could wait for the fourth of January although it is so near. Come along honey. I can talk better than write. Come and come, well and philosophical. . . . Good bye, ever your own Ell.

From January through April, Lt. Col. Bennet Riley's Second Infantry pursued Halleck Tustenuggee's band throughout the upper St. Johns River area. By this time Riley and his men had gained some manner of fame for their exploits and for their ability to endure hardships in the field. One newspaper noted that "Riley can sleep in the swamp like an alligator," while later adding, "we like the Colonel's appearance—he has the go-ahead look about him."[22] Finally, in May, Halleck Tustenuggee and eighty of his people surrendered, and that same month Anderson's Second Infantry received orders to leave Florida.[23]

---

21. Samuel P. Heintzelman, a native of Pennsylvania, graduated from West Point in 1826. Appointed first lieutenant of the Second Infantry in 1833, Heintzelman moved to Florida in 1835 and served as quartermaster until leaving for Columbus, Georgia, in 1837. He returned to Florida in 1838, serving there until 1842. Heintzelman fought with distinction during the Mexican War and served on garrison duty in California during the 1850s. Serving in the Army of the Potomac, Heintzelman achieved the rank of general and fought in nearly every important battle in the eastern theater during the Civil War. See Cullum, *Biographical Register,* 1:295–96; and Heitman, *Historical Register,* 1:521.

22. *St. Augustine Florida Herald and Southern Democrat,* December 24, 1841; January 7, 1842.

23. Ibid., May 6, 1842. For the Second Infantry's actions against the Indians from January to May, see ibid., February 4, 25, April 29, 1842; *Savannah Georgian* as quoted in *Army and Navy Chronicle,* December 30, 1841, p. 411; January 29, 1842, p. 27; February 12, 1842, p. 59; March 19, 1842, p. 140; May 21, 1842, p. 281.

As James Anderson's service in the Second Seminole War was winding down, he and Ellen were preparing to leave Florida in spring 1842 for his next posting. George settled down in Newnansville, though exactly when is not clear. On June 12, 1841, he wrote to Mannevillette in Europe regarding the settling of Charles's estate. On November 21, 1841, George wrote to Ellen from Charleston, noting that he had been acquiring goods. Back in Newnansville soon after the first of the year, George bemoaned the need for a good paper currency; Congress, he hoped, would adopt better currency. In his view success against the Seminoles would never be achieved unless the Floridians themselves took the field in sufficient numbers to defeat the foe. The U.S. Army in Florida was, in his view, "3,000 good for nothing, drunken scapegoats, the scourings of other countries. An army is, or ought to be, filled with natives. One thousand of them would do more service than the above Brandy-drinking sons of guns."[24]

General Worth's relentless attacks pushed the Seminoles deeper and deeper into the peninsula. Campaigning right through the summer months, Worth kept the pressure on until many Indians, including Coacoochee, Tiger Tail, and Halleck Tustenuggee agreed to emigrate west. Simultaneously Congress passed the Armed Occupation Act, legislation calculated to garrison the frontier with settlers on what had been Indian lands south of the Alachua County line. Introduced by Sen. Thomas Hart Benton of Missouri, the act provided that any head of household or single male could claim a 160-acre tract, build a cabin, occupy it, cultivate at least five acres, and after five years secure title to the land. A federal land office was established in Newnansville, and almost 950 claims were issued. The town boomed as new settlers poured in.[25]

Remaining tribesmen fled to the lower Peace River and the Everglades. By spring of the next year Worth's aggressive tactics had resulted in all but a remnant of the Indians being either killed or removed from the territory. Worth declared the war over in August 1842. Only roughly three hundred or so Indians were allowed to remain on a small reservation in the lower peninsula.[26]

24. George Brown to Mannevillette Brown, January 7, 1842, transcription in possession of James M. Denham.

25. On the Armed Occupation Act, see Schafer, " U.S. Territory and State," 217–18; James W. Covington, "The Armed Occupation Act of 1842," *Florida Historical Quarterly* 40 (July 1961): 41–52; Sidney Walter Martin, *Florida during Territorial Days,* 93–96; Brown, *Tampa before the Civil War,* 84–87; Brown, *Florida's Peace River Frontier,* 65–68; and Tebeau, *History of Florida,* 149.

26. On this phase of the Second Seminole War, see Mahon, *History of the Second Seminole War,* 274–320; Covington, *Seminoles of Florida,* 96–109; Mahon and Weisman, "Florida's

By spring of 1842 George and Edward had opened a store in Newnansville. With Edward's financial assistance George was well on his way toward establishing a business presence in Newnansville. Writing Edward, who was investigating medical opportunities in Macon and Albany, Georgia, George kept him abreast of his business activities and of the latest news in Newnansville. Some of Edward's former patients missed him: one complained of worms, another was "uneasy about his 'yard' [penis], but has to grin & bear it." Another had the bolts. Eleven days later George mentioned that he had attended the superior court and noted that Joseph Smith and John L. Doggett had asked about Edward. He also had witnessed a murder trial in which George Mackay had made a speech in favor of the accused, "making a damned ass of himself," and "at the same time in a lame contemptible affair as I ever heard, one that did more injury to the poor criminal than good. This man and another," he continued, "was sentenced to hang."[27]

Corinna returned to Newnansville in February 1842, staying apparently until September, when she temporarily rejoined Ellen in New York. Before she left Florida, however, Corinna wrote several letters to Mannevillette in Paris.

[Corinna Aldrich to Mannevillette Brown]

Newnansville [to Paris]

Feb 12th, 1842

My very dear Brother—I have not heard from you in several weeks which makes me quite uneasy. I hope the fault lies with the mail contractors. Since my last you perceive we have returned to this detestable city of the woods—(I think I have not written you since our return—as G told me he had written the week we arrived & 'tis but one month since we left St. Augustine—) We do not think of remaining here & I have only come to settle with this business—I hope to leave for middle Florida in about three or four weeks at farthest from this.

We left Ellen & Mr. Anderson at Palatka. Mr. A's health—however—is somewhat impaired & he has applied for leave and will no doubt obtain it. If

---

Seminole and Miccosukee Peoples," 196–98; Prucha, *Sword of the Republic,* 297–303; Edward S. Wallace, *General William Jenkins Worth: Monterey's Forgotten Hero* (Dallas: Southern Methodist University Press, 1953), 51–55; Sprague, *Origins, Progress, and Conclusion of the Florida War,* 286–493; and Tebeau, *History of Florida,* 168.

27. George Brown to Edward Aldrich, April 13, 24, May 7, June 2, 1842, Anderson-Brown Papers, USMA. Chandler Hastings and James Greer were hanged on June 2, 1842. See Denham, *"Rogue's Paradise,"* 209.

so—they will get in a visit before we move & then go North to visit Mr. A's relations in Virginia. If they start out not too early, E & I will accompany them. I hope you will accompany them—I hope you will meet us & return with us. I think you can do a fine <u>business</u> in <u>your</u> way—South—particularly in Florida —but you must not venture here before Frost. My health is suffering much from this climate & 'tis one great reason for our contemplated move. Another summer in East Florida would use me up. George's health is good—he has gone to Charleston—we expect him back next week. He & Edward will immediately go west—to arrange for a move. Do you get news papers? I suppose you have heard . . . what a row old John Quincy Adams has tricked up in Congress with his abolitionist petitions & his petition of some crack brained Yankees to secede from the union or rather to divide the northern & southern states. It was proposed to expel the old ninny for insulting the House—how it will end I don't know. I suppose as all such affairs do, in smoke—but he ought to be <u>turned</u> out. He is crazy—no doubt.[28] 'Tis near time for Congress to adjourn & nothing is yet done to set the currency to rights—or any thing else. Probably the session will be polarized.

Ed & I will miss the city when we go North. E. has some considerable accts—yet to collect—hurt arm is still with me. Aunt Hall with Ellen—both well & in fine spirits. Ell writes me the baby grows very fast & rapidly increases in knowledge of good & evil. Don't you want to see your nephew? If you want to see him & us half as much as we do you, you will not stay away much longer. Young [Charles] Cushing of Portsmouth—grandson of old Jacob Heap is here—intending to practice law—"What a fall <u>is</u> <u>this</u> my countryman"—He is out of health however—& 'tis believed Florida can restore a lost limb— by some. Let them come & try it.—toes & elbows may sprout but it will be out of old shoes & jackets! Unless <u>the</u> <u>war</u> <u>is</u> <u>ended</u>—East Florida is now done for fortunes—for health—& for happiness. Even should the war end—it will be

---

28. This is a reference to Adams's continued opposition to the "gag rule" in the House of Representatives that prevented the reading of antislavery petitions. Corinna refers here to an incident that occurred in January 1842 in which Adams offered a petition to Congress from citizens of Haverhill, Massachusetts, that called for a peaceful dissolution of the Union. Some members called for Adams's censure, but it was not accomplished. See Charles M. Wiltse, *John C. Calhoun, Sectionalist, 1840–1850* (New York: Russell and Russell, 1968), 70; William W. Freehling, *The Road to Disunion: Secessionists at Bay, 1776–1854* (New York: Oxford University Press, 1990), 350–52; and William Lee Miller, *Arguing about Slavery: The Great Battles in the United States Congress* (New York: Alfred A. Knopf, 1997), 429–44.

years before planters can get under way again. It is reported that 20,000 Germans are to be sent here by mule train. It would be a fine plan—but too good to be true.

We have been putting out some fruit trees around our domicile & about the lot. They look very pretty—but we must leave them & I don't much regret it—should matters improve here—we can at any time return. If not—it will be well we are off—in spite of trees & shrubbery.—we shall rent to a good tenant —& trust to luck for the rest. Edward is in his office—it joins the house. He says I must remember him & tell you anything so you would come & see us. Aunt Ann is reading the paper by the fire—the negroes are getting dinner & playing in the yard as is usual on Sunday—it being a kind of holiday with them. Are you aware that all our additions are separated buildings from the house?—& Do you know that we have had quite an old jacketless winter—scarcely a cold day. Indeed 'tis too warm most of the time for any fire, & doors & windows all open. Orange trees will soon recruit with a few such winters.

Yesterday Dr, Aunt Ann & I had a long ride <u>a cheval</u>. It was oppressive until we got in the woods. You will be surprised perhaps that we venture—we go in protected places I assure you. Have you heard the Indians have been at Mandarin—I think I wrote you from St. A. Well, again they have been there, & been pursued—Two soldiers killed on our side,—One Indian killed & one run down & taken out of 18 or 20.[29] Thus it ever is—they get the better of all engagements and thus I fear it will ever be—Col Worth—has removed his head quarters from Tampa to Palatka—why—I don't know. Mr. Cushing admired your paintings of the runaway horse & the portrait of Add [Adelaide]. I have them both. I have also two <u>old</u> paintings for you—of the weeping & laughing phylosophers—they are said to be very fine—come & get them. Ann says I must give her love & tell you she will be too old to see you—if you don't make haste. I wish you would take a likeness of yourself and send it to me.

One Mr. George Mackay is here practicing law—he says he was introduced to you in N.Y. [H]e has the exterior of a gent—but his character is after the Burrett[30] order—whether pretty or not—I cant say. He and his brother keep

---

29. Corinna is referring here to the attack of Halleck Tustenuggee's band of twenty warriors on Mandarin in late December 1841. The "band murdered four people and burned two buildings." See Mahon, *History of the Second Seminole War*, 305; Sprague, *Origins, Progress, and Conclusion of the Florida War*, 400; and "Mandarin Massacre," *St. Augustine Florida Herald and Southern Democrat*, December 31, 1841. See also *St. Augustine Florida Herald and Southern Democrat*, January 7, 1842; *St. Augustine News*, December 25, 1841; and *Savannah Georgian* as quoted in *Army and Navy Chronicle*, December 30, 1841, p. 411.

30. This is a reference to Samuel L. Burritt, a Duval County lawyer, judge, and legislator.

bachelor's hall.[31] . . . I am in hopes to be pleasantly quartered in middle Florida Deo Volente by the time you get here. God speed you & bless you is the prayer of your fond sis, C.

[Corinna Aldrich to Mannevillette Brown]

Newnansville [to Paris]

March 13th 1842

Dear Brother—Your very kind favour in reply to Elle's & mine epistle from St A is very welcome. I am glad to hear your thumb is not seriously injured. I have felt very uneasy about it. In regard to the articles you may have purchased for us—dear—whatever the amount I will as soon as possible remit you—but if you have not gone over one hundred dollars—that is fifty on account of each—do not exceed that amount. When we wrote—we had no idea but that <u>Uncle Sam</u> would promptly pay his debts—but as yet he has been very delinquent. Edward has much due him & will in the course of five or six weeks go to Washington & if possible affect a settlement. Still he may not be able to and in such case it would be impossible for me to remit you more that the above sum. If you have not done so, do not buy shoes or gloves—we can get such articles here or any where—& as our funds are small we wish you to lay them out in the best articles or such as we could not afford here—say Valencia[32] & Brussels[33]

31. Corinna is referring to George and Captain John Mackay, natives of Georgia. George supplemented his legal practice as deputy surveyor. See Carter, *Territorial Papers,* 26:1025. John Mackay graduated from West Point in 1829, joining the topographical engineers soon thereafter. Serving in Georgia, Alabama, and Louisiana before traveling to Florida with the Second Artillery in 1837, Mackay was primarily employed constructing maps and building roads in Florida from 1839 to 1843. His most significant contribution was the supervising, along with J. R. Blake, of the "Map of the Seat of War in Florida Compiled by Order of Brig. Gen. Z. Taylor, Principally from the Surveys and Reconnaissance of the Officers of the U.S. Army, Head Quarters of the Army of the South, Tampa Bay, Florida, 1839." The map also acknowledged the assistance of James W. Anderson and several other officers who provided "important information" in the "compilation of this map." Extensive comments on the map are in *Army and Navy Chronicle,* August 8, 1839, pp. 88–89. Later he conducted surveys of the Choctawhatchie and Holmes Rivers in West Florida. He died in Savannah in 1848. See Cullum, *Biographical Register,* 1:341; and Heitman, *Historical Register,* 1:670.

32. "A mixed fabric mainly employed for waistcoats, having a wool weft with a warp of silk, silk and cotton, or linen, and usually striped" (*OED*).

33. "A costly kind of pillow lace made in Brussels and its neighbourhood, noted for the thickness and evenness of its texture and the delicate accuracy of its forms" (*OED*).

laces—French capes & collars wraught[34] work—and get us each enough black silk velvet—jet black velvet for dresses—say 15 yds each—that is, 30 yards—and if your money holds out yet—30 yards of jet black satin—but by no means [spend more than] a hundred dollars—for fear we should not be able to remit you as soon as you may need it. If you can afford to lay out any for us & wait until the summer—I can then pay you easily—but if you will need it as soon or before you reach home—don't expend over one hundred. You understand me—dear. It is not that we would not remit you several hundred—but that we cannot—you know not how scarce money is. I am in hopes it will be more plenty another season.

We are thinking about going west. I don't mean far—but west from this—to some of the new counties—where every thing is more plenty & health better. Ed & I will start on an exploring expedition in the course of two weeks—on the way, will if possible sell our carriage & horses to raise the wherewith to go to Washington—this may seem strange but is impossible to raise the wind any other way. E cannot collect here although he has much due him—because Uncle Sam owes every body as well as him—consequently no business can go on until the great wheel is started at Washington. I hope that may soon be. E will move it—one spoke—if it is to rotate at all. We would not part with our horses—but we expect to spend the summer or part of it north—& we don't care to keep them in our absence—besides the great expense—they would be neglected.

Ell is now at Palatka, Mr A's station—and the headquarters of the army. They, (she & mr A) will spend the summer North. I shall go & stay with them some time. In the Fall if we live they will have to come & stay with me. Edward says he hopes to meet you & bring you back with us—I hope so—no doubt you could do well South—any where.

You bet Ell's child is a girl—we have named it Edward Willoughby—for E & his father—so you've lost—the next will be named George Mannevillette—you must pay up the cash—I wrote Ell word you bet me. I sent your letter to her—in writing her again dear—don't speak of her eyes—she has been very nervous about them—but seems to have got over it—she has a cataract on one eye—but it is scarcely perceptible—she intends to have it taken off this summer. The baby is all daddy. I am afraid it will not look at all like our family. Aunt Hall is staying with Ell now—she is such a great nurse Elle cant spare her to

---

34. Obsolete spelling of *wrought*. Used as an adjective, *wrought*, when referring to "textile materials, especially silk," means "manufactured; spun" or "decorated or ornamented, as with needlework; elaborated, embellished, embroidered" (*OED*).

pay me a visit. Ann and G are with me—both well. Indeed—we are all in good health. I hope you are ditto. I long for you to get home—dear—& E is anxious to see you too—we all are—so hasten along. Don't push yourself to the <u>least</u> inconvenience about the articles for us. . . . because we can better do without the <u>duds</u> than you without the needful. . . . Ell writes in love & kindest wishes & prayers for your safe return—you must spend the first six weeks with me— yours ever C

[Corinna Aldrich to Mannevillette Brown]

Newnansville [to Paris]
March 27th, 1842

My Dear Brother,

I have seated myself to write you a farewell epistle from this delightful country—before another mail day I expect to be on my way to Georgia. Edward, as I told you—returned here for the purpose of settling up his business. He has, however, but partially succeeded. The delinquency of Uncle Sam has not only kept him out of funds due from that source—but has hung like [an] incubus[35] over his private affairs & prevented any thing like a final settlement. Most of his debtors have given him their notes—collectible when Uncle Sam "ponies up" & he can ask no more. I regret it in as much as I did hope to be able to send you two or three hundred to lay out in nick nacks for me—but I can't do it. Whatever you may have already expended on our account—that is Ell & I—I will remit you, so soon as you let me know the amount, because I know you want it, but unless you can wait until you return home to be [reimbursed], don't make any further purchase on our account. You may get the black velvet for dresses that I spoke of in my last & indeed any thing else you please—wraught capes & collars—laces & black satin &c. if you can wait to be paid until you come to see me. I shall no doubt by next summer or Fall be <u>flush</u> & able to pay interest. You understand me dear. It is not that we would not delight to have the articles, but we would rather never see such things than put you to a penny's inconvenience & so I must urge upon you not to expend a dollar more than you already have, unless you can wait until the Summer at least for a return. We most want jet black silk velvet drapes & wraught capes—next blacks satins & laces. I tell you which is most important—as you may be able to get some of the articles—if not all—shoes & gloves . . . won't keep in the south—neither [will] coloured velvets, silks, or satins—only jet black will wear at all. Enough of this.

---

35. "A person or thing that weighs upon and oppresses like a nightmare" (*OED*).

Don't bother your dear self, but come to see us, & if you have not a second coat we'll be so happy to see you we won't remark it!—Edward says you must visit us because he will secure you ample business. We are going to Thomasville [in] Thomas county Georgia—a pleasant, healthy town in the Western part of Georgia—and offers great advantages to E—George will join us there next fall <u>Deo Volente</u>. He is obliged to remain here during the Spring & settle his business—he will also attend to E's. We you see are the <u>pioneers</u>. Hope we'll prove good ones this time. Mr. A's regiment will be ordered North this Spring. If so, I shall pay Nell[36] a visit in the Summer & she promises to return with me in the Fall. God grant we may all meet together. Once more, what a happy season it will be. Indeed I am so pleased with the prospect of getting out of this place, I can scarcely keep from jumping for joy & yet we have the best house & the prettiest lots in the town. I rent out the house & furniture until we get a house elsewhere. George & Aunt Ann board with the tenants.[37] They intend to take other boarders. [O]ur house is quite large & well calculated for such business in such a place. George will spend the Summer North & [in] the Fall will come with us. Mr. A's health is better—mine also, but we intend to go off in season & escape a return of the chills & fever. I am very happy dear that your throat is so much better. So be careful of it—Your nephew is daily improving in health & intelligence—his mother tells me—he seeks most diligently among his petticoats for his great toe & if not permitted to put it in his mouth—crys [*sic*] lustily—for toe! I have made him a little jockey cap & shall send it next week by Dr. A's brother—who is at present paying us a visit. . . . I am writing with a steel pen & 'tis strict indeed. Excuse errors. . . . You must address George here for the present. Ell at Palatka & me Thomasville—have E & G send love—adieu again—C.

[Corinna Aldrich to Mannevillette Brown]

Palatka [to Paris]
May 12th, 1842

My very dear Brother,

Your favour of the 3rd Feb. came to Palatka in the boat with your humble serv't. I had been travelling for several weeks, and I assure you I was not a little

---

36. Nickname for Ellen.

37. By this time George was well on his way to establishing his business in Newnansville. He, Edward Aldrich, and Edward's brother Louis were discussing joint ventures and consulting one another regarding business affairs. On May 7, 1842, he informed Edward that their supplies would be shipped via Port Leon, as the steamer *General Clinch*

gratified to meet with a letter from you, as well as to find Nell, and her <u>family</u> in fine health. In regard to your advice about sending the needful, Nan[38] & I have before written you. You are not aware of the difficulty of collecting <u>cash</u> in this country—no matter where—scarcity & depression pervades the Union. In travelling through Georgia & Carolina the last month, I have had an opp'y to judge of the state of our finances myself, and I know not whence relief is to come—our politicians are self interested and disordered in opinion—but one thing is certain—<u>something</u> must be done—or our country perish. In the course of two or three weeks, Mr. Anderson expects to be ordered North. Edward has sent me here to go with them and as well—for I am still afflicted with aches and ails—they tell me only change of climate can cure. . . .

The following fragment from Corinna to Mannevillette was written between January 22 and June 7, 1842.

. . . I shall return [to Florida] very early in the Fall in order to be prepared for a visit from Mr. & Mrs. Anderson & from my brother from Europe. I only hope G[eorge] & E[dward] will select a pretty place, & a healthy one. Aunt Hall is here—she <u>will</u> keep house for Ell. Don't choose to act like a visitor. She's an odd one—but she will take care of No 1 as long as she "breezes" as our negro Charles says. Ann I left with the tenants of our house at New—to secure the rent. She will board there until we get fixed elsewhere. Ellen expects to go to Detroit or Buffalo where, dear, you will find us, if you get to <u>America</u> before the first of Sept.—and God willing after then you will find us on our way South. I shall let you have the earliest information of my aboding place. Ell & I talk often of who shall have the first visit, but I tell her it must depend on circumstances, and I'll be content to be first or second so I am honoured at all.

Do you see what a fuss our good people at large have made about Boz— alias Mr. Charles Dickens. I think they make fools of themselves. He'll go home & give us another dish of Trollope.[39]

---

had broken her shaft. He also advised Edward to lease a good building with the idea of making a store of it.

38. Nickname for Ellen.

39. Frances Trollope (1780–1863) was an English author who traveled in America in 1830–32 and returned to England to publish her unflattering *Domestic Manners of the Americans* in 1832. She was the mother of novelist Anthony Trollope. Corinna's hunch about Dickens was right; America worshipfully welcomed him in 1842, but he too became disturbed by American manners and institutions, offending many Americans in his *American Notes* (1842). Dickens arrived in Boston on January 22, 1842. After touring most important American cities Dickens left America on June 7.

Do you know that the voters of the little state of R. Island have made a great fuss & agreeable to their charter—only he can vote, who has 150 dolls—it seems the <u>majority</u> had not that & each party have elected their own Governor—and are about to fight it out. The President has ordered a portion of the Army to keep the peace in case of civil feud. Where it will end, remaineth to be proved but I suppose like [nullification]—in words & smoke. It makes something to talk of, just now.[40] For my part, I long to get out of Florida. We are daily expecting the order and shall go directly to New York, then I said send all I can of the needful. If Government were not bankrupt we should be flush—but so it is—and we must bear it. . . .

On May 25, 1842, the Second Infantry departed Florida for its new posting at Buffalo, New York.[41] James and his family had arrived in Buffalo by August.[42] Corinna, Edward, and James's sister, Virginia, also journeyed north. Over the next several years Ellen and James remained in the North, except for one brief visit to Palatka. When Corinna wrote to Mannevillette on September 12, she had probably been there for at least two weeks since she said that she had already sent him two letters and was waiting for a reply; she noted that Edward planned to return to Newnansville.

> . . . Did I tell you my wayward lord had returned again to East Florida & he
> & George have concluded to try their fortunes another year in that delectable

40. Corinna is referring to the "Dorr Rebellion," involving a conflict over suffrage, with Thomas Dorr challenging the constituted authorities of Rhode Island over voting rights as prescribed in a new state constitution. Dorr led a revolt and was eventually arrested. See William G. McLoughlin, *Rhode Island: A Bicentennial History* (New York: Norton, 1978), 126–36; and Eric Foner and John A. Garraty, eds., *The Reader's Companion to American History* (Boston: Houghton Mifflin, 1991), 916.

41. *St. Augustine Florida Herald and Southern Democrat,* May 27, 1842.

42. Established in 1839 due to increasing tension along the U.S.-Canadian border, "Poinsett Barracks" first held troops in 1840. Located on the highest ground within the Buffalo city limits, it would be known as Buffalo Barracks. The post occupied one city block and housed over six hundred soldiers and officers with their wives and children. The post offered officers' wives excellent social opportunities, including frequent parties and balls. However, as relations improved with Canada, the need for the post diminished. By 1846 the post was abandoned, many buildings were torn down, and the officers' barracks was converted to a private residence. The structure survives today as the Wilcox Mansion, the Theodore Roosevelt Inaugural Historic Site. See *Theodore Roosevelt Inaugural National Historic Site* (Buffalo, N.Y.: Theodore Roosevelt Inaugural Site Foundation, 2000), 18–19; and Merton M. Wilner, *Niagara Frontier: A Narrative and Documentary History* (Chicago: S. J. Clarke, 1931), 378–79.

*Corinna Brown Aldrich,
circa 1840s, painting by
M. E. D. Brown. Courtesy
of Mannevillette Sullivan
and Jane and Raymond
Gill.*

Law Notice.

THE SUBSCRIBERS have formed a co-part-
nership in the profession of Law, and will practice in the several Superior Courts of the Eastern
District of Florida, to wit, in the counties of St
John's, Musquito, Duval, Nassau, Alachua. Hillsborough, and Columbia, and in the COUNTY COURTS,
of St. John's, Alachua, and Columbia. Letters or
business should be directed to Wm A Forward, St.
Augustine, or Louis Aldrich, Newnansville, or to
Forward and Aldrich, at either place. Business confided to either will receive the attention of both.

December 1st 1842.

WILLIAM A. FORWARD
LOUIS ALDRIDH.

N. B. F. & A. will also act as agents (for such as
may desire their services) in the purchasing and sel-
ing of lands in East Florida.

Law notice, Louis Aldrich and William A. Forward partnership. St. Augustine Florida
Herald and Southern Democrat, *January 9, 1843.*

place. The inducements, however, are greater than they have ever been before. The passage of the Hon. Mr. [Thomas Hart] Benton's bill for the armed occupation of Florida will no doubt settle up the country in a few years. Emigrants, they write me, are already thronging there from all the states—so that the roads are thronged with travellers, and the villages with strange faces. One excellent provision is that no person can hold the bounty of land 120 acres unless he builds a house upon it, and makes other improvements suitable for a white man to live in. By this means the mal will be kept out, and the country inhabited by respectable people and those who have something to begin with. The land is rich enough for such even to jump at the advantages offered. George seems quite delighted at the prospects held out to him. God grant him success—he will deserve it—for he is an upright, honest & industrious young man. I hope too, my dear Manne, there will be inducement sufficient for you to become one of us. I have no doubt of it. For I know of many wealthy & respectable families who are moving there now. Edward wrote me of 3 or 4 last week—that we know from middle Florida —and many also from Georgia. Indeed if half of expectation is realized, it will be one of the most desirable _states_ in the union. It will be a state very soon. Micanopy will be the seat of Government.[43] Ellen & Anderson are going out to spend the winter with me. It is a Heavenly climate in Winter. You must be sure to come to me, dear, as soon as you get to your native shore. Though rough the soil & rude the home, I am sure a warmer welcome cannot greet you elsewhere. I am expecting Edward every day—but shall not go south before the middle of October. . . .

Corinna remained in New York for the rest of 1842. In one undated fragment she urged Mannevillette to resist the many temptations to sin in Paris. She wrote from Buffalo to Mannevillette on October 24 that Edward was coming there to take her back south. Corinna expected to pass through New York City in December and hoped that Mannevillette could meet her there. Though she left a welcoming letter at the Howard House, noting that she was headed to

---

43. Since 1838, when Florida's constitutional convention met in St. Joseph, division of the territory was a major political issue. Generally those in East Florida favored division because they resented the fact that Middle Florida, because of its greater population and wealth, tended to dominate and direct political affairs in its own interests. As a corollary to this, many in East Florida opposed the admission of Florida as a state while a substantial majority in Middle Florida favored it. See Brown, *Ossian Bingley Hart*, 60–61; Dodd, *Florida Becomes a State*, 31–47, 63; Doherty, *Whigs of Florida*, 5–7; and Sidney Walter Martin, *Florida during Territorial Days*, 259–66.

Florida and that Ellen was in Buffalo, Mannevillette would not return to America for seven more years.[44]

Meanwhile, Edward's friends had put his name forward as a candidate for the legislative council. As the *St. Augustine News* reported on October 1, 1842, Alachua County Whigs had nominated Aldrich as a candidate for a senate seat once they learned that their first choice, Francis Sanchez, had decided, practically at the last minute, not to run. The journal spoke well of Edward, noting that it would use its "best efforts to effect his election, as we understand he is a good and TRUE DIVISION MAN." Edward's late entry in the race hurt his vote-getting potential. As one supporter noted, "because of his professional duties" and travel, Edward was unable to campaign in Columbia County or even to visit several settlements in his own county. Running last in a field of eight, Edward's bid for elective office was unsuccessful.[45] Nevertheless, Edward's brother Louis was well on his way to establishing himself in the area. In November he was admitted to practice law in the superior court for the Eastern District of Florida, and on December 1 he announced a law partnership with William A. Forward.[46]

The next year (1843) was one of little correspondence for the Brown-Aldrich-Anderson family. James and Ellen remained together in Buffalo where James served as regimental adjutant. Corinna, Edward, and George remained in Newnansville, but all traveled frequently that year, and though no letters survive from Ellen, one from George and some from Corinna reveal the family activities during that time. On February 2, 1843, George wrote from Savannah to Edward in Newnansville explaining that he had been detained in Savannah due to ship problems but that he would be back soon. Discussing various items that he had bought and shipped back to Newnansville for their store's stock, he expressed his gratitude in being able to leave town knowing that Edward could handle the business at home. A letter from Virginia Anderson to Ellen dated April 11, 1843, noted that Ellen was in St. Augustine with Corinna while Virginia was in Buffalo. The correspondence resumes in spring 1843.

44. Corinna Aldrich to Mannevillette Brown, October 24; November 12; December 12, 1842, Anderson-Brown Papers, USMA.

45. Old Alachua to the editor of the *News,* October 15, 1842, in *St. Augustine News,* October 22, 1842; *St. Augustine News,* October 29, 1842; *St. Augustine Florida Herald and Southern Democrat,* November 21, 1842.

46. *St. Augustine News,* December 19, 1842; *St. Augustine Florida Herald and Southern Democrat,* January 9, 1843; *Jacksonville (Florida) News,* October 1, 1847.

ST. AUGUSTINE:

Monday November 21, 1842.

"Principles and the People."

The Election

Counties and Precincts.	F. L. Dancy,	J. G. Cooper,	J. C. Pelot,	Gabriel Priest.	L. D. Hart,	J. M. Hanson.	William Cone,	E. S. Aldrich.
St. John's.								
St. Augustine,	149	146	148	147	123	138	117	124
Picolata,	2	3	3	2	3	5	2	3
Palatka,	25	25	25	25	6	6	6	6
North River,	5	6	6	6	0	0	0	0
Duval.								
Jacksonville,	40	45	38	45	89	84	77	74
Black Creek,	35	35	29	42	28	26	26	5
Mandarin,	32	38	32	33	26	32	30	31
Breward's,	19	24	16	19	3	1	0	0
St Johns Bar,	3	3	3	3	10	10	10	10
Alachua.								
Chucuchatta,	27	29	19	18	12	8	5	8
Homosassa,	1	17	10	8	4	5	15	5
Waccahoota,	6	23	13	19	14	6	16	0
Miconopy,	21	28	24	15	23	25	23	18
Fort Clark,	2	10	8	10	2	60	0	8
Newnansville,	45	62	62	48	38	25	19	54
Fort King,	11	11	8	11	4	4	5	6
Hatchet Creek,	3	2		6	7	3	3	
Ft. Fanning,	1	10	2	3	7		10	3
Charly Emathla	3	9	13	15	2	1	3	3
Anutteliga,					7	7	7	7
Columbia.								
Alligator,	36	76	60	50	55	39	17	
Carver's,	11	23	21	13	12	1		
Sapp's,	3	6	5	14	22	19	15	
Min'ral Springs	30	36	34	16	24	17	7	
Cone's	2	9	0		12	9	13	
Osteen's,	2	3	2	2	24	8	25	
Basin Sinks,	5	6	1	6			5	
Ellis's,	5	25	12	4	9	4	15	
New River,	19	27	17	2	37	10	20	2
Fort Call,	3	6	11	4	25	24	13	
Johnson's,	17	19	12	5	17	2	9	
Nassau.								
Court-House,	36	36	36	36	7	7	7	
Fernandina,	4	4	4	4	1	1	1	
Frink's,	8	23	?	8	15	15	19	
Brandy Branch,	6	25	5	2	23	23	23	
Kirkl'ds & K F	27	35	26	21	15		7	
Hillsborough.								
Tampa,	26	26	26	26				
Manatee					9	9	9	9
Mosquito.								
Enterprise.					21	21	21	
	669	919	733	684	739	595	582	383

"The election." St. Augustine Florida Herald and Southern Democrat, *November, 21, 1842.*

[Corinna Aldrich to Mannevillette Brown]

Newnansville [to Paris]

April 30, 1843

I have not written you, <u>mon cher frere</u>, for two or three mails passed, in consequence of being overrun with company. This may sound strange to you, coming from this isolated place, but the fact is—since the close of the war—or better cessation of hostilities, for there are still Indians in Florida, hundreds daily flock into the country to look up lands—to speculate on—& to take up those tracts offered by government—under the armed occupation law. There is no doubt—in a very few years this territory will be more thickly settled than any of the Southern states—& far more prosperous—owing to the richness of the land, and healthy sites for building—& dear, need I add, I look forward to the time when it will be advantageous for you to spend at least your winters with us. Fort King is already started as a town—should the territory be divided—that will be the seat of government. E has taken up 160 acres of beautiful land adjoining—said now to be worth 2,000 dollars—and George another of scarcely less value—under the new law. That is—Gov gives the land—provided we improve & live on it a certain period—4 years . . . we expect to remove there this Fall. I think it will be a better location than this—as there is already a larger population in that vicinity than about here. The election for delegate comes on to-morrow & it is hoped the present incumbent Mr [David] Levy—will be reelected—though a loco-foco.[47] Our folks are whigs—but give him the preference.

I am happy dearest, to hear you are at length engaged in business likely to be profitable. . . . E has not yet collected from any source but hopes to in fact as soon as the mustre rolls are sent from our dilatory officers in Washington—& if Levy is elected—he will no doubt get his funds from Uncle Sam. He intends to lay his claims before Congress—about three thousand is due him—& all to whom he mentioned the matter while there—advised him to adopt that course.

I do hope you will come down in the fall. I expect A & Ell to spend next winter with me—& I trust you will meet us then—We hope to be at our new

---

47. "Loco-foco" is a derogatory term for states' rights Democrats. See Michael F. Holt, *The Rise and Fall of the American Whig Party: Jacksonian Politics and the Onset of the Civil War* (New York: Oxford University Press, 1999), 109. This battle was particularly acute in Florida. See Thompson, *Jacksonian Democracy;* Doherty, *Whigs of Florida;* and James M. Denham, "The Read-Alston Duel and Politics in Territorial Florida," *Florida Historical Quarterly* 68 (April 1990): 427–46.

home—Fort King. There we shall have very pleasant & intelligent neighbors—Col [Gad] Humphreys[48] & family—Col [John M.] McIntosh[49] perhaps Gen [Duncan Lamont] Clinch—all their lands are near—so we can ride to see each other at any time & it will be very pleasant—& the villages will be but a walk for us—only for a hundred yards. I hope your health is good—mine is vastly improved—& Nell writes me word hers as well as A & the baby's is prime—Buddy runs about & talks very plain. I want to see the little scamp (he is very bright & full of mischief) but I shall not be able to go on this summer—as they expect to come out in the Fall—& Edward says he cannot spare me—he wants me to be with him while he is building.

I have had a great bother in my domestic affairs this week[. A] negro woman I hired to wash ran off & carried all she could grab. We found her—& discovered she had not only robbed me, but some of the neighbors—they whipt her & I discharged her. So we are missing a washer but have one engaged. If E could but collect from any of his creditors—we might buy one. I am in hopes I shall be able ere long. As for the 50 you desired—it would have been sent had it been possible—but it was not. Whenever it is I will send you twice the amount if you need it. I feel very bad about it, & so does E—but you know nothing of the scarcity of money now—to what it used to be—I never knew the time I could not get that trifling amount before—whenever I wanted it—& I look forward to the time again—but we must get a new President first—Aunt Hall writes me she has had a partial paralysis of the nerves of her feet & is quite lame—I intend to take our barouche & go down for her the first of next month. I think she is lonesome & nervous—possibly I may be able to arrange that matter for you through her—if she is not too stingy to loan me—she is very close—I would have asked George but he has recently met with a heavy loss—& I knew could not well spare that amount. He will do well,

---

48. Gad Humphreys, a native of Connecticut, joined the U.S. Army in 1809. A veteran of the War of 1812, he was honorably discharged in 1821 at the rank of lieutenant colonel. Soon thereafter, in 1822, he was appointed as the first Indian agent of territorial Florida. Generally solicitous of interests, Humphreys was unpopular in many quarters. He was eventually removed from his post by President Andrew Jackson in 1830. He continued to reside in the Fort King area long thereafter. See Heitman, *Historical Register,* 1:555; Mahon, *History of the Second Seminole War,* 70–71; Covington, *Seminoles of Florida,* 50–51, 63; and Sprague, *Origins, Progress, and Conclusion of the Florida War,* 19–71.

49. John M. McIntosh is listed among the signers of the petition from settlers of the Newnansville area asking Congress to pursue removal of the Seminoles [more aggressively]. See Carter, *Territorial Papers,* 26:876.

however . . . and will undoubtedly be a rich man if he lives & sticks to his business. Vance is well—indeed we are all in good health & spirits—the weather is fine, the trees completely shade our house—and we are as cool as need be[. W]e only want George & Nell with us to be very happy & I trust in God that time is not distant—write soon. Ever your own fond sister.

Corinna

[Corinna Aldrich to Mannevillette Brown]

Newnansville [to Paris]
October 20, 1843

God bless your dear heart, my brother, I am truly grieved that neglect of mine should have caused you one hour's anxiety. Indeed I have written you often since I came back from LaGrange, yet not as often perhaps as heretofore—for I have been much perplexed in mind, and we have had a great deal of sickness. At one time we had <u>seven</u> down with fever & each one in separate rooms—among the patients my <u>two</u> best servants were included. You may judge I was as the old woman replied when Anderson asked her if she were not afraid to live alone in the woods, lest the Indians should attack her; which she said "sometimes—she was powerful flustrated," but in addition to sickness at home, E was far from well & constantly on the go—& then I knew poor Ell was very sick though not dangerously so, in Buffalo—so that with one source of anxiety and another—looking for letters from you & her, & yet dreading to receive them lest they brought bad news—night watching and nursing & &c. I should not deny it if I were told I had left undone everything that I ought to have done. But dear, I was rejoiced to get a letter from you, the first I believe for 2 months, if not three.

Are you never coming home, dear? Your letters interest me very much indeed, yet I cannot but wish you would in one little corner confide to your sister some little idea of your business prospects. You ask me if I sent that money? No dear, I could not. Long since we expected funds from Washington, but our only hope rests now on the new secretary. Should our agent not be successful with him, E. will have his claims brought before Congress. He ought to have done it last session, but it was too late. He will certainly do [this] & I think I can safely promise you assistance in the Spring, or perhaps sooner. Still my dear brother, if your circumstances are such that 50 or 100 would greatly aid you now, let me know & I will send it to you. But if it will do as well three or four months hence—I can better then send you double. Just at this time cash is very scarce. . . . Well Dear . . . has brought me a candle—but with this awful steel pen I scarcely hope to finish my letter more nicely than I began. Someone has taken my knife from my desk. I'll find it by next mail. By the way—how do you succeed in <u>talking</u> french. I am trying to brush up mine. I do not despair of visiting France yet. Write soon. . . . Corine

P.S. Did I not write you Ell has a daughter—born 4th August & called Corinna—

In November, Ellen and her children arrived in St. Augustine on board the schooner *Stephen and Frances.*[50]

[Corinna Aldrich to Mannevillette Brown]

Newnansville [to Paris]

December 29, 1843

I have not written you for two or three weeks of late, Dearest Brother, yet I am sure you will forgive when I tell you of half I have had to prevent me from writing. In the first place the illness of poor Aunt Hall kept me occupied all the time soul & body & then her death—not unexpected, but sudden in truth, I know not whether I have written you since or not. She died on the 6th, inst. after a long & [tedious] illness—during which, however, she suffered but little bodily pain. We expected for weeks she would die & yet we put it off. E. told us she could not live long—he was obliged to go to Jacksonville. I was all ready to accompany him, but she was so very sick, I did not like to leave her. E's business was on her account & as medical treatment was of no avail—except such directions as he left to make her comfortable & she desired him to go—he left—to return & find her not. She died the day before E. returned—about 12 o'clock. She was perfectly conscious of her situation at last but the night before was delirious, & asked repeatedly for you & every member of the family. I never had a greater trial of feeling—but thank God it is past. It is a scene we must all sooner or later go through—& it is our duty dear brother to strive to be prepared. I hope, Dearest, in the many blessings you now enjoy, you do not forget the Giver and that the time will come when you must give an account of your stewardship. I know of nothing that has given me so much gratification as your letters speaking of your success in painting. I have ever felt that a bright career was before you & I only tremble lest in the flush of triumph, you overlook the one thing needful. It is good for me that I have witnessed Aunt H's sickness & death. I had begun in the recent dawning brightness of our fates to forget these things—but I trust it is not too late for me to think of them & I pray that our Good Creator will lead us all in the paths of peace & Eternal as well as Temporal happiness.

---

50. *St. Augustine Florida Herald and Southern Democrat,* November 13, 1843; *St. Augustine News,* November 11, 1843.

I have received letters from dear Nell the last mail telling of her health & her little ones. Dear Manne, having none of my own—they are very dear to me. I live for them & you must excuse me, if I sometimes play a mother's part in writing of them & her. All the past week—indeed all the time since the death & burial of Aunt H. I have had a house full of company. . . . ([T]here is no good publick house here) I had the Judge—the Marshall & the Attorney General of the Territory with me.[51] Whenever in St. A.—I have received great hospitality from the families of each & I was glad of this opp'y to return it. As for our health—we are all doing well. We have each Vance Ed, G, & J Louis A—(the lawyer who is now staying with us—) & mineself—have all suffered from the old fashioned Influenza—now called the Tyler Grippe[52] or La Grippe—but are all convalescent. I think I have never had such a cold since my childhood. By the way, I omitted to mention another of my guests—Capt. Anderson's brother [Benjamin Franklin Anderson]. He is now with us—has been in the Navy but resigned & contemplates planting being tired of a sailor's life— though every inch a <u>sailor</u>.

I forgot to say—Aunt H. made a will, bequeathing whatever might remain of her property to Ellen & I—but precious little I fear there will be. Ed promises me if possible he will save the plantation for our—for all our sakes—as there are graves on it dear to our hearts. I have just been interrupted by a visit from two young ladies & now it is nearly dark & the mail closes at sunset. . . . We are all well & send lots of love—E & G & Aunt A. . . . Adieu, God bless & keep thee. Thine own, Corrine.

That winter Ellen penned several letters to Mannevillette from Buffalo Barracks. She informed him that "my two little children grow fat and troublesome like other people's little ones"; Ellen noted that "I generally write to Corinne with Master Willoughby climbing the back of my chair and pulling first at the pen and then at the paper. . . . I have had to do battle in order to get rid of him to day. As soon as ever he sees me making preparations to write, he seems to think it his part to the fun to tease me and goes to work as regularly as I do." Complaining of Buffalo's "dismal" climate and longing for Florida, "where the

51. No doubt Corinna hosted the following Eastern Judicial District officials during the fall term of the Alachua County Superior Court: Judge Isaac Bronson, U.S. Marshal John Beard, and District Attorney Thomas Douglas. See Denham, *"Rogue's Paradise,"* 215–16.

52. This is obviously a sarcastic reference to President John Tyler's unpopularity among ardent Whigs such as the Aldriches.

·*REGULAR*
CHARLESTON AND SAINT AUGUSTINE PACKET
STEPHEN & FRANCES.

The undersigned takes pleasure in inform
ing the citizens of Saint Augustine and the
Public generally, that he has newly fitted
up the above vessel in a superior manner for the
accommodation of Passengers, having added to her
former conveniences an extensive and airy cabin on
deck, with state rooms; and hopes by strict attention
to his business, to receive such share of the public
patronage as his merits shall deserve.
Freight and Passengers taken on as reasonable
erms as by any other vessel.
July 2, 1841.   LOUIS COXETTER.

"Regular Charleston and St. Augustine packet Stephen and Frances." St. Augustine
Florida Herald and Southern Democrat, *November 15, 1838.*

sun shines," Ellen predicted that James's next posting would be Jefferson Barracks, near St. Louis.[53]

Then on May 2, Ellen complained to Mannevillette about the burden of
being a woman. She told him, "you men know nothing of the disappointments
and anxieties of life. . . . Do you imagine your once fair sister the idle literary
person she used to be? Alas! no such thing! Instead of literature and science,
imagine her thinking of eggs and potatoes. Instead of conversing with agreeable friends, scolding disagreeable servants. Always running about to no purpose, Always trying and never succeeding." She also had grown weary of army
life: "I think the popular ideas of garrison life are very erroneous. So far as I
have seen it, nothing could be less gay, more secluded . . . and monotonous."
Virginia Anderson also joined them that summer. Predicting that Henry Clay
would be the next president, she observed that there was much excitement
about politics among her women friends. Finally, not long after the contest, she
wrote to him deploring Polk's election. She told him that she had expected to

53. Ellen Anderson to Mannevillette Brown, January 6, 1844, Anderson-Brown
Papers, USMA.

be back in Florida by this time but that money problems had kept her from going.[54]

Meanwhile, back in Newnansville, George kept Edward in St. Augustine informed of his business activities. His slave Charles had run away, had returned, and was dispatched to Black Creek on an errand. He provided a detailed account of the Fourth of July celebration in Newnansville. George congratulated Edward on his decision to reside permanently in St. Augustine, urging him to stick to his decision. Aunt Ann, George mentioned, had also tired of Newnansville and intended to go to St. Augustine.[55]

Louis Aldrich continued his law practice in Newnansville for the next two years. Alachua County court records make frequent references to him; in 1845 he became a probate judge.[56] Delving into politics, Louis, unlike his Whig brother, was a Democrat. He and five other representatives from Alachua County joined men from other East Florida counties at a Democratic convention, calling for a Palatka meeting to be held on July 9, 1844, for the purpose of nominating four senatorial candidates, to "take into consideration the subject of division," and to form "the more effectual organization of the Democratic Party."[57] While collaborating with George on the purchase of land and other business matters, Louis was elected to the Florida House of Representatives in 1846 and 1847, and the next year he was elected to the Florida Senate.[58] Sometime soon thereafter Louis left the state, joining hundreds of other Americans who flocked to California after the Mexican War (1846–48). Settling in Sacramento, he prospered and was elected judge of the Tenth District of California.[59]

Meanwhile, that summer Edward and Corinna tried to escape the summer heat in St. Augustine. Aunt Ann joined them. Corinna seemed comfortable in the Ancient City and hoped that Edward's medical practice would flourish.

54. Ellen Anderson to Mannevillette Brown, May 2, July 29, October 24, December 28, 1844; January 2, 1845, Anderson-Brown Papers, USMA.

55. George Brown to Edward Aldrich, June 14, July 6, 1845, Anderson-Brown Papers, USMA.

56. See Alachua County, Inventory and Order Book, Book 2, 1841–57, 203, Court Records (Microfilm Copy) in Florida State Archives, R. A. Gray Building, Tallahassee; Alachua, Hillsborough, Benton, and Marion Counties, Superior and Circuit Court Minutes, 1844–50, pp. 15, 18, 19, 24, 25, 98, 120, 135, 136, 139, P. K. Yonge Library, University of Florida, Gainesville.

57. *St. Augustine Florida Herald and Southern Democrat,* May 21, 1844.

58. Phelps, *People of Lawmaking in Florida,* 1.

59. *St. Augustine Ancient City,* January 24, 1852.

Updating her brother with family news, she also offered a vivid portrait of her surroundings.

[Corinna Aldrich to Mannevillette Brown]

St. Augustine [to Paris]

October 21st 1844

I was truly rejoiced to get a letter from you—my dear brother—after so long silence. I had hoped and feared each week as no tidings came—until I was half crazy with apprehension. I am most happy to hear you are doing so well— and trust it may so establish your reputation—that you may not hesitate to make us a visit. We are very pleasantly located here, and Edward has a very good practice—That is—he has all there is. And though it is provokingly healthy—he has more than enough to meet our expenses. In the <u>winter</u> here, however, is the Physician's harvest. Then the city is filled with invalids, and they all employ a Doctor. I have no doubt, you might make a trip profitable. We shall see when you come. I have no doubt you could get just as much as you could do in a winter—& <u>some</u> in summer—strangers are just now coming in, & denizens returning. Every mail night a posse arrives, & every packet,[60] & vessel brings its complement of visitors, & strangers.

Gen. Worth is still in command of the Garrison—he is very gay—and his officers & staff form an attraction to those who are too sick to bear the rigors of a northern winter & yet when here, will scarcely admit they are invalids. The old Gen. is very likeable & entertains a great deal of company. He has a large family—two grown daughters—one married who has a baby the like of which never was born—& lots of others—all of which I doubt not you might paint. . . .[61] I expect a visit from Ellen, & her family this winter; & George tells me he will pop in on us. . . . G— is now in Charleston. He will pay us a short visit on his return. He is still doing business in Newnansville—but I am in hopes he will go to the sea board another year. He is now doing very well—but it is a sorry life, that of being in the woods. I did not realize how miserable it was

---

60. Short for *Packet-boat,* a vessel "plying at regular intervals between two ports for the conveyance of mails, also of goods and passengers; a mail boat" (*OED*).

61. Worth remained in St. Augustine until September 1845 with his wife Margaret and his two daughters, Josephine and Mary, the latter of whom was married to Capt. John T. Sprague, who served on Worth's staff. The couple lived in a coquina house near the colonel. See Wallace, *General William Jenkins Worth,* 21, 55.

☞ Dr. E. S. ALDRICH, having removed to St. Augustine, tenders his professional services to the citizens. He will attend with promptness to all calls, by day or night, either in town or country. Office in Dr. Poujaud's House, opposite to Mrs. Aguair's.   July 16.

☞ Drs. E. S. ALDRICH and J. E. PECK, having associated themselves in the Practice of Medicine and Surgery at St. Augustine, may be found at the Office now occupied by Dr. Peck, or at their respective dwellings.   3   Aug. 6.

Medical notices of Dr. E. S. Aldrich. St. Augustine Florida Herald and Southern Democrat, *July 16, August 6, 1844.*

until I have become settled in a civilized place. We have here all the advantages of town & country. It is not a very large place, you know, but the society is refined, & it is innocently gay. Should Clay the whig candidate for President be elected—we shall no doubt have some changes in our circle—but some for the worse—All my hope is, if the Whigs beat—E may get his dues out of Uncle Sam—now none but loco focos—get what is owed them—& they get more than their due. By the last mail—there was good news from Georgia—but the issue is doubtful.

Edward is gone in the country for a few days of business. I expect him back to-morrow. His health is good—so is Aunt Ann's and mine is better than it has been—. . . . Aunt Ann says I must tell you—if you will come home—she will go to France with you—She is the same old six pence—ready for a journey, or a jig, as ever—In fact she is younger (as she fancies she is) than I am. We have lots of balls, & parties, & those kinds of amusements, but no theatre, or any thing of that sort—Still I never knew any one to come here that did not enjoy themselves & wish to return—there is a kind of fascination about it—that bewitches all who come. . . . We have delightful weather now—neither too hot—or too cold. As I sit at my desk in my bed room up stairs—I can look out on the beautiful North River—bounded by the Island of St. Anastasia—&

above on the right lies the harbour just opposite the old Fort. The breakers dash up on either side making the cliffs on either shore look as if dusted with snow—In a bright sunlight this is one of the prettiest views in St. A—But my paper & the gathering twilight warns me to close. . . . your devoted sister, Corinna

Chapter Eight

"Going and Coming"

Back to St. Augustine

During January and February 1845 the Brown-Aldrich-Anderson family reunited in Florida. After visiting Edward and Corinna in St. Augustine and George in Newnansville, James returned to Buffalo Barracks in March, leaving Ellen and the children in St. Augustine with the Aldriches. Ellen remained in St. Augustine for nearly a year until leaving in May to join James in Buffalo. James was transferred to Fort Gratiot, Michigan, in September 1845.

[Corinna Aldrich to Mannevillette Brown]

St. Augustine [to Paris]
January 19, 1845

The first date of the New Year, my Dear Manne, I give to you, I wrote you just before I left here for Charleston, Dear; and think I have not since, for indeed since my return, I have been so feeble, I have done nothing, but lie in bed, and take physic—until last Thursday, when a ball at Gen. Worth's roused me up; feeling better, Ed. & Aunt A. persuaded me to go, I went, and have since been as well as usual. I have been for several months, suffering from general debility—and nervous irritation, giving up for a few days, upon the slightest cold, or any fatigue—E. thought a voyage would do me good, & sent Ann, & I off to Charleston—no doubt this trip would have had the desired effect, had we not had so long, and uncomfortable a passage; both going and coming. The ordinary time is 36 hours—we were 6 days on the way there, were blown out to the gulph, put back to Savannah, with the loss of our main sail & other damage—went up to the city & passed a night with a cousin of E's (this was, however, an agreeable [diversion. We v]isited Lockspur Island about 4 miles up the Savannah River & 18 from the city—Sav. is building a very large & beautiful Port on this Island, which we had the pleasure of inspecting, & then put to sea.

While in Charleston it was very cold, and I had much to do—shopping & buying a negro for Ell & I—Under such excitement I forgot the cold & knew not I was fatigued until we again set sail—Then not having ever been seasick, all other passengers being so, I felt the need of ease. Aunt A & our servants were flat on their backs—it was cold, & gusty, we could keep no fire, & were out 5 days! I assure you we felt, when we landed, as if there were "<u>no place like</u> home," one night during a heavy blow, Vance bawled out to me, "Corin we should have thought it hard to have been put in the house of correction, but we have put ourselves in solitary confinement, in a <u>nastier</u> place, <u>voluntarily</u>!" I could tell you some tales of our jaunt that would amuse you—but must keep them for your <u>ear</u>. . . .

Col. [Sylvester] Churchill, <u>The</u> <u>Inspector</u> <u>General</u> <u>of</u> <u>our</u> <u>Army</u>, took tea with us last week—I wrote to him of it (your picture) he took quite an interest; I will do all I can for you—but if you could only once <u>visit us</u>, <u>I could do more</u>. No doubt you could get more than <u>fame here</u>—I think the officers would <u>patronize you</u>. & if so <u>citizens, of course</u>. We have 4 companies here, & most all the officers are married—It being head quarters, we have all the aristocracy of the Regiment, you know—It has been quite gay since the Hollidays —but I have not joined in any festivities until I went to Gen Worth's—at which I wore a <u>new dress</u>, & being <u>just from Charleston, it</u> was '<u>all the go</u>.'

One anecdote I must tell you of our voyage—Aunt A had been so long in Florida, everything was new & strange!—The day we were blown out to the gulph—it was drizzly, and cloudy:—our main sail was gone, the gaph[1] broken, the waves very high—the vessel rolling, & every thing rolling <u>in her</u>. Vance was very sick, but up she mounted. I said "Where are you going?" To see what . . . is the matter; just then the table in the cabin, started and run on the casters bang against our state room door! She called—the mate chanced to be passing, & let her out! It was just dinner time, & they thought she had come to dine—one had a plate in his lap, another soul was ducked with the pitcher of water, & others were holding on to any thing they could; she braced herself up with a lurch against the partition, & began her inquiries.—her voice trembled, and she was so vexed, yet tried so hard to keep her temper I thought I would die a laughing —My door was ajar—she told them it was the first time she ever was with sailors that couldn't keep a reckoning or take an observation; & it would be the last. They told her when the sun came out they would find out where we were, & let her know—She came back to me with the assurance that we should land in France & see you before we found <u>St A</u>. or <u>Charleston, either</u>—She laid down, my berth was above hers—I thought I would comfort her, & laid down; she popt out her head to look up,—I forgot I had called to her, and spit right

---

1. A gaff is "a spar used in ships to extend the heads of fore-and-aft sails which are not set on stays" (*OED*).

in her face! At first she said she thought the devil was in me, as well as every-thing else! But when she saw I did not intend it—she laughed as heartily as I did—we concluded to try, & wait with patience for deliverance—which came in due season—Take it all in all it was a curious farce, & one I shall long remember—I hope when you return, dear, it will be with a Capt who is a <u>sailor</u>—Heaven guided our helm—I am still expecting Ellen—but have writ-ten her to take the land route—. . . . [Corinna]

[Corinna Aldrich to Mannevillette Brown]

St. Augustine [to Paris]
February 29, 1845

I have not heard from you for several weeks my dear Manne, neither have I written you for as long a time for the reason of the arrival of Capt. Anderson, Nell & the little ones. So unexpected was their visit at last, that they took us quite by surprise—though I assure you, it was not the less happy a meeting—They came about two weeks since, we having been warned of their coming only by one mail—Nell is very thin in flesh, but says her health is good. Ander-son never looked better & the children are both well & pretty—The little boy is quite recovered, the girl is a fairy-like little thing, just fit to paint—fair, & deli-cate, with dark eyes, & curly locks—I think she resembles her mother, but some say she looks like me! It would be no small vanity in me however, to cher-ish the opinion. Edward is all father and a fine little fellow he is too—We can afford to be proud of them.

Dr. A. & Capt. A. left a few days since for Newnansville—I suppose they wish to recall the days "Auld Lang Syne"—I know not what else would have prompted such an excursion, to persons who knew so well the privations, & fatigue of such a jaunt—We expect them back in a few days from this,—Also George will return with them—on his way to Charleston—He still holds on; & wisely, to old Alachua—He is doing well there & when one is, in times like these—It is foolish to seek to do better—Anderson will go north again in two weeks from this—his leave will then have expired. Ellen & the children I intend to keep as long as I can. Their stay, however, will depend on circum-stances—If the 2nd, as is expected, is ordered in the summer to Detroit—She will go there, but if to Orregon as is apprehended she will remain with me.[2] At

2. Corinna is referring here to the potential of war breaking out between the United States and Great Britain over the Oregon boundary dispute. The dispute was not settled until June 15, 1846, roughly one month after the United States declared war on Mexico. On the Oregon question, see John S. D. Eisenhower, *So Far from God: The U.S. War with*

all events, I hope to keep her several months; & then, should she resolve to go—I will try and accompany her. . . .

I had got thus far, Dear, and Nell came and requested me to accompany her to church—This which I did—and heard a very nice sermon—Ellen is anxious to have her little ones christened while here—I think she will after the gents return—How I wish you could be here with us all—but I trust in God the time is not distant when we shall all be reunited—While in N.Y. Ellen visited Mrs. Schoolcraft's picture gallery. She says she saw several very fine paintings, but no one was present to tell her the artist's names—I hope to see some of yours when we [go]. . . .

If Col Churchill arranges E.'s affairs for him, in Washington—there will be nothing to prevent us from a trip North in the Summer—I hope about the time you may return & we can all come south together—If I should go—I shall leave my home in Aunt Ann's care and yet I fear to [mobilize] these happy thoughts—I have had so much disappointment in my life. I begin to feel that except in religion there is no happiness this side the grave—Ellen does not appear very well today—She is very thin—but does not complain—still I fear she is not altogether as well as she would have me think—All the others are well—My own health is improved very much—E. has bought me a pretty little pony—and I think so long as I take regular exercise I shall get fat but she will be poor as long as she has the worry of children—

By the way, did I tell you her little girl is called Corinna? I will tell you a little anecdote, but you must not call names in your answer—as I have never mentioned the matter before Edward—While Ell was at the Waverly House in New York—She went to the parlour to see an old friend of Capt. A's—a lady present asked Nab's pardon and then left the room—about an hour after—she received a card from J. W. Pomeroy[3] says she thought best to receive his call & such confessions ensued as caused Anderson to call him an ass. She says he judges it was he that was bit & not me! He told A—he should always feel that he was at fault—that I would not have him; he behaved so bad, etc, etc. but that since then he had reformed!—but A. says he has not, that he drinks and gambles—He is married, & has two children—The eldest is called "Cora Corinna"! . . . He thought the name beautifully poetical—I should think

Mexico, 1846–1848 (New York: Doubleday, 1989), 59–60, 68; and David Alan Greer, "Oregon Territory," in Frazier, *United States and Mexico at War,* 303.

3. Corinna's former fiancé.

he would be glad of any other association—for I gave him a lecture when I dismissed him from my presence that he cannot forget—although he sent his love to me—& begged my forgiveness—truly he is an ass—I am sorry he has discovered where I live—for I should not be surprised, if he were to be troublesome —I will endeavor to avoid him—but if we should meet—I will take all idea out of his head—of any regret or fancy that I repent. Ell says his wife is a bitch—ugly—& coarse—that they seemed to be poor & not truly happy. . . . By the way, . . . we were young when we knew the villain—but as soon as I had an opp'y to look into his character—I saw & trembled—Indeed it was a happy escape at the last—but I feel he was the Devil's agent to ruin our happiness— & indeed he blighted all our youth—Still we should rejoice that his career of vice & folly was checked ere too late—he might have corrupted us for Eternity —I merely mention the matter as an anecdote of our early years—the recollection of such events may make us better by the contrast of a happy present— with a sad fact—it is like having rode on the brink of a Precipice near to death—but enough of him, & his follies, & vices I leave him to his maker. . . .

We were out to a party at Gen. Worth's on Friday last & speaking of painting, the General expressed a wish that some accomplished artist were here to take the likeness of his only son—a little boy . . . & very pretty—I think there would be many to patronize you—but we shall see—

Aunt Ann is making apple dumplings & mince pies—would I could hand you some—Do you know I have become a famous housekeeper? We do not have to <u>cook</u>, however—unless we fancy—for we have a . . . excellent man cook—but Ann is like all old ladies—she likes to be busy to speak of it afterwards. Poor old thing—I suppose anything to do, better than idleness to those who neither read, write or think! Don't you want some shirts? I will have some made for you if you will send directions. I must close with our united love—It is time dearest—for the mails to close—Ever yours, Corinna

[James Anderson to Ellen Anderson]

[Buffalo Barracks, New York, to St. Augustine, Florida]
April 16, 1845

My Dear Ellen—

Would you believe it? I hold in my hand this afternoon your kind letters of the 5th and 7th which left Augustine (as postmarked) on the 8th making only 7 days & a little over on the route—It gives me much pleasure to hear that you are all so well, but it would give me more to meet you all at the door some day not very distant, as it is—the gratification is just to get a letter from you as you must write me a few lines every week as I do you—You speak of Bud & sis in general terms, but must recollect that my mind dwells much on bud's lameness & give me particulars as regards it—I feel much gratified at his improvement, but remember when I left Florida he limped scarcely at all & if he is not as well off now, though it would be a sad disappointment, you should let me know it—You ask how Virginia likes her visit,—she has no doubt spent her time agreeably but does not appear to fancy Mrs. [Arabella] Riley very much—she thinks as you did formerly that she is not very amiable—Particularly to Miss I. I imagine she is unbearable at times—Miss I. vents her spite particularly on Mrs. Richardson,[4] telling her to her face that she influences Mrs. Riley—If she does, no doubt it is for Mrs. Riley's good that she does so—Virginia must be as glad to see you back as anybody but your humble servant. As to my desires upon the subject, you should know them by this time: for I don't believe I have said much else in my previous letters—well the fact is—you must come home as soon as you well can—for I despise the kind of life I am leading & if it was not for fear of losing [money]—I would go out to [board] tomorrow. By the end of this month I will send you funds & as soon after as you can conveniently, Ellen, come home—tell me at what time you start from Augustine, how you are to come & at what house you intend to stop in New York—if you had no particular house in your mind stop at the American Hotel—but wherever house you intend to stop let me know & I will go to New York to meet you.

We have little or no news here, Mrs. Albertis has had a miscarriage & came near dying—Mrs [Hannibal] Day has another boy. . . . It is as dull here as I ever knew it at this season—we have commenced drilling & dress parades—but the weather is too cold for me before breakfast so I lay a bed—The Colonel is much tickled with the [lithograph] of Col Worth, has had it handsomely framed & displays it on his mantle piece.

Have you seen by the papers that the State of Missouri have given the old fellow a Sword? It is quite a feather in the Colonel's cap—The Colonel owes all his good luck to making me his adjt.—hem—After all the Colonel is of the eighth & long may he live to wear his honors. I have just told Margaret that you were coming home by the first of June, at which she is much rejoiced—I am very glad you have got rid of that spot on your nose—at times it looked . . . as if it might become much worse—I envy the warm weather you speak of, ours is disagreeable. It will probably remain so for a fortnight to come—Nearly all

---

4. Probably the wife of Lt. Israel Bush Richardson of the Third Infantry, who graduated from West Point in 1836 (Heitman, *Historical Register,* 1:828).

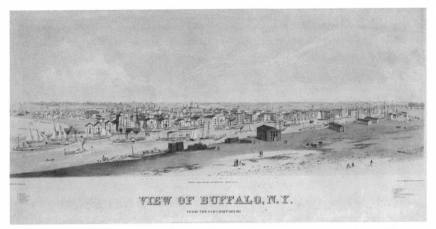

View of Buffalo, New York, circa 1848. The Mariners Museum, Newport News, Va.

the city of [Pittsburgh] has been burnt down. . . . millions of dollars damage—
The pickles you left are good & I commenced eating them but had to quit as I
found they disagreed with me as usual—I am as healthy as a buck & have no
care but in your absence. . . .

Tell the doctor his cigars proved too good, for I could not keep them. I
passed them off as Florida cigars made of Florida tobacco—The Floridians
ought to be obliged to me—I suppose there will be much scrambling for office
among them in Florida—has the doctor had anything to say to Levy? What is
the trouble with the Doctor's father, is he used up in money matters? . . . Tell
Mrs A that I would be very glad to come back, but would much rather meet
her here. That she must pack up & come on with you & I cannot get along
without you after the 1st of June—so be a good girl and come back; as to my
housekeeping—I don't keep house—Margaret does everything. I do not even
know what I am going to have for dinner, nor do I care—since the good fish &
[oysters] diet I have had while away. I have become very indifferent as to Buffalo fare & never bother myself about my meals—Virginia looks very well—
she writes to you by last mail—God bless you all—Kiss bud & sis for me—I
wish I could see you all tonight

—Yours truly W

No news about moving now as I believe we will [not know] anything until
about the 15th June by which time you must be here if not sooner—I shall
expect you by the 1st June. I believe, to read my letter, one would think I was
just married, well I care not—it must be that I love you as much, if not more
than ever—Your own W.

[James Anderson to Ellen Anderson]

Buffalo Barracks, New York [to St. Augustine]
April 27, 1845

My Dear Ellen:

On the 24th of this month, I wrote to you enclosing $150 & I write this letter which I think will reach you by same mail; the check requires your signature before it can be paid; so that if it misses reaching you by any accident, I do not lose it. I wish you to notify me as soon as you receive my letter of the 24th. At the same time that I send this, I send a paper or two for the doctor containing the gist of Rumours of War &c. Brother Johnathan has been swaggering & blustering for the past year how easily he could lick John Bull & what a great fellow he was, & what he intended to do & all that & as soon as John Bull blusters back a little, every body seems to think there is going to be a fight right off. But I do not think it will come off yet quite. Bobby Peel & Jimmy Polk both stand pledged to maintain, each their undisputed right to Oregon. What the end of it will be, I cant say—but it will probably be a year or two, any how, before we have a war. England, I think is determined not to see us extend our territory & principles much farther on the continent even without a struggle— as Bennet [Riley] says, "Oregon is not the true 'Casus Belli'"[5]—

My ankle appears to be getting well very fast—the Doctor thinks I will be out in 8 or 10 days—as well as I can recollect, it is the first time I ever was laid up with lameness. The sick folks here are all getting better. No more cases of Scarlet fever have occurred in Garrison & the old cases are nearly well. Mrs. Russell[6] (Miss Waite's sister) is married. Mrs. Day apologized to Virginia about our visit there. She said that she did not know we had been there until she came up stairs—she has heard since we did not like it. Capt. Day has been to see me most every day since I have been confined. I had a visit also from Mrs. Riley & Mrs. Richardson—the latter is going home in a few days. They are all very kind to me, but nobody's attentions can supply yours—

"That what we have, we prize not to the worth"
"Whiles we enjoy it, but, being lacked & lost,"

5. Latin: "reason for war."

6. James refers to the widow of Capt. Samuel L. Russell, Second Infantry, who was killed on February 28, 1839, in an action with the Seminoles near Key Biscayne, Florida. On March 16, 1839, Anderson and thirteen other officers met at Fort Fanning to issue a series of resolutions in memory of the late Capt. S. L. Russell. See *Army and Navy Chronicle,* March 28, 1839, p. 207–9; May 23, 1839, p. 328–29; and Heitman, *Historical Register,* 1:854.

"Why there we lack its value—there we find"
"The virtue that possession would not shew us"
"Whiles it was ours—"[7]

I think Shakespeare must have written the above when he was separated from his wife.

You must not forget to write me, what day you start from Augustine & what route you are going to take to come on in order that I may meet you if necessary in New York—I shall expect you to start by the 15th next month. I wish you however to consult your own comfort & convenience, remembering that my desire is great to have you home. I hope the Doctor & Mrs. Aldrich will come with you also—at any rate you must insist on Mrs. A's coming—the trip would be of great advantage to her. How come [Albert] Nunes to take the [St. Augustine] "News" in hand—is it not in other words Levy's paper or organ— as soon as I saw it under its new colors, I suspected Levy to be at the bottom of it.[8] Although Levy eats pork, yet is he a renegade Jew—& the people of Florida will some day find out the Shylock.[9] President [Anson] Jones of Texas has no doubt been bribed by Foreign Influence to oppose the annexation question as also [Sam] Houston, as both of them are raising every obstacle to its consummation in spite of the wishes of the people of Texas—The President (Jones) will not assemble [the Texas] Congress to act on the Resolution & unless Texas accepts before January next, the law passed by our Congress falls to the ground.

There is no danger of our Removal for the present. How come on Bud & Sis—I want to hear their prattle. I hope you enjoy your own health. The weather now is getting very pleasant. The grass is green & the trees are budding. Radishes & lettuce are making their appearance. Now is the time for you to change climate with advantage. Start now & get ahead of the fevers—Don't forget the box of shells—Remember me to the Doctor & Corinna & Miss Ann—take good care of yourself & if necessary come all the way by land. I shall then see you the sooner. God bless you—

As ever yours W.

7. James quotes from Shakespeare's *Much Ado about Nothing* 4.1.218–22. Line 220 should read as follows: "Why then we rack the value; then we find"; "rack" here means "stretch." It is unclear whether James is quoting from memory or from a text.

8. On April 12, 1845, Thomas T. Russell, the proprietor and editor of the *St. Augustine News,* a staunch Whig paper, announced that he had relinquished ownership to Albert A. Nunes. From that issue onward the paper promoted the Democratic Party. Previously the staunch Whig organ had continually denounced David Levy and other Democrats.

9. Shylock is the greedy and vengeful Jew in Shakespeare's *The Merchant of Venice.*

[Ellen Anderson to James Anderson]

St. Augustine [to Buffalo]
May 5, 1845

My Dear Will,

Your kind letters of April 11th and 16th arrived together by the last mail. One day's difference in the time of mailing your and Virginia's letters appears to have made a difference in my receipt of them. I observe they were written on the same day but mailed, one on the 11th and one on the 12th. My dear fellow, the reason I have not mentioned Bud's lameness more particularly is precisely because I have no change to mention. You say he limped scarcely at all when you left. In truth, I cannot see that he limps at all now, but I do not think I could have asserted this much before. And still, that deformity of the hip does exist, although not in the smallest degree increased, and it may be that it diminishes, but you see it must diminish considerably before I would venture to believe it. I rub it twice a day with salve and its improvement would be very rapid, if I could perceive it from day to day, whereas the Doctor did not promise that I should see an improvement under six weeks. His general health is excellent and he appears in every way improved. He has lost all that irritability which rendered him so hard to take care of; I even think he has grown prettier than he was. The great improvement in his temperament I attribute to the medicine the Dr. has given him. I tried this morning to move his leg from right to left (which you remember was always the difficulty). To my surprise he instantly stiffened the limb from hip to toe and held it so with all the strength of his muscles. He seemed to be in play but I could not persuade him out of the notions. For your satisfaction I have asked the Dr. to write down the name of the medicine he is giving Bud, lest I should make a mistake. Here followeth a copy: "Hydriodas Potassae in solution ointment of the same," familiarly called "Iodide of Potassium." The Dr. is going to write down a course for me to pursue after I shall have left here for home, and says, if any of his old symptoms return, he must be sent on to Florida to him again. But I do not think he has any apprehension that they will; for he said he thought Bud would recover anyhow as he grew up from the effects of the disease, but the course of medicine he put him on could not do him any harm and would hasten his cure, as I told you in my last letter.

Sissy has quite recovered from her crossness, although she has no more teeth through, but there is one all but through. I fancy it gives her no further uneasiness. She is now as lively and sweet-tempered as ever. I have weaned her entirely, the Dr. advising me to do so, and I could the more easily do it, as we have two fine cows from the country and she can have as much milk as she needs and that which is of good quality—the latter being more than I can say for the St. Augustine milk which we buy.

My dear Will, I will get to Buffalo by the first of June if it be possible. I will start by the first opportunity after I am in possession of sufficient funds to start with. At present I have about $60.00 which you know would not be sufficient, more especially as there is no vessel going from here direct to N.Y. There may be one still in the course of two or three weeks, but I have not heard of any as yet. There was one expected out from there by Char. but it has been lost. Moreover I found upon inquiry that The Baltimore packet will not return here before the first of August which will be too late for me of course. I now think I shall go in the <u>Stephen</u> and <u>Francis</u> from here to Charleston and from there to New York, but I shall write you particularly about it the last thing I do before I start. Also, if I go by way of Charleston, I will write to you from there, so that you will know more precisely what time to start to meet us in New York. I should be delighted to have you come to meet us.

I read your letters over and over again. . . . I don't want you to be lonely certainly, where it is in my power to prevent it, you should never feel an unpleasant emotion, and yet I cannot feel sorry that you miss me. Oh my Will you little know how dear to me is [the] thought that you love me. And when I read your letters I cannot help thinking you do a little bit. But I wont bother you with prattle.

Edward has been sick the last week and confined to the house. In consequence of which I have stayed at home because Corinna was obliged to stay. Mrs. Barrett is spending a week at Gen. Worth's. Mr. B. promised E. that when he came for his wife he would pay him some money, but for my own part, I do not believe any of these fellows will pay at all, unless forced to do it and E. is not the man to force things. I suppose the property will be of value one of these days. Should it become so when our children are of age to educate, it will be particularly acceptable, and this is all I hope from it. Corinna is determined to come with me although she will have to work to get Edward's consent to it. He don't want her to go, but I think it will be of essential benefit to her. I have no doubt she will come. Give my love to Virginia. I wrote to her last week. Her experience at the Col's will not do her any hurt. It is well for some to find out there is not always paradise whenever there is a smile. Your joke on Mrs. Casy is jostled a little out of the truth, I am of opinion. "Total abstinence" is Mrs. C's own remedy which I <u>have heard her</u> recommend more than once as infallible. If old C. told this story as you state, I rather guess he has put his wife's word in Mrs. L's mouth. Certainly it is not new to me, except as coming from Mrs. L. I could not help laughing to think you were so enamored by it. My health is excellent. Nevertheless I'm afraid I'm in the predicament they all deprecate.

Certainly, I have very strong reasons for thinking so, but as it is always possible that one may be mistaken in the early stages of these affairs. Why I try to persuade myself that I may be so. I should not have mentioned it if you had not asked me about it. Take good care of yourself and I will come back as soon as ever I can. I shall hold you to your promise of being "a good boy." And I, for my part, shall do what I always [have.] Your good wife Ellen.

In the spring of 1845 the United States and Mexico continued their war of words over the U.S.-Mexican border and the offer by the United States to purchase California. U.S. relations with Great Britain were also tense because of British opposition to the U.S. annexation of Texas and the ongoing boundary dispute over Oregon. Moreover, many feared that in the event of a war between the United States and Mexico, abolitionist forces in Great Britain might induce that country to join Mexico as an ally. Indeed, the sentiment among many in England to halt U.S. expansion was strong.

[Corinna Aldrich to Mannevillette Brown]

St. Augustine [to Paris]
May 19, 1845

I ought to have written you, my Dear Brother—several weeks since, but circumstances have prevented. Last week the Dr. was quite sick with chills & fever—and my time & attention were fully occupied. Ellen said she would write you, but her eyes trouble her so much whenever she over tasks them, that I persuaded her after having written Anderson, to defer writing you until this mail, and now, Edward is so well, I prefer to write myself. Why have I not heard from you of late? I begin to hope you may be coming home—alas! it would be a joyful event—almost too good news to be realized—but my dear Manne, would it not be best for you to come at once?—By our last papers— we had most belligerent threats—both from Mexico, & England!—Indeed, Mexico has declared <u>war</u>—This, however, would be but a flea bite—did not old England threaten too—now if E. does fight us—it will be a hard one. We are unprepared, so say the <u>wise ones</u>, & will get a good <u>drubbing</u> before we wake up to the importance of meeting John Bull with his own weapons. They have been for years making ready:—they have an Army & Navy that would swallow ours at a meal!—we have nothing to cope with them. Our Navy, & Army, are crampt [*sic*] to death, and I do not blame them for rejoicing at the prospect of war. They who have been reared from their cradles to such station —ought not now in their old age, or even in maturity, to be turned out on the world, to seek occupations they know not how to fulfill—& now if we should get in a war with John Bull—Congress, & the <u>sovereign people</u> will find out their use—& I hope regret their niggardly conduct. Raw militia may do to fight Indians, but they will find that discipline is requisite to meet a civilized foe—I think too, it will result to our benefit in more ways than one. Politics & factions are ruining this country—and much I fear if we are not set to fighting strangers—we shall get at it at home. We have a Loco Foco President & they of course rule. I only hope <u>brag</u> will prove a <u>good dog</u>.

I suppose you are aware that Florida is a state. It has made no little stir in the political world—such fighting to see which party shall get the ascendancy. I suspect to my regret it will be a loco foco state. I would fain have it whig. Many of the big Fish of Georgia are here now—aiding the good cause. Viz —[John] Berrien[10] Jacobs,[11] & [Alexander] Stevens[12] [*sic*],—all members of Congress, & talented men. We are now electioneering for the first Gen Assembly—to be held next month I believe also for Governor, & Representative to Congress. We are yet in doubt, both parties are making great efforts. They wished Edward to run for Representative, but I begged him not. No man's

10. John Macpherson Berrien was born in New Jersey in 1781 and migrated to Savannah, Georgia, with his parents one year later. He graduated from Princeton and was admitted to the bar in Georgia upon his return. He served in the War of 1812. After serving as a solicitor, judge, and Georgia legislator Berrien was elected U.S. senator in 1825, resigning in 1829 to become President Andrew Jackson's attorney general. Falling out with Old Hickory, Berrien resigned his post in 1831, left politics briefly to practice law, and in 1841 was elected U.S. senator as a Whig, serving in that capacity off and on until finally resigning that post in 1852. He died in 1856. See *Biographical Directory of Congress, 1774–1971* (Washington, D.C.: U.S. Government Printing Office, 1971), 586.

11. Corinna is most likely referring to Seaborn Jones, born in Augusta in 1788. After attending Princeton College he was admitted to the bar in 1808. Living first in Milledgeville, Jones relocated in Columbus, where he was elected to the U.S. Congress as a Democrat in 1833, serving until 1835. Reelected in 1845, Jones served one more term in that body. He died in Columbus in 1864. See *Biographical Directory of Congress, 1774–1971* (Washington, D.C.: U.S. Government Printing Office, 1971), 1207.

12. One of the leading Whig statesmen in the U.S. House and Senate, Alexander Stephens was born in 1818 in Taliaferro County, Georgia. After graduating from the University of Georgia in 1834, he was admitted to the bar and practiced law in Crawfordville. Serving in the state legislature 1836–42, Stephens was elected to the U.S. Congress in 1843 and served in six succeeding congresses until 1859. In 1861, after the secession of the southern states, Stephens became vice president of the Confederate States of America. Jailed briefly after the Union victory, Stephens resumed his political career, serving in three successive congresses from 1873 through 1882. He died in 1883 shortly after he was elected governor of Georgia. See *Biographical Directory of Congress, 1774–1971* (Washington, D.C.: U.S. Government Printing Office, 1971), 1749.

character is safe in such times. Lying is the order of the day—& the aim of each seems, to excel in the vices. Besides it is so out of E's province that it would ruin him (that is his fortune, if not his good name).[13]

I suppose you got my letters all about Ellen & her little ones. Anderson has had a sprained ankle—since he returned to Buffalo—but at the last out was recovering. He has made it a race nevertheless to get Ellen home. He has begged her so hard to follow him, that I cannot prevail on her to stay the summer with me, as I hoped. We expect (for it is agreed that I must go on with her—) to leave here on the 30th inst—Take the steamboat to Savannah, & thence to New York—by the Line Packet "Exact"—which advertises to sail on the 2nd June—Ergo, if you get this—answer it to Buffalo—as we shall, <u>Deo volente</u>, be there ere this reaches you. I hope <u>you</u> may be able, Dear, to meet us there, & return South with me, <u>in the Fall</u>. Indeed—'tis probable Ellen will return with me—for A. will be ordered to the frontier if the war begins. We shall know to night. Gen Worth told me—at a party a few nights since, that he hoped to march to the Capital of Mexico—You must not come home after they begin to fight—so come <u>before</u>. Aunt Ann is fat & hearty—she says you must not wait until the Privateers get out. Indeed you must not. I did not know it was so late Dear—but as the last minute has come—I must close—I ought to have begun earlier—but indeed I have been so busy since I concluded to go with Ell—that I hardly have my wits about me. You see I never had an idea but she would stay with me—and it makes a vast difference in my wardrobe besides household affairs—for though I leave Vance as nominal housekeeper —& though she generally holds that office—it is like the loco foco appointments —a sinecure to her—she is the face & hands, I the machinery—or better main spring. George is well. I expect he will be here before we leave. . . . Dear Manne tell me if you are making more than a living—& truly if you do that—Don't deceive me Dear. [Corinna]

[Ellen Anderson to James Anderson]

St. Augustine [to Buffalo Barracks, New York]
May 26, 1845

My Dear Anderson,

Once more I write from this detestable city, but it is for the last time. On Friday we leave here and arrive in Savannah so as to take passage in the brig Exact which leaves that city on the 2nd June, being towed out of the Savannah River

13. Edward had previously run unsuccessfully for a seat in the Florida legislature. See previous chapter.

by the steamboat—So there is to be no delay. The passage from Savannah to N.Y. is normally made at this season of the year in five or six days, so you can judge what time to start in order to meet us in N.Y. I received a short letter from you yesterday and very short it seemed after the one of last week. You will understand why I am not away from my previous letters. I could not well help myself although I have been very very sorry to disappoint you even in a small degree. You must not expect to see me looking like the blooming rose, Dear Will, because you see, I have gone to seed and it "ain't natural." It has been my misfortune to have been in this way or nursing, which is just as bad, ever since we have been married, which, to say nothing of the influence it has on my personal appearance, renders me so nervous, low spirited and incapable of exertion that I get sick of myself and fancy my friends are sick of me. Oh how different I should feel could I come home well, but when I look forward to all I must go through with I am utterly dismayed. However, I do not wish to give you the blue devils. Indeed I don't mean to have them myself anymore than I can help. I suppose I ought to mention that E. received a letter from the Col. by the same mail as mine. The business he will attend to. Also the old fellow's cane shall be forthcoming, as good a one as I can get for him. Sisy has cut four more teeth and is cutting more. She looks almost as seedy as her Mama; however, neither of us are sick. Bud is in excellent health and looks well. Mrs. Aldrich is improving, and the Doctor is without room for improvement.

I have just received an invitation from Mrs. [Sophrina] Bronson to spend the evening with her so I must hurry along and get through with my letter in order to dress myself for it is late in the afternoon now. I was going to write and put my letter in the Savannah post office myself but I fear it might not get to Buffalo so soon as by this boat and perhaps not soon enough for you to hear from us in season to start from New York should you think fit to come meet us so I began my letter later in the day than usual. Indeed we should like to have you come right well. The only drawback is the expense and I suppose that is the only one in your mind. I know not what to advise you and so I will not advise at all. Only I will say this and whichever or whatever you do it shall be done the best and I know you acted from the best motives. Mrs. [Eugene] Van Ness and family, except the Major, are going along in company with us. The Brig <u>Exact</u> is the best of the line and very fine indeed: so they say. So you see we have a fine prospect before us and I sincerely hope we may arrive safely and find all well. All the news I gather now I will put in my pocket and keep until I meet you, for I do not expect to write again. God protect and bless you. Excuse me, dear Will, from writing any more tonight as the darkness has come and Corinna will be hurrying me to be ready.

Yours ever, Ellen

[George Brown to Ann Dearing]

Newnansville [to St. Augustine]
August 25, 1845

Dear Aunt Ann

I received last mail a letter from Major [John] Beard[14] offering me 300 dollars for the place of Charles & yours on St. Johns River. And I have written him in reply, that I will make the sale providing you give your assent. The price I consider very fair under all circumstances; to be sure, it <u>cost</u> more, but as it stands it is of no use to you, and probably <u>never</u> <u>will</u> <u>be</u>, and should the house get destroyed by fire, or accident, as it certainly will unless occupied, the place will be worth nothing, as the <u>land</u> is of no <u>value</u>. I advise <u>you</u> <u>by</u> <u>all</u> <u>means</u> <u>to</u> <u>sell</u>, but consult your <u>own</u> <u>wishes</u> entirely, as you are mostly interested in the matter. Should you sell, the money could be invested for you much more profitably than where it is now sunk. You could invest in Bank shares, or I would take it—and give you liberal interest; or I could buy you a little negro that could <u>grow</u> <u>worth</u> <u>more</u> every day, unlike a house, which diminishes in value. Please let the Doctor know what you decide and he will inform <u>Miss</u> <u>Beard</u>, the matter now stands until you say yes or no. . . .

[George L. Brown]

[Ellen Anderson to Mannevillette Brown]

Fort Gratiot, Michigan [to Paris]
March 27, 1846

My dear Mann,

Your letter of Oct. 9th was received by me one or two days since. So you see it was upwards of five months in reaching me. You will perceive by the heading of my letter that I have changed my location from Buffalo to Fort Gratiot, which is on the river St. Clair in the state of Michigan. We left Buffalo about the beginning of September, and three days after our arrival here, I added to the number of inhabitants one little daughter. So you see I have not been idle although I have not answered your letter. . . . But for the reason of <u>my</u> not answering your letter, my good Brother. I will frankly confess. It was because it was so disagreeable to me. You will recollect that you in that letter asked me for money. Now you might as well ask me for my gizzard, as poor Aunt Hall used to say, for I have as much of one as the other. Money! good Mann, never but twice or say three times in my whole life have I had money that was my

14. John Beard was U.S. marshal for the Eastern District of Florida.

Fort Gratiot, Michigan, circa 1840s, as James and Ellen Anderson would have remembered it when they lived there from 1844 to 1845. State Archives of Michigan.

own to do as I pleased with and I am going to tell you what I did with it, for I desire to preserve your good opinion in this matter, although after I had received that last letter I supposed I must give it up. Well then the first money I ever had, beyond a little change, was twenty five dollars which you sent me just before you went to Europe. You may depend I thought a great deal of it, but Charlie, with whom and on whom, in a great measure, I was then home, why! I gave it to him only excepting enough to buy myself a quire of paper, a bunch of quills, and a pen & ink. My next money was upwards of a hundred dollars. I have forgotten how much, which Mr. Anderson gave me to furnish out my wardrobe when in New York. Seventy five of this I sent to you and considering the circumstances I did not think it more than the twenty five I had received. However it was not to repay the old debt that I sent it, but out of good will as I would again if I had it. But I never told Mr. Anderson that I done this, for to say truth I would not have been willing to. I spent the remainder of the money to such good advantage that I have no doubt he thought I spent it all in cloths. My third money was a hundred dollars the proceeds of some property Aunt Hall left me and I spent it in going down to Florida to make Corinne a visit. So much for all the money ever possessed or ever likely to be by your humble servant. Of course when you asked me for money you must have thought I possessed it. I can easily conceive of the reasoning which leads you to such a conclusion, but I fear the day has gone by when the old man will fork out the cash to me as he has done. But certainly at the time of receiving your letter and ever since he has been burthened by a debt contracted to relieve his brother—a fellow who is not worth the pains he cost or that every cent of his money beyond what it cost us to live goes monthly to [make] payments. In the course of two or three months we shall be relieved from this Vampire and then possibly I may have a dollar to help a brother in distress. One thing I must remark that I never knew whether you received the money Corrine and I sent at that time. . . . I'll venture to promise in [Corinna's] name without fear of your being disappointed that if you will come and visit me, she will come and meet you, I don't care where I am. She is very differently situated from what I am. She has no children and her husband dotes upon her and upon nothing else. He lets her do just as she pleases and she pleases very much to take journeys. . . . Ever Yours, Ellen

Corinna wrote Mannevillette from St. Augustine on January 12, 1846, that the town was very dull with the army gone and that Edward was still having trouble collecting his fees. Thus Edward had decided to relocate his medical practice to Pensacola, a port town bustling with activity as the army and navy mustered forces there preparing to battle Mexico.

With a population of approximately 2,000, Pensacola was one of Florida's three largest towns. The 1850 census listed Escambia County as having slightly over 4,300 persons, with whites outnumbering slaves by a ratio of two to one. The county had the largest free black population of any county in the state with 375, most of whom would have resided in Pensacola. White men outnumbered women by a ratio of approximately three to two. Founded by the Spanish in the middle 1500s and then abandoned briefly, the settlement served as the capital of Spanish West Florida until the brief British occupation (1763–83). After the American Revolution, West Florida reverted once again to the Spanish. From that time until the United States acquired the Floridas in 1821, Pensacola served as a seat of the declining Spanish colonial power in the upper Gulf of Mexico and as an Indian trade center and port. Even after the transfer of flags Pensacola remained home to many Creoles. Under U.S. rule, as in St. Augustine, many of the former Spaniards became actively engaged in civic, commercial, and political affairs.

The sisters would have found many similarities between St. Augustine and the Escambia County seat—not the least of which would have been the substantial military presence. Soon after the Americans acquired the gulf port they established a large naval installation there, and much of the commercial, economic, and social activities reflected this military footing. Thus urban activity in Pensacola revolved around the inner city down to the dock areas, Cantonment

Clinch, and the naval yard at Warrenton. Forts McRae (on the west shore of the bay's entrance), Barrancas (facing directly toward the opening), and Pickens (on Santa Rosa Island) guarded Pensacola Bay. Although favored by one of the best harbors on the gulf, Pensacola had no major river linking it to the interior. Also like St. Augustine, lands in the interior were not as fertile as those in Middle Florida. Accordingly, Pensacola's growth leveled off by the 1850s. Pensacola's chief advantage was its easy access to the gulf ports of Mobile (sixty miles) and New Orleans (175 miles) to the west and Apalachicola (125 miles) to the east.[15]

[Corinna Aldrich to Mannevillette Brown]

Pensacola [to Paris]

April 18, 1846

. . . and you must remember—Dear—that where I am is home. You must visit Ellen, and George, but my house is your home. Indeed, Dear, we have been knocked about a good deal—in search of a resting place—and we have tried many—but I think we have at length hit on one which will be permanent. We are most pleasantly located here—have a fine garden—fruit and flowers in abundance—and a very comfortable house—with room and to spare—I shall keep your room in order—had we not been very unfortunate of late in being cheated in buying some negroes—we would not be out of funds— but no matter—our means will not long be straitened. E. is a good Dr—is very much liked wherever he practices—and is [winning] on the people every day here. But you must not expect a very large or populous town. It is a large naval Depot; and that, and the 3 forts in the mouth of the Bay, give it importance. But the town itself is no larger than St. Augustine—yet there is lots more money, and more business, indeed. St. A. is falling away so fast—I doubt if there will any town remain, after a few years. There is nothing to support it. Here we have—(beside the prospect of a railroad-) a Navy yard—a dry dock—3 forts— and lots of ships even in the Bay—both merchant & Naval—75 thousand dollars is paid quarterly off among the Army & Navy every three months in this place—of course there is a plenty of the needful for circulating medium—and it is a poor chance if we don't get hold of a little of it.

15. On Pensacola, see Denham, *"Rogue's Paradise,"* 39–40; Herbert J. Doherty, "Antebellum Pensacola, 1821–1861," *Florida Historical Quarterly* 37 (January 1959): 337–56; Ernest F. Dibble, *Antebellum Pensacola and Its Military Presence* (Pensacola, Fla.: Pensacola Bicentennial Series, 1974); and George F. Pearce, *The U.S. Navy in Pensacola from Sailing Ships to Naval Aviation, 1828–1930* (Pensacola: University of West Florida Press, 1980).

MEDICAL.

DR. E. S. ALDRICH (a graduate of the Medical College of South Carolina) tenders his services to the citizens of Pensacola and vicinity in the practice of Medicine, Surgery and Obstetricks. Three years observation in the Hospitals of Charleston, (where the most scientific and approved practice is pursued) and sevreal years subsequent experience in a large private practice, and as acting Surgeon in the Army in Florida, have enabled him to keep pace with the modern improvements in Medical science, for treating not only diseases incidental to the climate but also those resulting from other causes.

He will attend with promptness to any calls in the city or country, by **Day** or **Night,** and promises due attention to his patients, with moderate charges, and to the poor his services will be cheerfully rendered gratis.

N. B. Office on Palafox street, next door to the Reading Room of the Florida Democrat. At night he may be found at his residence on Intendentia street, next door to Rev. Mr. Peake's.

April 18, 1846—3—tf

Medical notice of Dr. E. S. Aldrich. Pensacola Gazette, *April 18, 1846.*

It makes me feel very bad—dear—to read over your letter but in truth—Manne, I am not at fault. You know I would do any thing in the world to <u>bring you home</u>. And why not come?—How is the spring—G will aid you—and you can come to <u>three</u> homes. Ellen will expect a visit—she is at housekeeping—though almost out of the world now. George is keeping bachelors hall at Newnansville—and no doubt there you could get business for a while—but <u>here is your home forever</u>. My house is large. I have no family. <u>I claim</u> you. And Edward and Aunt Ann expect and desire to see you. I don't know much about the resources of the place as to your profession—but I believe you would have <u>plenty</u> to do—so many rich families—so many dashing officers of the Army & Navy—No doubt they would afford you employment. . . .

I wrote you on our arrival here—but as you may not have received the letter—I repeat we left St. Augustine in Jan. soon after my return for the North—went to Key West—then to New Orleans and from that eternal city —came here. . . .

Corinna again wrote to Mannevillette on May 23 to urge him to come to Pensacola, and she elaborated on every reason why he should do so. For instance, she explained that in New Orleans and Mobile, "merit is patronised and appreciated—and the people are wealthy and liberal! And you could come and stay with us, you know, until you get acquainted, and feel at home, then go round to all these places. . . . We are most delightfully situated—<u>not</u> extravagantly— but we have every thing comfortable, a fine society—pleasant rides, & walks, fine bath houses—good spirit in abundance, &c &c . . . E. & I. have beautiful saddle horses; and you shall ride, & walk, & talk, & bathe, at pleasure." She also considered the political reasons why he should come then: "I suppose you know we are at war with Mexico—as yet we have been more than conquerors—yet the matter is but just begun, and who can say how it will end? I want you to come home before England gets a finger in the pie—although I trust no such evil as a war with Brittainia[16] will fall upon us now. At first Mexico was laughed at, and a hand full of men placed at the cannon's mouth, to defend us. Now 50,000 sol. are at the order of the President and ten millions of dollars; this looks as if the administration regarded the affair as more than a flea bite, unless forsooth, the preparation for a war with Mexico hides a deeper cause of apprehension. Be that as it may—I am writing to urge you to <u>come home</u>—now—now—." As his sisters continued to move, George remained in Newnansville.

16. Archaic spelling of the Latin name for Britain.

[George Brown to Ellen Anderson]

Newnansville [to Fort Gratiot, Michigan]
June 29, 1846

Dear sister,

I acknowledge my indebtedness to you for two letters and not only to you but to a dozen others at least. It is a failing I have to be behind with all my correspondents, save business. It is something in my favour to say that it is my punctual attention to the one sort that causes my tardiness to the other. Your letter of May 19th was rec. during my absence in Charleston, from which today I returned a short time since. My trips to C. are frequent taking up nearly one third of my time. I am pleased to know of the continued good health of yourself and Anderson & the juveniles. I would like to see your children there—though I do not wish my eyes to be gladdened at your or Anderson's detriment, for I certainly should consider it such did you visit Florida consequent upon the Captain's being ordered to Texas. I am anxious as himself for his military fame and promotions, but not in such a war—Mean . . . and unworthy as the motives are which brought on the fray; the end will be still more so, unless speedily brought to a close. I honor the unfortunate brave men who have suffered in the cause, but to our President Mr. Polk (the pronunciation of his name indicates his breed and his brains) and his admirers will be meted a different reward - - - The negro question we hear, is no longer a question; that it will soon be settled on just and amicable terms—this is my earnest wish. I am opposed to war when it can be avoided by any fair compromise. I am also against such commotions from a selfish view. A war falls heaviest on those who buy and sell merchandise—I am one, and do not wish to be ruined from an excess of "American patriots." It will do well for those who are at ease in their possessions, or for those who have something to lose, to sing such <u>patriotic</u> strains—but for us who are struggling in the world peace, and peace only is to be desired; and I think we love our land as dearly as the noisy brawler who spouts his nonsense from every bar-room that will give him credit.

I have ever been a strong opponent of Mr J. C. Calhoun. I retract all my harsh words and hail him as his country's best friend. Have you read Genl. Scott & Mr. Secretary [of War William L.] Marcy's correspondence? the Genl. you will recollect commences one of his letters by saying that he had recd. one of Mr. Marcy's just as [he] was sitting down to a hasty <u>plate of soup</u>, hence he is called Marshall [Fearless]—Mr. Marcy and the whole tribe in Washington can do nothing to injure Genl. Scott, the people know his history, and <u>theirs</u>. They will make him president with a little more abuse.

Our village is progressing a little by the aid of <u>saw</u> <u>mills</u>. Mrs. [Zilphia] <u>Standly</u> is building a large prime hotel, which will be quite a house—the old lady still drives ahead "point blank" and have too, a new piano in town, the tum te tum therefrom can be heard all hours of the day.

My old bachelors establishment is badly in want of a fair spirit for its minister. I certainly shall [fix] myself to somebody before long. I have had an adventure of late which I will tell you of, if you will remind me when I <u>see</u> <u>you</u>—I cannot trust it upon paper.

I hear from Corinna often. She seems pleased with Pensacola; I trust [she] remains so. She amuses me as usual with Aunt Anne's whims and oddities—I suppose you hear the same—a curious old lady our Aunt; yet Corinna could scarcely do without her—like [Saw Slick's] clocks they become fixtures and necessaries by their daily associations.

Give my love and best wishes to Anderson, Miss Virginia, and the "wee things."

Affectionately Yrs
George L. B.

Chapter Nine

"I Live on Hope"
Pensacola

With the outbreak of the Mexican War, James's unit left Michigan in July 1846, traveling down the Mississippi River toward Mexico. Soon thereafter Ellen and the children traveled to Norfolk, Virginia, staying briefly with James's relatives. From there Ellen, the children, and Virginia Anderson made the trip to Charleston, where George met them and escorted them to Florida.

By the spring of 1846 the Aldriches had relocated from St. Augustine to Pensacola. Ellen, the children, and Virginia joined them in the fall. Aunt Ann also continued to reside with the Aldriches. Though failing in health, she contributed to the family by sewing, looking after Ellen's children, and cooking her specialties, apple dumplings and mince pie. But once the family settled in Pensacola the primary focus of the family's attention was James's welfare in Mexico.

Roughly the same time that James's unit left Michigan for Mexico, George Brown wrote Mannevillette from Newnansville of the family's activities.

[George Brown to Mannevillette Brown]

Newnansville [to Paris]
July 18, 1846

My Dear Brother

. . . I am still in business at this village, and have slowly, but I hope surely, prospered. My trade is large, though of a <u>small</u> <u>kind</u>. My customers are a curious sort of people, very different from the close-calculating folk of New England. My [receipts] are mostly in raccoon hides, and "sea Island" cotton. Of the last I ship this year about 200 Bales. I purchase it in the seed from the plantations, and grow it on my own. . . . Altogether I have much to be glad for, and much to complain of, still being of a contented sort of a disposition, I live on without a murmur, and manage to enjoy myself. I keep an old Bachelor's establishment, no woman as yet having touched my tender spot. I am pretty much of an old Bachelor too, having singular notions, am much addicted to pets,—a tame raccoon, and tame paraquet being part of my household—most gladly would I welcome your face within my house.

Corinna & Dr. Aldrich and Aunt Anne are now living at Pensacola, some 300 miles from Newnansville—they are all well and happy. Dr. Aldrich has there a good practice and is very popular with the people of P. so says a gentleman from there. Ellen & Captain Anderson are at Fort Gratiot Michigan. Ellen is the mother of three children. She will have a dozen if nothing unfortunate occurs. Capt. Anderson is daily expecting orders to Texas—and Mexico in which case, she and her Juveniles will visit Corinna at Pensacola.

The war in Mexico, I presume, astonishes the <u>natives</u> of Europe. It is indeed a shameful affair, but now [commenced], must be carried on with energy. I hope it will soon terminate. The Oregon Treaty with Great Brittain, carried out by last Steamer to Liverpool. . . . gives much joy to the inhabitants of the U.S. of all parties. It was so unexpected, that the transition from gloom to brightness was perceptible in every face. I dreaded the prospect of a long and tedious war with England. I am as patriotic as my neighbors, still my <u>amor patris</u>[1] is not so very extensive as to lead me to sacrifice my life and the means whereby I live in a foolish unholy and unnecessary quarrel. War ever falls heaviest on those that buy and sell mdse.

Why do you not visit us—we are not changed in hearts and mind, however time may have made inroads on our Phizes. We are all very anxious that you should return home. You need have no apprehensions as to pecuniary matters and you can find, what you can boast of, <u>three</u> homes here, with me; or Corinna; or Ellen. Indeed, if you wish to see us all again, you ought to return this year—for another season may make the small number of us left, still less— life is of little certainty in a southern climate, and though I still keep in excellent health, I have seen those more robust than I, snatched away by a blighting fever, without scarcely a warning. . . . I am

most affectionately thy brother
George L. B.

While George, Ellen, the children, and Virginia were planning to meet in Charleston, Aunt Ann in Pensacola became extremely ill. She died in September, three months after joining the Episcopal Church. Ellen, Virginia, and the three children, Edward Willoughby, Corinna Georgia, and Ellen Mannevillette, had arrived about one week before her death. Edward was busy establishing his medical practice and drugstore.

1. Latin for "love of country" or "patriotism."

With the departure of James for the Mexican War, James and Ellen resumed their correspondence in an intense manner.[2] Upon leaving Ellen in Michigan, James first wrote Ellen on September 1 from New Port, Kentucky, a recruiting station just across the Ohio River from Cincinnati. Within ten days James's outfit was in New Orleans preparing its descent on Mexico. On September 16 his unit reached Brazos Island, near the Rio Grande. After a long, sleepless night on the beach James shared his thoughts with Ellen of the rough road ahead, noting "Florida was not a touch to this country, nor were our hardships there so severe as they will in all probability be here. In an hour or two we will leave here for the mouth of the Rio Grande' & from thence we shall go to Camargo. . . . 'tis said the Mexicans are quite hostile & are getting brave since the return of Santa Anna. No doubt they are hostile but I do not believe they will meet us again in open fight. Their policy is to let us alone & the Country will use us up." Sickness and bad morale has already begun to decimate the ranks. Volunteers were "leaving the country sick & disgusted by hundreds." James concluded by informing Ellen of the great hardships his fellow officers' wives were experiencing. "This is a horrible country . . . for . . . women," he wrote. Those who had decided to come along were "heartily sick of it already & would I doubt not give much to be back at Gratiot, where they ought to have stayed at the first—there is not the least comfort for a lady here & unless we are stationed on this frontier after the war is over & build ourselves comfortable posts, there is no chance for the army ladies to come here. But keep up your spirits, Ell. I show you the worst side now, so that you may be able to look at things here in their proper light. Matters may alter for the better & cannot for the worse unless we are whipped which I do not expect."[3]

2. James's activities in Mexico are beyond the scope of this book, and most of his letters to Ellen while he was on campaign are not included here. They are all published, however, in James M. Denham and Keith L. Huneycutt, "With Scott in Mexico: Letters of Captain James W. Anderson in the Mexican War, 1846–1847," *Military History of the West* 28 (spring 1998): 19–48. For more on the phases of the Mexican War he was involved in, see appropriate sections of Eisenhower, *So Far from God;* K. Jack Bauer, *The Mexican War, 1846–1848* (New York: Macmillan, 1974); Justin H. Smith, *The War with Mexico,* 2 vols. (1919; reprint, Gloucester, Mass.: Peter Smith, 1963); Otis Singletary, *The Mexican War* (Chicago: University of Chicago Press, 1960); and Richard Bruce Winders, *Mr. Polk's Army: The American Military Experience in the Mexican War* (College Station: Texas A&M University Press, 1997).

3. James Anderson to Ellen Anderson, September 17, 1846, Anderson-Brown Papers, USMA.

Virginia Anderson, Ellen's sister-in-law, lived with the Andersons and Aldriches for extended periods of time and accompanied Ellen and her children on trips. Courtesy Elizabeth Traynor.

Although the mail service was slow and apparently not always reliable, Ellen did receive some of James's letters to Pensacola, and she stayed informed of the army's movements through Pensacola newspaper accounts.

[Ellen Anderson to James Anderson]

Pensacola [to Mexico]
December 16, 1846

My Dear Will,

The last date I had from you was the [2nd Nov] and now I am even in doubt as to where you are. But I live on hope, every mail I think will bring me a letter or some hint of your movements in the papers. I suppose you are with Col. [Bennet] Riley. There is a gent. here who says he knew Col. R. a long time ago but he fancies the Col. has forgotten him. Judge [Benjamin D.] Wright[4] is the

4. Benjamin D. Wright was a native of Pennsylvania and longtime resident of territorial Florida. Arriving in Pensacola in about 1823, he was appointed to the territorial legislative council by President James Monroe the next year. In 1825 he was appointed U.S. district attorney, serving until 1831. In 1841 he became mayor of Pensacola. Wright owned and operated the *Pensacola Gazette* until 1839 but continued to write editorials for the paper until 1846. See Carter, *Territorial Papers,* 22:913, 23:400, 25:431–32, 151–52, 363; Knauss, *Territorial Florida Journalism,* 20–21, 63–65; and Denham, *"Rogue's Paradise,"* 214.

man. I told him I did not believe the Col. had forgotten him or anyone else with whom he had ever been acquainted, for he did not seem to me a man likely to forget. Lt [Jeremiah Mason] Scarritt[5] came home the other day on sick leave. I have seen his wife but she could give me no news of you. But she promised to bring her husband to see me as soon as he was well enough to go out. I hope I shall not have to wait so long however to get news of you.

We are all well here. The children go to school and the baby trots about. There is very little variety in our life. We get up late as of old, and go to bed later; a practice I try hard to reform but I have almost come to the conclusion that this course is the natural one and the contrary against nature. This is a dull place but under present circumstances it suits me all the better for that. I suppose it is more dull than usual from the naval vessels being kept in the Gulf so much and still more from the death of the episcopal clergyman—a man who appears to have been very much beloved, and for whom all the ladies appear to think it necessary to put on the longest possible face for the longest possible time. Think of their keeping the church (pulpit) covered with black from three weeks before Christmas until Easter—refusing to take it off even for Christmas. Such is their determination.

I suppose by the time you get this Christmas will have come and so my dear Will I wish you a very merry one. I hardly hope my wish will be gratified, for I have an idea you put the fairest colors on the picture in describing your situation there and it must be bad enough even at your description. I think of you a great deal especially when I have something nice to eat—you will laugh at this. I cant help laughing at the idea myself, but it is because I am haunted by the idea that you have such miserable victuals. Virginia is well and has finished her dress so I suppose she will be writing to you before long. Our time is a good deal occupied just now but after a week or so we shall be much more at leisure. You see when we first came here all Corinna's friends, and there are a good many of them, called on us, and they have the most old fashioned way of making calls of an hour length so that two or three will take up a whole afternoon, (either in receiving or pay—for you know we must return as we receive). Then followed poor Aunt Ann's sickness and death on which account we thought it proper to put on mourning and there being but one mantua[6] maker in the

---

5. Jeremiah Mason Scarritt graduated from West Point in 1838 and became a second lieutenant in the Sixth Infantry. He became brevet captain on September 23, 1846, for "gallantry and meritorious conduct in several conflicts at Monterrey, Mexico." He died in 1853. See Heitman, *Historical Register,* 1:863.

6. A loose gown worn by women.

place, and she not to be trusted, we (Corine and I), had to make our own and we have not quite finished yet. V's dress is a coloured one. I mentioned it lest you should think we were foolish enough to have her put on black.

We are now about returning our calls for the first time and here I suppose is the proper place to speak of "the society" as it is called. Old Bowton of Port Huron once spoke to me of the want of "society" at that delightful ("otherwise") little place. Not knowing how to get round the matter of having to deny the existence of good society in the very place where it was denied and having often been in that dilemma; it occurred to me that good society was like Peddy's flea "put your hand where it is and it ain't there." . . . But this place is one or two touches above Port Huron. Although there is nothing that could be called living in style here. All the better for me. To say nothing of my not feeling much interest in style just now on other accounts, I want to save a little of my monies so that when you come out of Mexico we may pay all the debts and have enough to go to housekeeping with comfortability, without contracting any more. That is all I care about so far as money is concerned. It is storming hard so that we have had to close the blinds which makes it so dark that I have run off the tracks a little but I hope you will be able to decypher [*sic*] what I have written. Virginia and Corine send their love to you. Bud and Sis speak of you often. As for the baby the principal object of her affection is a little 'nigger' who lives with Corine, whoes [*sic*] business it is when not otherwise engaged to tend the baby and who appears to be fond of so doing.

Com. Stewart is ordered to the Gulf Squadron. Com. [David E.] Connors to be recalled. The <u>Pennsylvania</u> and <u>Ohio</u> ships of War are also ordered to [Vera Cruz]. I don't know whether this is news to you but it is to me and so I put it down. God bless and take care of you, my own good Will. Good bye, Ever yours, Ellen

[James Anderson to Ellen Anderson]

Monterey, Mexico [to Pensacola]
December 27, 1846

My Dearest Ell,

I cut short my last letter, leaving you under the impression that we were all pushing onto Saltilio; after sending off the letter an express arrived from Saltilio which changed the whole face of matters. Our orders were countermanded immediately & we were ordered to march next day the (23rd) for Victoria on our back track. I had a relapse of fever & stood it out until night in camp with the intention of going on, but I had to give up at last & am now here. The fever has left me & if I could get tonics or quinine, I could soon get up, but such things are not in our Hospital at this place. I shall stay here until I recover entirely, when I shall go to the mouth of the Rio Grande & from there join the Regiment, as it will be most convenient. In consequence of being detained here, I shall not probably see a letter from you for a month or two which grieves me much. . . .

I hope to be able to be with the Army before anything is done, but as there is no use being sick with my company, I shall wait until I am well before I join. I run the risk any how of enclosing in this letter a Treasury Note for $100 for you & shall direct it under cover to the Doctor in hopes of its going safe. In a few days I shall be able to procure another when I will send that also. It makes me feel melancholy now when I write to you, which is caused altogether by my not getting any letters from you & knowing that I am out of the track of getting them for some time. But I should not repine, for I know you are safe with your friends & I ought to have no uneasiness on that score, but a letter sent from you every week would be a great blessing. Direct your letters as usual. I am in hopes to be with the company in 3 or 6 weeks at farthest & would be with them sooner were it not on account of the roundabout way I have to join it, perhaps by Tampico. . . . Give my love to Corinna & tell her that her nice long letter deserves a return at my hands & if I ever get my strength I shall most certainly answer it.

Give my love to Virginia & tell her to write—write—write—if she don't write me that often even if only a few lines, I won't forgive her for it. Tell the Doctor I wrote to him some time ago, from this very place, but he does not appear to have got the letters, as Corinna said nothing about it in her letter. Love to Miss Ann & plenty of love for Yourself & the little ones. Kiss Bud Sis & baby for me. I should like to see you all but am afraid even to dwell on the idea. Time. Time alone will show forth the truth of all matters & with this war I wish I could say ended my military career. I have no farther desire to remain in after it is over—nothing but the l'argent[7] binds me to the service. Patriotism, honour, glory, all have evaporated somehow or other & I am become a sober, common sense man, laughing at all flights of fancy whether in the fields or drawing room. I hope you will get the money safe. I know you must have been much fatigued when you arrived at Newnansville or you would have written me a few lines—it was a hard journey inland for you & the children. Good Bye. God bless you. I can only live on the hope of one day being all together.

As Ever Your own Willo—

7. French: "silver" or "money."

On January 2, James wrote Ellen that his health was improving and that he was "getting more & more anxious to join my company." He also expressed to Ellen his gratitude to her brother George: "I feel very grateful to George for his kindness—had he not given you his protection & aid at the time he did (I do not know what you would have done), for I feared you were not equal to undergoing it alone & knew that you feel somewhat uneasy at the undertaking yourself. I assure you, I consider myself fortunate in having such Relatives as Corinna, George & the Doctor. God knows what would have been our present situation without their kindness & attention. We must make it up some of these days. As to Corinna, she gave me a hard rub in her letter & I did not scold her, but asked her future forbearance."

James wrote the next day,

There is some talk that we are to make a demonstration against Vera Cruz as soon as sufficient force can be collected for that purpose & probably such may be the next affair. The Mexican papers breathe nothing but war to the death and as Santa Anna is now president of Mexico, there is in my mind but little possible doubt that the war will be continued. I shall endeavor to start from here now in 3 or 4 days so that I do not wish you to change the address of my letters. Direct to Capt. J. W. Anderson 2nd Infantry, Army of Occupation Mexico & I think I will receive all my letters some time or other. Mention particularly the Regiment I belong to, as our letters are assorted by Regiments. I endeavour to write you regularly once a week but sometimes I am unable to write for a greater length of time on account of being on the march & there being no mode of sending off any letters. I shall continue to do so & in the event of anything extraordinary oftener—however letters can only be forwarded about once a week as we do not have an express oftener unless something extra occurs.

On January 14, James wrote Ellen of the Battle of Monterrey (September 20–24), including details about the battle and a sketch of the battlefield. His letter of January 15 includes a lively discussion of the fandango, an old Spanish dance, and descriptions of Mexican houses and plants.[8] On January 28, 1847, he provided Ellen with an update of his movements, noting that "the troops have been assembling in this vicinity: preparatory to the Embarkation—as yet no troops have left here: Genl. [Winfield] Scott says however that he will be very much chagrined if he has to delay over a week. Genl. Worth is encamped with

---

8. See Denham and Huneycutt, "With Scott in Mexico," 25–30.

his commands a few miles above on the River & at this point there are about 1500 men, other troops will soon be down also. There is some talk that we are all to embark for an Island about 60 miles south of Tampico; however, but little is known on that subject. When we do start from this point, our operations will no doubt be as expeditious as possible."

James asked Ellen to fill him in on the latest political news. He was especially interested to know if she had "looked at the proceedings of Congress lately? I see that a Bill has passed the House by a large Majority for raising more regulars for the War only, as well as adding one Major to each Regiment in service to be taken from the Captains of the army. Should they promote the oldest Captain in service to the Majorities, I shall be made a Captain by it. There is a strong chance of promotion for me, but still I dislike the features of the Bill. As soon as you see the passage of the bill by the senate I wish you would send it to me. As every thing here just now is in preparation, of course we have but little news."

Once again James confided to Ellen that she had made the right decision to join Corinna and Edward in Pensacola: "It seems to be tacitly acknowledged by all here that this is no place for our families. The only lady that I know of who has been here was Mrs. Ogden, wife of Capt. [Edmund Augustine] Ogden Qmaster,[9] whom you saw in Buffalo—& she went back immediately. Should the war ever end & our Regiment stationed at some particular point here, so that we can make a few comforts around us, all of us will be for sending for our families & I shall be among the first." The next month (February) found the army, commanded by Gen. Winfield Scott, preparing for its assault on Vera Cruz, as James informed Ellen.

[James Anderson to Ellen Anderson

Tampico, Mexico, to Pensacola]
February 22, 1847

My Dearest Ell,

. . . we still are encamped near the mouth of the river, with the transports in full view waiting for the elements to subside. I presume from appearances that the embarkation will commence tomorrow. I cannot give you any additional Army News—nor have I a chance of getting another letter from you at this

---

9. Edmund Ogden was a native of New York who joined the army in 1827. Ogden served with the First and Eighth Infantries before his appointment as quartermaster in 1838. In 1848 he was brevetted major for meritorious conduct. He died in 1855. See Heitman, *Historical Register,* 1:756.

place. I hope however to the last & as there is a large Steamboat lying outside waiting for the surf to run down in order to cross the bar, I may yet get one. Genl. Scott left here day before yesterday for the South & as I hear only waits for the force from this place to join him, to commence the fandango at Vera Cruz. Should we be attacked on landing there may be some hard fighting for us. . . . We have to land our heavy siege pieces & columbiads, the latter carrying balls over 100 lbs weight—& the infantry will have to protect & the navy cover the operation. Should we however succeed in landing without opposition, Vera Cruz is ours without much ado & the principal strife will be nearer the City of Mexico, unless the Mexican Government ask for peace.

I have now seen the banana, the plantain, the cocoanut, the orange, the lime, the lemon, the citron, the shadduck, the pommegranite [*sic*], the pine apple & other fruits not known in the United States, growing & I suppose as we get farther within the tropics the vegetation will change still more. I took a gun today & went into the woods back of us & met nothing but noisy parrots, parroquites [*sic*] & Mexican jays, one variety of each of which I killed more to satisfy my curiosity than anything else, but when I got back to camp, I found myself covered from head to foot with ticks & had to strip off my clothes & smoke them to get them off. The red bugs & ticks are a great nuisance here.

With this letter you will receive my pay accounts for the month of February which Major [Eugene] Van Ness[10] will pay whenever you call upon him for it & should you wish the money before he comes to Pensacola to make his payment, all you have to do is to get the Doctor to send on the accounts to him & he will send you the money. There appears just now to be but little dissipation among the Regulars. Every thing appears solemn as if on the eve of some great crisis & yet it is generally known that the Mexicans are in a bad plight. The news, however, of Genl. Taylor's defeating Santa Anna is not true, as we have information from San Louis to within eight days ago & he had not then left there. Strange as it may appear all the dread among officers and men as to the approaching campaign is of the sea voyage & most of them would rather march 500 miles than go 100 by water—as to myself I have no dread of the sea & am glad we don't have to <u>march</u> to Vera Cruz. I cannot say to you that you need feel no anxiety on my account, for the future is uncertain to us all & in battle the chance of a man's death is certainly increased. I can only say that I feel confident of living to the end of the war & if it don't last too long, a few years

---

10. A native of New York, Eugene Van Ness joined the army as paymaster in 1838. He was promoted to the rank of colonel in 1855. He died in 1862. See Heitman, *Historical Register,* 1:983.

longer. Our regiment is in good order & I believe will behave well & Genl. Scott says it shall have the chance to shew itself—by the bye. . . .

The troops here are all healthy & from what I have seen of the place & vicinity I believe with proper police, the yellow fever would scarcely ever make its appearance here. God bless you. Good night. Love to all—kiss bud, Sis, & baby for me—I will close this after I hear that our embarkation from this point is certainly decided upon so that you may know to an hour what time we leave here, a thousand thanks for your letter of the 21st of last month, it makes me feel as if you & I were growing young instead of old.

As Ever Yours

Willo

February 23, 1847

Dearest I have only to add that we are off. yours truly

Willo

[Ellen Anderson to James Anderson]

no. 11 [Pensacola to Mexico]

February 25, 1847

My Dearest Will,

I promised in my last letter to write more frequently a great deal and beautifully I have kept my promise. I feel mad at myself for letting so many days slip by without performing it but I have nothing new to offer by way of excuse. I kept a-being busy and the time slipped by without my noting it. But as I have had no letter from you in the mean time I cannot help thinking you are where my letters cannot find you let me write as often as I will. However I do not intend that this idea shall deter me from writing as I of course, cannot tell what letters you will receive or what you will miss. Corine and the Doctor have gone to New Orleans. The latter to purchase drugs and the former a cook. The Doctor is about to open a drug shop in partnership with Mr. [J. M.] Shippy[11] formerly of St. Augustine. It appears about the most reasonable notion I have ever seen the Doctor start up and at present is quite a hobby with him. He is very much improved in his habits and so is Corine and there is room for more. E. does not of course give up his practice at all. He is to set Shippy up in the business and they are to divide the profits between them. Success attend them.

---

11. J. M. Shippy was a native of New York (U.S. Manuscript Census, Population [1850], for Escambia County, Florida, p. 295).

I will just mention in this letter for fear you should miss the others that I have received both the $100 and the $50 you sent me. I do not think I miss getting any of your letters, sooner or later they all come to hand. I wish mine to you could have the like success. It appears to me you do not get more than a third of them. I am waiting anxiously for a letter from you now. It is rumoured here that there has been another battle, but from what they say I conclude you were not there, you know it can make no difference in the fact if I say I am glad of it. I want to hear that you are right well again and what prospect there is of your coming home.

We are all in good health. Bud cut the top of one of his little fingers almost entirely off last week. He stumbled and fell striking his hand upon a hatchet that had been most carelessly left in the way. The cut was entirely through the bone. But it has healed without any sort of trouble and is now almost entirely well—a fully good proof I think that his blood is in a healthy state. He and sis go off to school every morning like they were born a-doing it. Bud's schoolmistress complains that his memory is too good in which account she has to find a new lesson for him to read every day. He played her a trick by bringing his book home and getting Virginia to read it through to him. Perhaps you do not understand the difficulty, but I do because I make him read to me sometimes. You see he will try to read without spelling the words and you cannot be sure that he is reading and if you make him spell he will pronounce according to his recollection not according to the sound of the letters and you catch him by the mistakes he makes. The baby runs about and plays and jabbers with Bud and sis and fights too, like the toughest of them. She speaks some words quite plain. Sis tells every one who enquires after you of her that you have gone to 'Mexicole' to kill the birds. I suppose she gets the notion from your going gaming at Gratiot. She says: "One day my pa (paw as she pronounces) brought me home a bird and it scratched and scratched and scratched." And I think she remembers when you brought home a wounded bird at Gratiot. She has a great fancy for inventing. For instance I will say to her "Sis tell me something." She will hesitate a moment and commence "when I was a little boy" (that is a great thing with her) "I once had on a white jacket and white pantaloons and a white hat and I was dressed all in white." This or some other nonsense. She will tell you with a degree of gesture and earnestness that is very funny in one so little, especially as what she says is pure invention. They call her a liar, but it does not appear to me that she intends to deceive at all, but she amuses herself and her listener by imagining. She has not forgotten you at all nor the sugar plumbs you used to give her. She often describes the wonderful things you are to bring her from Mexico. Indeed whenever she wants or desires any thing she either asserts that she possesses it already or you are to bring it from Mexico.

Virginia is well and sends her love to you and says I must tell you she wishes you would come home.

I believe the regiment bill has passed for Volunteers. I do not see so many papers now as I used to. E. does not bring them home. One little item I saw which was, that when the committee on military affairs reported that the army did not need a Lt. Col. their report was received with shouts of laughter. Nevertheless they continued to get the bill before them again and I do not know how it was settled but I suppose you do by this time. Sis has just told me that when you come from Mexico you are going to put two pockets in the apron I made her. I have most horrible ink and the old nick seems to have been abusing my pen so that I can scarcely write legibly.

I do not expect Corine back for a week. I keep house in her absence. It is pretty tedious business. I have not been here long enough to take an interest in the people. I am slow to form attachments anyhow, and there is no one here remarkably interesting although I ought not to say it as they are all very polite to me especially now that Corine is away. Last night we had a room full of company, and as I felt pretty stupid I set them all to making candy to entertain themselves and they seemed very well pleased. I cannot tell whether Virginia enjoys herself here or not. She is never very communicative to me and I seldom attempt to draw anyone out. I suppose however that she has nothing to communicate. God bless you

Ever yours
Ellen

On March 9, James participated in the successful amphibious assault on Vera Cruz. From a camp near the landing he provided Ellen with a detailed description of the assault. Later in April he related an account of the Battle of Cerro Gordo and his observations on Mexican customs.[12]

[James Anderson to Ellen Brown Anderson]

Xalapa [Jalapa], Mexico [to Pensacola]
May 5, 1847

My Dearest Ell,

I have just received your letter (no. 15) of the 13th April in which you state that you have received my letter of March 29th & that you have also seen Thomas Young. I am very sorry that I could not know beforehand that the <u>Princeton</u> was to go to Pensacola or I might have sent you some little matters

---

12. See Denham and Huneycutt, "With Scott in Mexico," 31–39.

as curiosities of the country. Let me beg you my dear to forget my whining about not getting letters. At length they are all reaching me in good season but there is one letter that has never reached me & I did not know it until I got your last—it is the one in which you say you told me of your money matters & how you stood. I have asked you to tell me, in order that I may govern myself accordingly in remittances & as 'our young folks' grow bigger & of more consequence, I must manage to become less so & spend less money on myself. I am afraid I have been too selfish in my many solicitations for letters, letters, nothing but letters from you & the strain of your last is so sober that I cannot help thinking I have required too much, if so—you must not hesitate to say so, do what you can for me in the way of correspondence, remembering always that your letters are to me more than aught else. You speak of my standing a chance of getting tired of the old story, if you were to write very often or rather every day. Don't you think I would get a lecture if I were to make such a remark of you. I know that I have the advantage of you in our correspondence, having at all times things upon which I can dwell that will be interesting to you, while you are tied down to the same scenes and the same duties every day; but you must remember that you are my home & that you can mention no detail of home that will not be interesting.

The question of our being stationed at Vera Cruz was never agitated. The 1st Infantry are stationed there. I have now had five letters from you since I have been in Xalapa. Poor old Margaret. I doubt whether she ever will suit any body as well as she suited me & I doubt whether I shall ever have another cook to please me as well as she did, which is saying a great deal, as I am pretty fond of the good things of this life & can enjoy a good dinner as well as any of my neighbours. I must mention [a few] words more of money matters. Let the matter with George rest for the present. I suppose he had [the] idea connected with your interest or he would not have loaned the money to Louis Aldrich. Had I known these facts however some months sooner, they would have saved me some uneasiness. I wish you to keep & appropriate all the money I have sent you & will send you from Mexico to the use of yourself & the children. . . .[13]

[Ellen Brown Anderson to James Anderson]

[Pensacola, Florida, to Vera Cruz, Mexico]
May 27th, 1847

13. For the rest of this letter, see Denham and Huneycutt, "With Scott in Mexico," 39–40.

My Dearest Will,

Your two nice long letters of April 29th and May 5th I received day before yesterday & I have so much to say in reply to them that I hardly know where to begin. I am very far from supposing you have nothing else to do, my own best Will, than writing to me, although if I did so suppose my obligation to you would be none the less, for what could gratify me more than that you spent your leisure in writing to me? But my Dearest and my best of all husbands, I cannot express what I feel when I reflect how many things you have to occupy your time and attention. If you were never separated from me, I should never half-know you. I recollect I closed my last letter to you with the expression (written in play) that your letters were the best part of you. I can scarcely think you misunderstood me, but after the letter was gone it worried me some for fear you might take exception at it. If you did, you must take what I say now as a comment on it. Oh my Will keep on, write to me, write to me, yet do not worry yourself either, write to me just as you have done. You have no idea of the happiness you confer. You actually make me better, for I cannot help thanking my Father in Heaven for all his blessings bestowed upon me, unworthy as I am, and I try to do my duty that his blessing may not be withdrawn from me. I have not written to you for more than a week, and I blame myself continually for not writing to you oftener. One reason is for two or three days I was sick not very sick but still too sick to write. You know I have always been subject to slight billious attacks, and I suppose I always shall be but I am getting to know them too well to let them run into fevers. I said this was one reason and the other is the want of a good servant. Just now I have none at all, for I discovered the one I had to be a thief and of course dismissed her but she was good for nothing apart from that. Now I am on the look out for a new one; meantime I find the entire charge of the three youngsters somewhat fatiguing. Still I had much rather be without than have one in whom I [had no] confidence. Bud and Sis are delighted with their medals. I have strung them on ribbons and tied them around their necks, and put all my little stock of latin on the stretch to try and translate the inscription on them.

You say I must give you my impression of Mexico in order that you may tell whether you have been accurate in your descriptions. My Dear Will that would be to send your letters right back to you. I am satisfied that your descriptions are most excellent and as for the vividness of my impressions I feel as if I had been the whole journey. Do not worry yourself with the idea that I let money matters trouble me. It is true I give a thought to them but it is in a reasonable sort of way. You must recollect I am human as well as yourself and more like you perhaps than you imagine. Don't you think both of us require a check [rein]. If you had received the letter it would have informed you that I mentioned the matter more because I thought you would expect me so to do, than for any uneasyness [*sic*] it gave me. I do not call your complaints of my not writing "whining" by any means. I think you had good reason to complain. Virginia wrote to you last week and says I must tell you she intends to write again next week. You can't imagine what a funny little thing the baby is. She is just at the most interesting age now. We say every day how you would delight to play with her, but Dear Will if I go on in this way you will feel as if you could fly away to get home. May Gen. Scott prove a prophet. Let us have peace or I am afraid there will be found a woman and small children making tracks in the direction of Mexico. As for Jalapa or any other place without doubt I should like it just as well as Gratiot. It is not the place but how I am fixed there that I care about.

I am sorry my letters have not seemed cheerful sometimes. I try to be cheerful and for the most part I succeed. I feel that I have a great deal to render me contented but Dear Will do you remember what the old phrenologist there at Mrs. Day's told you about me? His eloquent sum up of my character was "She is as melancholy as the mischief." I suppose you have forgotten it, but it made an impression on me because I thought there was some truth in it and the nature will peep out sometimes when one is not aware of it. But I am not melancholy neither; only I seem to get so when I am thinking or writing. But I say again and again I have much to make me happy and I am so. God bless you My Dear Dear Willoughby. I am very glad you give so good an account of your health. I have already written to you that I have received the Daguerreotype of the Mustacheos. [Tell] Schureman I send my compliments to him and I give you all joy of your picturesque appearances. This letter is written abominable but I hope you will be able to read it. I did not feel like writing nice today. Good bye.

Ever yours,
Ellen.

James's letter of May 5 was the last to reach Ellen and probably the last that he wrote. On May 6, Gen. Winfield Scott sent Gen. William Worth with his three thousand troops to Puebla, near Mexico City. The rest of Scott's army followed on May 28. Thus with this movement and the stations between Puebla and Veracruz being evacuated on June 4, the American force was almost completely cut off from all communications from the coast. While James and his comrades settled into their three-month occupation of Puebla in preparation for their final drive toward Mexico City, Ellen, the Aldriches, and George in Newnansville waited anxiously for information from the front. On July 26, George provided Mannevillette with an update of the family's activities that summer. Asking that his brother return home, George explained,

We have looked for you year after year until hope is nearly exhausted. You will find here warm hearts, to bid you welcome home, beating with love toward you, such as a brother and sister only can show. Should you come this fall you will find us all in Florida. Corinna still resides at Pensacola, Dr. Aldrich is doing a good practice there. Ellen and her family (3 children) are with her, but her stay there depends on the <u>War</u> in Mexico. Capt. Anderson is there fighting his best. He was in the "battle of Cerro Gordo" in Genl. Twiggs command. Genl T. was in the hottest part of the battle. Most earnestly do I hope for the termination of the war. It is a disgrace to the United States, however glorious may seem the victories. It is a war of Mr. Polk's and if not ended sooner will end with his administration, which will as surely fall at the next election, as that the sun will set. . . . You will see in the person of your brother, how easy it is to transform a "Yankee" to a southern "Cracker"—Living in log-houses and eating "hog and hominy" transforms a person almost as soon as the light does the colour of a chameleon. Yet let the outward man change as it may, my <u>insides</u> are the same as when I last saw you, years, long years ago. The crops in this country will be very large this season, abundant enough to supply all Europe, should it again be afflicted with short crops, as it was last year. . . . Let me hear from you often—though I trust our correspondence will soon cease by our being brought together.

affectly your brother
George L. Brown

Meanwhile, also that July, Gen. Winfield Scott's forces made ready for their final assault against Mexico City. Scott organized his twelve thousand troops into four divisions. As part of David E. Twiggs's division, James's Second Infantry under the command of Bennet Riley marched out of Puebla toward Mexico City on August 7. Anderson's brigade was the first to enter the Valley of Mexico. Ten days later the rest of Scott's force was approximately five miles south of Mexico City. Over the next three days Anderson's unit jockeyed for position along the southern approaches to the city while sparring with Mexican troops under the command of Gen. Gabriel Valencia. Then, finally, in a dramatic morning attack on August 20, Riley's troops routed Valencia's forces, opening the southern approaches to the city. By the end of the day, after the battles of Contreras and Churubusco, Scott's army had pushed the demoralized Mexicans behind the gates of the city. That afternoon, however, in an attack against the Churubusco convent, James was mortally wounded. Struck by a musket ball in the neck, he died at ten o'clock that night. With mail cut off from Mexico, Ellen likely first learned of her husband's death from newspaper accounts.[14] Months later, in a letter written from Mexico City, Capt. Henry W. Wessells, James's West Point classmate who was with him on that final day, provided Ellen with a full account of what had happened.[15]

[Corinna Aldrich to Mannevillette Brown]

Pensacola [to Paris]
September 28, 1847

Alas, My Dear Brother, sad has been the causes of my not writing you of late. But I believe I have written you since poor Edward's illness. He was very ill for three weeks, but has quite recovered—and we had just begun to look forward again to a brighter future—when the news came of Terrible battles in Mexico, & among the slain, our beloved friend & brother—<u>Anderson</u>—It was a tremendous stroke for poor Ellen—indeed we were all overwhelmed with grief—not only for the loss and most <u>untimely</u> death of one so dear to us all, but our sympathy for our dear afflicted sister makes it still more intolerable to bear. I know, dear Manne, that these events, however chance like they appear to us, are controlled by Him who suffereth not a sparrow to fall without his notice, & permission. Yet it still seems dark to us, that he should be snatched away—just in the very prime of his life, & usefulness; just when the star of his destiny seemed to shine the brightest—Oh! we looked forward to so much pleasure, we hoped to have you all at home & to be so happy—but he is gone—and now I only look about, & wonder for whom next the mandate will be sent!

You must try & come home to us, once more, Dear Manne—we long to see you—but we fear to hope again—Oh! trust in God! My brother, and endeavour to be prepared—when your summons comes! . . .

We have sad news again to day from Mexico—but our selfish hearts tremble no longer. All our hopes & all our fears are set at naught. He for whom we hoped and feared so much—sleeps beneath the sod. The clang & tumult above him, will no more disturb, the shouts of history will not reach his ear—nor the groans of dying comrades trouble his repose.

We have not yet heard the particulars of poor A's death. There seems to be so much confusion & fighting down there, that no one has time to write us. We

14. Anderson was listed among the dead in the *Pensacola Gazette,* September 11, 1847. See also *Jacksonville (Florida) News,* September 17, 1847.

15. Henry W. Wessells to Ellen Anderson, October 26, 1847, and February 27, 1848, in Denham and Huneycutt, "With Scott in Mexico," 44–47.

only know a terrible fight ensued on the hordes of Mexico (the city) & that he was killed after distinguishing himself, by much skill & bravery. Our loss was great but we gained the day. Since then another battle has been fought & the report to day is that we have lost in the two battles about 3,000—the enemy more! Gens Worth, [Gideon J.] Pillow & [Persifor F.] Smith are said to have fallen—Gen Scott wounded—but we have no official account of anything as yet & wont have for some days. I suspect all is confusion & riot there. Scott has possession of the city, 'tis said, at last, but at what a sacrifice. Indeed if President Polk don't rue the day he fought with Mexico, he can't have any feeling. His brother passed through here yesterday, en route to the field. He looks as if he had preserved his body—beforehand—coddled in liquor—I recon all these old fellows tipple enough—else they would do better. The manner in which our army has been sacrificed is dreadful to think of. Had Gen Scott had men &c enough, he might have intimidated the Mexicans—but they did not fear him. He had but about 8,000 in all & they over 30,000. Of course, the victory for us, is the greater—but not worth <u>one</u> of the noble hearts it hushed in death. Why my dear Manne our country will be in mourning from end to end & that for the brightest and best of its sons. It is feared, if relief is not sent to Scott soon, his whole army will be cut off. As it is, he can't have enough to keep the city . . . long in his hands. I presume he will have a reinforcement, as soon as possible—but it ought to have been sent before. I did hope for Peace. . . . I feel as if I did not care & yet I know I ought to feel for those who may suffer. But it is thought we are no nearer peace than when we began.

I must close this, dear—for I have not yet written to George. I want to do so—& beg him to come to see us, & do you try and come by & by. You must not come until after frost, say the last [of] October. The fever is raging now in New Orleans & Mobile—1000 dying daily. . . . All send love—we are all well. Write soon & come soon.

[Corinna]

[Corinna Aldrich to Mannevillette Brown]

Pensacola [to Paris]
November 22, 1847[16]
. . . I have not heard from George since our sad bereavement. He wrote E a short letter from Charleston, which he lost or mislaid, and therefore I can only say he was well, & promised to do all he could for Ell—Poor thing—she is not

---

16. The first page of this letter is missing.

in any need at present but pretends to bear her lot. Edward ever has been & still is a brother & more to her. He would not listen to any . . . for her living with us before, and surely he would be grieved at such a prospect now. Ellen says she feels all his kindness, but by & by she desires to do something, that she may lay up against her children. . . . I tell her yes, by & by, to <u>satisfy</u> her—The Doctor's profession affords him a very handsome living and an occasional something to lay by and [he] does . . . want to put it by for me, and what do I need it for but her & her children—Dear Manne, it is & [especially] to be a cause of gratitude in my heart, that I have a home to give her & all, and such a husband to receive her—for indeed he feels like a brother to you all, and I love him the better for it—Little Corinna is begging me to quit writing, she wants me to play—Here comes the doctor, he will [play] with her. We have such a nice large home—six rooms [and the basement]—a parlour large—I am writing in what Ed calls his study—it opens into the dining room—I suppose you know every southern house has a figg in front, if not all round, out there the two little girls are now at play—I do long to see you dear, but why speak a fact so evident—You must be with us as soon as possible. I ask no more—I have stayed from church this evening on purpose to write you—as the Dr. & I propose leaving tomorrow for Mobile. The Dr. has a little business, and as the sickly season is surpast, he thinks the jaunt will be of service to both of us.

You say I have not told you Ed. was well—Indeed, dear Manne, you cannot receive all my letters—I do not think him so entirely well as before his illness—yet he is the best judge & he declares he is in good order. My own health is much improved within a month or so—I have been taking <u>iron</u> regularly, & it has greatly benefitted me—Ellen too is in better health & spirits than a while back—indeed my brother, dear Ell is far more cheerful & resigned to her lot than I ever thought she could become. She declares her trust is in God and in that trust she is happy—Oh a blessed one it is my brother, would that we could cast all our care on Him, for he says He careth for us—& if we but have faith, we need have no fears—Don't think it is a usual custom to spend my sabbaths on <u>letter</u> <u>writing</u>—No dear, I have not done so for a long while, but I could not think of leaving town without replying to your kind letter—lest some accident should prevent my writing on the way, & thus delay too long. I have suffered from suspense too much myself to let others feel one hour pain from such cause that I could relieve. Will is gone to church with his man and with Virginia, who, by the way, is still with us. She talks of going to Norfolk—but I don't suppose she will leave before spring if at all—I shall write George either tonight or <u>en</u> <u>route</u> for Mobile. I don't think [it is] the sick[ly] season because [it] is in the papers regularly—you ask if you can visit us from New York via Newnansville

—certainly but it would be out of your way—yet you can soon ascertain the [route] once in N.Y. You can scarcely not be aware of the improvements in travelling dear, just as you left the U.S.—vast indeed they are and oh may you soon witness them dear, and may I have the happiness ere long to welcome you to my home & hearth . . . your <u>devoted</u> sister, Corinna

Chapter Ten

"We Are Nearing Our Desired Haven"
Key West

During the remaining months of 1847 Corinna, Virginia, the widowed Ellen and her children, Edward Willoughby (eight years old), Corinna Georgia (six), and Ellen Mannevillette (four), coped with the loss of James. Then, on the night of January 2, 1848, while Edward was away, they were awakened when their Pensacola residence caught fire. Despite prompt assistance of those nearby, the house burned to the ground.[1] This event no doubt strengthened Edward's determination to leave Pensacola. Soon the family moved once again to Macon, Georgia, arriving on January 19. The family rented a house a few days later. On February 10, Corinna and Ellen traveled to Charleston to buy new furniture. But Edward's second stint in Macon was even shorter than the first. The town proved unsatisfactory, and by October the family had moved to Marietta.[2] After depositing Corinna, Ellen, and the children in a boarding-house, Edward returned to Florida, this time to Key West. As the new year dawned, Corinna received the following letter from her husband.

[Dr. Edward Aldrich to Corinna Aldrich]

Key West, Florida [to Marietta, Georgia]
January 8, 1849

My dearest Corinna,

It is very cheering to my heart to be able to rescue you from trying suspense, as I am convinced I shall, when you have read my report of Key West. I am agreeably disposed toward the place. Firstly, as brother Stevens would say, the population, instead of being six or seven hundred as I supposed, numbers nearer <u>three thousand</u>. And there are as many pleasant families here as you will

---

1. *Pensacola Gazette,* January 8, 1848.

2. Corinna Aldrich to Mannevillette Brown, March 3, May 7, August 27, October 25, 1848, Anderson-Brown Papers, USMA.

Bird's-eye view of Key West, circa 1855

find in any southern town of the same population—and in praise of the climate, <u>enough cannot be said</u>—The sea breeze is so exhilarating, and the gardens look so green and fresh, that I can [scarce realize] the impression that I am still in <u>Uncle Sam's</u> territories. You know what delightful nights we had in Pensacola & St. Augustine in the spring and summer[? W]e have such weather here all the time. The island is six miles long, and there are many pleasant walks about, in different directions.

I arrived here (in the Island after a delightful passage of little over two days) on Wednesday evening. Next day I was sent for to attend two negroes belonging to Mr. Fontane—then a Capt. [Reason] Duke sent for me to attend his wife [Jane], she came here from one of the neighboring keys for her medical treatment.[3] She has a daughter also expecting in a few days to be confined, and I have every assurance that I shall be employed in preference to either of the other physicians, for the opposing faculty are not held in much respect. One is old. Dr. Peachy, hospital surgeon, & his partner, Dr. [Thomas A.] Pinkney [Pinckney]—the latter is brother in law of Judge [William] Marvin, <u>& his clerk</u>.[4] The Judge is now absent at Tallahassee, he is expected back shortly.

3. Captain Reason and Jane Duke were well known in the Florida Keys. He was a successful wrecker and operated the Cape Florida lighthouse. By the middle 1850s the Dukes had relocated to Tampa, where they established a hotel, the Florida House. See Brown, *Tampa before the Civil War,* 125.

4. Theodore A. Pinckney, born in Ontario County, New York, arrived in Key West in 1836. Sometime thereafter, with William Marvin's help, he was appointed inspector of customs and surgeon in the marine hospital. Marvin discusses this matter in Kevin K. Kearney, ed., "Autobiography of William Marvin," *Florida Historical Quarterly* 36 (January 1958): 206. See also Hammond, *Medical Profession in 19th Century Florida,* 499–500. A native of New York and one of the nation's leading experts on maritime law, William

Joseph Lancaster, his wife Annie, and their daughters Eliza and Laura were friends of Ellen and Corinna in Jacksonville and Key West. Florida Supreme Court.

Judge [Joseph B.] Lancaster now resides here, with his family.[5] He is also absent for a short time at Tallahassee. There are no troops here now, & . . . I . . . was allowed to occupy buildings of the barracks. By next return of the boat I shall be able to tell you definitely what I shall do. I shall have no difficulty about getting a house either at the barracks, or nearer the center of the town. Two of those handsome residences of the barracks are still unoccupied. Ossian Hart is

Marvin served as U.S. district court judge of the Southern District of Florida in 1847–63; see Manley, Brown, and Rise, *Supreme Court of Florida,* 78–83.

5. One of Florida's leading Whig politicians, Joseph B. Lancaster served on the Florida Legislative Council (1825, 1840–44, serving as speaker in 1843–44). He was also the former port collector and mayor of Jacksonville, judge of the Southern Judicial Circuit, and a member of the Florida Supreme Court. See Manley, Brown, and Rise, *Supreme Court of Florida,* 128–31; Brown, *Ossian Bingley Hart,* 73–74, 84, 92; Denham and Brown, *Cracker Times and Pioneer Lives,* 150–51; and Phelps, *People of Lawmaking in Florida,* 56.

also living here with his family, practising law[6] I have met with many old acquaintances & patients—and all try to persuade me to stay here. We have three handsome churches, & a fourth new building. . . . [T]here is a society here of sons of temperance & about one hundred & fifty members. The place is improved much since the severe storm, it is rebuilt in a more substantial manner.

I did not enumerate all my patients. I was called on to attend a little girl this morning, & before going out operated on a Capt. of a schooner for elongated uvula palate—I removed it very much to his relief—he is stopping at present at the hotel with <u>his</u> wife, a very pretty woman but she has [ptyregurm?] on her eye—has been in New York & placed herself under a nervous old physician for the whole summer at a cost of near three hundred dollars without being relieved—I suspect he was too nervous to operate—I shall operate on her in a few days and I feel sure of success. Indeed I am already in a better practice than I have ever had in Georgia, and best of all <u>it will pay</u>. The Marine hospital is worth 1200 dollars a year. And as old Peachy is a <u>loco [foco]</u>, I hope by and by to supersede him. The cholera is so severe in N. Orleans that some fear . . . of its coming here. I do not myself think it will come, and I sincerely trust that such a calamity may be averted.

We had a great many foreigners on board as passengers to Havanna. Among them was a son of the rich Jew, [a] Rotchchild of Paris. I found him very sociable, & a thorough republican. I have not yet been able . . . to dispose of Mariah, but there are two persons wanting to buy, but as she gets constant employment I thought I would wait until next return of the boat and I will then remit to you. I do sincerely trust you will be able to get along in money matters until then. If you have not yet gone to housekeeping I think <u>you better not</u>, but try & sell all goods & chattels except such as you can conveniently ship in small compass via R. Road <u>to Charleston</u>—but dispose of <u>everything you can</u>—for one <u>fact is most certain</u> I cannot return to Marietta to live. I can do better anywhere on the sea board. Mind to sell all you can, for the expenses of moving goods per sail was enormous. I was charged only to Augusta $5.25 for my extra baggage—but I insisted on deduction in consideration of paying for two seats & I only received $1.00.

6. Ossian Hart, a native of Jacksonville, was a son of Isaiah Hart, with whom Edward had boarded when he first arrived in Florida in 1836. A prominent Whig politician, Hart was solicitor of the Southern Judicial Circuit. He and his wife Katherine had resided in Key West since November 1846, migrating to the town from Fort Pierce after the devastating hurricane that struck the east coast of Florida that year. See Brown, *Ossian Bingley Hart*, 66–68.

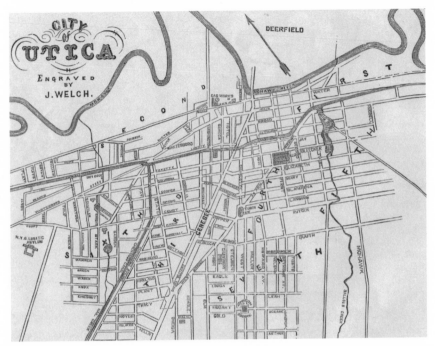

Utica city plan. Utica, New York, City Directory, 1849.

Baggs Square, Utica, New York, circa 1850. Oneida County Historical Society.

I hope you got my letters from Savh & Augusta, also the box . . . from the latter place Augusta. . . . I examined all the goods in [L. S. Switts's] store at Savh & he also went out & got some other specimens but I do not see anything as pretty, as the piece I took down, so I told him to credit the bill the amount of the dress, & that you would probably be over in the course of the winter & so make a selection then. I was disappointed dear—but really, he had not a piece of goods that I could call at all pretty.

Mariah behaves herself well, & I hope to be able to make an advantageous sale of her[,] but if I knew you would get cash enough for the furniture for present purpose I would keep her—For she [may earn] 50cts a day with ease. If I sell her, I have made up my mind to retain the child, & let her keep her in charge until she gets older. I never knew a finer little negro. Mariah . . . says she likes Macon better than here—I doubt not she does. . . .

While Edward was shuttling his wife and her sister's family through Georgia in preparation for their move to Florida, Mannevillette Brown was just returning to the United States after what a Utica, New York, newspaper called an extended "residence in Italy and France," where he studied "art among the noblest galleries of the world."[7] Upon his return to Utica, Mannevillette boarded first with Thomas and Sarah Walker, his old patrons,[8] with whom Corinna and Ellen had corresponded while Mannevillette was in Europe. Mannevillette soon took up residence in the fashionable Baggs Hotel in the heart of Utica's thriving business district. He frequently joined the guests entertained weekly at the Walkers' residence.[9] Soon to become Utica's mayor, Thomas Walker was a law partner of future senator Roscoe Conkling. Mannevillette also reacquainted himself with other city leaders such as Joshua A Spencer and Francis Kernan.[10] During the decade when Mannevillette was away, Utica experienced dramatic prosperity and population growth. By 1850 Utica contained nearly twenty thousand native-born citizens and immigrants

---

7. Undated Utica, New York, newspaper clipping, Anderson-Brown Papers, USMA.

8. Courtney, "M. E. D. Brown," 71.

9. According to one account, Sarah Walker entertained handsomely: "Mr. and Mrs. Walker met the most prominent people in art and literature . . . and many of these distinguished individuals became guests at their house . . . which contained about the best collection of pictures in Utica at the time, some of them being portraits painted by Artist Brown" (undated newspaper clipping, Walker Family Biography File, Oneida County Historical Society, Utica, New York).

10. David M. Jordan, *Roscoe Conkling of New York: Voice in the Senate* (Ithaca, N.Y.: Cornell University Press, 1971), 6–7; Bagg, *Memorial History of Utica,* 184–85.

from many parts of the world. The town boasted canal and railroad links that served a flourishing industrial economy based on banking, woolen and cotton mills, and other manufacturing industries.

As the young artist readjusted to life in the United States, his thoughts fell naturally to his sisters in Florida, especially Ellen and her children. He and George were determined to assist her in any way they could. They expressed this determination both to Ellen and to each other. Soon after arriving in Utica, Mannevillette wrote Ellen, "I am sorry I never knew personally your husband, but I shall try to prove my good will towards him by giving it all to his dear children whom I long to see."[11] Likewise, George wrote Mannevillette of his own feelings regarding Ellen and her children. "Ellen's little family," he noted, "seem to give a promise that the race will not be extinct in the present generation. Losing their Father, Poor Anderson, cannot be made up to them. Yet you and I, Heaven aiding us dear brother, will raise them up in the world as he would wish them to have been raised. Before his death, I felt like an old bachelor, who was satisfied to knock along through life, content if, when death called, I could square up with all and go. Now, I feel these little children acting on me continually to heap up something where rust doth corrupt.[12] In short, I feel like a man of family."[13]

On April 11, Edward and the family set out from Marietta for New York to visit Mannevillette and purchase goods for use in Key West.[14] By May, after a short visit, Corinna, Ellen, the children, and Virginia boarded a steamer bound for Key West. On May 26, Corinna sent her brother the following account.

[Corinna Aldrich to Mannevillette Brown]

Key West [to Utica, New York]
May 26th, 1849

My Dear Brother,

As we are nearing our desired Haven—after the tedious passage of 15 days, I am resolved to drop you a line, despite the rolling and tossing of our barque!

11. Mannevillette Brown to Ellen Anderson, February 24, 1849, Anderson-Brown Papers, USMA.

12. Matt. 6:19.

13. George L. Brown to Mannevillette Brown, June 3, 1849, Anderson-Brown Papers, USMA.

14. Corinna Aldrich to Mannevillette Brown, April 21, 1849, Anderson-Brown Papers, USMA.

for I know you will be very anxious to hear of our safe arrival, and as the <u>Samson</u> is bound to Apalachicola, and the steamer <u>Isabel</u> must have already gone on her way, if I do not improve this chance, I may not have another before the 15th or 16th June when the <u>Isabel</u> will again return—She makes but two trips per month.—I can give you no account of our future home, that is all in the distance, and as to our voyage—it has been without excitement or novelty to me—we had one tolerable blow, the first night we neared the Bahama Banks —ever memorable from old Columbus landing, although dreary and barren enough to look upon—The next day, however we were becalmed, and we have had but slight winds since—which accounts for our long passage. At Abaco Island—the negros came off in boats bringing shells and fish to offer in exchange for bread & meat—and <u>all</u> <u>you'll</u> <u>please</u> <u>to</u> <u>give</u> 'em. They are the most greedy beggars I ever met with—but certainly excusable—for their land is but a heap of sand and rocks, and they poor and ignorant. One old grey beard, who is nominally the governor—or a sort of driver appointed by the black Prince of Nassau to keep the lesser darkies in order—came out in a light boat, and introduced himself as His excellency John D. Ellis—Governor of Abaco. He proved the greatest beggar of them all, but our captain has a true sailor's heart, and gave to them all, liberally. They were not as free in return as I expected—but held on to their fishes & shells for a price! I bought a pair of the latter—more in charity, than admiration, however, as they were not choice specimens.[15]

15. Corinna's encounter with Afro-Bahamians is typical of the continual interaction between these folk and ships passing along the Florida coast during the nineteenth century. Economic and social exchanges were common. With the collapse of the Bahamian economy in the late 1800s, Afro-Bahamians began migrating to South Florida to seek seasonal agricultural work. When Miami emerged in the late 1890s, Abaco blacks seeking economic opportunities helped to found Coconut Grove and Miami. Thus some of these blacks selling provisions to Corinna's party may well have been the parents of those who eventually relocated permanently in Florida. See Marvin Dunn, *Black Miami in the Twentieth Century* (Gainesville: University Press of Florida, 1997), 1–19, 34–44, 51–73, 95–100; and Paul S. George, "'Colored Town': Miami's Black Community, 1896–1930," *Florida Historical Quarterly* 56 (April 1978): 432–35. Bahamian blacks and their progeny had significant impact in Florida into the twentieth century, taking on leadership roles in civil rights struggles in their communities. As Robert W. Saunders has written, "[M]any influential Blacks in Key West and Tampa either were born in the Bahamas Islands or descended from Bahamians. . . . Bahamian traditions remained strong in these families and were passed down" (*Bridging the Gap: Continuing the Florida NAACP Legacy of Harry T. Moore* [Tampa, Fla.: University of Tampa Press, 2000], 27–28).

We have been beating about among these reefs and Islands for the last six or seven days. This afternoon we crossed the Gulph Stream. and to-morrow Morning, we hope to reach Key West. At all events—if you receive, you may be sure we are there! I shall write you a long letter by the next mail, and hope then, My dear good Manne to give you a favourable account of our proceedings. Virginia and Ellen were quite sick the first few days—and Edward and the children a little so—but all are now well—and seem to enjoy the bright clear atmosphere—especially at night. I believe no where on earth are there <u>such</u> moonlight nights as in this latitude—so clear—the breeze so soft and so refreshing—you laugh, but I tell you, My Dear Manne, it is not the heat of a southern clime that is so very objectionable—but the long long season. This is what debilitates. If we had no more warm weather than you have at the North—no one would complain of the heat. Our nights are always pleasant.— I see the wind is breezing up now, and I must hurry through or my candles won't hold out while I drop a line to George. There is a lantern in the cabin, but it only serves to make darkness visible[16] the candles are flowing in rivers down the sides. We have had several rainy days that were so agreeable! It is not charming to have a small gale, a rough sea—torrents of rain—all of consequence confined to the cabin—one half confined to their berths & the others obliged to lie down because they can't stand up! Oh! then how I wish myself on shore! Yet we soon forget it, and in time get used to it, as well as to the dreary monotony of a cabin. All the folks, save the little ones, are on deck—but I hear them coming down.

. . . I do hope, when next I go abroad—I may not have to furnish a house— have but so much to do it with and so many hours to do it in!—Oh no—I never will put myself in just such a fix—yet I would do it all, and twice as much. . . . E . says if Gov. gives him the surgeon's birth,[17] he will let Elle & I—come on with George in the Fall, and join you in a trip to New England. Would it not be nice?—I had some pretty dresses made up to visit Utica, I tell Ell as I did not wear them—I intend to reserve them until I go north again, if I come out, like the ladies of Langollen in the style of another century!—again good night, Dearest. Write soon and direct to Key West Florida via Charleston per steamer Isabel. Tell Mrs W[alker] to write me. By & by if I live—I will send her some fruit—it is not in season now—but soon will be—there I must stop—Ever your own devoted sister,

Corinna

16. See Milton's *Paradise Lost,* book 1, line 63.

17. Variant spelling of *berth:* "A situation or office on board a ship or . . . elsewhere; a situation, a place, an appointment (Usually a 'good' or 'comfortable' one)" (*OED*).

The next day the party arrived in Key West. When the family reached the island city, it was well on its way to becoming Florida's largest and most cosmopolitan town. Key West's population approximated 2,500 people, about 550 of whom were black. Men outnumbered women by a ratio of two to one. The town was an important maritime, fishing, and wrecking center. On October 11, 1846, however, three years before the sisters arrived, a hurricane had devastated the island. One of the most powerful to hit Florida in the nineteenth century, the storm took fifty lives and swept away almost every physical structure.[18] By 1849, however, the town had been essentially rebuilt and its economy was booming. Its docks and business section bustled with activity. As the southernmost settlement in the United States, Key West was a key naval and customs center. Its navy yard, hospital, and customhouse were focal points of the community, as was the U.S. admiralty court presided over by Judge William Marvin, one of America's most distinguished jurists. One of the chief pursuits of many in Key West was the wrecking business. Key West was surrounded by dangerous reefs, and ships passing through the Florida Straits often foundered offshore. Skilled salvagers (known as wreckers) saved lives and cargo at great personal risk to themselves. While they enjoyed great profits, wreckers often enjoyed a dubious reputation.[19] Ellen and Corinna witnessed and commented on their handiwork to their brother Mannevillette.

Situated atop the Caribbean, the community enjoyed extensive commercial relations with the Bahamas, Cuba, and other English and Spanish West Indian and South American colonies. Much of the white population of Key West and other keys to the north was composed, at any given time, of cockney fishermen (Conchs), whose turtling and fishing expeditions brought them to the keys from the Bahamas. These seasonal trips, beginning in the early nineteenth century, eventually led to permanent settlement. Key West's population also included large numbers of soldiers, mariners, and newcomers to American shores, making it one of the most diverse communities in the nation. According to the 1850 Monroe County census, Key West's residents hailed from almost every state in the union and from such faraway places as Norway, France, Italy, Prussia, Gibraltar, Minorca, Sweden, Corsica, Denmark, Holland, Portugal, Canada, and Austria. Three years after the Aldriches arrived, a visitor reported that the town boasted 650 houses, twenty-six stores, ten warehouses,

---

18. Jay Barnes, *Florida's Hurricane History* (Chapel Hill: University of North Carolina Press, 1998), 59–60; Brown, *Ossian Bingley Hart,* 68–69.

19. Dorothy Dodd, "The Wrecking Business on the Florida Reef," *Florida Historical Quarterly* 22 (April 1944): 171–99.

four churches, a courthouse, a jail, a customhouse, a marine hospital, and large military barracks. Just offshore he found twenty-seven wrecking, coasting, and fishing vessels in a harbor that easily accommodated vessels needing twenty-two feet of draft.[20] As well-educated, intelligent women, Corinna and Ellen might well have expected to enjoy a cosmopolitan society with intellectual opportunities rarely available on the Florida frontier where they had resided previously. During the following months, as Edward organized his medical practice and worked to secure appointment as surgeon of the marine hospital, Corinna and Ellen offered their impressions of their new island home to Mannevillette.

[Ellen Anderson to Mannevillette Brown]

Key West [to Utica, New York]
June 7, 1849
Moschetotown

My Dear Mann,

Just imagine yourself down in the bushes, in a swamp, anywhere, where the moschetos[21] are the thickest, and fancy how delightful it would be, to live there, night and day, without reprieve or intermission; to eat, sleep, read and write there, and you will have an idea how we enjoy ourselves at Key West. The children, poor little things, suffer a great deal. I do not know how I might like the place, if it were not for the intolerable annoyance. It affects my health. I have been quite sick the last two or three days. Last night, I had a violent nervous headache, but I took some medicine, and to day I am a great deal better: for which I am glad, not only because to day is the first mail day, since our arrival, and I am determined to write to you and George, let the case be what it might. Hitherto, I have never written, when it could be avoided, if I was out of spirits.

20. For general information on Key West, see Walter Maloney, *A Sketch of the History of Key West, Florida* (1876; reprint, Gainesville: University of Florida Press, 1968); Jefferson B. Browne, *Key West: The Old and the New* (1912; reprint, Gainesville: University of Florida Press, 1973); Denham, *"Rogue's Paradise,"* 54–57; and Brown, *Ossian Bingley Hart,* 68–74. For other contemporary descriptions of Key West, see Kearney, "Autobiography of William Marvin," 179–222; Thelma Peters, "William Adee Whitehead's Reminiscences of Key West," *Tequesta* 25 (1965): 3–42; Rembert Patrick, ed., "William Adee Whitehead's Description of Key West," *Tequesta* 12 (1952): 61–74; "What I Saw at Key West," *Pensacola Gazette,* May 8, 1852; *Tallahassee Florida Sentinel,* May 11, 1852; James M. Denham and Keith L. Huneycutt, "'Our Desired Haven': The Letters of Corinna Brown Aldrich from Antebellum Key West, 1849–50," *Florida Historical Quarterly* 79 (spring 2001): 517–45.

21. Obsolete spelling of *mosquitoes* (*OED*).

I believe it has been a bad plan, for it has occasioned me to put off writing until I lost all inclination to write at all. But you have said as much to me about writing under all, and every circumstance, that I determined to begin anew in this respect. So, if you get crossgrained letters from me, you will please to recollect this: for my letters are mighty apt to smack of the humour I am in, even if I try to avoid it.

I have made sundry inquiries about schools here, and find they have nothing but a. b. c. schools in the place, and of them only two. How they pay I have not yet heard, but I was saying, I feared I should find myself somewhat in the predicament of the western editor, who, when there had been an earthquake, gave as an excuse for not sending out his paper, that it took both hands to hold on his trowsers. There is neither an earthquake, nor have I a shaking ague,[22] but it will take both hands here to scratch moscheto bites. We shall see. I am afraid the climate will render me so bilious that I shall be good for nothing here. It takes the life out of me. In fact I am, as when they say of people that they have got out of bed backwards. I came down to Key West backward and I shall never feel right about it until I go back and come down in a good humour.

We have a very pretty house here but altogether too small for the size of the family. However, it is very pretty and pleasant to look at, that is something. We have any quantity of coconut trees and almond trees, and also dates although the last I have not seen, but still the island is a most desolate and miserable looking place. They say there is plenty of money here, and there ought to be something of the kind or I don't know what could induce people to live here. What I dislike greatly is, the impossibility of getting a drop of pure cold water. All the drinkable water is caught in great reservoirs, which they call cisterns, by means of spouts around the eaves of the houses, just as they catch rain water at the north, and is no better than that.

We were three long weeks from the time we were on board the vessel at New York until the arrival at Key West. Our passage was tedious but otherwise not very disagreeable until the last night, when we took our first taste of moschetoes, on coming toward the shore. We had one storm, which we knew nothing about until it was over, and drifted about for two or three days in calms in the gulf stream; which latter would have been pleasant to me, if it had not been so disappointing to everyone else on board, inasmuch as I heard a great

---

22. *Ague* refers to "ague and fever" commonly associated with malaria, a common malady in southern climes, especially the tropics. The disease was transmitted by mosquitoes and recurred at intervals.

deal of the curiosities of the gulf stream, thereby. We have been here not quite a fortnight. I suppose you know we only have a mail here once a fortnight. Corinna received three letters from you: Mrs. Walker's remark about our coming up to see your pictures made me ache. Because it would have delighted me a great deal to have had it in my power to act as she supposed we would have done, but alas what use is it to me to have wishes and choices if I do not have even the habit of uttering them. This is to be enclosed with the Doctor's and Corinna's letters and I shall have the ring enclosed also[;] all I fear is its getting crushed. Give my love to Mrs. Walker and the other ladies. It is very warm here as you might expect, but most of the time the heat is alleviated by a good breeze. Good bye. May God bless you.

Yours Ellen M. A.

[Corinna Aldrich to Mannevillette Brown]

Key West [to Utica, New York]
June 8th, 1849

Dear Brother,

I was very glad to receive your three kind letters by the last mail. I am happy to learn also, that you reached Utica in time to see your good friends before their departure. I should think it was a warm season to visit Europe, but I suppose they expect to be absent a long time. I wrote you by the vessel via Apalachicola on the day of our arrival, but before we reached the land, our voyage was so long I thought you might feel anxious about us although there is little danger from storms at this season. We landed on Monday morning the 28th and never were poor souls more glad to find a haven—for we had been becalmed on the reefs, or among them, and were well nigh devoured by <u>mosquitos</u> and <u>sand flies</u> and alas! these same pests are the bane of Southern Florida. Were it not for them, this land would be a paradise. The climate is lovely—The sea breeze almost constant—and last but not least, <u>money plenty</u>! There was a wreck brought in last week worth 140 thousand dollars—and another this week. And there the wreckers—wharf owners—&c., all get heavy salvage—besides the goods are sold at auction, and great bargains often made.

I began this yesterday, Dearest, but finding out the boat would not be here before to-morrow, I deemed it best to defer until the last minute that the news may be as fresh as possible—you may judge how these confounded mosquitoes bite by the way I write. I have to scratch between each word. All the consolation is they come only in spells. This month is said to be the worst & in winter they are not troublesome—but sometimes I think they will kill me, out & out! Still I think this must be a delightful residence in winter. We have a very pretty home—and a large yard full of trees—cocoa nuts full of fruit—almond—

dates & tamarinds. This place is said to be the jewel of the island. There are many larger houses, but none so full of shrubs & trees. These are a great protection from the sun.

Edward has just come in. He has mounted a regular sombrero with a brim six inches wide. Virginia is writing at the same table—the children are running around us—& Ellen is writing in the parlour. She will drop you a line. I intend to write George. Edward is writing to Washington—he is very desirous of obtaining the appointment of surgeon of the Hospital & really I think he ought to have it. With it, he would soon get ahead here but without I do not think the practice would compensate him for the privation of living in such a mosquito hole. I mean he could do as well in many a pleasanter location—Pensacola or even in New Orleans. In fact, I tell him if he does not proceed—I would remove there in the fall. We could do so with little expense and once <u>located</u> in New Orleans, he could not fail. . . . One reason why I like New Orleans is because I think it would be a fine place for you as well as Edward and for George—also. All trades thrive there.

This place has greatly improved since I was here before. There are many new & handsome houses & ware houses—also Gov[ernment] is building a large fort and the Barracks are manned and various improvements as well as a large increase in the population, but still it has no charm for me. We had a fine <u>serenade</u> last night for young Spaniards came round in the moonlight and regaled us for an hour or so. I do think they have the brightest moonlight here of any place in the world, but these mosquitos, alas, "the trail of the serpent is over it all"[23] & in my last I wrote of visiting New England with you this summer, but I am afraid, Dear, it will be too expensive a jaunt for us to think about unless Ed gets the talisman from Uncle Sam. You see Ell won't go without the children. Then we must take a servant and the expense would be more than doubled thereby. She wants me to go on my own to see you, but I don't like to leave her. Virginia & the Dr. say they would take good care of the little ones—and I have no doubt they would be more comfortable than in travelling—at least the two little ones. But we shall see. If my health should fail me, I shall be obligated to go on towards the Fall to recruit.[24] I could take a packet from here to New York & the expense would not be much, even for her & me. . . .

I know I would like right well to be with you a while on any terms. I do want to see your paintings so much. Manne, you must get a <u>wife</u>! Then we

23. Thomas Moore, *Lalla Rookh: Paradise and the Peri* (1817), line 206.
24. *Recruit* in this sense means "to refresh one's spirits or health."

could pay you a <u>visit</u>! . . . I am selfish in regard to you and George, but not so much so, but that I [do not] want to see you happy and I believe if you were each <u>happily</u> married you would be a great deal happier. But be sure you make a <u>right</u> choice. If I were only an old maid, how nicely you & I could live together—The girl we brought out has so far proved herself worthy. I don't know what we should have done without her. We have one new woman left who does our cooking and washing. So we get on very well. We had a time in putting the house to rights, but it is nearly settled now. As to the cooking, that is not much. The market is very poor fish & turtle—turtle and fish are the varieties with an occasional stake of tough beef. No vegetables and but little fruit. Indeed people ought to make money here and I expect they do. That is—the wreckers and merchants. The lawyers also do well, but how the Drs. fare remains to be proved. Were I alone, thousands would not tempt me to live through a summer here. In winter no doubt 'tis pleasant enough. All those who are able send their families away in the summer. However, the nights are cool and pleasant—there is none of that salty, suffocating weather you feel at the north. It would be hard if there were not some blessings where there are so many evils to endure. People say they get used to the mosquitos. I hope I shall if I must live here. Now my arms & neck are just as raw as if I had been blistered. But I won't grumble any more. I did not mean to do so for I came voluntarily although I must say I did not know what I was coming to neither did Edward—for we had only been here in winter. And I can't bear to say anything to worry him—for I am sure if he could, he would bear all for us. I will try & be patient until we find out whether 'tis best to remain or against. And consolation is—he is not losing here—and it will cost no more for us to go to Pensacola or New Orleans hereafter than if we had not stopt here—as this is the best rent. I expect I have tired you out dear; but I had to blow out.

When I write you again, I will try and give you some idea of the town or whatever it is called. It contains three thousand inhabitants—all squatted together on the Gulph shore. We went up in one of the observatories or lookouts where the wreckers go to play <u>their game</u>—and we had a fine view of the village. It is about as large as St. Augustine and built after the same style—narrow streets—& low houses. More of this hereafter. I must close dear or I shall be eaten up alive. I hope in the next mail there will be a [renewal] of this crop at least. Ellen & E are both writing you. You have to take all at once, as there are but two mails a month. You must write Dear—so as to have your letters reach Charleston on the 14th and 30 of each month. The boat leaves there on the first and 18th of each month. You must give my love to Mrs. Walker. . . . Tell her I will send her a barrel of Cocoa nuts by & by. Our trees are full.

They look very pretty and of all sizes on the same tree from the blossoms to full grown fruit, although not yet ripe. It is a very graceful tree, I wish I could draw that I might give you more idea of our place. I will try as soon as the mosquitos die off a little. I may be able to give you a hint. You can fill up the picture. God bless you dear Manne all send love ever yours Corinne.

[Corinna Aldrich to Mannevillette Brown]

Key West [to Utica, New York]

June 21st 1849

We sent you a whole budget of letters the last mail, My dear and best of brothers, but as we have only two chances per month, I doubt not you will be glad to hear from us again. I was disappointed not to get any letters by this mail, yet I ought not to have been—for no one could know whether we were here or not. We shall probably get plenty next time—and that will not be long—at least as so far the time has passed quickly. There is no antidote for discontent or ennui like occupation—that I learned long ago—and consequently keep myself always busy. Indeed we have had plenty to do since we came. To set a house to rights—at best is no trifling matter—but when it's small and inconvenient, the difficulty is great. We have the consolation, however, of having what is called the prettiest place on the island, and really when I look upon it in the moon light particularly I am quite charmed.

The foliage of the cocoa nut is, as a lady remarked the other day, "so very oriental." There is a good deal of shrubbery about the yard, and every thing grows so luxuriantly—The hybiscus, the oleander, the jasmine, the popinac or acacia, the plantain almond, fig, lime, & etc. The flowers on many of these are gorgeous—and stand up like quaint nosegays. While the dark green leaves of the almond & lime contrast magnificently—I could describe a charming place, indeed—and not exceed the truth—yet to look upon, it is not really so. If it were not for the dread of the hurricane, I think they would make a beautiful place—but they are wholly discouraged since the storm of 46—that destroyed all the gardens—indeed it laid waste the city—blew down houses—uprooted trees—and made havoc every where—But the house we live in withstood the gale, and I don't think it probable we shall ever have such another. Edward is doing very well in his practice and seems to be gaining popularity every day. He books on an average ten dollars per day, and yet there is not much sickness. Every body seems to fear the cholera, but I see no cause for alarm. The air is so pure & the wind sweeps over the whole island let it come whence it may.

We have become acquainted with several very pleasant families—and altogether there is far more civilization and refinement than I had any idea of meeting. In a few years, if no misfortune should happen to retard the prosperity of the place—I think Key West, will stand a fair competition for refinement and intelligence with any of our older southern towns. Most persons here get rich, and as their treasures increase, they incline to comforts and refinement. They build houses—plant gardens, and send their children away to be educated. There are three or four young ladies here now, who have but recently returned from New England boarding schools—Moreover you can tell directly you see them—you know they were not "brought up" in these parts! we have an <u>artist</u> a Miss [Julia] Wall—she has several paintings in oil of her own execution —I am not judge enough to decide on their merits—but I should not deem them very fine. However, I could not do as well. She is not pretty but a good natured fat laughing girl, full of fun & frolic. Her Pa has the biggest house—& is about the richest man—and she runs about & amuses herself—leading, I doubt not, a very merry life despite her having been seven years at the north.[25] There are two young ladies here. The Misses Lancaster—(their father is judge of the Supreme Court) who amuse me not a little.[26] One is rather passe—the younger is very sentimental. I talk to her, or rather wind her up & set her going, just to hear her unwind—last evening she spent the evening with us, and it was too funny to hear her descant on the beauties of the night. Although she is not far wrong there, for I do think we have the loveliest moonlight nights here I ever saw—you think I am not taking much trouble in my penmanship. The truth is Dear, I have had so many things to prevent my writing until to day that I am now obliged to hurry to get through. I have scribbled George a few lines—and want to write one letter on business and one for Jane the girl we brought from N.Y. En passant, mon cher frere, she proves quite a treasure in her way. I like her very much—but we have the meanest sample of a negro for a cook & I am much afraid she will spoil her. I try hard to keep them apart but it seems impossible. Kindred spirits will draw together—where both are ignorant—'tis a difficult thing to steer among them—I find it so—I want

25. Julia Wall (seventeen years old) resided at Aaron Frierson's residence (U.S. Manuscript Census, Population [1850], Monroe County, Florida). Her father, William H. Wall, was not recorded by the census taker. Corinna's August 11, 1849, letter mentions that he had gone to Cuba. William Marvin noted that Wall "had been baptized in the Church of England but educated and brought up among Roman Catholics in Spain" See Kearney, "Autobiography of William Marvin," 202.

26. Eliza (twenty-seven) and Laura (twenty-two) lived with their parents, Joseph B. and Annie Blair Lancaster.

Edward to sell the old imp, and either hire, or try another, for 'tis like a ticket in a lottery to buy a negro—sometimes you get a prize. But I try to be satisfied —and let all things take their course.

One comfort we have is a delightful climate—the breezes here are charming —so cool & refreshing. The mosquetos are not half so bad as represented. They only last a few days—the first fresh breeze sends them all off. I thought when we first arrived, (it happened to be during an attack of the varmints) I thought they would eat us alive—without pepper or salt—indeed we were almost mad with them, and people told us, by way of a marvel, that they hadn't begun to come. It was all moonshine, however, so far they have gone and have not returned—only occasionally, but not worse than elsewhere at this time of the year. By the way—I see the cholera is in N.Y. are the people alarmed? I feel as if I wanted to fly, when I think of sickness—If it were not for my implicit trust in God—and belief that He over rules all destiny, I should be tempted to start off to day—& try what I could do—I wish I wore pantaloons. . . .

But 'tis time enough to talk of these matters—We all keep well—The children often talk of you & name their dolls for you—Last evening young Mr [William B.] Lancaster came in & they thought it was you—it was quite a disappointment. Dr. is in his room that he has appropriated mixing medicine— Ell has left off writing being tired out & is rocking sis—Villette is flying round. Virginia is dressing—The sun is about going down—and as the twilight here is very brief—I must [steal] away. . . .

> Ever truly & affectionately yours Corrinne

[Ellen Anderson to Mannevillette Brown]

> Key West [to Utica, New York]
> June 22, 1849

Dear Manne

I cannot bear to let a post slip by without saying a few words, since you are fond of getting letters, even if there be nothing in them. Corrine has already written to you, and I intend to get her to post this, my word or two, inside her letter. First of all, our grand enemy, the mosquetoes, are not nearly so bad as they were. This is a great comfort, as it renders the place endurable. Secondly, the school I think I can get, but I don't think it will pay well. I have not, as yet, taken any positive steps, I have only, as it were, felt the pulses. There are but two schools in the place, both inferior, and prices accordingly. I should have been more energetic, but I have been so discontented that it has paralized me. For the first fortnight, I thought I could not, for the mosquitoes all but threw me into a fever, and they made the children suffer so much, that my very heart died within me, now, they are not so bad, I feel rather more reconciled. I don't know what I shall do, however.

Yesterday I took in my hand a veritable piece of California gold and guessed its worth to be about $100. It was weighed afterward and found to be worth about ninety-six dollars: so you see I had a pretty good guess. Also I ran my fingers through a quantity of very small pieces which I suppose to be, what they call, the gold dust, and got my finger nails filed with it, and immediately, I thought, if every one should take such a tax out of it, it would very much decrease its value, so I picked it carefully out of my nails, and put it back again. It gives one such an idea, of the reality of the stories we have heard, to see these things. And it will give you a further idea, to know it was handed about in a bit of common paper, done up in the most careless manner. A gent carrying it to the north, for a friend, brought it here for the Doctor to see.

I expect the constant wrecking brings a great many curious things to this place. The other day, we were shown a great number of statuettes, as they are called, Little statues, three or four inches high, illustrative of Mexican people, and customs. They belonged to the French minister, who was taking them home; the vessel he was on board was wrecked, and they, with the other cargo, had to be sold to pay salvage. I could not help feeling sorry for the poor fellow, who had to lose them. If giving any person a vivid idea is a proof of the skill of an artist, these were the work of no ordinary hand, for they were the most life-like things I ever saw. They were executed in wax, and coloured to resemble life.

Let me give you an idea of our life here. I get up in the morning between six and seven varying considerably in the time, by the time I get dressed (I take it leisurely, having no one to care whether I am up or down) breakfast is generally ready. If it is not, I read until it is. After that I go into Corinne's room, and chat with her a spell, then I devote about an hour to teaching the children. This is not much, but it is long enough for them. After that I sew until dinner, which is generally between two and three. After dinner we dress our selves, and, if we do not have any calls to prevent us, we walk out, and return the calls we have received. We return between six and seven, take a lunch instead of tea, for the lights call in so many moschetoes, that a regular set tea does not seem desirable, then walk a spell, on the piazzas, and at ten o'clock go to bed. This is a general outline, but it wants a vast deal of filling up to give you a correct idea. It is easy to describe the great currents of the ocean, or give a general idea of the shape of the land, but who can tell of its many under currents, or describe the immersed indentations upon its shores. Just so in life, what shoals, what quick-sands, what undercurrents forever influence it? What unthought of circumstances back all our judgements? By the way, I remember an amusing instance of this. When James Hennard was out on the St. John's river, Florida, near Mandarin one of the healthiest spots on earth, so healthy that a physician cannot make a living there for want of patients, a most indisputably healthy spot, he received a letter from uncle Halliburton, asserting most dogmatically that the place was not healthy and proving it by the facts (which were facts too) that the river was wide and shallow & etc. They made poor Jim go home, although he was getting better of the complaint which induced him to come. This was a white swelling in the knees. After his return, he had his leg amputated and he is now poor fellow in his grave. And I have heard the Doctor say, more than once, had he remained in Florida, he would have been alive now, so far as that disease is concerned. So much for human judgement, when I said the circumstance was amusing I meant the letter not poor Jim's fate, of course.

As for the victuals we eat, there is great complaint of not being able to get anything, and it seems as if they had good reason. Although, for myself, if I can get something, and that something wholesome, I am not likely to grumble, and that much we can have here. We get various West Indian fruits here. I have already seen two varieties that I had never seen before I came, but I don't think "the north" need cry for what she misses. We get fine pineapples here. I eat[27] them for the first time here last night, and I see the Doctor has bought some more to day. The children are well, but they do not look so rosy as I would like to see and I think they never will in this climate. Every one here looks tanned, and freckled, and pale. I don't believe what-we-call-fresh-looking is ever seen here, but as I have not seen all-the-world of Key West, I may be mistaken. Corinne looks pale. She does not look near so well as she did when she left Marietta. . . . Give my love to Mrs. Walker and her daughter. How much Corinne and I would like to see them. Perhaps Corinne may but I drag too many anchors, and it is time I found a harbour and rested there, although I am a rover by nature. . . . Ellen.

[Ellen Anderson to Mannevillette Brown]

Key West [to Utica, New York]
July 6, 1849

My dear Mann,

. . . Within the last two or three days, we have had the moschetoes again. I believe you were informed that they are not perpetual. Certainly if they were, I would not, and indeed could not, remain upon the island; if I did, it would be

27. This was an acceptable past-tense form of *eat* in the nineteenth century.

under ground, not upon it; for they do set me distracted, and I think they are almost gone. But indeed, if it were not for these annoyers, I should go quite into raptures about the extreme loveliness of the climate, nothing could exceed it. The heat, even when it is hot, produces none of that lassitude, which one feels in inland places, but it is so tempered by constant winds, coming on every hand over the ocean, that it is seldom exceedingly hot. I suppose you are aware that we are in the region of the trade winds, here. I do not believe there is a place in the union, where they have finer weather than they have here. The nights are lovely beyond expression. Next to climate, geographers, generally, describe the face of the country soil and productions, but of these you have been told before, and they are no great things anyhow.

They had all sorts of doings here, day before yesterday—Independence Day. The masons and the Sons of Temperance marched about, they had an address, fired guns, and ended finally with a ball in the evening. All this sounds very large, but the place is small, and of course the doings were small in proportion. It was a sort of imitation of great things. It often amuses me to observe how much places are like individuals. People in remote places, country folks and small craft every where, fuss themselves to death to do, what is done in large cities, and by great folks, and they succeed in doing exactly what the said great folks don't think it worth while to do. You may depend, there is a great deal in this idea although I have not happily expressed it. Places are as marked in their character as individuals, and, what is more, have precisely similar characteristics. But I think I will not write you a composition on the subject, to day. We went to hear the address on the Fourth, which was (pretended to be) extempore, and was very good. We were also invited to go to the ball, but did not go. The children have not been very well the last week, but they are getting better; also miss Virginia is somewhat indisposed, I am quite well, and Corinna is as usual. I have not commenced my school yet, and fear I shall not. Schooling is very cheap here, and good in proportion. Someone told a converted Indian Preacher, that he had very poor pay; to which he replied, "yes very poor pay, and very poor preach." And so it is with the schools here, very poor pay, and very poor teach. Whether or no they would pay very good pay, for very good teach, I can't tell. People in general are better judges of the price, than of the quality of the article. But I am not in a very great hurry. I told you, I should not tell you any news. I'm only talking on paper, that you may see my pot-hooks having been assured by you that the sight of them would be agreeable, even though they did not carry much news or information. They have several cupolas here, as they call them, a sort of observatory, for looking out for vessels. (I suppose you are aware that wrecking and its accompaniments, make the place.) Also a light house. We went up into the last, and one of the former.

From the top of either, you can see the whole extent of the island, and see the sea all around it. Although I knew that the island was small, yet I was astonished to find how very small it is.

They talk about it being six or seven miles in extent, but I think they must include a long narrow strip which stretches away to the west. To my eyes which I am aware are inexperienced, the main part does not appear to be more than two miles in extent. There is not a living tree of what would be called, at the north, good size, on the island. I mean of course to except those planted in gardens in town but even there they are not large. There are a good many dead ones, but they are not large. I fancy they have been killed by the gale. I have just been down in the parlour to receive a call from two ladies, very pleasant persons, but they told me no news. You have no idea how bad I do want to see your pictures, and I want to see you too. You must give my love to Mrs. Walker and the young ladies. I am in hopes I shall be able to come on to the north, in the course of the next year, and if I do, you must . . . take the children's likeness, because I want them, for my own comfort and satisfaction. It is true they will not remain likenesses long, but I wish to have them to look at, when they shall have children to remind—or rather to keep in mind what pretty little things they were. And then I sometimes fear that they may die, and then how highly I should prize a likeness of them. You see I remember what you said about it, but perhaps you have yourself forgotten. Don't you think you may fancy to visit Havanna some of these winters? I shall try hard to take a peek at it next winter, and preparatory thereunto, I shall make an effort to learn Spanish, this summer I am disappointed in one respect, in that I expected to find plenty of persons here, who could speak the language; but such is not the case. In this, the place differs from St. Augustine and Pensacola. I find it hard to get a teacher even, and that, as it were, within a stone's throw of Havanna. Every body here hails from, and talks about Nassau, an English town on one of the Bahama islands, the birth place of the Dr's mother.

To day is the 7th, for I began this document yesterday. The wind blows "powerful" as the crackers say. You have no idea how I dread the Fall, and its storms, but I believe it is a good sign, as what one anticipates seldom happens. As I anticipate being frightened, perhaps I shall not be. I am taking strychnine to try and benefit my eyes, although without much encouragement that it will do any good: but I think my general health is benefited by it, at the same time that it renders my nervous system more than ordinarily sensitive. We hear that George is about to get married. I don't know how much truth there may be in it, but I have written him a long letter containing many excellent hints, which, if there is any occasion for them, are, of course, too late. I thought of this, and so I told him, he could forward them to you, or hand them to some <u>malade</u>[28] of his acquaintance whom they might benefit. Corine is writing letters, by the side of me, which may account to you for my changing the colour of my ink. There are two ink stands on the table. Miss Virginia is in the parlour below writing. Dr gets plenty of practice. Children are playing. Their grand delight being to fancy themselves the parents of innumerable children. I was talking to Willy one day about getting a living, choosing professions, and such things. He had asked me what it meant? ("making money") and he interrupted me to ask if there was not such a profession as Mothers? . . . ever yours, Ellen M. A.

[Corinna Aldrich to Mannevillette Brown]

Key West [to Utica, New York]

July 8, 1849

Mon cher frere. I deferred writing your letter until to day in order that you might have the latest possible news. I believe Ell has thereby forestalled me in telling you all there is. One thing would amuse you—here it is—the funny kind of fuss and rumpus a wreck of dry goods knocks up here among all classes. For my part I wonder how the merchants make a living. I suppose, however, they buy in quantities and lay by until the novelty is over. Most persons too are improvident. There was a good deal of wisdom, in old Jake Sheaf's advice to give the poor a little at a time & often. He said if they had a chest of tea they would put a pound in the pot and it is somewhat the case with all of us. We hate to use the economy with a small quantity, that we do when pinched a little in weight or measure—n'est pas?[29] My french is weak. . . .

[Edward] is still trying to get the appointment of surgeon at the Hospital & indeed he ought to have it. The man who is surgeon at this time is absent & has been since before we came—& the one who is surgeon pro tem is also clerk of the court and moreover is one who once held the office, under Van Burin I believe, and was turned out . . . He being at that time also deputy collector, it seems he is a monopolist. He approved his own accounts and thereby got seventeen hundred dollars for medicines at the Hospital for one year. A sum sufficient, the Dr. says to defer the expenses for a major Hospital, but this is not all. This man Pinkney? is a loco foco and clerk of the court. I don't see how one man can hold two offices which call for such opposite abilities. . . .

---

28. French: "sick person." Ellen apparently means "someone afflicted by love."
29. French: "isn't it so?"

George, I suspect is getting rich, and my dear Manne, I think your chance is <u>fair</u> <u>too</u>. I am right glad you are doing so well but if we live out the winter, I want you to come out and go to Savanna with us. You could get 2 or 3 hundred for a portrait there—here even. A dauber came last winter & he had 100 for his productions. I wish you could see them. Every one, you know, likes a pretty picture will pay for it, whether they are judges of the execution or not. . . . Ell is just come in from church. Do you know Charles Adams, of Portsmouth notoriety, is our pastor? She is abusing me, because my dress is soiled. The fact is I have to wear white most of the time & as I often go to my pantry—to stir up cake & pastry. I am apt to get a lick. Last evening I went into the kitchen to call the cook to take out breakfast and Jane and I killed two big scorpions. Their bite, however, is misrepresented. It is by no means so poisonous as many believe, not more so than a wasp or a bee! Still they are so ugly, we can't but deplore them. . . . I never saw one half as large before—and these I am told are small.

To turn to a more interesting if not more agreeable theme, I must reply to your hints respecting your love farce—for I can give it no better name. If you told me all and truly of the matter—believe me dear—there is no harm done. I have this mail written George a long chapter on the subject of matrimony— and I will venture, my dear, as I have had experience, to repeat some of my sage advice to you. I don't know why people should jest and make light of the matter, the most important event, not only to the parties concerned, but ultimately, I repeat, the most important event of our mortal life—to the whole human race. Reflect my dear, how all important to you, your friends, to your children, is a happy marriage. And what a purgatory an ill matched pair create. Verily a crust of bread where love is, is better than all the gold of California if it shine only upon hearts at variance. I believe in the most refined, the most exalted love—in the perfect mirror of thoughts, feelings and sympathies. In an attachment where no sordid notions of wealth or avarice dare intrude—and this is the only kind worth the seeking. Moreover, my good Brother, love to be lasting <u>must</u> be based upon intimate knowledge of a character we <u>esteem</u>. Love the result of fancy, only intoxicates, and wears off with the excitement which produced it. But there is a kind of slower & more lasting growth, and the only kind worth having. Ponder well on what I say & never believe yourself won in a day. Nothing would please me more than to see both you and George happily married and surely no regrets could be more poignant than to know the reverse were the case. As I said before, however, I don't think you are badly wounded. I know too well the <u>symptoms</u>. He jests at scars, who never felt a wound![30] Are

---

30. Shakespeare's *Romeo and Juliet,* act 2, scene 2, line 1.

you tired of what I say? n' importe [no matter], My prayer is that you may one day be able to say—as much happiness as mortals are permitted to enjoy is mine, for my wife is "all my fancy painted her," and like good wine improves by age. . . . Good-bye dear yrs C.

[Corinna Aldrich to Mannevillette Brown]

Key West [to Utica, New York]
July 21st, 1849

My Dear Manne:

[T]he steamboat ceases to run until the first of October or after what are thought the hurricane months. The mail will at interims be carried by sail vessels. It is a great disappointment to us outlanders thus to be cut off from our only chance of regular intercourse with the world! We are in hopes to get a peep now and then, however, as we are bound to have a mail twice a month, somehow. It is said they have two fine vessels engaged. Still, if you should not receive our documents so from July, thereafter—you will know to what cause to attribute it. . . .

When we first came here—the mosquitoes were so intolerable and being told they would increase rather than diminish, Ell & I resolved on flight at any hazard. But that evil is remedied. 'Tis true, we are still amazed by the varmints, but they are by no means so intolerable as they were. Indeed, I do think this is a heavenly climate. I never was in a place where the cool breezes were so constant as here—or so refreshing—but that is all we get now of the luxuries of life—no fruits. In fact, there is no market—a bit of good beef is a rarity—although we have such granddaddy turtles—They would pass for beef in haunch stake. . . .

We actually <u>feed</u> on <u>watermelons</u>. They are the only fruit we get except West India productions and most persons are afraid to eat them. I have a glass of ice water by my side which is also quite refreshing. What a blessing it is—I don't know how they existed without it in the olden times—The discoverer for preserving it should be knighted. You see, I have taken you at your word—that the letter would not be too long. Indeed I did not know until just now that I had written so much which proves that it interests me and you are <u>bound</u> <u>to</u> <u>be</u> <u>interested</u>. I intend dear to make the most of you before you get that <u>little</u> <u>wife</u>—because I <u>know</u> I cannot hold the same place then as now! Don't shake your head, it must be so, and I shall be content—because I only desire to see you happy & beloved. I wish you could feel the nice breeze we are enjoying. As I sit at my bedroom window, I look out through the coconut trees on the wide gulph & watch the breeze as it ripples o'er and wonder that anything so calm & lovely can be tossed into such a tempest as nearly to overwhelm us.

By the way, is Mrs. Walker fond of flowers? I could send her some. I will enclose you a specimen of a kind of Jessamine, the Spanish Jessamine 'tis called & grows here luxuriantly. The perfume is delightful & very strong. If she likes to cultivate anything of the kind, let me know & I will cut some slips for her & also get her some seeds. I intend to send her & you a lot of coconuts by & by— some are nearly ripe, others will not be until winter. They are all sizes on the trees from the blossom to the full grown fruit. We have tamarinds and dates just starting forth. This place we live on might be made very delightful. When the doctor gets the Hospital I intend to lay by enough to buy it—if we live long enough. However, I don't much care. 'Tis no use to try and count on the future. It rests with One who oversees all our plans. Ell & I are resolved to learn the Spanish language & it being one present amusement, I mention it, although the end thereof is far off I reckon. . . . I have no <u>news</u> to add but our united love we heartily send. Take good care of your dear self and believe me your grateful and affectionate sister. [Corinna] P.S. I have lost the jessamine I will press another. I send a tamarind.

[Ellen Brown Anderson to Mannevillette Brown]

Key West [to Utica, New York]
July 21st, 1849

My Dear Mann,

Corine received a letter and some little books from Mrs. Walker by the steamer. Mrs W.'s letters give the very best impressions of her character, and make me feel a strong desire to be personally acquainted with her. You are very fortunate to have such persons for associates and friends. As for the young lady, whoes[31] letters and whoes' wreath of Flowers were sent, I think she more than justifies all your good opinions of her. She must have been, indeed, a wonderfully lovely, talented, and extraordinary being. It is so seldom that youth, beauty, and talents, (the most general blessings of Earth) when combined, are devoted to the love and praise of Him, whoes gift they are! It is sad and true, that the most favoured of mankind, in worldly things, are the least apt to remember and praise their Creator.

That your friends in this family, appear to be exceptions to this general rule is the most remarkable and interesting thing about them to me, although they have plenty that is interesting besides. Religion makes every person more or less interesting, who is sincerely interested in it, but when a character, otherwise highly endowed is strongly under its influence, human nature rises as it

---

31. Obsolete spelling of *whose* (*OED*).

were into a new, indeed a new creature! I cannot express the feelings with which such persons inspire me. I love them with the profoundest love, and I begin to perceive how easy it would be to love God with all the enthusiasm and devotedness, which is acceptable to Him, could we but realize his character and associate with his angels. They make some such impression on me, as do the sky, and stars, and lovely natural scenery.

I had a letter, by this last mail, from Major Wessells, dated 17th April 1849. He had just arrived at Monterey, California. Although there is nothing in his letter, which may not be gleaned from the newspapers, still there is a reliableness and a genuineness about a letter from one you are acquainted with, which a newspaper never can have. . . . The gentleman who wrote it, is entirely to be relied upon. He expresses a hope that I obtained the box and rifle, which were left for me at the Quartermaster's storehouse. Have you heard any thing from them? Had I not best write to the quarter-master at N.Y.? Don't forget to answer these questions in your next letter. One of our neighbors has a bathing house near here, and just sent us an invitation to go and pay it a visit with her, so I quit my letter and went, and now I have just returned. It is a fine large bathing house, and although I don't think I coveted it, yet I am sure I wished I had one like it. I tryed very hard to swim but without success. but, I think, if I had one of my own, and could go into it every day, I could soon learn.

This is the last regular trip of the Steamer, as she will be laid up during the hurricane months, as they are called: these are August, September, and October, so now I shall begin to look out for squalls and you may look out not to receive your letters so regularly. There were certain hints in Mrs. Walker's letter about you, about which I can only say, you appear to be in good hands. If I were on the spot, I should probably have much more to say. The young lady, who esteems it a misfortune to be an heiress, don't know the world, I fancy, not that I think money so much to be coveted as some do, but really it is a great thing to be independent, even as a wife. If the person fears being loved for their wealth, I should think it was easy enough both to judge of, and to test the matter. But after all, and alas for the bitter truth of it, I do not believe all the caution, of which man and woman are capable, can prevent mistakes in getting married. It is an old and hackneyed remark, but not the less true for all that, that it requires one set of qualities to win lovers, and quite another to retain the hearts of spouses. Now I fancy that for this latter purpose, money is unequalled. But after all, as the old negro said, human nature is mighty uncertain, and this may serve for a consolation to the disappointed, as well as a warning to some others, not to believe too much.

It has been said of knowledge, that the roots are bitter and the fruits are very sweet: the very contrary of this is true of knowledge of the world: If it have any sweetness, it is at the roots, all the rest is bitter, and yet it seems necessary to acquire it, in order to behave with common sense. Thus you see I am obliged to run on just with my thoughts, as, it appears to me, I have exhausted the subjects which the island affords, and to tell of the family, would be only to repeat what I have said before, at least until there shall be some change. . . . Ellen

Eleven

"I See I Am Fiz-z-z-zing Now"

Summer and Fall in Key West

Corinna and Ellen wrote faithfully from Key West to George in Newnansville, keeping him informed about conditions in their new home. George replied often; apparently in good spirits, he wrote about such entertaining topics as the comparative traits of different Florida pests:

> Mosquitoes, when too thick, are certainly very annoying, but could I exchange every flea that daily crawls and many are now "going it" over my "damnation body," for a mosquito flying around it, I should make them "<u>jump</u> at the chance"—A flea steals upon you ere you are aware, and when you put your finger on him, he has done his mischief and gone. A mosquito, on the contrary, heralds his approach and gives you a chance to carry into execution the threat of the [bitten] Irishman—"to knock the devil [down] his length." Besides this advantage in the daytime, a good net secures you at night—so you see you have the advantage over us, as far as this annoyance . . . is concerned."[1]

As they were with Mannevillette, the sisters were greatly concerned that George make a wise decision when marrying, so George kept them updated regarding his marriage prospects:

> [D]uring the past year, I have been engaged <u>according to report</u> to nearly every lady of my acquaintance. Nor need you apprehend anything from my choice—I am passed[2] the day when a pretty face would be chiefly sought for. She, whoever she may be who is to share my lot through life, must have a <u>mind</u>—<u>this can</u> be found out before marriage. The temper, habits, & etc. of

---

1. George Brown to Ellen Brown Anderson, July 3, 1849, Anderson-Brown Papers, USMA.

2. Alternate spelling for *past* (as a preposition), still current in the nineteenth century.

a lady are like the secrets of the Hall of Eblis,[3] only to be known when it is too late to retreat from the consequences. I could bear well with most any failing in a wife, save an empty head. I would take one as ugly as Parson Peabody and as big as Sheriff Oates, if she had the talents of the one and the good nature of the last, providing those qualities could not be obtained on other terms. I have not concluded to quit the world, and retire in this wilderness, and hope yet in my travels to light upon some damsel worthy to be loved. . . .

George also provided his sisters with the latest news of Indian disturbances in the lower peninsula:

We have some bad Indian news to day. They have killed a Mr. [William] Barker at Indian River, and wounded Mr. [James] Russell the collector at Charlotte harbour—and broken up the Indian River settlement. Whether it is a small party only, or the beginning of another "war" I cannot yet say, as we only have the express news. I trust however that it will end by the apprehension and punishment of the rascals concerned.[4]

[Corinna Aldrich to Mannevillette Brown]

Key West [to Utica, New York]
August 11, 1849

My Dear Manne:

A boat having touched in here from New Orleans—My Dear Manne, and bound to New York—I cannot let slip the opp[ortunit]y to drop you a line. She leaves again in the morning, so I have only time to say how d'y do?—If she were to remain a few days—I should be tempted to put myself on board instead of a letter—for I feel greatly like taking a trip but am not ready. Nevertheless, I

---

3. Eblis is the principal devil or evil spirit of Islamic belief. George may be referring to the concluding episode in William Beckford's gothic novel *Vathek* (1786), in which the hero journeys to the fabulous hall of Eblis and is doomed to eternal torture.

4. George Brown to Corinna Aldrich and Ellen Anderson, July 27, 1849, Anderson-Brown Papers, USMA. For the hostilities George refers to, see James W. Covington, "The Indian Scare of 1849," *Tequesta* 21 (1961): 53–64; Covington, *Seminoles of Florida,* 112–20; James W. Covington, "Billy Bowlegs, Sam Jones, and the Crisis of 1849," *Florida Historical Quarterly* 68 (January 1990): 299–311; McReynolds, *Seminoles,* 264–66; Canter Brown Jr., *Fort Meade, 1849–1900* (Tuscaloosa: University of Alabama Press, 1995), 1–8; Brown, *Florida's Peace River Frontier,* 80–84; and Michael Schene, "Not a Shot Was Fired: Fort Chokonikla and the 'Indian War' of 1849–1850," *Tequesta* 37 (1977): 19–37.

mean to come by and by!—I want to see you, and Mrs. Walker, and also to show you I can behave pretty—and above all, I want to bring you back with me! I think a visit here would benefit you in many ways—If you could only see the portraits one Ms. [Julia] Wall daubed here last winter—and then went over to Cuba, and did likewise—carrying off no small quantity of doubloons! . . . We all continue in good health. Indeed I do think this is one of the most healthy places in the world—and yet they contrive to keep the Dr pretty busy—he has 3 or 4 patients to visit every day—notwithstanding we have neither yellow fever or cholera. . . .

We have a rumour by a boat from Tampa Bay—that the Indians have again taken to arms and are murdering—plundering & setting fire as of yore—this, if true, will be a pretty business for Uncle Sam, inasmuch as, the war was thought to be ended long ago—by poor old Gen [William Jenkins] Worth! For me, I always thought it would be their joking—They have only bided their time! We know, for certain, that a party of Indians attacked a settlement about 3 weeks since at Indian Key—about 180 miles above this, on the Florida coast, and killed several persons—routed the balance and burned the houses!—last week, they ran off 18 families on Peas creek, above Tampa about 30 miles—killed the Indian agent, and fired the store. This was the very way the war began before I was told. Thank Heaven—we are quite as safe here as if in New York. You have no idea, My dear Brother of the horrible suspense of lying down at night—with the probability of being routed out of bed before day, by an Indian war whoop!—It seems to me—for years I never slept without one eye open!—I would awake at the tread of a spider—and jump at the sound of a cricket! suspecting a decoy in every sound.—I shall never forget the first night I slept in Georgia—out of the reach of savages after having passed three years in this state. It was like being in Paradise—and yet there was no real danger—I know it now but then I did not—and when I saw they set fire to a house not a quarter of a mile from ours, & heard them yell—I don't think it was cowardice to dread their coming closer! I feel sorry for the poor settlers about the wilds of Florida. They will all be broken up, and the poverty and distress consequent upon these moves is only second to being scalped!—I say again Thank God we are out of harm's way. This island is 160 miles from the main land—They will scarcely venture that far by water—and if they should I think we could swamp them ere they landed.———

The children are flying round with their dolls. They have all the family! But my dear Manne—they are so full of boils—in fact, all the children in town are so—'tis said—it prevents their having fevers—so I suppose 'tis the lesser evil—but it makes them look bad—Ell & I are digging away at the Spanish language—I expect Ell will accomplish it—as she is like she was of old—let every thing else go, & drive at the main stay—whereas I see so many other nails to hit on the head—I fear I shall never get through—however I plod along. The weather is tremendous about this time. How is it with you? Indeed 'tis too hot to do any thing—and I do feel so good for nothing—I think sometimes I will lie down and let everything go—then I arouse myself and so the time goes by—I could not believe it was so late as the 10th Aug—when I began to write.—One might suppose the time passed merrily. . . . Your devoted sister Corinna

P.S. We have just heard by a vessel from N.Y. the vexatious intelligence that a <u>noted</u> <u>quack</u>—one Dr. Jones[5] was hired to quit this place—has been appointed Hospital Surgeon—But as he is very unpopular—and no kind of a physician it is hoped his appointment will not be confirmed by the senate. Edward says—Dear Manne—that he intends to get certificates of this fellow's <u>incompetency</u>, and a petition for his removal—and send them on to Washington—& try & get the appointment yet. Is it not too bad—that politicals should have the power to put such a man in such a station. I pity the poor fellows he may have to close. I would not let him physic a cat for me—E will get all the private practice—however indifferent Uncle Sam may be to his patients—E will write you by the mail—but mean time—Dear—if you have any opportunity to favour E's course—I would be glad. We have the sloop of war <u>Germantown</u> just arrived—no news. The people speak of petitioning Congress for E to have the Hospital.

[Ellen Brown Anderson to Mannevillette Brown]

Key West [to Utica, New York]
August 16th, 1849

My Dear Mann,

The mail having at length arrived, I suppose the time for its departure will arrive also; so I shall undertake to write you a letter, although I have a pen and ink of about the meanest quality: and when ones ink will not flow ones ideas are apt to refuse to flow also. No matter, <u>it</u> <u>will</u> <u>be</u> <u>a</u> <u>letter</u>. <u>You</u> <u>understand</u>.

We have been having the torrid zone here, in good earnest. Oh but it has been hot! To-day, the wind blows a little and it is somewhat cooler. Do you reflect that we are but one degree from having the sun vertical. It made me feel so hot, when I was reminded of it.

---

5. A native of Virginia, S. F. Jones first arrived in Florida in 1840, practiced medicine in St. Augustine until 1844, and then moved to Key West. While there he became active in the 1848 presidential campaign of Zachary Taylor. He served until 1854. See Hammond, *Medical Profession in 19th Century Florida*, 322–23.

Willy has been writing you a letter; it does not do him much credit, but I shall send it, because he will break his heart, if I do not. You must write him an answer to it, if you have time, if not, get some small body, with little to do, to write one for you, as all his gratification consists in receiving and opening <u>his</u> epistles; not but he can read them, but he does so love to have a letter sent to <u>him</u>.

If I were with you, I would write your letters for you. How would you like to have an amanuensis? The school does not come on at all. I have some idea I could get one, but it would not pay well, and I assure you, I must be remarkably well paid, to be induced to remain in this place another summer. In the mind I am now, I would rather live at the north, in an almshouse. As for the children, you would not know them for the same: poor little things, the heat, and, worse than that, the bites make them look abominable! The fact is Mann, that sometimes I am ready to burst, for lack of safety valve, whereby to let off steam, and I see I am fiz-z-z-zing now. Oh me! Do you suppose this a letter from a crazy woman? When blood boils, should it not fiz-z, as well as water; and did you never hear of one's blood boiling?

I am so cold, and calm, and bear, with so much equanimity, both small and great misfortunes; that doubtless my blood is not blood, but only a cool sort of lymph; and my head is not filled with brains, but only with very simple pudding. Such no doubt is my appearance, but I think I shall take both my pudding and sauce to another location, if I can accomplish it by any means; for both of them will get hot, if they are continually heated. Are you mistified? I shall leave you to solve the enigma as you best can.

You ought to see Villette, she is running about dressed up in one of Will's old jackets, and with her clothes stuffed into a little pair of pants, she looks very funny. I have just had to send them all out of the room they bother us so. The floor shakes, when they run about and that makes us make all sorts of erases and such. I say us, and by so saying, I mean Corine and myself. Miss V. A. for whom you feel "a family affection" is down stairs, and whether or no she feels the same for you, I am unable to inform you, because she has not informed me, as indeed she never does inform me of anything. Every one to his taste, if she don't fancy me, happily I do not lose in my own esteem there by, only I am sorry on her account, as I think I can be a faithful friend and as is usual with folks of that sort, I have hard work to avoid being a bitter enemy. But I am fiz-z-ing again.

Have you ever read Vanity Fair?[6] Do you remember how we tryed to get it in New York? Well, we borrowed it here, and a very entertaining book it is,

---

6. Ellen refers to William Thackeray's satirical novel published in 1847.

containing some most accurate likenesses of 'humans' as the Florida crackers say. I have a great mind to undertake "A Vanity Fair" in America. I think I could do it. If I only had a study all to myself, and if and but, and if, and but, and if, and but, and so on. You see we are studying Spanish; this I am doing [again you] start to go to Cuba, (where old Wall has gone . . . and where he will make a fortin'). I am going too, when you go. We'll go together, ahem. The mail closes this evening at six, and although I do not believe it will get out of town, I must nevertheless close up mine epistle, and put it therein; or it, the letter not the mail, will not go at all. So good by. May God bless yours.

Ellen

[Corinna Aldrich to Mannevillette Brown]

Key West [to Utica, New York]
Aug. 17th, 1849

I have at last received your very kind letter Dearest Manne—The old mail Boat contrived to find our shore after a voyage of thirteen days. Indeed we are looking out for the vessel of the 15th—she ought soon to be here—as this is awful business to have a line from the world only twice a month in anticipation and not get that! I did not know or at least did not appreciate the daily mail—until I came to this outlandish place, and in good earnest if it were not for the loaves & fishes[7] I would not stay here—I never would have come—if E. had not been promised the Hospital and now behold Dr. Jones is appointed there—a man who is scarcely capable of spelling his own name correctly—you ask if you shall press the matter—I fear 'tis too late now even the good people here do not think it so—for they have got up a petition to have the said D. Jones removed & Edward appointed in his place—the charge preferred is a heavy one, that of incompetency, but whether he has political influence enough to retain him in office despite the responsibility remains to be proven. E. has just come in with the petitions got up in his behalf—he says he intends to send a copy of the same to you in order that your friend Mr. W. if so disposed—may know what grounds to go upon. 'Tis true E is not much of a politician but he is a good Whig—and his influence is very considerable although he makes no fuss about it. However, this business is not looked upon as a political affair, but all parties have united to remonstrate against the injustice of having such a man placed in such a position. You know all the poor fellows out here in the gulph who may chance to fall sick, can only rely on the Hospital and 'tis hard they should not have a competent physician. This fellow attempted to perform

---

7. For the miracle of the loaves and fishes, see Matt. 14:14–21.

the simple operation of lancing a child's gums and slit its tongue so it bled to death! But this is only one of many & far worse blunders. He spells jolly with a g & rat with a w—wrat!! But enough of this. . . .

There are so many strangers here. We spent last evening with Miss [Julia] Wall—the belle of the city. She has or thinks she has a talent for sketching. I told her of you—she expressed a desire to see you. She is a <u>ringing</u> belle her Pa sounding at the rate of millions—Budd is writing you—and so is Ell—I think you will get a budget although we have only until dark to make up a mail—En passant—that news of George was all gammon.[8] In fact I did not believe a word of it—but somehow Ell got a kink in her brain that it might be true & we both loaded and fired at him—resolved to know the worst. I am very glad it was not true—not that I object to his marrying, far from it—as your Aunt Mary used to say, I wish he would, that we might have somewhere to <u>go</u> & <u>take</u> <u>tea</u>—now & then!! But I want both him & you to look out for the right kind of lady. Be sure no wealth can compensate for lack of feeling—and a flirt you may depend—has never a warm heart. They may feel for themselves but not for others! & wide is the difference. May you never experience it!—I am coming on to see you Dear, if I live—I want to talk to you on this & other subjects—particularly do I wish dear to make you a <u>little</u> <u>more</u> <u>selfish</u>—It sounds like a most heathenish Doctrine—but really Dear—there are those in the world who mentally & physically live like parasitick[9] vines upon the limbs & trunks of trees deriving all their sustenance therefrom, yet apparently so green & thrifty in themselves—we can't believe they are without a root! Well people are not unlike plants—although I trust all are not parasites. I find I have not room to carry out my metaphor—n'importe . . . for my own part I see so much of the shuffling and scrambling for California sand—in this same place. I am sometimes tempted to take to my heels & seek my fortune by myself. But I am stopt by the reflection that I should want to come back & see how the poor things I left behind were getting on—and to speak in earnest 'tis this same feeling, Manne, that makes me hesitate to go North now. But I shall brave it yet—I am resolved—if I live to visit you this fall—I shall try hard to bring you back too. So <u>be</u> <u>ready</u> <u>my</u> <u>boy</u>. I believe I must close and drop a line to George & also one to Mrs. W. G's last letter was in fine spirits. He says when he intends to take a sleeping partner he will let us know. I hope you will ditto. . . .

God bless you dear Corinna

---

8. "Talk, chatter. . . . Ridiculous nonsense suited to deceive simple persons only" (*OED*).

9. Obsolete spelling of *parasitic*.

[Corinna Aldrich to Mannevillette Brown]

Key West [to Utica, New York]

Sept. 3rd, 1849

. . . I had hoped to have left here, ere now for your good city, but circumstances alter cares. E's not getting the hospital made me think I ought not to go now—and the cholera that it was best not to, until cold weather—and moreover as it is to feel the cold weather in part, that I undertake the journey. I think I shall defer my visit until November. I see by the papers you have warmer weather than we do—but not so much of it—and we have no cholera, & or yellow fever or any other dreadful disease, indeed Dear Manne, this is a fine climate. The only trouble is, it debilitates me, but I am in hopes E. will get on so I can take a trip off once in a year or so—and that will invigorate me again. I believe he wrote you of the petitions that have been sent on in his behalf. Fortunately the fellow they have appointed here is incompetent. There could not be a better plea for a removal I should think, but whether it will have any weight in these degenerate days, is hard to say. I see the old President [Zachary Taylor] is gone East. I wish him joy of the stuffing he [will] get. If he gets any fatter, he'll be fit to kill, when he gets back! I wish he had staid in Washington long enough to have received E's petitions, but suppose "'tis all fa the best."

Ell is very busy making clothes for the little folks—she says she will write you. As for me, I have been repairing damages in my <u>gentle man's</u> wardrobe the past three weeks—for the first time in my life. He never would let me sew for him, but necessity knows no law—and as it is next to impossible to get sewing well done, and as the girl we brought out with us, proved to be a good sewer—he consented for us to try & like many another once begun he has kept us at it—last week I cut him a black sack coat and it fits first rate: also a pair of white pants! Do you remember the brown vest I made for you? in days lang syne [long ago]. . . .

I tell you Manne 'tis getting <u>warmish</u> here. How is the weather with you? & how is the cholera? We have no epidemick here as yet. Indeed it is very healthy—although the Dr. finds something to do. He averages about 6 or 7 dolls pr day good and sometimes more—in fact he books more—but 'tis not all <u>sure pay</u>. But his average practice is better here than it has ever been when out of Gen. employ—money is plenty—and gold & silver the circulation medium—you never see old ragged bills, or any thing of the sort. At Marietta & in fact all through Georgia every thing is <u>notes</u> and credit, and precious little pay at that, but here every man handles his doubloons! I want you to come, and take a few—I think you would enjoy a winter out here. 'Tis thought there will be a great many strangers here this winter and I do think it the best climate by far for invalids I ever was in—the temperature of the atmosphere is so equal and so dry, far more so than Upper Florida or West. . . .

P.S. I forgot to tell you Ell & I were studying Spanish & we get on famously. Last week we had to make a call at a house where not one could speak English. We made out quite a chat. They seemed to understand all we said—after a few weeks more study—we intend to go to see them to <u>practice</u>—'Tis getting dark

Good night and God bless you Dearest Ever yrs C.

[Ellen Anderson to Mannevillette Brown]

Key West [to Utica, New York]
Sept. 3rd, 1849

My Dear Mann,

The weather here goes on in regular degrees of comparison hot, hotter, and hottest. It certainly must have arrived at hottest in the course of the last two or three days. I am all the time wondering and contriving how I shall get away from this place next summer. I say next summer, because then, if nothing happens meantime, I shall have the money to pay mine passage. It will be due me from Government.

I have not only been feeling the pulses, but (listening looking) at the tongues of these people to see what is the state of their systems in respect of having young ideas cultivated, but indeed I find not a symptom, which would indicate blood-letting on that account. To speak without metaphor, they will let me have the young sprouts to cultivate, but I must do it very cheap. 'Vel' now I think if I must work for very cheap, I will go some where else to do it—for here I am boiled, fried, stung and blistered. My children, who were pretty children, are turned into ugly children, and, in short, I cannot tolerate the idea of passing my summers in Key West, and as I cannot pass my summers elsewhere and my winters here, it follows that I must find means to pass all my time elsewhere.

My plan is this—to get a situation as instructress in some school, where my children could be pupils. Under such circumstances it would about take my salary to pay for their schooling, but for the coming three years I shall be able to clothe myself, and in that time, could I only commence flying, I fancy my wings would become so strong that I could fly on my own account i.e. take the superintendence of a school, which, I think, ought to maintain a woman and three children but all I can say is that if it will not, <u>something else must</u>. I can fancy that all this is very disagreeable to you, but indeed my Dear Mann, I can only say, out of the fullness of the heart the mouth speaketh,[10] and unless I talk

10. Matt. 12:34; Luke: 6:45.

about some such matter, I fear I shall not write at all, because I can think of nothing else. I feel that I must bestir myself, for the time passeth and the years draw nigh,[11] when I shall have no pension to fill up the chinks and corners of my expenses and I dread those coming years, <u>if they should come to me as I have experienced them in years past, worse than death.</u>

No man knoweth the thoughts of a man, save the spirit of a man that is in him.[12] I insert this passage of scripture because I can fancy it will furnish a good hint in reply to your reflections on all I have said. I fancy I know what you will say but perhaps not. I don't know that it is worth while to trouble you with these matters, but I believe I have said so before. I quite envy Corine the prospect she appears to have before her of seeing your pictures this winter. I think they would be the principal thing I should be thinking about if I were coming north! I hope she will be able to come, and I hope she will enjoy herself, she needs recruiting very much. I would come with her if I were able, but it is easy to see that if I should get my two foots on the continent again, I should run away. They would not get this Buonaparte on board a vessel bound for St. Helena again. It is a wonder to me now, what I came here for, except to cost money, while it was scarce. Bless my stars what a helpless individual a woman is! What a ninny she can be. If it was not wicked I would wish myself a man. I would put my two legs into a pair of trousers and take the longest kind of steps, I don't know where. The fact is, Mann, a woman, having children, not having money, not having youth beauty or facinations [*sic*] is a nuisance, a scum on the face of the Earth, a blot, and a nastiness in creation, and such is your humble servant and sister. Ain't you proud of me? I really don't think this letter is fit to send, for I have set down and let my thoughts just sprawl themselves out upon it. So you see what beautiful thoughts I have but sometimes I am a great deal more refined and if you wont lay this letter to heart, I will promise to write you a most refined and ladylike epistle next mail, and I will get into a good humour on purpose for it. You would be astonished could you know how amiable I am sometimes, but to day I feel like an old witch. Give my very best love to Mrs. Walker and her family and in particular to the two young ladies, whom I take for granted to be very sweet and lively, having been raised by so excellent and sensible a mother. God bless you my Dear Mann. May he bestow upon you grace, wisdom, and strength is the prayer of your sister.

Ellen

11. Eccles. 12:1.
12. 1 Cor. 2:11.

[Ellen Anderson to Mannevillette Brown]

Key West [to Utica, New York]
September 13, 1849

Dear Manne,

... I will write an order to the Quarter master at New York, and that there ought not to be any expense to be paid upon the box and rifle so long as they are in Uncle Sam's keeping, it is at his cost. I will send the order to you, and you get the things, if you can, without putting yourself to too much trouble but don't worry yourself about them.

There has considerable rain fallen here in the course of the last two or three days which makes it much cooler, and renders us much more comfortable. Save this, I have no news to tell you. The children look somewhat better than they did. I teach them every day, and that, with my Spanish and my sewing, makes up my occupations. There is very little visiting here, so that society does not interfere with one much and positively nothing else to interest one in the smallest degree, except to watch the vessels sailing in and out of the harbour, which, by the way, is oftentimes a sight pretty enough. I can get along better than most people under such circumstances as these, because I am fond of solitary occupations. I am mistaken if the little "island far off in the ocean" is not a very nest of scandalmongers, and for the very reason that they have nothing upon Earth to take up their attention but one another's business. As one hears the rumbling noise in volcanic countries, which threatens and precedes the irruption, so here we hear the symptomatic sounds, and I suppose in due time shall witness its consequences.

Give my love to Mrs. Walker. It makes me feel more acquainted with her to learn that she is acquainted with my friend Mr. Wessells. He was the most intimate friend my husband had, and since his death, has evinced the kindness of a brother for me. I am sorry indeed to hear of poor Mary's death. Does Mrs. W know his present wife? and what sort of a woman is she? As you speak of his eldest daughter, I suppose he has other children. I have never seen him but once since he was last married, and then only for a short time.

I do not mention my school project because I should have to say the same things over and over again. I shall not be able to decide, finally, before the first of October, as to whether I can get at a school at a decent price, or not. It is next to impossible to get a room to begin with, but I shall see. As I have said before, I am not anxious about it. You must know that this is quite a hobby of mine. I believe any child, not an idiot, can be made smart if well trained. The question is what is a good training? And to this I should reply in detail only that I had rather reply in practice. So to the children again. Sis spells very well, (she is a good student but Will was born, I think, with innate ideas of spelling, for he does not love study.) And she reads well, only I have exercised her so long in one book, that I had almost made her like the old woman who could read nobody's bible but her own; however I have found it out and now I intend to teach her the other words in the language. She is remarkable at getting a lesson, she will commit to memory anything in reason that you give her, whether she understands it or not, which latter occasions me a good deal of puzzle as to whether she does understand or not. Besides reading and spelling she studies natural Philosophy (on a small scale) and Geography. Villette knows her letters, and can spell owl, she also spells most other words with the same three letters, except nag which she spells "og." And now my Dear Manne over and above and by and through all other things, I endeavor to raise my children to be religious, believing all other knowledge or accomplishments utterly unavailing to render them happy or useful except as I shall succeed in that. I wish them to be taught musick as soon as they shall be old enough, and it is about the only thing, conceited beast that I am, that I do not feel able to teach them, and bitterly I regret that by hook or by crook, I did not contrive to foster this accomplishment on to my finger ends, for be you sure that if I had got but a small quantity of instruction, I would by this time have made large use of it. But I intend the children shall be taught. Villette will have fine musical abilities if one can judge from one so young. Georgia has not so good an ear but she will make up for it by hard trying. Willy also has a good ear. . . . Goodbye may God bless you, yours Ell

A debate arose between Mannevillette and Ellen regarding her desire to work; in one letter he explained his opposition to her plans:

> But tho' strongly tempted, I shall not criticise or advise you but rather give you new matter of reflection. Now my dear sister of our family you are the only one that has any babies—and for that reason I can tell you that you are of especial interest to each and all of us. This is not said because any one has said so to me, but rather because circumstances convince me of it. Now for my part of the interest. I here promise you, so long as heaven will permit me, to give you yearly the same amount of money that you now receive from the United States Government. You may henceforward draw on me in any way shape or manner or at any time that you see fit for the whole or part of said income. . . . I know what you want, it is what we all would like, and that is independence, but I defy you to get it—no position in life will produce it. No man can be more independent in this world than I am. There lives not a man

to whom I feel the slightest dependence and yet I dare not act what I feel, for it would be the height of folly.[13]

Ellen's response follows.

[Ellen Brown Anderson to Mannevillette Brown]

Key West [to Utica, New York]
Oct. 8th, 1849

My Dear Mann,

Your two letters of the 13th and 23d Sept. have been received by me, and I have a great deal to say in reply to them. So much, indeed, that I fear I shall not say the half of it. For the matter of the advice, which you would have given me, and did not, and, finally, sum up in a direction to send forward my anticipations to another world, I must reply, that I endeavor to do so. But, my good brother, should not one do something else, besides? I think we have duties to perform, in regard to this present life, which, if we neglect, we shall as much tarnish our Christian characters, as we should by neglecting the important duty to which you refer me. And one of those duties which weighs upon my mind, is the duty of taking <u>proper</u> <u>care</u> of myself and children. I do trust in God; he is my only dependence. But, will God aid if I foolishly sit still and say, may I be fed and clothed? That is not the sort of faith we are directed to have for our neighbours, and, I opine, is not the sort we should have for ourselves. St. Paul directs that he who will not work, shall not eat.[14] Now I can't think of doing without the latter and I am very willing to do the former; but I had rather do some kinds of work than others; and had rather work for some people and in some places than others. Who is without preferences? Not that I consider that I work at present, but I say I am willing to; although to set about it, is about as dis-agreeable to me, as it is to most persons, who are not used to it. Again, My Dear brother, I bear in mind that, having food and raiment, we should be therewith content, and also that we should take no thought for the morrow [etc.][15] but do you not suppose these directions to be intended to relieve us from anxieties, and not to prevent us making any exertions? Now, before me lies the certain fact, (which I at least feel bound to believe,) that the pension which at

---

13. Mannevillette Brown to Ellen Anderson, September 23, 1849, Anderson-Brown Papers, USMA.

14. Thess. 3:10.

15. Matt. 6:34.

present supplies my necessities will at the end of three years be paid me no more. 'Tis true that three years is a long time, and before it expires I may die. But, I think, (I may be wrong,) that in regard to this matter I should act as though I expected to live.

You tell me you will give me the same amount of money as the government does, well my dear Mann, <u>if you are able to give it</u> me, I shall not hesitate one moment to accept of it, and I feel greatly obliged to you anyhow. But don't offer or promise me this money and then pinch and deny yourself, to pay it to me. That is what I am afraid [of]. I should feel so afraid to use my money, if I obtained it under such circumstances, that it would not do me any good. <u>Now do not deceive either me or yourself in any such matter</u>. You see there would be no sense in such a proceeding, because I <u>insist</u> that I am both able and willing not only to look out for number one, but also <u>two</u>, <u>three</u>, and <u>four</u>.

I get 'powerful' dis-contented sometimes and sometimes have written to you and George when I was in these humours. Whether or no I have cause you cannot judge, for the <u>cause</u> of my discontent I have never mentioned: only my <u>means</u> <u>for</u> <u>its</u> <u>remedy</u>. If it be the effect of a deseased state of mind, I can only say, with other invalids, having the desease,[16] I must take measures to cure myself of it.

Is it not just possible, my dear Mann, that instead of judging—(as one is directed, in the bible, to judge, of a tree, by its fruits)[17] by my actions, that you judge me by the actions of other peoples—(or judge one tree by the fruit of others) a kind of judgement much more common, than reflected upon. I don't know that you do; for I do not pretend to any great self knowledge, nor am I very certain of what you may have wished to say to me, that you did not say. Only this I know, that I wrote you a letter setting forth that I intended to break out in a new place as the Georgians say, and you overlook all the subject matter of mine epistle, and offer to give me money, and George serves me the same way, now it is true, that I might go ahead with any plans without troubling either you or him about them; but I did not, and, if I can make it out clearly to myself, I will try and tell you the reason. You are both of you old, oh no, not old! Ye are bachelors pro. tem.[18] Vel[19] 'sich'[20] "domestic ties" sometimes seems very desirable. May be you might fancy to have a housekeeper or, may be you

---

16. Obsolete form of *disease* (*OED*).

17. Matt. 12:33; Luke 6:44.

18. Latin *pro tempore:* "temporarily; for the time being."

19. This seems to be a mock German pronunciation of the English *well*.

20. Ellen seems to be mocking the southern or cracker pronunciation of *such*.

might know of a 'siteravation'[21] which might just suit, or on the other hand, it may be, (for how do I know) you may be aristocratic in your feelings, and a whole train of considerations may cut in there. Now if you are poor and proud, I could keep at a distance, if you are poor and needy—of affectionate relatives—I could come into your neighborhood. And last of all, if you are rich and choose to maintain me, until you get married, I am at your service. Only I would not like to be a stumbling block in the way of the latter event, and so preparatory to taking care of myself, whenever I should [shall] think fit, you must not quarrel with me, for laying up treasures after my own peculiar fashion, which are not upon Earth as the bible forbids, nor yet exactly or entirely in Heaven, as it directs, but in my heart.[22] I intend to make myself an accomplished teacher, if I can, and keep it by me as the nobleman did his trade, against the day when I need it. I have not any property, and never shall have any, and I think brains was given me instead. I don't feel as if I was altogether wise and good, my dear Manne, but I believe I try to do what is right. . . .

[Corinna Brown Aldrich to Mannevillette Brown]

Key West [to Utica, New York]
Oct 9th, 1849

. . . Dear Manne, I am sick to day—right sick, I have these attacks often, so often that I take them as a matter of course, and so does the family—yet 'tis hard to bear. I have almost turned wrong side out, three times since breakfast—and still feel as if there were more to fling up, as the darkies say! n'importe, I am coming on to see you, and I think that will greatly benefit, if it does not cure me. You & Mrs. W.—both seem to think December a more pleasant month than November. Be it so—it will suit me as well, to come then. I calculated on leaving here the middle, or last of next month—(November) If no untoward event should happen to detain me.

The white girl whom we brought out with us, is very anxious to go back—she is not contented, and 'tis not to be wondered at. She has no acquaintances, or company of her cast, save the negroes. She says she would not have staid a week with any one but me—and if I do not go on, she will remain with me until Spring. However, as I hope to go—I am not sorry she wishes to do likewise—as I could not so well go all alone—and I would rather have one in her capacity, than a companion. I do not at all deem it advisable for Ellen to take the children on at this season. Indeed I would not attempt a winter journey

21. *Situation.*
22. Matt. 6:19–22; Mark 10:21; Luke 12:21, 18:22.

with three such little travellers unless it were unavoidable. It is neither agreeable or judicious. These are my sentiments, not <u>hers</u>. She is resolved to go north in the Spring, and then I know no objection. I love all children—her's, as if they were my own, and I believe I am perfectly sincere when I say, if I had <u>one even</u>, and did not choose to leave it behind—I would stay with it—I would like to have her go on with me—but that she won't hear of—and I don't know as she is to blame. They are nice little children and well worth caring for. As to my object in visiting you at this seemingly untoward season—I am rather selfish in my views. I feel as if the journey would do me good in body, and mind. I want to see you, and talk to you dear, and I want to see Mrs. Walker. Again I believe a journey in cold weather more beneficial than in summer—if my mind can be relieved of care and anxiety—[etc. etc.]—

The <u>Isabel</u> is arrived from Cuba and I must make my hay. She only remains an hour—but we are not allowed the quarter of that—I don't know why they close the mail so early unless to make people prompt. If I had written on Saturday, as I ought but I was sure there would be time enough. On Sundays I don't write letters unless I cannot do it at any other time. Budd & Ell are both writing you, and poor little sis thinks she is doing the same. Children are so imitative. They went to the funeral of a little child a while ago—and they have scarcely done ought else, but <u>bury</u> <u>their</u> <u>dolls</u> <u>since</u>. Virginia and the Dr. are visiting below stairs. Ell, I & the little folks above. They all desire their love—and I must close—as my time is up—I hate to send you such a scramble, dear, but you must take this or none. God bless you, and keep you from all harm. I trust I may soon see you, and won't I be so happy. I would like it better if Ell could join me—but we cannot have every thing as we wish. For me—I am grateful for what pleasures are permitted me. Again Dearest May God bless you. I shall write you the mail before I leave. You say you will meet me in N.Y. that will not be necessary dear, unless you choose—as I shall go on with some gentleman from here, and shall have Jane with me—who is a faithful and trusty Irish<u>er</u>— and knows N.Y. like a book. I may bring her with me—as she <u>may</u> return with me—her wages are low, & you know servants travel for half price. I would not speak of these matters dear—but may as well, as think. While you and E & G have to work—I must and will at least be reasonable! Adieu dearest. We have had no storm as yet—but 'tis daily <u>expected</u>! In fact, the weather has been very calm and hot. But to day is lovely. We have what is called a Norther—but not one of the frigid or very boisterous kind; only just cool enough to equalize the atmosphere—and, par consequence, the temper of some individuals of the sanguine temperament. The wise ones say—there is no danger of a storm while the wind is North—I am in hopes we shall not have a regular blow out.

We had news last evening from Tampa Bay—Headquarters of Gen. [David] Twiggs. The report is—He had a-talk with Billy Bowlegs: (who by the way is straight as an arrow I'm told) Billy devised six weeks armistice to consider— Gen Twiggs refused the time. Billy then said he "had warriors to last him <u>ten</u> years and he [Twiggs] could fire away at the pile"!—If this be true, & we have another 7 years war in prospect and we have no reason to doubt the summary. The talk was by appointment—we are out of harm's way-. . . . [Sincerely Yours, Corinna]

[Corinna Aldrich to Mannevillette Brown]

Key West [to Utica, New York]
Oct. 23rd. 1849

To our surprise & almost dismay dear Brother, we learn the mail will close at six o'clock tonight instead of the day after tomorrow her usual time. This happens in consequence of the steamer's being obliged in the interval of time to her next trip, to go to New York for some repairs to her machinery! What a nice chance it would be for me to go on if I were ready. That is an objection I could easily miss out, however, if she did not charge so exorbitantly, 50 dollars or 55 I don't know which. 'Tis true, this is no more than the regular passage by steamer via Charleston—30 from here to C. & 25 thence to N.Y. but I can take passage in a fine packet, one of those which run to New Orleans, frequently touch in here for one half or less than half—the only difference to me will be in time, and as I am on no very important errand, the delay of a few days will make no material difference. Many persons think it more safe to go by steamer, but as to that I place my trust in a higher power than any element of earth. God will protect me and carry me as safely in a packet as a steamer. I know if I had my choice, unbiased by expense, I might choose the <u>Isabel</u>, as she is a fine boat & I know her Captain & still I would rather come on a <u>packet</u> or not at all or in any way to incur such outlays. I feel I ought not to indulge. Edward's practice here will do no more than keep the pot boiling unless it should vastly increase this winter. It may, as often invalids resort here & probably will this season in preference to going to Florida while the mainland is harassed by marauding Indians.

Do you hear any thing of the war! Whether it is a war, or not! We are, as it were, out of the land of truth. Such garbled reports are brought as none can digest or credit. The last was that Billy Bowlegs (who, en passant, is . . . nearly straight in his pedestals!) was to have a talk, which means, a speech made up by Uncle Sam & put in his mouth by an interpreter, but any how he was to meet Gen. [David] Twig[g]s, and say whether he would fight or run away. I believe they will play at beau peep with our people until they are all <u>exterminated</u>. We hear also that Wild Cat, who was sent for by Gov. to prevail on his brethren to return with him to the far west, passed through Alabama since, all painted, plumed, and armed for <u>war</u>![23] He is a cunning Indian and I am surprised that after all his perfidy he should again be trusted in a matter of so vital moment. This concerns not us, however, "fight dog, fight bear, my dog went there"—I forgot George, but I don't believe he will be wiry enough to put himself in their way. . . .

Now I think of it, I will put you up a barrel of coco nuts fresh from the trees! I will direct them to the care of Mrs. Walker. I wish you had sent an address, but I will try & have them reach you. They will be in N.Y. in 5 days from this! I send them in the hull or outer shell as 'tis said they keep better. You must not eat too many of them at a time. The milk won't hurt you, they make nice <u>pies</u> & <u>puddings</u>. You must present Mrs. W. with a dozen from me & tell her if I were sure she would get them I would send her a barrel. When I come on I will bring these flower seeds. There are great varieties of cactus. . . . I can leave home better when Ell & Virginia are here. I should not be willing to leave Edward <u>all</u> <u>alone</u>, for any time.

I heard from George last mail, he had been to Charleston & hastened his return as the <u>bilous</u> & yellow fever prevailed there. I reckon G is making money! & I am glad of it. I want to see you & him independent. Poor Ed will never do more than make a living here unless he gets that Hospital & that I fear he is not politician enough to obtain. But political & influential friends may do it for him. You have no idea dear, of the rancorous feeling, the bitter envy, jealousy and all unkindness which influences these office seekers and holders. They would tear each other's eyes out to rob another of his office, or to turn out or put in one of their party. I am disgusted with them. Let them scramble on, 'tis a regular scramble business & I do not desire to see my husband in the mess. If he can by fair & open means obtain the appointment, I hope he may succeed —but on no other terms do I want it & I believe He who permits evil & punishes it and blesses those who trust in Him, will order all things right. . . . Ever your. . . . sister Corrina.

---

23. Corinna was mistaken regarding Wild Cat's return to Florida. Federal authorities requested his support in urging Billy Bowlegs and the remaining Seminoles to emigrate west, but he refused and was not among the party. As Corinna wrote this letter Wild Cat was moving his band of Seminoles from the Arkansas Territory to Mexico. See Porter, *Black Seminoles,* 127–28; Jane F. Lancaster, *Removal Aftershock: The Seminoles' Struggles to Survive in the West, 1836–1866* (Knoxville: University of Tennessee Press, 1994), 80–86.

[Ellen Brown Anderson to Mannevillette Brown]

Key West [to Utica, New York]
October 23rd, 1849

My Dear Mann,

Your half sheet of the 8th Oct. I received yesterday. It was <u>multima in parvo</u>[24] if you will excuse a little Latin; I fear my last to you was <u>parvum in multo</u>.[25] I had a great mind to commence this one as I was saying and go straight on with the old subject, but I think I ll drop it, for the present, because however much I talk, I only talk around certain ideas, which I do not and shall not, express, and this is why I ~~talk~~ write so much, to so little purpose. But mind I don't give up the point viz. that you do not know me, although your letter is a good one, being as letters written in a hurry often are, the concentrated essence of a long talk.

Here it is the 20th Oct. and the people have not yet had their storm. About the 10th it came on to blow pretty hard, and look very threatening, whereat many, nay almost all the families, nailed up their windows, and packed away their goods and chattels, preparitory [*sic*] to being hurricaned; but no hurricane came, and although the wind has continued to blow, off, and on, ever since, they have quite given up the idea of having one. So I suppose this year will be remarkable for this omission—(If that be the proper word to use).

One old (or perhaps I should not say old, because although an old wrecker he does not appear to be an old man) one wrecker then, is so discouraged at the lack of storms this Fall, that he has determined to go to California. I wonder now what your idea of a wrecker is! A piratical sort of fellow, whiskers and beard outside, and rascality in? Is that it? La me, how "distance lends" the romantic, as well as "enchantment, to the view."[26] La me! Man, they are tall, short, fat, lean, and universally ugly, like men every where else. Some are liberal, others stingy, they have wives and children who are neither beasts, angles[27] nor cherubs. There is not a Meg Merridies nor a Nanbeest Brown; no, nor a Nina, upon the island. They live in comfortable houses, grumble about expenses, and persue[28] their avocations in as business-like a manner, as any shopkeeper you could find; The rascality being with the one, as with the other, in the counting room, not upon the sea. Upon the sea, they are the ablest of seamen;

---

24. Latin: "much in a little."
25. Latin: "a little in much."
26. Thomas Campbell, *The Pleasures of Hope* (1799), part 1, line 7.
27. Obsolete spelling of *angel*.
28. Obsolete form of *pursue* (*OED*).

necessarily so: for it is their business in calm and storm, to go to the relief of distressed vessels, and their arrangements for this purpose, are as business-like and systematic as those of any other trade or calling and a wrecker may be as honest and as honourable a man as any other, and yet not have to quit his trade for conscience sake.

You want to hear about the children. 'Vel' I feel as if you knew all about them already, nevertheless, as you make the request and I might be supposed to take an interest in replying to it, I shall devote a word or two to them. I shall begin by replying to your last question first: their health is at present good, but they have suffered so much from the heat, moschetoes and above all from the biles,[29] with which their faces especially have been covered, that they are not at all so good looking as when you saw them, and besides they are all three quitting the pretty and growing into the ugly age but the biles have scarred their faces very much, but the doctor thinks they will not be permanent, and so I hope. Will I think is of good size, rather large of his age; and so also is Miss Vilette, as we call her, (the youngest), but Georgia is small, which brings the last two to be pretty nearly of a size. The eldest is indeed the smallest except that she is slightly the tallest. If you have not forgotten it, why of course you remember, that I have told you my husband, and so were all his family, father, mother, sister, and brother, as far as I have known of them, tall, and our folks you know were not short, so it [is] reasonable enough that my young ones should be of good size.

As for their dispositions, I, their mother, think they are remarkably amiable children, whether or no I am a good judge others must determine. I speak very sincerely on this, as I think I do on all other subjects. (My penmanship must delight you, but somehow I am not in the write-good-humour to day and I am afraid I never shall be again, until I get some deacent [*sic*] pens, and some good ink to encourage me.) Now comes "their studies" Ah!!! I shall astonish you with a catalogue of them; but you must bear in mind their ages, and that the instruction is according thereunto. Master Will reads well, and spells very well, and writes tolerable well, all three without regard to his age, and with regard to his age, he studies, Geography, Arithmetic, Grammar, reads history, and writes composition. I am aware that this last exercise will make you laugh, when you consider the age of the pupil, most, nay everybody would think it rediculous[30] but I have my own notions about educating children, and you see there is nobody to interfere with me, no not even taking sufficient notice to

---

29. Obsolete spelling of *boils.*
30. Obsolete spelling of *ridiculous.*

laugh at me. I wish Will in addition to the above to commence the study of some language other than English, but I have not yet started him fairly, and for this too I have my reasons, which I will give you when you shall have occasion for them. If you will get married and have some babies and let me educate them, I will engage to make geniuses of every one of them, and not bring on the great bugbear the brain fever[31] either. [Rest of letter is missing]

Corinna wrote to Mannevillette on November 22 from the Howard House in New York City, where she had arrived after a rough voyage by steamer. No correspondence from Corinna, Ellen, Edward, or Mannevillette survives for the next few months; Corinna returned to Key West sometime in March 1850. The sisters' last few Key West letters unfold their plans for departure from Florida.

[Corinna Brown Aldrich to Mannevillette Brown]

Key West [to Utica, New York]
March 21st, 1850

I am not "mad" my Dear Brother, nor fevered by the coveted wealth of California! Indeed, I think, if an examination were made, my brains would prove as sound, as any, in this tribe! However, I am not going to decry my neighbours. All things considered, I cannot but approve of the course, Edward is about to take: and sound or crazy, if I had the means, I would go with him, to California! Not that I suppose, gold is to be picked up in the streets, or won without toil, and privation more, perhaps, than elsewhere. But, as the effort is greater, so is the reward. I believe with the exertion he would have to make here, for a living; he can there, in a few years acquire a competency, if not a moderate fortune. Whatever you may suppose, I do not act or talk without reflection; and the best result of reasoning, of which I am capable. I did not put this idea in his head, either; I found him full of it when I came home; and I can only say now as then, I had no objection to urge against it, except, that I endeavored to impress on his mind the privations he must undergo and I believe, further, he is fully aware of this and willing to bear it, in the hope of ultimate success.

In regard to Ell & I, we are going to St. Mary's Georgia—the birth place of the Doctor, and present residence of his father. 'Tis a quiet little village, quiet as the grave, where the grass grows in the streets, and the fennel runs rank by

31. "A term for inflammation of the brain 'and also for other fevers, as typhus, with brain complications'" (*OED*).

the wayside. Still it has its advantages. There are several old families who make it a winter residence. 'Tis on the Atlantic, or near it. We can live comfortably & economically—it is generally healthy and it is George & Edward's wish that we should for the present, <u>locate</u> <u>there</u>. I also like the idea of having <u>a</u> <u>home</u>, although Ell & I do not admire the place. Still, we will go there and may learn to like it better. One gratification will be, seeing George two or three times a year and possibly, you may be induced to pay us a visit. In consideration of this plan, Dear, we shall <u>not</u> <u>need</u> <u>assistance</u>. <u>Now</u>, you must understand me, and not put yourself out, because, <u>if</u> <u>we</u> <u>needed</u> <u>it</u>, <u>I</u> <u>would</u> <u>say</u> <u>it</u>, knowing you would aid us. George has promised, if we go to St. Mary's, to get us a house & we will ship from here our bedding & such articles of furniture etc. as is advisable. I shall write George this mail & tell him, we accept his offer, & will go to St. Mary's but we cannot get there, right off. I shall go to N.Y. with Edward, to see him comfortably off. In the mean time, <u>Ellen</u> <u>and</u> <u>the</u> <u>children</u> <u>will</u> <u>remain</u> <u>here</u>, <u>at</u> <u>board</u>; <u>until</u> <u>a</u> <u>favorable</u> <u>opportunity</u> <u>offers</u> <u>to</u> <u>take</u> <u>her</u> <u>&</u> <u>the</u> <u>things</u> <u>to</u> <u>St.</u> <u>Mary's</u>. She will get there as soon as I do. While in N.Y. I shall get such articles as we may need. I have a woman who I have engaged to hire, by the year, at $12 per month. This will hire us all the servants we will need in St. Mary's. The price of labour there, is so much less. George says he will supply us with our groceries, from Charleston. We can hire a nice house for from $8 to $10 per month. We pay $25 per month for the one we occupy here, and 'tis small, & inconvenient, though pretty. We could not remain here or I would do so, but living is very expensive and the climate so debilitating, that even the Dr. is pulled down by it and worse still, the mosquitos are intolerable!

The children are playing around me so that I cannot write a word straight, but you must not <u>judge</u> <u>me</u> <u>on</u> <u>paper</u>, Dear. I told Ell after I mailed my last letters to you, that I believed you would think I was <u>tipsy</u> or crazy! I would not have sent them, if I had not supposed it was the last chance, I should have to write you. Ed <u>then</u> thought of going right off. We are <u>now</u> awaiting a packet for N.Y. and the next letter you get from me, will, if I live, <u>be</u> <u>mailed</u> <u>there</u>. You must write me there, in reply to this. I hope you approve our plans. You can write Ell <u>here</u>, until she leaves for St. M. She will probably be here one more mail, <u>if</u> <u>not</u> <u>two</u>, but she will not need any funds as she will have $120 from Washington (her pension) next mail. And George sent her <u>a</u> <u>supply</u> by last mail. I tell you this Dear, lest you should suppose she would be in need of funds & put yourself out, to remit her. Edward will leave me sufficient to take care of me comfortably, for six months, and at the end of that time, he hopes to remit me, <u>from</u> <u>California</u> and <u>I</u> <u>have</u> <u>no</u> <u>doubt</u> <u>he</u> <u>will</u> <u>be</u> <u>able</u>; <u>however</u>, you may think of it, at any rate 'tis worth the hazzard [*sic*]. If he is successful, he will send for us—but of that, hereafter. <u>You</u> <u>must</u> <u>not</u> <u>forget</u> <u>the</u> <u>portraits</u>, Dear, <u>I</u>

want them to ornament our parlour. We intend to live so nice, & snug. You must come to see "the ladies of Llangollen."

Will you be able to come down to N.Y. to see us? Virginia will go on with us, but she will proceed to Chester (Penn.) Edward and I will remain in the city, a week or two. You think he can't get a passage before May, I tell him so, but he says he has much to attend to there. We will go to a private boarding house. . . . He has a Brother in N.Y., also one in California. The latter writes he is getting on finely. He is a Lawyer, & to be depended. [The last page is lost.]

[Ellen Brown Anderson to Mannevillette Brown]

Key West [to Utica, New York]
March 21st, 185[0]

My Dear Mann,

Your letter of March 5th I received last mail. I am sorry your spirits are not as good as they have been. But pray do not let my affairs be an additional uneasiness to you. George sent me, by the last mail sufficient money to pay all my present expenses, so that I am quite four handed just now, as I over heard a Yankee woman express it. My mind is not in good order for writing a letter to day as we are all making preparations to move, and for the life of me I can think of nothing else. In as much as boarding here is expensive and the only comfortable house is crammed, I have made up my mind to go directly to St. Marys. There I will board until we get to housekeeping, and I am farther induced to do this from the reflection that there will be no doctor here (whose opinion is worth sixpence) after Edward leaves, and the whooping cough is prevailing, and the small pox in the hospital: these you will admit are urgent reasons for, and I see nothing against my going, except that George asked me to wait until he could make preparation for me, but I think if he were here he would withdraw his request. So good bye my Dear. Write to me at St. Marys, and from thence I will write to you again yours

Ellen

[Corinna Aldrich to Mannevillette Brown]

Key West [to Utica, New York]
April 7th 1850

Dear Manne

Your letter to Ellen, as she is gone, I took the liberty of reading. I suppose ere this, you are in receipt of our last documents which explain the cause of her absence. We are unluckily detained here, and probably will be, a few days longer, by contrary winds. We are daily expecting a packet the Wassasea (I think that is the name) bound to N.Y. We have sold out, bag and baggage (almost) and are now <u>at</u> <u>board</u> in the most <u>recherché</u>[32] Hotel of the Island. My room is exquisite, having one window with two <u>panes</u> out, and six <u>pains</u> in. A white bottom curtain, an apology for one, hangs alone; draped in the middle by a bit of rope, in lieu of fancy cord. My bed is not quite down, but very palmy, being made of the <u>leaves</u> of that graceful tree. A sort of desk that once was fine but now usurped by rats & roaches constitutes our washstand with an odd bowl & Ewer—an old fashion card table, that trembles on its spindle legs, like some time worn veteran of eighty—yet telling of porcine wrath and piney in its bits of still adhering veneering while its double leaf assures us, that our ancestors also knew the hazard of a lie! An uneven floor all stained with grease & "back-ing," an old chair that must have been upon the reef judging from its piebald aspect and an old hearth, or horse rug that also has smelt salt water, serves as a carpet. The walls are planked, if not paneled; while the wasps and spiders have tapestried them & trellised the rafters! I have long thought a good hotel would do a great business here & am now convinced of the fact—were it not for <u>pride</u> I would start one, it would be as good as California. Though I should have to get Edward out of [the] way. He says the last employment he would undertake would be to take boarders! Our present lodgings form a strong contrast even to the home we have just deserted—and that is the <u>crack</u> residence of the Island. We have a daguerreotype of it. I will show it to you sometime.

Do you think you will be able to come to see us while in N.Y.? I can't say when we will be there, however, all things now, are against us. We look out every day for a packet and trust there may be one this week. We have been ready now for ten days. I did not think, when Ellen left, the next trip of the Isabel would find us here. Yet it is so, she is in tonight from Savannah. My next I think will be dated from New York but you must not be [alarmed] if you do not hear from us as soon as you expect. We may be kept here a fortnight yet & may have long passage also, although at this time of year it is not probable. I have written George & shall endite an epistle to Ell. She will be very [surprised] to learn me still here. She left in such a hurry, supposing we would also leave that week. But I have no doubt 'tis all wisely ordained and will be all right in the end. . . .

Good bye dear Ever yours Corrina

---

32. French: "exquisite, refined, sought after."

Chapter Twelve

"The Uncertainty of Our Lives"
After Key West

In early spring 1850 Corinna, Edward, and Virginia left Key West, arriving in New York City on April 26. Soon after arriving Virginia left the family to visit friends in Chester, Pennsylvania. Edward set his plans in motion to build a new life for himself, Corinna, and perhaps Ellen and her children in California. His brother Louis was prospering in the Golden State, and he hoped that San Francisco might offer financial rewards. After buying drugs and other supplies he set out by steamer on May 13 for San Francisco. After arriving safely that summer he notified Corinna that his prospects were not good because there were already too many doctors and quacks there, though he still hoped for a hospital appointment. In October he wrote to Mannevillette that he was doing well but had many expenses.[1]

Meanwhile, Ellen and the children joined Corinna in New York after boarding for a brief period in St. Marys, Georgia, with Edward's father. Financial concerns dominated the sisters' thoughts that summer, but George and Mannevillette continued to assist them. "I am determined she [Ellen] shall not work as long as I can help it," George wrote Mannevillette earlier that year; "I will take care of her and her children until your affairs enable you to do your part, which I know you will cheerfully do as soon as the world wags well with you." Mannevillette likewise was determined to live up to his commitment to match her federal government widow's pension.[2]

In the fall the sisters received word from Florida that George was to be married to Matilda Stewart, whose family resided on a plantation, Liberty Bluff,

---

1. Edward Aldrich to Corinna Aldrich, July 28, 1850; and Edward Aldrich to Mannevillette Brown, October 31, 1850, Anderson-Brown Papers, USMA.

2. Ellen Anderson to Mannevillette Brown, June 6, 1850; George L. Brown to Mannevillette Brown, April 22, July 15, 1850; and Mannevillette Brown to Ellen Brown, September 23, 1849, Anderson-Brown Papers, USMA.

forty miles from Newnansville. With Mannevillette's and George's financial support, the sisters made their way to Florida late that year. After arriving in December the sisters divided their time between Newnansville and the Stewart plantation. Attending dances and meeting new in-laws, the sisters found a happy respite at George and Matilda's wedding.[3] After a six-month visit to Florida the sisters were on their way back north. Returning by way of Portsmouth and Boston, they were back in New York City by November. From December to June the family moved five times: to Chamber Street; to 673 Broadway; to 521 Broadway; to Brooklyn, where they boarded with a friend; and finally to 99 St. Mark's Place.[4] To say the least, the family's living situation was unsettled. Thus, as Ellen commented to her brother in the winter of 1852, "The uncertainty of life is proverbial, but, I think, the uncertainty of our lives beats the proverb."[5]

Meanwhile the sisters continued to keep track of loved ones in Florida and California. George and Matilda's first child (Adelaide) was born that summer. But the news from Edward in California was not good: he had lost all of his belongings in a fire; he had made a series of bad investments; and he had difficulty finding satisfactory employment. Even so, the family learned from their brother George in Florida that Edward wanted Corinna, Ellen, and the children to come to California that summer. But Corinna resisted. George promised to assist them financially in making their journey, but their plans to move to California never materialized. Edward would never see Corinna again. In a startling letter to his brother-in-law Corinna's desperate husband reveals a secret that had been haunting the family for years.[6]

[Edward Aldrich to Mannevillette Brown]

San Francisco [to Utica, New York]
15 Feb. 1854

3. Ellen Anderson to Mannevillette Brown, January 11, 1851, and Corinna Aldrich to Mannevillette Brown, March 10, 1851, Anderson-Brown Papers, USMA.

4. The editors wish to thank Raymond Gill for his investigation of the New York City sites where Corinna and Ellen lived; all of the buildings are now gone.

5. Ellen Anderson to Mannevillette Brown, February 22, 1852, Anderson-Brown Papers, USMA.

6. George Brown to Mannevillette Brown, August 17, 1852; Corinna Aldrich to Mannevillette Brown, July 17, 1851; Edward Aldrich to Mannevillette Brown, November 11, 1852; and George Brown to Corinna Aldrich, June 6, 1853, Anderson-Brown Papers, USMA.

My dear Brother

Your two letters have been received. The first one in time to have answered by last mail, but my heart was so wrung with agony at the confirmation of what I have some time suspected, from her style of writing, & her hand writing, that I could not possibly write to you, or to her.

It is about the first time since I left home, that I have failed to write Corinna. You did well to write to me. Would that I had been informed sooner, that by this time, my plans might have been matured, to have gone on for her. At present it is almost impossible, unless I knew her salvation depended on it, then I would sacrifice anything & everything rather than stay away from her.

My dear friend what can I advise, what can I do to save her?

To recover her, and make her good, & happy once more, I would consent to anything, for a kinder heart never beat than hers. Oh, what is best, I could not bear to have her treated harshly. And if she does not change for the better, I could not write for her to come to me. She would disgrace herself, & perhaps die on the way, for in those packet steamers, rum flows as freely as water, & the women generally drink as much as the men. If need be I must go home to her, tho' I make any sacrifice. At present I must bear all to you. Oh, exert your utmost to save her, & whatever you do to save her I must & will approve. Kindness I think will avail more than a harsh course would. Would to God I had never parted from her.

Do write me some particulars about that Asylum, its discipline, government etc. Send me a pamphlet as I suppose they are to be had, or write me full part[icular]s on this subject! Write soon. If there is no other remedy, that must be resorted to. But my God I would not have her placed in solitary confinement, shut out from the world & her friends. No, she must see them & if it must needs come to that I will be one of those friends to return & cheer the [poor] unfortunate.

But she must be reformed & saved, and I will advance any sum that may be necessary to that end.

Do you whatever is best =While that habit continues, it would be difficult if she were here for me to place much restraint over her. For my practice often calls me away for hours & sometimes for days. This community is composed of the most depraved of human materials & unless she makes up her mind to resist every temptation she would have many bad examples before her. But I believe I could influence her. There is one thing I must explain to you in regard to her. There is one habit which she has been addicted to for years, that of taking one or two doses daily of Morphine—Were she placed under any kind of restraint, it would be wrong & impossible to withhold that from her, except at the expense of her life. And it is a habit which she can never overcome, it has become necessary to her very existence and I never saw any very bad effects from it. She generally required a dose of it every morning & again at midday—it was the only thing that would check the intolerable night & day sweats & pains in the bones to which she was subject. I tried all things as substitutes but without avail, and I am sorry to say that she could not survive if the usual quantity of Morphine was withheld. But all liquors are deadly poison to her. Do bear this in mind in your management of her.

I have written her a long letter, urging her by every argument to reform, and it may have its [weight]. If not, we must use other means. But let me know if possible, before you take any stringent measures with her. I did not write her word that I had heard from you. I told her that I had feared this thing, from the kind of letters I had received from her for a long time past. When I rec'd your first letter, the same mail brought two from her dated 4th & 19 Dec. Poor thing, she spoke so affectionately of you, and said were but George & I with her, her measure of happiness would be complete.

I do not believe that she is aware of how badly off she was when you were there. I know you have great influence with her. Do make one more personal effort, go & see her, and speak plainly to her, see if my letter has the desired effect. Tell her what must be the inevitable results of a persistence in such a course of conduct, her own misery & that of all connected with her, a death of shame & oh most horrible the death of her soul. May God avert such a calamity & bless and save her is my heart's fervent prayer. Ever yrs Sincerely & Affectionately

Edward S. Aldrich

P.S. Who is the man [J. Egbert] Farnham she speaks of—are they boarding him[?] If so I should veto it. If he is a boarder perhaps he has been the agent to introduce the cursed poison to my table. Let me know all soon as possible for I shall be in wretched suspense till I hear again. If need be I must go on, for to save her I will do anything—Once more good bye and thanks to you for writing. I have hopes that my letter to her will have the desired effect. I have written her word not to ship the furniture when she breaks up housekeeping but to sell if it will bring anything, as I shall board them when they come on, & the market here is over stocked with furniture & as cheap as in N. York.

I have made her but a small remittance this mail only fifty dollars and told her that owing to the hard times & some pecuniary disappointments that it would be necessary for me for the present to economize.

Yrs Truly
Ed. Aldrich

Throughout the rest of the year Corinna's addiction and its treatment occupied Ellen and her brothers. But Ellen also was not well. Her eyesight continued to deteriorate. Nevertheless she maintained her determination to educate the children and hoped to spend the extra money from her brothers, after rent and expenses, to educate the children beyond the "solid branches," which she could handle herself. She hoped to buy a piano and pay for music and dancing lessons for the girls. Edward kept in touch with his wife and his sister and brothers-in-law, and it seemed for a time that Corinna's condition might improve well enough for her to join him in California. But it was not to be. Corinna Aldrich died in the Bloomingdale Asylum on November 30, 1854.[7]

From his home in Newnansville, Florida, George eulogized their sister: "This event does not take me by surprise at all, yet it seems sudden and I feel that our little band will miss her much now she is gone. I grieve for her loss as much as a brother can, still I knew her situation and the facts of her case were such, that I cannot lament that she has left this earth when her days for so long a time, (and no hope for a better change) have been days of suffering. I shall remember her only as she was in times gone by."[8]

After Corinna's death Ellen continued to worry about her children and her financial situation. As always, money was extremely scarce. Edward suffered serious financial setbacks in California. To earn some extra income Ellen moved to a house on West 36th Street and began to take in boarders. She also subleased part of the house to a family. But her woes continued in subsequent months as she endured disputes with her boarders, repair problems, and other financial difficulties. In March 1856 she pawned her watch to help pay the bills. Georgia and Villette were attending a school that gave them a half-price arrangement, and Will was attending a free public school. Over the next two years Ellen moved frequently.[9]

---

7. Ellen Anderson to Mannevillette Brown, June 6, 1854; and Edward Aldrich to Mannevillette Brown, April 14, August 15, 1854, Anderson-Brown Papers, USMA. Corinna's death certificate lists the cause of death as "inanitio," exhaustion due to lack of sufficient food. The Bloomingdale Insane Asylum grounds are now occupied by Columbia University; one building from the asylum remains, currently housing the Foreign Student Center.

8. George Brown to Ellen Anderson, November 30, 1854, Anderson-Brown Papers, USMA.

9. Ellen Anderson to Mannevillette Brown, January 17, May 3, 20, August 4, 1855; May 20, August 4, 1856; and Edward Aldrich to Ellen Anderson, February 28, 1855, Anderson-Brown Papers, USMA.

*George Long Brown,
circa 1850, painting by
M. E. D. Brown. Cour-
tesy of Mannevillette
Sullivan and Jane and
Raymond Gill.*

Letters and financial assistance from George became more irregular, and then in October 1857 Ellen learned that George had died in Charleston. According to a local official, George's "death had caused a great gloom to settle over the community in which he lived; he was esteemed and beloved by all who knew him." George's body was returned to Florida, and he was buried on the Stewart plantation beside his second child, Claudia, who had died about the same time. Several months later Ellen learned that Matilda had given birth to a son, George Jr. Nearly a year and a half later Ellen received word from Matilda's father that her daughter, age three, had died.[10]

According to his attending physician, George died of "congestion of the brain," but Ellen's friend J. Egbert Farnum, who visited Charleston not long after George's death, provided Ellen with more details on July 1, 1858:

> Everybody spoke in the highest terms of George but there was a hesitancy on the part of his intimate friends to communicate particulars in regard to his death; finally, I came across his most intimate friend in Charleston, a Mr.

10. George died on October 8, 1857. See James B. McLin to Ellen Anderson, October 20, 1857, letter in possession of Elizabeth Traynor; John D. Anthon to Mannevillette Brown, October 13, 1857; Ellen Anderson to Mannevillette Brown, November 10, 1857, January 28, 1858; Mary Stewart to Ellen Anderson, February 17, 1858; and E. Stewart to Ellen Anderson, October 4, 1859, Anderson-Brown Papers, USMA.

Miles and I asked him leading questions, informing him that I was a connection, and wished the particulars for your information. He spoke very feelingly about George—said that he attended him through his illness, and was with him when he died and then went on to tell me that to the surprise of his friends, George had drunk immensely during the last three years, but in a very quiet Manner—his business became involved in consequence, and going on from bad to worse, he . . . died at the "Mills House" from the effects. Another reason was given out to the world, and few knew the real facts of the case. His property would not cover his liabilities, but by a law passed in Florida the widow receives one half of what her husband dies of, personal and real estate, and no claims of any nature can affect it, consequently, Matilda is left well off. . . . [Mr. Miles] said that during the spree which George was on, he sent for his book-keeper and that he informed him that George had been in the habit for nearly three years of drinking from 2 to 3 quarts of brandy a day![11]

J. Egbert Farnum had become acquainted with Ellen and Corinna sometime after Edward's departure for California, but his exact relationship to the sisters remains mysterious. Tom Henderson Wells has referred to Farnum as an "adventurer of the most violent nature." Born in New Jersey and educated in Pennsylvania, Farnum fought in the Mexican War and participated in the Narciso Lopez and William Walker filibustering expeditions before meeting Ellen in New York. From 1858 to 1860 Farnum penned Ellen dozens of letters from Charleston, Washington, D.C., and a Savannah jail, where he was incarcerated for his involvement with the notorious smuggling slave ship *The Wanderer*, apprehended off the Georgia coast in December 1858. In a highly politicized and publicized trial that riveted the nation, Farnum and his compatriots were charged with the federal offense of piracy on the high seas. Farnum kept in constant contact with Ellen during his incarceration and trial. He even was successful in having Ellen enlist the support of one of her old friends from Florida, Sen. David Levy Yulee, on Farnum's behalf. Farnum was eventually acquitted of piracy. Ironically, he joined the Union army at the outbreak of the Civil War. Serving with distinction, he attained the rank of general.[12]

11. Transcripts of the letters Farnum sent to Ellen from July 1, 1858, through May 17, 1860, were provided to the editors by Mannevillette Sullivan. The originals are included in the Anderson-Brown Collection. They are hereinafter cited as Farnum Papers.

12. Tom Henderson Wells, *The Slave Ship Wanderer* (Athens: University of Georgia Press, 1967), 10, 63–72. Becoming a member of the 70th New York Volunteers, Farnum

Although the Farnum saga is beyond the scope of this book, Farnum's relationship with Ellen raises some fascinating questions. While it is unclear whether they were lovers, it is clear they had intimate feelings toward one another. Ellen's letters to Farnum have not survived, but his strong feelings for her and her children are evident. "You are constantly in my thoughts Ell," Farnum wrote on one occasion, "and nothing but the grave itself can ever bury the deep heart felt gratitude and love I entertain for you. Through you, I have once more become a sober and responsible being, and I trust with God's help ever so to remain. Keep up your spirits, try to get good health, and in any event remember that I will strive henceforth to do right. Give my love to Georgia and tell her, that we must soon be married—my bachelor life begins to hang heavy on my hands. Kiss my other wife [Villette] for me. Love to Wumps [Will] and to yourself everything you wish. Your boy, Egbert."[13]

Not surprisingly, Farnum's incarceration seemed to strengthen his longings for Ellen. "I feel, here in my solitude, how little I have appreciated your unwavering love and devotion to me," Farnum wrote from the Savannah jail, "and from my inmost heart I pray to God for your welfare and happiness. You have been the first, and the only <u>relative</u> on earth to me, that is, since I have grown to man's estate. But for you, I should have been dead long ago. You are entwined around my affections to such a degree that it seems that you belong to me, and you do not. Is there anything on Earth I would not do to ensure your happiness! No Ell, there is <u>not</u>!" A few days later he wrote to her, "I feel as though you were my wife, my sister, my mother, my friend." In several letters he asked her to tell the children to write to Uncle Farnum, and sometimes he referred to Ellen as "Ma," or "Mama," perhaps playfully picking up names the children had for her, perhaps teasing Ellen for being older than he, and perhaps joking about her signature, "Ellen M. A.," standing for Ellen Maria Anderson.[14]

Meanwhile the year 1859 was a comparatively good one for Ellen. She learned that her pension had been increased to three hundred dollars per year and that three hundred dollars in additional benefits would also be forthcoming. She

---

fought in the battles of Fredericksburg, Chancellorsville, and Gettysburg. After the war Farnum became inspector of customs in New York City. He died in 1870. See James Grant Wilson and John Fiske, eds., *Appleton's Encyclopaedia of American Biography* (New York: D. Appleton Company, 1888), 2:412.

13. J. Egbert Farnum to Ellen Anderson, January 27, 1859, Farnum Papers.

14. J. Egbert Farnum to Ellen Anderson, February 1, December 17, 20, 1859; March 28, 1860, Farnum Papers.

M. E. D. Brown, circa 1860, self-portrait. Courtesy of Elizabeth Traynor.

also learned that her friend Senator Yulee would use his influence to have Will appointed to West Point. Will's acceptance to the academy seemed practically certain by the time Ellen learned that James's old commander, Gen. Winfield Scott, had written a letter of recommendation for Will to the secretary of war. Despite her poor eyesight, her health was generally good that year, and she considered ways to make money. "[T]here is very little hope for a woman with <u>encumbrances</u> as a family of any sort is most poetically called." She added that she remained frustrated at not finding some occupation in life: "It seems strange to me that I can't do something as well as other people. A lady asked me 'if I knew what I was fit for?' I told her 'no'—she said she could tell me. 'I was fit to be a lady.' I don't know whether she meant it for a compliment or not."[15]

Also that year Ellen again tried her hand at a literary career. For one publication she reviewed a new novel, *Beulah,* written by Augusta Jane Evans.[16] In

15. Ellen Anderson to Mannevillette Brown, February 27, March 19, December 30, July 18, September 4, 1859, Anderson-Brown Papers, USMA.

16. This work initially appeared in 1859. For a recent edition see Augusta Jane Evans, *Beulah* (1859; reprint, edited with an introduction by Elizabeth Fox-Genovese, Baton Rouge: Louisiana State University Press, 1992).

November she wrote a lecture for a lawyer in exchange for some legal work. By spring of the next year she was exploring the possibility of writing for a newspaper. There was even some discussion of a regular salary, but as Ellen explained to Mannevillette, "To write, I must have a mind as free as possible. Pots and dishes and cooking and servants and scrubbing don't agree with writing. Neither can one sew and write at the same time, but I have tried to accomplish all of these things together and broken myself down with hard trying. I sometimes think I can never be good for anything again, and indeed but for the children's sake, I have no ambition. I like to write because it absorbs my attention, and keeps me from thinking of unpleasant things, but I have no relish for society. Everybody sickens me, sooner or later." A few days later she lamented her plight once again: "I have two great prejudices to overcome. First I <u>am</u> a woman. Second I am <u>not</u> famous. I was seeking literary employment last winter, when a gentleman advised me to pursue this course, and would have paid me ten dollars a week to begin with if I could have kept up as I began, but alas I became so blind and sick that the thing was impossible. . . . You say that paradise is not in this world and that the devil is. No doubt that is so, and the latter is after me with a sharp stick certain."[17]

While Ellen waited anxiously for notification of Will's acceptance to West Point she worried about Villette's and Georgia's future. Villette had a talent for painting, and Mannevillette offered to teach her. Georgia, Ellen hoped, could eventually teach school and that year began exploring opportunities along that line. Finally, that spring, Ellen received official notification that Will had been admitted to West Point. Senator Yulee offered personal congratulations on March 21. Ellen recognized the prestige of this appointment and relished Will's opportunity for a free college education while following in his father's footsteps at the U.S. Military Academy. This was something that Ellen had dreamt of for years. But the unsettled national political situation made Will's admission bittersweet. Within months after Will had enrolled at West Point, relations between the North and the South degenerated into a full rupture. During April through June 1860 the Democratic Party, the last remaining national party, divided over slavery. The split made possible the election of Republican Abraham Lincoln in November. Lincoln and his party stood firm against the expansion of slavery in the territories. This was so threatening to the majority of white southerners that the election triggered talk of secession. South Carolina seceded from the Union in December, followed by Mississippi, Florida,

17. Ellen Anderson to Mannevillette Brown, November 4, 20, 1859; May 13, 16, 1860, Anderson-Brown Papers, USMA.

West Point quarters of cadets Edward Willoughby Anderson and Frank Masi. Pencil drawing by Edward Willoughby Anderson, courtesy of Elizabeth Traynor.

Alabama, Georgia, and Louisiana in January 1861. That month in a letter to Mannevillette, Ellen revealed her own sentiments while at the same time informing him of her advice to Will: "I have advised him to remain where he is until called upon to fight the South, when he can ask to be excused. . . . I declare when I think of the suffering, confusion, starvation, and slaughter which impends over the country, I wish I were a man that I might go on a crusade to preach peace. I think the earnestness of my feelings and my knowledge of the subject—(you will laugh at this, but I do understand it—) would make me influential."[18]

18. Ellen Anderson to Mannevillette Brown, May 20, June 11, August 5, 1860; January 17, 1861, Anderson-Brown Papers, USMA.

Throughout 1860 and 1861 Ellen and Will corresponded often. Though she advised him regarding his studies and about settling into the routine of West Point, the political climate of the academy and the tenor of national politics dominated their correspondence. Will's inclinations clearly were with the South. As the year came to a close, it seemed increasingly likely that the Union would dissolve. To Will's indications that he was prepared to leave the academy Ellen advised him to "remain where you are until called upon to fight your own brethren, then sheath your sword and tell all men, law or no law, you will only draw it for your country's enemies." One month later she revealed that she would support her son if he was determined to resign.[19]

Meanwhile, Ellen had become seriously ill. However, she felt some improvement because Edward had returned from California and had begun treating her illness. Edward had left San Francisco on September 12, 1860, and had arrived in New York by January 1861. He planned to head south as soon as he could. Ellen was prepared to go with him. "This decision of mine may involve the loss of my pension," she wrote Will, "but it will influence your whole future, which is not to be weighed one moment against a paltry three hundred dollars per year." Still, she urged Will to stay put for the time being because the conflict could be resolved peacefully: "I think the Union is gone. Civil war is the thing now to be avoided. In case of an amicable settlement, you will know perfectly what to do when the time comes. If this thing is not amicably settled, the whole country will fall into the direst anarchy and confusion."[20]

While Ellen sparred with Mannevillette over the nation's political climate, the disagreements between her and her brother had no bearing on their strong familial bonds. "I would rather you be right than me," she wrote Mannevillette; "I hate to see the country going to destruction. . . . I see the indications of the coming tempest in every part of the political sky. The lightening[21] of passion blinds men's eyes. Its muttering thunder deafens their ears, and there is no voice of peace powerful enough to be heard in the storm, no hand strong

19. For an account of Will's years at West Point and nineteen family letters, mostly between Ellen and Will, see Sullivan, "Letters of a West Pointer," 599–617; see also Ellen Anderson to Edward Willoughby Anderson, December 31, 1860, on p. 607.

20. Dr. Edward Aldrich to Mannevillette Brown, October 10, 13, 1860, and Ellen Anderson to Edward Willoughby Anderson, January 28, March 23, 1861, Anderson-Brown Papers, USMA; Ellen Anderson to Edward Willoughby Anderson, January 28, 1861, in Sullivan, "Letters of a West Pointer," 607.

21. Obsolete spelling of *lightning* (OED).

enough to stay its effects, no head with wisdom enough to inspire confidence during the trial." She told Mannevillette that she was ready to go south with Edward to seek out some family land, apparently in Florida, and live there. But she had no money to leave New York, so she waited.[22]

In April, Will's situation at West Point grew more precarious; on April 12, Confederate forces in Charleston fired on Fort Sumter.[23] On April 15, President Lincoln called for seventy-five thousand volunteers to suppress the insurrection. Two days later Virginia seceded from the Union. Simultaneously authorities at West Point ordered cadets to take an unconditional oath of loyalty to the Union. Will informed his mother that he had refused to take the oath. Ellen traveled to West Point personally to meet with Will and assess the situation. She returned to New York City on April 20 and wrote to Will the next day, urging him to resign immediately. But she also enclosed a letter from Mannevillette expressing the opposite view so that he might consider it. Ellen's clearest statement of her position appears in the following letter to Mannevillette.

Tuesday Morning. April 23rd [1861]
179 East Twentieth street [New York, N.Y.]

Dear Mannevillette,

Yours dated Sunday 20th was received last night. I perceive that I must write My Declaration of Independence.[24]

22. Ellen Anderson to Mannevillette Brown, January 30, 1861, Anderson-Brown Papers, USMA.

23. Edward was in Charleston that month and provided Ellen with an eye-witness account of the firing on Fort Sumter, which she relayed to Will (Ellen Anderson to Edward Willoughby Anderson, April 19, 1861, Anderson-Brown Papers, USMA).

24. Ellen took the position held by many white southerners in 1861—that they were merely doing what their forefathers had done in 1776—that is, they were declaring their independence from an oppressive government. In their view their rights were being trampled upon. The Republican victory of Abraham Lincoln—a party and a president opposed to the expansion of slavery into the territories—and also their permanent minority status in the Union convinced many that a government based on the notion of the "consent of the governed" was no longer possible. Thus they believed that they were merely seceding from the Union to preserve self-government. For more on this, see James M. McPherson, *Battle Cry of Freedom: The Civil War Era* (New York: Oxford University Press, 1988), 241; William J. Cooper, *Liberty and Slavery: Southern Politics to 1860* (New York: Knopf, 1983), 267–68; Emory Thomas, *The Confederate Nation: 1861–1865* (New York: Harper, 1979), 37–38; and Emory Thomas, *The Confederacy as a Revolutionary Experience* (Englewood Cliffs, N.J.: Prentice Hall, 1971), 1–2, 23–38.

1st—I have as much right to make the South my Country, as the German has to make the United States his country.

2nd—All governments rest upon the will of the governed.

3rd—The South announced through her constituted representatives, in Congress assembled, that, in certain contingencies, she could not remain a part of the United states. Those contingencies arose. The South asked for a peaceable separation. It was denied her. She has resolved to take it by force. She fights for the preservation of her homes and firesides. I think she ought to do it. While I have health to speak or nerve to act, I will uphold the cause which I consider right. "If this be treason, make the most of it."[25]

Ellen M. Anderson.

Dear Mannevillette,

What you will object to in the above, is, I suppose, the assertion that the South fights for the preservation of her homes and fire sides. I form my opinion from having had my home in the southern country. In this consists the fatal blindness of the North: that they cannot see this necessity.

Here are brethren going to cut each other's throats about what is truly a misunderstanding. It is horrible!

A gentleman said to me, a few days since, "It is surprising! Every Southerner I meet talks as you do."

Why then do you not believe us? said I. "What would you have us do?" said he, "would [you] have us act like a pack of cowards?" This man asserts constantly that he is a friend to the South.

As for the slave trade, its principal depot is here in the city of New York. This also I know of my own knowledge. The North gets the money, and the South gets the blame.

You must believe that I, at least, am convinced of the stern necessity there is for the South acting as it does, when I defy ruin and death, for myself and my children, rather than oppose it. I cannot even give it the seeming opposition of silence.

Here I am in the midst of a community in the wildest state of excitement, with every man, woman and child in it, (except one or two boys,) so far as I know, opposed to me in sentiment. I am protected by my sex. They may try to reach me through Will. Now judge if my opinions are likely to be founded upon want of thought or selfish interest.

25. This quotation is Patrick Henry's response to members of the Virginia House of Burgesses that the remarks he had made regarding the Stamp Tax (1765) were treasonous. See John B. Boles, *The South through Time: A History of an American Region* (Englewood Cliffs, N.J.: Prentice Hall, 1995), 97.

Edward Willoughby Anderson in his Confederate uniform, circa 1861. Courtesy of Elizabeth Traynor.

Will is here. I don't know whether he will remain in the city or go South. On that point he must judge for himself. He is in equal danger either way. God rules over all.

Yours,

Ell.

P.S. Of course I need not tell you Will has resigned. He has not yet received its acceptance.

After leaving West Point, Edward Willoughby Anderson proceeded immediately to the home of his father's family in Norfolk, Virginia. Enlisting as a lieutenant in the Virginia Provisional Army, Will eventually was assigned to the Engineer Corps of the Army of Northern Virginia. Meanwhile, Ellen's health deteriorated rapidly. Under the care of Dr. William Van Buren, whom she had known in Florida, Ellen was being treated for a breast ailment.[26] Ellen grew

---

26. Edward Willoughby Anderson to Ellen Anderson, June 24, September 30, 1861, in Sullivan, "Letters of a West Pointer," 616.

sicker every day and worried about what would become of her daughters when she died.[27] In Ellen's last surviving letter her concern for the girls was paramount: "Dear Mannevillette, I write to ask you, if you can come down and take care of my girls, in case of my death? . . . We are without a single friend in the world. All have gone. Acquaintances and friends have fled from me. Besides I have no confidence in human nature."[28] Ellen still hoped that the girls, unlike herself, could eventually be self-supporting: "The girls are very capable. Georgia could teach in English branches and . . . in part, pay her own expenses. . . . which would in a short time take care of herself entirely. Villette wants more instruction because her health has been so feeble, she has not been able to study so hard as Georgia, but her abilities are as good."[29]

჻

On August 5, 1862, Ellen Anderson died of breast cancer at the Convent of the Sisters of the Dust in Gramercy Park. She was buried with Corinna in Greenwood Cemetery, Brooklyn, New York.[30]

27. Ellen Anderson to Mannevillette Brown, February 20, May 28, 1862, Anderson-Brown Papers, USMA.

28. Ellen Anderson to Mannevillette Brown, June 6, 1862, Anderson-Brown Papers, USMA.

29. Ibid.

30. Eugene J. Bockman to Raymond Gill, May 11, 1982, City of New York, Department of Records and Information Services, Municipal Archives, Genealogy and Family Records, copy in possession of the editors.

Epilogue

Ellen Anderson was the last of the Florida pioneers from the Brown family, but the extended family's correspondence resumed after the Civil War and continued until nearly the end of the nineteenth century. At the Civil War's end Capt. Edward Willoughby Anderson was among the soldiers in Gen. Robert E. Lee's Army of Northern Virginia, which surrendered to Gen. Ulysses S. Grant in April 1865. Chief of ordnance in Gen. Cadmus Wilcox's division, Will had served in the Engineer Corps for the duration of the war.[1] Throughout most of the war Anderson served on Virginia coastal fortifications. In the last year of the war, once those fortifications were evacuated, he fought in the war's final battles in the Richmond area. Severely wounded at the Battle of Cold Harbor, he recovered and was appointed assistant chief of ordnance on General Lee's staff. He was then promoted to chief ordnance officer on the staff of Maj. Gen. W. D. Pender, and at war's end he held the same position on General Wilcox's staff.[2] Immediately following the war he attended the City College of New York. After settling in Washington, D.C., Will studied law and became a patent attorney. In 1867 he married Elizabeth Felicia Masi, the sister of his West Point roommate Frank Masi. Will and "Lizzie" had seven children and had a long life together until Lizzie's death in 1903.[3]

After serving the Confederacy as surgeon Dr. Edward S. Aldrich returned to Florida and established a medical practice in Jacksonville. On August 11, 1865, the *Jacksonville (Florida) Herald* announced that "Dr. E. S. Aldrich, physician and surgeon, late of San Francisco, may be consulted at his office at Mrs. Hadsell's Mansion House, or at the Drug Store of Mr. J. Jones." Two years

---

1. E. W. Anderson to Gen. F. C. Ainsworth, September 4, 1909, Mannevillette Sullivan family genealogy materials, copies in possession of the editors.

2. "Remember Before God the Soul of Edward Willoughby Anderson Who Departed This Life Thursday, September Second, Nineteen Fifteen," Mannevillette Sullivan family genealogy materials, copies in possession of the editors.

3. Brown-Anderson family genealogy chart; undated newspaper clipping of the obituary of Edward Willoughby Anderson, copies in possession of the editors.

Elizabeth Felicia Masi Anderson was the sister of Edward Willoughby Anderson's roommate at West Point. Courtesy of Elizabeth Traynor.

Georgia Anderson, Ellen's daughter, sometime after the Civil War. Courtesy of Elizabeth Traynor.

Villette Anderson, Ellen's daughter, sometime after the Civil War. Courtesy of Elizabeth Traynor.

later Edward had relocated to Lake City. Notifying Mannevillette of his whereabouts, Edward added that most of his relatives had died in the war but that he hoped to see Mannevillette and Ellen's children at some point in the future.[4]

It is not clear what happened to the girls immediately after Ellen's death, but apparently Mannevillette honored his sister's dying wish and came after them. Georgia and Villette Anderson never married but lived together in various places, including Utica, New York; Hartford, Connecticut; and Washington, D.C., where they moved in 1870 to be closer to Will and Lizzie. But tensions between them and Will's wife and in-laws caused problems. "The poor things misconceive and misconstrue all we do, and we cannot help it," Will wrote

4. The *Jacksonville (Florida) Herald* as quoted in Hammond, *Medical Profession in 19th Century Florida,* 9; Edward Aldrich to Mannevillette Brown, July 5, 1867, Anderson-Brown Papers, USMA.

his uncle Mannevillette on one occasion.[5] On that same day Georgia wrote to Mannevillette, "We are ready to come back. We can find no way to maintain ourselves here." Exasperated, Mannevillette insisted that Will find the sisters a boardinghouse in Washington, D.C.

Georgia suffered from chronic poor health. She died in 1874 at the age of thirty-one from a stomach ailment. Villette came closer to her mother's wish of living an independent life. She worked for a time drafting inventions in Will's law office. "I like the work very much," she wrote her uncle in 1870.[6] Although apparently not as sickly as her sister, Villette suffered from various ailments that often kept her from her work. Plagued by head pain, drowsiness, and bowel problems, Villette worked when she could but throughout her life received financial assistance from Will and her uncle Mannevillette.

Yet Villette was resourceful and hardworking. Along with her work in the patent office she engaged in domestic crafts. She often sent her uncle cravats she had made. She also made doll clothes for Will's children. Villette's work in the patent office seems to have stimulated her own inventiveness. In 1877 she tried but failed to obtain a patent for a shoe-lacing invention. She also invented a device to put on one's arm to increase comfort and speed when writing. As Villette grew older her health continued to deteriorate. In 1891, just after a visit to the Stewart plantation, Liberty Bluff, she died at the age of forty-six.[7]

At the outbreak of the Civil War, Matilda Brown resided on her plantation near Gainesville, Florida, with her daughter Adelaide (eight), her son George Jr. (three), her brother James M. (twenty-four), and her mother, Mary E. Stewart (fifty-two). But after the war times were hard and the family struggled. In 1870 George Jr. died of meningitis at the age of thirteen. In 1874 Matilda and Adelaide moved briefly to Knoxville and then Nashville, Tennessee, to be with Matilda's relatives. Adelaide seemed content in her new surroundings. Writing to her uncle after attending a ball, Adelaide noted that because she had "been shut up in the Country so long that any amusement now is a great treat—besides there is so little real happiness that falls to the lot of any of us that we should try to grasp every little sunshine that falls across our path."[8] But

5. Will Anderson to Mannevillette Brown, January 16, 1870, Anderson-Brown Papers, USMA.

6. Villette Anderson to Mannevillette Brown, August 14, 1870, Anderson-Brown Papers, USMA.

7. Villette Anderson to Mannevillette Brown, January 20, 1880, November 31, 1891, Anderson-Brown Papers, USMA.

8. Adelaide Brown to Mannevillette Brown, June 26, 1874, Anderson-Brown Papers, USMA.

the sunshine soon faded as Adelaide died of heart failure on February 25, 1875. Eulogizing his niece's death, Mannevillette wrote Will that "cruel as it may seem, Death was a great blessing to Adelaide. She was sensible kind and honest, and yet was so situated and brought up, as to be unfitted for the world in mind, body, and state. She was too lovely to live."[9] Matilda returned to Florida soon after Adelaide's death, residing in Ocala with her sister, Mrs. Leonard Dozier.[10]

Life seems to have been fairly comfortable for Will until December 1875, when his law firm was dissolved and reorganized. Unemployed and with a son ill from typhoid fever, Will suffered a nervous breakdown, an illness that Villette referred to in a letter to Mannevillette as "nervous prostration"; Will's condition became so serious that Lizzie's father, Philip Masi, considered sending him to an asylum for treatment.[11] Fortunately, Will's health improved and he was soon back at work. Early the next year with his father-in-law's assistance he opened his own law office. His business soon flourished, and he resumed an active and productive life. While Lizzie and his six children absorbed most of his time and financial resources, Will was active in the United Confederate Veterans. He also provided financial assistance to his aunt Virginia, who, like her nieces, never married and had difficulty supporting herself. Edward Willoughby Anderson died on September 2, 1915, at his residence at 1435 Chapin Street, and he was buried in Arlington National Cemetery.[12]

Though he was the oldest of the Brown siblings, Mannevillette Elihu Dearing Brown outlived all of his brothers and sisters to maintain an active correspondence with the younger generation. Finally seeing the Florida that his siblings had described to him in many letters, Mannevillette visited Matilda and Adelaide in 1871, taking pleasure in a steamboat trip down the St. Johns.[13]

9. Mannevillette Brown to Edward Willoughby Anderson, March 4, 1875, Anderson-Brown Papers, USMA.

10. Matilda Brown to Mannevillette Brown, October 13, 1891; and Matilda Brown to Edward Willoughby Anderson, September 10, 1896, Anderson-Brown Papers, USMA.

11. Villette Anderson to Mannevillette Brown, December 22, 24, 28, 30, 1875, Anderson-Brown Papers, USMA.

12. Eulogy of Edward Willoughby Anderson, undated and unsigned; undated newspaper clipping of obituary of Edward Willoughby Anderson, Mannevillette Sullivan family genealogy materials, copies in possession of the editors.

13. Mannevillette Brown to Edward Willoughby Anderson, February 10, 1871, Adelaide Brown to Mannevillette Brown, December 13, 1872, and Matilda Brown to Mannevillette Brown, November 13, 1891, Anderson-Brown Papers, USMA; Courtney, "M. E. D. Brown," 66–77.

*M. E. D. Brown, circa 1890s.
Courtesy of Elizabeth
Traynor.*

Although he enjoyed a long, distinguished career as an artist in Utica, New York, Mannevillette's circle of friends began to diminish, as did his movement among Utica's artistic elite. Then, just after his eighty-sixth birthday, a Utica newspaper made the following announcement: "The death of M. E. D. Brown occurred shortly before 4 O'clock yesterday afternoon in his rooms in the Tibbitts Block, 81 Genesee Street." Alone in his studio, the artist who had once "moved in first society and was one of the lions of the town" died without friends and almost penniless.[14]

Within days after the notification of his uncle's death Edward Willoughby Anderson traveled to Utica to arrange for Mannevillette's burial. Disposing of his personal effects, Will also dutifully brought his papers back to his home in Washington, D.C. In future years from time to time Will and his descendants read and drew inspiration from his mother's and aunt's experiences on the antebellum Florida frontier. If the letters of Ellen, Corinna, and their family speak with a loud and clear voice of their trials and tribulations, they also offer rare glimpses of women's world of that time and place. And yes, all together, "they do make a very interesting history."

14. *Utica Daily Press,* September 2, 1896; *Utica Morning Herald,* September 2, 1896; M. E. D. Brown Probate File, April 16, 1900, Oneida County Surrogates Court, Utica, New York.

Bibliography

Manuscripts

Anderson-Brown Papers. United States Military Academy, West Point, New York.

Biography File. Oneida County Historical Society, Utica, New York.

Biography File. Utica Public Library, Utica, New York.

Brown-Anderson Family. Genealogy and other records. Copies in possession of editors.

Fairbanks Papers. P. K. Yonge Library of Florida History, University of Florida, Gainesville.

Farnum, J. Egbert. Papers. U.S. Military Academy, West Point, New York. Copies in possession of editors.

Hall, James. Papers. P. K. Yonge Library of Florida History, University of Florida, Gainesville.

Miscellaneous manuscripts (cited individually). P. K. Yonge Library of Florida History, University of Florida, Gainesville.

Reid, Robert Raymond. Diary, 1833, 1835. State Library of Florida, Dorothy Dodd Room, R. A. Gray Building, Tallahassee.

Tappen, John S. Papers. State Library of Florida, Dorothy Dodd Room, R. A. Gray Building, Tallahassee.

Interviews

Gill, Jane and Raymond. Interview by Keith L. Huneycutt. Brooklyn, New York, March 24, 2001.

Sullivan, Mannevillette. Interview by James M. Denham. Belleville, Illinois, July 12, 1995.

Public Documents and Public Records

Ancient Records, Clerk of the Alachua County Court, Gainesville, Florida.

Carter, Clarence E., ed. *The Territorial Papers of the United States*. 26 vols. Washington, D.C. : U.S. Government Printing Office, 1934–62.

Court Records (Microfilm Copy) in Florida State Archives, R. A. Gray Building, Tallahassee.

Alachua County, Administrators Bonds, 1857–69.

Alachua County, Deed Records, Book A, 1846–52.

Alachua County, Deed Records, Book B, 1852–54.

Alachua County, Deed Records, Book C, 1857–59.

Alachua County, Inventory and Order Book, Book 2, 1841–57.

Alachua County, Marriage Records, 1837–49.

Alachua County, Minutes of the Circuit Court, 1868–74.

Alachua County, Record of Wills (Probate), Book A, 1840–59.

Court Records in P. K. Yonge Library of Florida History, University of Florida, Gainesville.

Alachua, Hillsborough, Benton, and Marion Counties, Superior and Circuit Court Minutes, 1844–50.

Alachua and Levy Counties, Minutes of the Circuit Court, 1850–57.

Florida Militia Muster rolls, Seminole Indian Wars, Florida Department of Military Affairs, St. Augustine.

Oneida County, New York, Surrogates Court, Probate Files, Utica.

Portsmouth, New Hampshire, *City Directory,* 1827.

U.S. Manuscript Census, Population, 1840, for Duval County, Florida.

U.S. Manuscript Census, Population, 1850, for Camden County, Georgia, and the following Florida counties: Alachua, Columbia, Duval, Escambia, Levy, Monroe, St. Johns.

U.S. Manuscript Census, Population, 1860, for the following Florida counties: Alachua, Columbia, Duval, St. Johns.

U.S. Manuscript Census, Slave, 1850, for Camden County, Georgia, and the following Florida counties: Alachua, St. Johns.

U.S. Manuscript Census, Slave, 1860, for the following Florida counties: Alachua, Duval, St. Johns.

Utica, New York, City Directory, 1849–50, 1853–54, 1854–55.

Newspapers

Army and Navy Chronicle, 1835–42.

Jacksonville Courier, 1835–37.

Jacksonville East Florida Advocate, 1839–40.

Jacksonville Florida News, 1846–57.

Macon (Georgia), Southern Post, 1838.

Pensacola (Florida) Gazette, 1845–52.

Portsmouth New Hampshire Gazette, 1819.

Portsmouth (New Hampshire) Journal of Literature and Politics, Rockingham Gazette and State Herald, 1833.

St. Augustine Ancient City, 1852.

St. Augustine Florida Herald, 1833–37.

St. Augustine Florida Herald and Southern Democrat, 1838–46.

St. Augustine News, 1838–47.

Savannah (Georgia) Daily Republican, 1840–41.

Savannah Georgian, 1836–40.

Tallahassee Florida Sentinel, 1852.

Tallahassee Floridian, 1836–40.

Utica (New York) Daily Press, 1896.

Utica (New York) Morning Herald, 1896.

Secondary Sources

Ambrose, Stephen E. *Duty, Honor, Country: A History of West Point.* Baltimore: Johns Hopkins University Press, 1966.

Bagg, M. M., ed. *Memorial History of Utica, New York from Its Settlement to the Present Time.* Syracuse, N.Y.: D. Mason and Company Publishers, 1892.

————. *Pioneers of Utica: Being Sketches of Its Inhabitants and Its Institutions with the Civil History of the Place from the Earliest Settlement.* Utica, N.Y.: Curtiss and Childs Printers and Publishers, 1877.

Baptist, Edward E. *Creating an Old South: Middle Florida's Plantation Frontier before the Civil War.* Chapel Hill: University of North Carolina Press, 2002.

Barnes, Jay. *Florida's Hurricane History.* Chapel Hill: University of North Carolina Press, 1998.

Bauer, K. Jack. *The Mexican War, 1846–1848.* New York: Macmillan, 1974.

————. *Zachary Taylor: Soldier, Planter, Statesman of the Old Southwest.* Baton Rouge: Louisiana State University Press, 1985.

Beckford, William. *Vathek.* Edited by Roger Lonsdale. Oxford: Oxford University Press, 1983.

Bemrose, John. *Reminiscences of the Second Seminole War.* Edited by John K. Mahon. Tampa, Fla.: University of Tampa Press, 2001.

Biographical Directory of Congress, 1774–1971. Washington, D.C.: U.S. Government Printing Office, 1971.

Blakey, Arch Fredric. *Parade of Memories: A History of Clay County, Florida.* Jacksonville, Fla.: Drummond Press for Clay County Bicentennial Steering Committee, 1976.

Blakey, Arch Fredric, Ann Smith Lainhart, and Winston Bryant Stephens Jr, eds. *Rose Cottage Chronicles: Civil War Letters of the Bryant-Stephens Families of North Florida.* Gainesville: University Press of Florida, 1998.

Bleser, Carol, ed. *In Joy and Sorrow: Women, Family, and Marriage in the Victorian South.* New York: Oxford University Press, 1991.

————. *Tokens of Affection: The Letters of a Planter's Daughter in the Old South.* Athens: University of Georgia Press, 1996.

Blumenthal, Henry. *France and the United States: Their Diplomatic Relations, 1789–1914.* New York: Norton, 1970.

Boles, John B. *The South through Time: A History of an American Region.* Englewood Cliffs, N.J.: Prentice Hall, 1995.

Boyd, Mark F. "Asi-yaholo or Osceola." *Florida Historical Quarterly* 33 (January–April 1955): 249–305.

Brighton, Raymond A. *They Came to Fish: A Brief Look at Portsmouth's 350 Years of History.* Portsmouth, N.H.: Portsmouth 350 Inc., 1973.

Brown, Canter, Jr. "The Florida Crisis of 1826–1827 and the Second Seminole War." *Florida Historical Quarterly* 73 (April 1995): 419–42.

———. *Florida's Peace River Frontier.* Orlando: University of Central Florida Press, 1991.

———. *Fort Meade, 1849–1900.* Tuscaloosa: University of Alabama Press, 1995.

———. *Ossian Bingley Hart: Florida's Loyalist Reconstruction Governor.* Baton Rouge: Louisiana State University Press, 1997.

———. *Tampa before the Civil War.* Tampa, Fla.: University of Tampa Press, 1999.

———. *Women on the Tampa Bay Frontier.* Tampa, Fla.: Tampa Bay History Center, 1997.

Browne, Jefferson B. *Key West: The Old and the New.* 1912. Facsimile reprint, Gainesville: University of Florida Press, 1973.

Buker, George E. *Jacksonville: Riverport-Seaport.* Columbia: University of South Carolina Press, 1992.

Bulwar-Lytton, Edward. *The Last Days of Pompeii.* Reading, Pa.: Spenser Press, 1936.

Bunyon, John. *The Pilgrim's Progress.* Edited by N. H. Keeble. Oxford: Oxford University Press, 1950.

Butt, John, ed. *The Poems of Alexander Pope.* New Haven: Yale University Press, 1963.

Callahan, Edward W., ed. *List of Officers of the Navy and Marine Corps from 1775 to 1900.* New York: L. R. Hamersly and Company, 1901.

Campbell, James T. "The Charles Hutchinson Letters from Territorial Tallahassee, 1839–1843." *Apalachee* 4 (1950–56).

Campbell, Thomas. *Pleasures of Hope, Gertrude of Wyoming, and Other Poems.* London: T. Nelson and Sons, 1864.

Cashin, Joan E. *A Family Venture: Men and Women on the Southern Frontier.* New York: Oxford University Press, 1991.

———. *Our Common Affairs: Texts from Women in the Old South.* Baltimore: Johns Hopkins University Press, 1996.

Clarke, T. Wood. *Utica for a Century and a Half.* Utica, N.Y.: Widtman Press, 1952.

Clinton, Catherine. *The Plantation Mistress: Woman's World in the Old South.* New York: Pantheon Books, 1982.

Coffman, Edward M. *The Old Army: A Portrait of the American Army in Peacetime, 1784–1898.* New York: Oxford University Press, 1986.

Coker, William S., and Susan R. Parker. "The Second Spanish Period in the Two Floridas." In *The New History of Florida,* edited by Michael Gannon, 150–66. Gainesville: University Press of Florida, 1996.

Coles, David J. "Edmund Pendleton Gaines." In *The United States and Mexico at War: Nineteenth-Century Expansionism and Conflict,* edited by Donald S. Frazier, 172. New York: Macmillan, 1998.

Cooper, William J. *Liberty and Slavery: Southern Politics to 1860.* New York: Alfred A. Knopf, 1983.

Courtney, Rosemary. "M. E. D. Brown (1810–1896): American Lithographer and Painter." *American Art Journal* 12 (autumn 1980): 66–77.

Covington, James W. "The Armed Occupation Act of 1842." *Florida Historical Quarterly* 40 (July 1961): 41–52.

————. "Billy Bowlegs, Sam Jones, and the Crisis of 1849." *Florida Historical Quarterly* 68 (January 1990): 299–311.

————. "The Indian Scare of 1849." *Tequesta* 21 (1961): 53–64.

————. *The Seminoles of Florida.* Gainesville: University Press of Florida, 1993.

Cullum, George W. *Biographical Register of the Officers of the United States Military Academy, West Point.* 2 vols. New York: D. Van Nostrand, 1868.

Cushman, Joseph D., Jr. *A Goodly Heritage: The Episcopal Church in Florida, 1821–1892.* Gainesville: University of Florida Press, 1965.

Cuthbert, Norma B. "Yankee Preacher-Teacher in Florida, 1838." *Huntington Library Quarterly* 7 (1944): 95–104.

Cutrer, Thomas W. "Winfield Scott." In *The United States and Mexico at War: Nineteenth-Century Expansionism and Conflict,* edited by Donald S. Frazier, 380–82. New York: Macmillan, 1998.

Daly, Lloyd W. *Aesop without Morals: The Famous Fables, and a Life of Aesop Newly Translated and Edited.* New York: Thomas Yoselof, 1961.

Daniel, James J. "Historical Sketch of the Church in Florida." In *Historical Papers and Journal of Semi-Centennial of the Church in Florida, 1888,* 3–43. Jacksonville, Fla.: Church Publishing Co., 1889.

Davis, T. Frederick. "Early Orange Culture in Florida and the Epochal Cold of 1835." *Florida Historical Quarterly* 15 (April 1937): 232–41.

————. *History of Early Jacksonville: Being an Authentic Record of Events from the Earliest Times to and Including the Civil War.* Jacksonville, Fla.: H. & W. B. Drew Company, 1911.

————. *History of Jacksonville, Florida and Vicinity, 1513 to 1924.* St. Augustine: Florida Historical Society, 1925.

Denham, James M. "Cracker Women and Their Families in Nineteenth-Century Florida." In *Florida's Heritage of Diversity: Essays in the Honor of Samuel Proctor,* edited by Mark I. Greenberg, William W. Rogers Jr., and Canter Brown Jr., 15–28. Tallahassee: Sentry Press, 1997.

————. "The Florida Cracker before the Civil War as Seen through Travelers' Accounts." *Florida Historical Quarterly* 72 (April 1994): 455–57.

————. "From a Territorial to a Statehood Judiciary: Florida's Antebellum Courts and Judges." *Florida Historical Quarterly* 73 (April 1995): 443–55.

————. "The Read-Alston Duel and Politics in Territorial Florida." *Florida Historical Quarterly* 68 (April 1990): 427–46.

————. *"A Rogue's Paradise": Crime and Punishment in Antebellum Florida, 1821–1861.* Tuscaloosa: University of Alabama Press, 1997.

————. "'Some Prefer the Seminoles': Violence and Disorder among Soldiers and Settlers in the Second Seminole War, 1835–1842." *Florida Historical Quarterly* 70 (July 1991): 38–54.

————. "Thomas S. Jesup." In *The United States and Mexico at War: Nineteenth-Century Expansionism and Conflict,* edited by Donald S. Frazier, 211. New York: Macmillan, 1998.

Denham, James M., and Canter Brown Jr. *Cracker Times and Pioneer Lives: The Florida Reminiscences of George Gillett Keen and Sarah Pamela Williams.* Columbia: University of South Carolina Press, 2000.

Denham, James M., and Keith Huneycutt. "'Our Desired Haven': The Letters of Corinna Brown Aldrich from Antebellum Key West, 1849–50." *Florida Historical Quarterly* 79 (spring 2001): 517–45.

———. "With Scott in Mexico: Letters of Captain James W. Anderson in the Mexican War, 1846–1847." *Military History of the West* 28 (spring 1998): 19–48.

Dibble, Ernest F. *Antebellum Pensacola and Its Military Presence.* Pensacola, Fla.: Pensacola Bicentennial Series, 1974.

Dickens, Charles. *The Complete Works of Charles Dickens.* Edited by Frederick G. Kitton. 15 vols. London: George G. Harrap, 1903–8.

The Dictionary of National Biography. Edited by Sir Leslie Stephan and Sir Sidney Lee. 22 vols. New York: The MacMillan Co., 1908–9.

Dodd, Dorothy. *Florida Becomes a State.* Tallahassee: Florida Centennial Commission, 1945.

———. "The Wrecking Business on the Florida Reef." *Florida Historical Quarterly* 22 (April 1944): 171–99.

Doherty, Herbert J. "Antebellum Pensacola, 1821–1861." *Florida Historical Quarterly* 37 (January 1959): 337–56.

———. *Richard Keith Call: Southern Unionist.* Gainesville: University of Florida Press, 1961.

———. *The Whigs of Florida, 1845–1854.* Gainesville: University of Florida Press, 1959.

Donne, John. *The Elegies, and the Songs and Sonnets.* Edited by Helen Gardner. Oxford: Clarendon Press, 1965.

Douglas, Thomas. *Autobiography of Thomas Douglas, Late Judge of the Supreme Court of Florida.* New York: Calkins and Stiles, 1856.

Dunn, Marvin. *Black Miami in the Twentieth Century.* Gainesville: University Press of Florida, 1997.

Dupree, Mary M., and G. Dekle Taylor, M.D. "Dr. James Hall, 1760–1837." *Journal of Florida Medical Association* 61(August 1974): 626–31.

Durbin, Larry., comp. *Camden County, Georgia, Cemeteries.* Jacksonville, Fla.: Southern Genealogist's Exchange Society, Inc., 1993.

Edwards, Lucy Ames. *Grave Markers of Duval County.* Jacksonville, Fla.: Privately published, 1955.

Eisenhower, John S. D. *Agent of Destiny: The Life and Times of General Winfield Scott.* New York: Free Press, 1997.

———. *So Far from God: The U.S. War with Mexico, 1846–1848.* New York: Doubleday, 1989.

Evans, Augusta Jane. *Beulah.* 1859. Reprint, edited with an introduction by Elizabeth Fox-Genovese, Baton Rouge: Louisiana State University Press, 1992.

Evans, G. Blakemore, ed. *The Riverside Shakespeare.* 2nd. ed. New York: Houghton Mifflin, 1997.

Fairbanks, George R. "Early Churchmen in Florida." In *Historical Papers and Journal of Semi-Centennial of the Church in Florida, 1888.* Jacksonville, Fla.: Church Publishing Co., 1889.

Falk, Peter Hastings, ed. *Who Was Who in American Art, 1564–1975: 400 Years of Artists in America.* 3 vols. Madison, Conn.: Sound View Press, 1999.

Faust, Drew Gilpin. *Mothers of Invention: Women of the Slaveholding South in the American Civil War.* Chapel Hill: University of North Carolina Press, 1999.

———. *Southern Stories: Slaveholders in Peace and War.* Columbia: University of Missouri Press, 1992.

Fleming, Thomas. *West Point: The Men and the Times of the United States Military Academy.* New York: William Morrow & Company, 1969.

Foner, Eric, and John A. Garraty, eds. *The Reader's Companion to American History.* Boston: Houghton Mifflin, 1991.

Forrester, Mary Lois. *Lest We Forget: A Town, Newnansville, Florida.* Alachua, Fla.: Privately published, 1999.

Foster, John T., Jr., and Sarah Whitmer Foster. *Beechers, Stowes, and Yankee Strangers: The Transformation of Florida.* Gainesville: University Press of Florida, 1999.

Fox-Genovese, Elizabeth. *Within the Plantation Household: Black and White Women of the Old South.* Chapel Hill: University of North Carolina Press, 1988.

Frazier, Donald S. *The United States and Mexico at War: Nineteenth-Century Expansionism and Conflict.* New York: Macmillan, 1998.

Freehling, William W. *The Road to Disunion: Secessionists at Bay, 1776–1854.* New York: Oxford University Press, 1990.

Gannon, Michael, ed. *The New History of Florida.* Gainesville: University Press of Florida, 1996.

Gardiner, Harold C., ed. *The Imitation of Christ.* Garden City, N.Y.: Image Books, 1955.

Garraty, John A. *The American Nation: A History of the United States to 1877.* 7th ed. New York: HarperCollins, 1991.

Garvin, James L. *Historic Portsmouth.* Somersworth: New Hampshire Publishing Company, 1974.

George, Paul S. "'Colored Town': Miami's Black Community, 1896–1930." *Florida Historical Quarterly* 56 (April 1978): 432–35.

Georgia Genealogical Magazine 32 (April 1969): 2187–91.

Gold, Pleasant Daniel. *History of Duval County, Including Early History of East Florida.* St. Augustine, Fla.: The Record Company, 1929.

Goldsmith, Oliver. *The Vicar of Wakefield.* 1766. Reprint, Norwalk, Conn.: Heritage Press, 1992.

Graff, Mary B. *Mandarin on the St. Johns.* Gainesville: University of Florida Press, 1953.

Graham, Thomas. *The Awakening of St. Augustine: The Anderson Family and the Oldest City, 1821–1924.* St. Augustine, Fla.: St. Augustine Historical Society, 1978.

Green, Fletcher M. *The Role of the Yankee in the Old South.* Athens: University of Georgia Press, 1972.

Greer, David Alan. "The Oregon Territory." In *The United States and Mexico at War: Nineteenth-Century Expansionism and Conflict,* edited by Donald S. Frazier, 303. New York: Macmillan, 1998.

Groce, George C., and David H. Wallace. *The New York Historical Society's Dictionary of Artists in America, 1564–1860.* New Haven: Yale University Press, 1957.

Hammond, E. Ashby. *The Medical Profession in 19th Century Florida: A Biographical Register.* Gainesville: George A. Smathers Library, University of Florida, 1996.

Harrison, Eliza Cope, ed. *Best Companions: The Letters of Eliza Middleton Fisher and Her Mother, Mary Hering Middleton, from Charleston, Philadelphia, and Newport, 1839–1846.* Columbia: University of South Carolina Press, 2001.

Heidler, Jeane T., and David S. Heidler. "David E. Twiggs." In *The United States and Mexico at War: Nineteenth-Century Expansionism and Conflict,* edited by Donald S. Frazier, 441–42. New York: Macmillan, 1998.

Heitman, Francis B. *Historical Register and Dictionary of the United States Army.* 2 vols. 1903. Facsimile reprint, Urbana: University of Illinois Press, 1965.

Holt, Michael F. *The Rise and Fall of the Whig Party: Jacksonian Politics and the Onset of the Civil War.* New York: Oxford University Press, 1999.

The Holy Bible: King James Version. Philadelphia: The National Bible Press, 1958.

Johnson, Timothy D. *Winfield Scott: The Quest for Military Glory.* Lawrence: University of Kansas Press, 1998.

Jordan, David M. *Roscoe Conkling of New York: Voice in the Senate.* Ithaca: Cornell University Press, 1971.

Juvenal. *Satires: A New Translation with an Introduction by Hubert Creekmore.* New York: New American Library, 1963.

Kearney, Kevin K., ed. "Autobiography of William Marvin." *Florida Historical Quarterly* 36 (January 1958): 179–222.

Kieffer, Chester L. *Maligned General: The Biography of Thomas Sidney Jesup.* San Rafael, Calif.: Presido Press, 1979.

King, Wilma, ed. *A Northern Woman in the Plantation South: Letters of Tryphena Blanche Holder Fox, 1856–1876.* Columbia: University of South Carolina Press, 1997.

Klos, George. "Blacks and the Seminole Removal Debate, 1821–1835." In *The African American Heritage of Florida,* edited by David R. Colburn and Jane L. Landers, 128–56. Gainesville: University Press of Florida, 1995.

Knauss, James Owen. *Territorial Florida Journalism.* Deland: Florida State Historical Society, 1923.

Lancaster, Jane F. *Removal Aftershock: The Seminoles' Struggles to Survive in the West, 1836–1866.* Knoxville: University of Tennessee Press, 1994.

Landers, Jane. *Black Society in Spanish Florida.* Urbana: University of Illinois Press, 1999.

———. "Free and Slave." In *The New History of Florida,* edited by Michael Gannon, 167–82. Gainesville: University Press of Florida, 1996.

Laumer, Frank. *Dade's Last Command.* Gainesville: University Press of Florida, 1995.

————, ed. *Amidst a Storm of Bullets: The Diary of Lt. Henry Prince in Florida, 1836–1842.* Tampa, Fla.: University of Tampa Press, 1998.

LeBeau, Bryan F. *Currier & Ives: America Imagined.* Washington, D.C.: Smithsonian Institution Press, 2001.

LeClercq, Anne Sinkler Whaley, ed. *Between North and South: The Letters of Emily Wharton Sinkler, 1842–1865.* Columbia: University of South Carolina Press, 2001.

"Letters of Samuel Forry, Surgeon U.S. Army, 1837–1838." *Florida Historical Quarterly* 7 (July 1928): 88–105.

Mahon, John K. *History of the Second Seminole War, 1835–1842.* Rev. ed. Gainesville: University Presses of Florida, 1985.

Mahon, John K., and Brent R. Weisman. "Florida's Seminoles and Miccosukee Peoples." In *The New History of Florida,* edited by Michael Gannon, 183–206. Gainesville: University Press of Florida, 1996.

Maloney, Walter. *A Sketch of the History of Key West, Florida.* 1876. Facsimile reprint, Gainesville: University of Florida Press, 1868.

Manley, Walter W., E. Canter Brown Jr., and Eric W. Rise. *The Supreme Court of Florida and Its Predecessor Courts, 1821–1917.* Gainesville: University Press of Florida, 1997.

Martin, Richard A. *The City Makers.* Jacksonville, Fla.: Convention Press, 1972.

Martin, Sidney Walter. *Florida during Territorial Days.* Athens: University of Georgia Press, 1944.

McCall, George A. *Letters from the Frontiers.* Philadelphia: Lippincott, 1868.

McLoughlin, William G. *Rhode Island: A Bicentennial History.* New York: Norton, 1978.

McMillan, Sally G. *Southern Women: Black and White in the Old South.* Arlington Heights, Ill.: Harlan Davidson, 1992.

McMurtie, Douglas. "The Beginnings of Printing in Florida." *Florida Historical Quarterly* 23 (October 1944): 63–96.

McPherson, James M. *Battle Cry of Freedom: The Civil War Era.* New York: Oxford University Press, 1988.

McReynolds, Edwin C. *The Seminoles.* Norman: University of Oklahoma Press, 1972.

McWhiney, Grady. *Cracker Culture: Celtic Ways in the Old South.* Tuscaloosa: University of Alabama Press, 1988.

Merritt, Webster. *A Century of Medicine in Jacksonville and Duval County.* Gainesville: University of Florida Press, 1949.

Miller, Blandina Dudley. *A Sketch of Old Utica.* Utica, N.Y.: Feirstine Printing House, 1913.

Miller, Stephen F. *The Bench and the Bar of Georgia.* 2 vols. Philadelphia: Lippincott, 1858.

Miller, William Lee. *Arguing about Slavery: The Great Battles in the United States Congress.* New York: Alfred A. Knopf, 1997.

Milton, John. *Complete Poems and Major Prose.* Edited by Merrit Y. Hughes. Indianapolis: The Odyssey Press, 1957.

Moore, John Hammond, ed. "A South Carolina Lawyer Visits St. Augustine—1837." *Florida Historical Quarterly* 43 (April 1965): 361–78.

Motte, Jacob Rhett. *Journey into the Wilderness: An Army Surgeon's Account of Life in Camp and Field during the Creek and Seminole Wars, 1836–1838.* Edited by James F. Sunderman. Gainesville: University of Florida Press, 1953.

Ott, Eloise Robinson. "Ocala Prior to 1868." *Florida Historical Quarterly* 6 (October 1927): 85–110.

Otto, John Solomon. *Southern Frontiers, 1607–1860: The Agricultural Evolution of the Colonial and Antebellum South.* Westport, Conn.: Greenwood Press, 1989.

Owsley, Frank L. *Plain Folk in the Old South.* Baton Rouge: Louisiana State University Press, 1949.

Paisley, Clifton. *The Red Hills of Florida, 1528–1865.* Tuscaloosa: University of Alabama Press, 1989.

Patrick, Rembert. *Aristocrat in Uniform: General Duncan L. Clinch.* Gainesville: University of Florida Press, 1963.

————. *Florida Fiasco: Rampant Rebels on the Georgia-Florida Border.* Athens: University of Georgia Press, 1954.

————, ed. "William Adee Whitehead's Description of Key West." *Tequesta* 12 (1952): 61–74.

Pearce, George F. *The U.S. Navy in Pensacola from Sailing Ships to Naval Aviation, 1828–1930.* Pensacola: University of West Florida Press, 1980.

Pennington, Edgar Legare. "The Episcopal Church in Florida, 1763–1892." *Historical Magazine of the Protestant Episcopal Church* 7 (March 1938): 3–77.

Peters, Harry T. *Currier and Ives: Printmakers to the American People.* Garden City, N.Y.: Doubleday, Doran & Co., 1942.

Peters, Thelma. "William Adee Whitehead's Reminiscences of Key West." *Tequesta* 25 (1965): 3–42.

Phelps, John B., comp. *The People of Lawmaking in Florida, 1822–1993.* Tallahassee: Florida House of Representatives, 1993.

Phillips, Rebecca. "A Diary of Jessee Talbot Bernard: Newnansville and Tallahassee." *Florida Historical Quarterly* 18 (October 1939): 115–26.

Porter, Kenneth W. *The Black Seminoles: History of Freedom Seeking People.* Revised and edited by Alcione M. Amos and Thomas P. Senter. Gainesville: University Press of Florida, 1996.

————. *The Negro on the American Frontier.* New York: Arno Press, 1971.

Powell, William H., ed. *List of Officers of the Army of the United States from 1779–1900.* New York: L. R. Hamersly & Company, 1900.

Proby, Kathryn Hall. *Audubon in Florida: With Selections from the Writings of John James Audubon.* Coral Gables, Fla.: University of Miami Press, 1974.

Prucha, Francis. *The Sword of the Republic: The United States Army on the Frontier, 1783–1846.* New York: Macmillan, 1969.

Rable, George C. *Civil Wars: Women and the Crisis of Southern Nationalism.* Champaign: University of Illinois Press, 1989.

Rawls, Walton H. *The Great Book of Currier and Ives' America.* New York: Abbeville Press, 1979.

Revels, Tracy J. "Grander in Her Daughters: Florida's Women during the Civil War." *Florida Historical Quarterly* 78 (winter 1999): 261–82.

Rivers, Larry Eugene. *Slavery in Florida: Territorial Days to Emancipation.* Gainesville: University Press of Florida, 2000.

———. "A Troublesome Property: Master-Slave Relations in Florida, 1821–1865." In *The African American Heritage of Florida,* edited by David R. Colburn and Jane L. Landers, 104–27. Gainesville: University Press of Florida, 1995.

Rohrbough, Malcolm J. *The Trans-Appalachian Frontier: People, Societies, and Institutions, 1775–1850.* Belmont, Calif.: Wadsworth Publishing Co., 1990.

Rowe, Anne E. *The Idea of Florida in the American Literary Imagination.* Baton Rouge: Louisiana State University Press, 1986.

Saltonstall, William G. *Ports of Piscataqua: Soundings in the Maritime History of Portsmouth, N.H.* Cambridge: Harvard University Press, 1941.

Saunders, Robert W. *Bridging the Gap: Continuing the Florida NAACP Legacy of Harry T. Moore.* Tampa, Fla.: University of Tampa Press, 2000.

Schafer, Daniel L. *Anna Kingsley.* St. Augustine, Fla.: St. Augustine Historical Society, 1994.

———. "'A Class of People Neither Freemen Nor Slaves': From Spanish to American Race Relations in Florida, 1821–1861." *Journal of Social History* 26 (spring 1993): 587–609.

———. "U.S. Territory and State." In *The New History of Florida,* edited by Michael Gannon, 207–30. Gainesville: University Press of Florida, 1996.

Schene, Michael. "Not a Shot Was Fired: Fort Chokonikla and the 'Indian War' of 1849–1850." *Tequesta* 37 (1977): 19–37.

Schlesinger, Arthur M., Jr., ed. *The Almanac of American History.* New York: Putnam, 1983.

Sheridan, Richard Brinsley. *The School for Scandal.* New York: Dover Publications, 1991.

Shippee, Lester B., ed. *Bishop Whipple's Southern Diary, 1843–1844.* Minneapolis: University of Minnesota Press, 1937.

Shofner, Jerrell H. *Daniel Ladd, Merchant Prince of Frontier Florida.* Gainesville: University Presses of Florida, 1978.

Silver, James W. *Edmund Pendleton Gaines: Frontier General.* Baton Rouge: Louisiana State University Press, 1949.

Simmons, William. *Notices of East Florida: With an Account of the Seminole Nation of Indians by a Recent Traveler in the Province.* 1822. Reprint, Floridiana Facsimile and Reprint series. Introduction by George Buker. Gainesville: University of Florida Press, 1973.

Simpson, John, and Edmund Weiner, eds. *The Oxford English Dictionary.* 2nd ed. New York: Oxford University Press, 1986.

Singletary, Otis. *The Mexican War.* Chicago: University of Chicago Press, 1960.

Skelton, William B. *An American Profession of Arms: The Army Officer Corps, 1784–1861.* Lawrence: University of Kansas Press, 1992.

Smith, Justin H. *The War with Mexico*. 2 vols. 1919. Reprint, Glouchester, Mass.: Peter Smith, 1963.

Sprague, John T. *Origins, Progress, and Conclusion of the Florida War*. 1848. Facsimile reprint, Tampa, Fla.: University of Tampa Press, 2000.

Stephen, Sir Leslie, and Sir Sidney Lee, eds. *The Dictionary of National Biography*. 1917. Reprint, London: Oxford University Press, 1970.

Sullivan, Francis P., ed. "Letters of a West Pointer, 1860–1861." *American Historical Review* 33 (April 1928): 599–617.

Tebeau, Charlton W. *A History of Florida*. Miami, Fla.: University of Miami Press, 1971.

Thackeray, William Makepeace. *Vanity Fair: A Novel without a Hero*. Edited by Geoffrey and Kathleen Tillotson. Boston: Houghton Mifflin, 1963.

Theodore Roosevelt Inaugural National Historic Site, Buffalo, New York. Buffalo, N.Y.: Theodore Roosevelt Inaugural Site Foundation, 2000.

Thomas à Kempis. *The Imitation of Christ: A Modern Version Based on the English Translation Made by Richard Whitford around the Year 1530*. Edited by Harold C. Gardiner. Garden City, N.Y.: Image Books, 1955.

Thomas, Emory. *The Confederacy as a Revolutionary Experience*. Englewood Cliffs, N.J.: Prentice Hall, 1971.

———. *The Confederate Nation: 1861–1865*. New York: Harper, 1979.

Thompson, Arthur W. "David Yulee: A Study of Nineteenth-Century American Thought and Enterprise." Ph.D. diss., Columbia University, 1954.

———. *Jacksonian Democracy on the Florida Frontier*. Gainesville: University of Florida Press, 1961.

Trollope, Frances. *Domestic Manners of the Americans*. Edited by Donald Smalley. New York: A. A. Knopf, 1949.

Varon, Elizabeth R. *"We Mean to Be Counted": White Women and Politics in Antebellum Virginia*. Chapel Hill: University of North Carolina Press, 1998.

Voorsanger, Catherine Hoover, and John K. Howat, eds. *Art and the Empire City: New York, 1825–1861*. New Haven: Yale University Press, 2000.

Wallace, Edward S. *General William Jenkins Worth: Monterey's Forgotten Hero*. Dallas: Southern Methodist University Press, 1953.

Walsh, John J. *Vignettes of Old Utica*. Utica, N.Y.: Utica Public Library, 1982.

Ward, James Robertson. *Old Hickory's Town: An Illustrated History of Jacksonville*. Jacksonville, Fla.: Old Hickory's Town, Inc., 1985.

Wells, Tom Henderson. *The Slave Ship Wanderer*. Athens: University of Georgia Press, 1967.

Wickman, Patricia R. *Osceola's Legacy*. Tuscaloosa: University of Alabama Press, 1991.

Wilner, Merton M. *Niagara Frontier: A Narrative and Documentary History*. Chicago: S. J. Clarke, 1931.

Wilson, James Grant, and John Fiske, eds. *Appleton's Encyclopaedia of American Biography*. 6 vols. New York: D. Appleton Company, 1888.

Wiltse, Charles M. *John C. Calhoun, Sectionalist, 1840–1850.* New York: Russell and Russell, 1968.

Winders, Richard Bruce. *Mr. Polk's Army: The American Military Experience in the Mexican War.* College Station: Texas A&M University Press, 1997.

Winslow, Richard E. *"Wealth and Honor": Portsmouth during the Golden Age of Privateering, 1775–1815.* Portsmouth, N.H.: The Portsmouth Marine Society, 1988.

Wolfe, Margaret Ripley. *Daughters of Canaan: A Saga of Southern Women.* Lexington: University of Kentucky Press, 1995.

Wright, J. Leitch. *Creeks and Seminoles: The Destruction and Regeneration of the Muscogulge People.* Lincoln: University of Nebraska Press, 1986.

Wyatt-Brown, Bertram. *The Shaping of Southern Culture: Honor, Grace, and War, 1760s–1890s.* Chapel Hill: University of North Carolina Press, 2001.

———. *Southern Honor: Ethics and Behavior in the Old South.* New York: Oxford University Press, 1982.

Yelton, Susan. "Newnansville: A Lost Florida Settlement." *Florida Historical Quarterly* 53 (January 1975): 319–31.

Yulee, C. Wickliffe. "Senator Yulee: A Biographical Sketch by C. Wickliffe Yulee." *Florida Historical Quarterly* 2 (April 1909): 26–43.

Index

Abaco Island, 236

Adams, Charles, 252

Adams, John Quincy, xxv, xxviii, 163

Adams, Mr. (of Portsmouth), 16, 17

African Americans, 8, 16, 39–40. *See also* Seminole Indians; slavery

agriculture, xxii, 15, 25, 27, 29, 37, 39, 112–13; fruits, 94–95; orange culture, 6–7, 28, 39, 43; potatoes (Irish and sweet), 43; silk culture, 10, 29, 30, 39, 94

Alachua County: described, 102

Alburtis, Mrs., 190

Aldrich, Corinna. *See* Brown, Corinna

Aldrich, Edward Sherman (E. S.), Dr., xix, 2, 51, 57, 59, 60–63, 72, 75, 104, 119, 123, 150, 155–56, 160, 191, 227; on conduct of the Seminole War, 76; on Corinna's addiction, 283; description of Jacksonville, 76; description of Key West, 229–32; on J. Egbert Farnham, 284; and marriage to Corinna, 64–65; and medical practice, 51–52, 72, 76, 97, 102, 113, 156, 162, 204, 209, 218, 224, 227, 232, 297; moves to California, 277, 281–84; moves to Jacksonville, 297; moves to Key West, 229; moves to Lake City, 299; moves to Macon, Ga., 76, 229; moves to Marietta, Ga., 229; moves to Mineral Springs, Fla., 93; moves to Newnansville, 102, 104; moves to Pensacola, 202–5, 208–9; moves to St. Augustine, 181; runs for legislative council seat, 173–74; seeks

appointment as surgeon of Marine Hospital at Key West, 232, 242, 251, 260, 262, 274; and slave ownership, xxv, 232; supporter of David Levy Yulee, 148–49; as surgeon in First Regiment of Volunteers, 51, 61, 64, 68, 69, 76, 102, 110–11, 112, 115

Aldrich, Letitia, 68

Aldrich, Louis, 150, 171, 173, 179, 181, 221; Ellen's description of, 160; migrates to California, 181; and politics, 181

Aldrich, Whipple, 65, 68, 191

Anderson, Benjamin Franklin, 179

Anderson, Corinna Georgia, 188, 194, 209, 229

Anderson, Edward Willoughby, 157–58, 166, 190, 194, 209, 227, 229, 261, 268; born, 153; and Civil War service, 295, 297; Corinna calls "Frogy," 155; dies, 301; and education, 276, 285; and family in Washington, D.C., 297, 299–302; marries Elizabeth Felicia Masi, 297; and nervous breakdown, 301; and West Point, 289–95

Anderson, Elizabeth Felicia Masi ("Lizzy"), 297, 299, 301; image of, 298

Anderson, Ellen. *See* Brown, Ellen

Anderson, Ellen Mannevillette ("Villette"), xvii, 209, 229, 261, 268, 276, 285, 290, 296, 299–300; portrait of, xix, 299

Anderson, Georgia, 268, 285, 290, 296, 299–300; portrait of 298

Anderson, James Willoughby, xvii, xxix, 3, 106–10, 115, 116, 126, 156, 166, 168; on Aldriches, 134, 139–40; on Buffalo Barracks, 170, 189–92; and campaigns, movements in Seminole War, 117–18, 119, 120–22, 129–50, 153–55, 160; courtship of Ellen Brown, 108–10; commendation by Col. William W. Worth, 152–53; daguerreotype of, 107, 223; death of, 225–26; and duel, 132–33, 137; on duty, 139, 214; on foreign affairs, 192, 193; on marriage, 124; and Mexican War, xvii, 208–11, 213–227; has money stolen, 137; on music, 138–39; on Seminole character, 140, 146; on Seminole War, 109, 115, 117–18, 129, 130–31, 145–46; transferred to Fort Gratiot, Mich., 185, 200; transferred to Pilatka, 153; on Yulee, 193

Anderson, Jane Willoughby, 106

Anderson, Villette. *See* Anderson, Ellen Mannevillette

Anderson, Virginia, 170, 173, 180, 190, 191, 192, 194, 208, 209, 212–13, 219–20, 227, 229, 261; image of, 211

Anderson, Will. *See* Anderson, Edward Willoughby

Anderson, William, 106

Anderson-Brown Collection, xxix

Andrews, Mrs. (Ellen's friend), 157

Arkansas Delegation, 131

Armed Occupation Act, 161, 172

Armistead, Walker, 105–6, 115, 119, 129, 135, 141

Army of Northern Virginia, 295, 297

Arpeika (Sam Jones), 64

Audubon, John, 24–25

Bagg's Square (Utica, N.Y.), 234; view of, 233

Baldwin, Abel Seymour 91

Baldwin, Eliza, 91

Barker, [William], 258

Beard, John, 200

Bellamy Road, 107

Benton, Thomas Hart, 161, 172

Berrien, John, 197

Bird, Edmund, 147

Bloomingdale Asylum, 285

Bolivar, [Simon], 36

Bowlegs, Billy, 272–73

Braddock, William, 42

Branch, Britton, 135

Bronson, Emma, 157, 159

Bronson, Gertrude, 157, 159

Bronson, Issac, xxvii; portrait of, 159

Bronson, Sophronia, 157–58, 199

Brown, Adelaide, 282, 300–301

Brown, Adelaide Mary, xxi, 1, 2, 164; death of, 6; etching of, 6

Brown, Charles Burroughs, xix, xxi, xxii, 1, 2, 5, 10, 66, 79, 112, 122; and African Americans, 40; and agricultural pursuits, 6–7, 10, 15, 20, 25, 27, 28, 29, 39, 43, 49, 62, 94–96, 98–99; builds, describes Llangollen, 81, 89, 92, 96; claims to have been deceived by George, 95–96; dies in Charleston, 124; estate of, 142; and medical degree, 96; in Newnansville, 104, 123; seeks sutlership, 118

Brown, Claudia, 286

Brown, Corinna (Mrs. E.S. Aldrich), xvii, xix, xxi–xxiv, 1, 2, 129; on John Quincy Adams, 163; and addiction, 283–85; on Anderson children, 155, 166, 176, 187, 188, 272; on Edward Willoughby Anderson, 155, 166, 176; on James W. Anderson, 112, 113, 116, 123, 143; on James Willoughby Anderson's death, 225–26;

on Armed Occupation Act, 172, 175; on Aunt Ann, 156; on Aunt Hall, 156, 176; on bloodhounds, 110–111; on Charles's death, 124–26, 146; on Charles's estate, 142; on climate in Florida, 63, 69, 163, 172, 241, 246; counsels George on matrimony, 252; and courtship of Edward Aldrich, 51–53, 57, 59, 60–61, 63; and courtship of Pomeroy, 7, 188–89; on crackers, 28, 29, 262; on Creeks, 21, 31–32; death of, 285; on Ellen, 188, 196, 226–27; fears slave uprising, 16, 21; on Fort King, 175–76; on house in Key West, 241–42, 280; on house in Newnansville, 112, 150, 164, 179; on house in Pensacola, 227; on husband's decision to move to California, 277; on Indian relics, burial mounds, 17, 113; on Jacksonville, 10, 28, 75; on Key West, 241–48; and literary aspirations, pursuits, xxviii, 7, 44, 45, 57–58, 63; on Mexican War, 226; and move to St. Marys, Ga., 278; and New York City, 172, 288; on Osceola, 32, 76; on Parisian fashion, 91; on Pensacola, 203–5; on politics, xxviii, 119, 122–24, 126, 143, 148–49, 166, 170, 175, 183, 196–98, 226, 262, 274; portrait of, 3, 171; and religious beliefs, musings, xxvi, 125, 126–27, 178, 227; and Seminole rituals (green corn dance, black drink, scalping, food), 32, 42, 114; on Seminoles and war, xxvi, 16, 21, 23, 26–34, 36, 39, 41, 63, 76–77, 90, 97, 104–5, 110–16, 118–119, 122–23, 143, 146–49, 163–65, 259, 273–74; on slavery, African Americans, xxiv–xxv, 39, 43, 119–20, 123, 164, 169, 176, 185, 236, 245–46; on St. Augustine, 182–83; 186; on subordinate status of women, 52–53; on

wandering nature of her family, 156 on wedding, 65
Brown, David (parson), 54–55, 60, 69, 72, 74, 85; on war-torn Duval County, 93
Brown, Elihu Dearing: privateering activities of, xix–xx
Brown, Elizabeth Dearing, xix, 1; death of, 2; portrait of, xxi
Brown, Ellen Maria (Mrs. James Willoughby Anderson), xvii, xix, xxi–xxiv; on Aldriches (in St. Marys, Ga.), 80; on American manners and human nature, 49–50, 80–81, 86–87; and children, 157, 179, 194, 199, 219, 222–23, 261, 267–68, 276, 285, 296; courtship and marriage to James W. Anderson, 108, 114, 128; on courtship, romance, and marriage, 51, 59–60, 66, 71, 78–79, 80, 85–86; on crackers, xxiv, 14, 88, 95; description of Key West, 139–40, 247–50, 267; description of Newnansville, 105; description of Pensacola, 212–13; dies, 296; and enrollment of Edward Willoughby Anderson at West Point, 289–95; and eyes, 73–74, 78, 80, 82, 196; falls out with Aunt Hall, 89, 92, 94; and fears of Civil War, 291–92; on Florida climate, 12, 50, 248; and friendship with Farnum, 286–87; on Hall plantation and Mandarin area, 13–14; on houses, construction of, 100–101; joins James at Fort King, 142; joins James in Palatka, 166; and literary aspirations, xxviii, 7, 69, 74, 289–90; on men, 59–60, 78–80; on mosquitoes, 89, 239, 246; moves to New York City, 281; on phrenology, 95, 99, 109; on politics, xxviii, 180, 290–95; portrait of, 3; and pregancy, births, 142, 151–53, 195–96, 199; on religion,

Brown, Ellen Maria (*continued*)
musings, xxvi, 1–2, 254–55, 269; on
Seminoles and war, xxvi, 14, 19–21,
36–37, 39, 92, 98, 100, 105; on society
in East Florida, 20, 38, 86–87, 105;
on slavery, xxiv–xxv, 39, 213; and
South's justification for seceding,
291–94; on teaching school, 240, 265,
267–68, 269; women, observations
on and subordinate status of, xxvi,
51, 59–60, 66–67, 80–81, 88, 180, 266,
269–71, 289–91; on wreckers,
275–76
Brown, George Long, xvii, xix, xxi,
xxii, 1, 5, 15, 30, 50, 62, 79, 90, 92, 94,
118, 128, 129, 176, 182, 187, 205, 215,
257; affirms determination to support Ellen and children, 235, 281; on
Aldrich family, 209; on Corinna
Aldrich's death, 285; on James
Anderson's death, 235; on business
in Philadelphia, 96; on business with
Charles in Newnansville, 114, 161;
on business with Edward in Newnansville, 156, 160, 162, 170, 173,
181, 208–9, 224; calls himself a
"Cracker," 224; dies, 286; and marriage, 250, 252, 257; marries Matilda
Stewart, 281–82; on Mexican War,
206, 209, 223–24; offers to sell Aunt
Ann's plantation for her, 200; plans
move to Florida, 77; plans to spend
summer in St. Marys, 150; on poli-
tics, 206; portrait of, 4, 286; purchases land at Fort King, 175; and
slave ownership, xxv; views on the
U.S. Army, 161
Brown, George Long, Jr., 286, 300
Brown, Henry Alexander, xx
Brown, Mannevillette Elihu Dearing
(M. E. D), xvii, xix, xxi, xxiii; advises
Ellen on "independence," 268;
arrives in Paris, 89; and art study in
Europe, xxiv, 62, 71, 85–86, 105, 123,

142, 234; dies, 302; and financial
support of Ellen, 234, 268–71, 281;
and lithography, xxi, 1–2, 8; moves
to Geneva, N.Y., 8; moves to Ithaca,
N.Y., 21; moves to Utica, N.Y., 8,
234; paintings by, xix, xxi, 2–4, 6,
164, 171, 289; in Philadelphia, 2, 5;
portrait of, 2, 289, 302; returns to
America, 234; spars with Ellen over
causes of Civil War, 292–95; travels
to Florida, 301
Brown, Matilda (née Stewart), xvii,
300–301; marries George Brown,
281–82
Buffalo, N.Y., 170, 173, 173, 179, 185;
letters from 189, 191; view of, 191
Burrett, Samuel, xxvii, 35, 71, 164

Calhoun, John C., 206
Call, Richard Keith, 34
Cao Hadjo, 64
Casey, Mrs., 137, 195
Cerro Gordo (Mex.), Battle of, 220,
224
Charles (slave of Aldriches), 154–55,
169, 181
Charleston, 185; Charles Brown dies in,
124; George Brown dies in, 286–87;
description of, 9–10, 119
Chocochattee region, 132, 133
Churchill, Sylvester, 186, 188
Churubusco convent, 224–25
City College of New York, 297
Civil War, 290–97
Clay, Henry, xxviii, 180, 183
Clinch, Duncan Lamont, 136, 176
Coacoochee (Wild Cat), xxviii, 64, 122,
141, 161, 274; attack on theatrical
troupe, 106; portrait of, 33
Cold Harbor, Battle of, 297
Cole, Mr. (sutler), 118
Conchs, 238
Conkling, Roscoe, 8, 234
Conners, David E., 213

Contreras and Churubusco, Battles of, 224

Convent of the Sisters of the Dust (New York City), 296

crackers, xxiv, 14, 28, 29, 36, 40, 72, 73, 94, 224, 250, 262

Creeks, 21, 31–32, 42

Critchton, Miss, 38

Currier, Nathaniel: and business relationship with M. E. D. Brown, xxi

Cushing, Charles, 163, 164

Dade, Francis L., 18

Dades Massacre, 18

Dale, Mr. 20

Danforth, J. B., 16

Davidson (soldier), 152

Day, Hannibal, 192

Day, Mrs. Hannibal, 190, 192, 223

Dearing, Ann, 1, 15, 27, 101, 116, 120, 123, 129, 143, 164, 166, 183, 185, 186–89, 200; dies in Pensacola, 209; first visit to Florida, 6; illness of, 70, 71, 102, 212–13; on militia musters, 40; moves, keeps house in Newnansville, 111, 156

Dearing, Delia (Dorothy). *See* Hall, Delia (Dorothy) Dearing

Dearing, Mary, 1, 7, 10, 15, 27, 49, 57, 80, 101, 116; death of, 103, 125; describes her cabin, 40; illness of, 44–45, 58, 70, 102; plans trip to New York, 84, 85

Dell, Bennet M., 104

Delony, Mrs., 80

Denham, James M., xxix

Dickens, Charles, 169

Doggett, John L., xxvii, 75, 85, 104, 162

Douglas, Louisa, 71

Douglas, Thomas, xxvii, 71; portrait of, 70

Downing, Charles, xxvii, 77

Downing, Rebecca, 77

Dozier, Leonard, Mrs., 301

Duke, Jane, 230

Duke, Reason, 230

East Florida: agricultural production in, xxii, 6–7, 10, 27; and Armed Occupation Act, 172, 175; description of, xxii, 7–9, 23–25, 93; houses in, 100–101; migration into, xxiii; slavery in, xxii

East Florida Railroad, 12, 16, 20

Ellis, John D., 236

Emaltha, Charley: murder of, 18

Emerson, Ralph Waldo, xxiii

Evans, Augusta Jane, 289

Exact (ship), 198, 199

Farnham, J. Egbert. *See* Farnum, J. Egbert

Farnum, J. Egbert, 284; on George Brown, 286–87; and filibustering, 287; and friendship with Ellen Brown, 286–88; and slave ship *Wanderer,* 287

First Regiment of Volunteers, 51

Florida, East. *See* East Florida

Florida Magazine, 74

Florida, Middle. *See* Middle Florida

Fontane, Mr., 230

Fort Clark, 102

Fort Deynand [Denaud], 153

Fort Drane, 41–42

Fort Eaton, 9

Fort Fanning, 143

Fort Gilliland, 102

Fort Gratiot (Mich.), 185, 209, 210, 223; letter from, 200; view of, 201

Fort Harlee, 102; view of, 103

Fort Holmes, 132

Fort King (Ocala), xxiv, 18, 108, 118, 119, 122, 132, 141, 143, 149; Aldriches purchase land in, 175; drawing of, 138; James and Ellens' house in, 128, 129, 134, 136; letters

Fort King (Ocala) (*continued*)
  from, 117, 123, 129, 131, 133, 134, 135, 137, 139, 144
Fort Marion (Castillo de San Marcos), 8, 24, 26, 64. *See also* St. Augustine
Fort Moultrie (Charleston), 64
Fort No. 12. *See* Post No. 12
Fort Ogden, 153
Fort Russell, 132, 137
Fort Tarver, 149
Forward, William A., 171, 173

Gaines, Edmund Pendleton, 31
Gatlin, Richard, 144
Gill, Jane, xiii,
Gill, Raymond, xiii
Grant, Ulysses S., 297
Greenwood Cemetery (Brooklyn, N.Y.), 296
Gunnison, John W., 13

Hall, Delia (Dorothy) Dearing, xxii, 7–8, 12–14, 29, 58, 65, 89, 92, 94, 96, 103, 111, 143, 156, 166, 169, 176; boards in Jacksonville, 111, 114; dies, 178; marriage to Dr. Hall, 5–6; portrait of, 4; in St. Augustine, 1–2, 5; sells, buys slave, 119–20, 123; visits Charleston, a "belle," 119–20; visits Newnansville, 114; will of, 179
Hall, James, xxii, 5–6, 8, 20, 26, 27, 29, 37, 45, 58, 62, 65, 70; death and funeral of, 71–72, 73; description of, 11
Halleck Tustenuggee, 141, surrender of, 160, 161
Halliday, Samuel F., 96
Hallows, Miller, 36–37
Halpatter Tustenuggee (Alligator), 64
Hammond, E. Ashby, xxix
Harlick Lustnugger, 140. *See also* Halleck Tustenuggee
Harney, William Shelby, 118
Harrison, William Henry, 123, 126, 143

Hart, Isaiah, 51
Hart, Ossian, xxvii, 231
Has-pi-tar-ke (Seminole chief): 153
Hernandez, Joseph, xxvii, 64, 158
Hernandez, Louisa, 158, 160
Hintzleman [Heintzelman], Samuel, 160
Hoffman, Lieut., 116, 122
Hopson, Nevil, 144–45
Horse, John (black Seminole leader), 64
Humphreys, Gad, xxvii, 176
Hutchinson, Charles, xxiii

Jackson, Andrew, 30
Jacksonville, 8, 141; description of, 10, 23–24, 28, 38, 75, 76; letters from, 64, 71, 74, 85; militia muster in, 15
Jacksonville Courier, 5, 69, 72, 74
Jacksonville Herald, 297
Jalapa [Xalapa], Mex., 221, 223; letter from 220
Jenks [Jenkes], Mrs. Hanna B., 157
Jesup, Thomas Sidney, xxviii, 42, 57, 62, 64
Jones, Anson, 193
Jones, Dr. (Key West Marine Hospital surgeon), 260, 262

Ker, Crogham, 158
Kernan, Francis, 234
Key West: description of, 229–32, 238–56, 267, 267; letters from 229, 235, 239, 241, 244, 246, 248, 251, 253, 258, 260, 262, 263, 264, 265, 267, 271, 273, 275, 277, 279; view of, 230; and wreckers, 238, 243, 248
Kincaid, James, 16
King Phillip (Seminole leader), 64

Ladd, Daniel, xxiii
La Grange (Hall Plantation), 64, 75, 76, 92; letters from 59, 62, 68, 81, 83, 86, 87
Lancaster, Annie Blair, 245

Lancaster, Eliza, 245
Lancaster, Joseph, xxvii, 245, 246; portriat of, 231
Lancaster, Laura, 245
Lapinski, Private, 137, 138
Larkin, Mr., 30
Leaton, Miss (sisters' friend), 19
Lee, Robert E., 297
Levy, David. *See* Yulee, David Levy
Levy, Moses Elias, 149
Lincoln, Abraham, 290
Llangollen (Charles's plantation), 81, 89, 92, 96; home also to Mary, Ann, and Ellen, 89; and Ladies of, 92; letters from, 91, 94, 95; sale of, 200
loco-foco, 175
Loomis, Gustavus, 139
Lucy (Ellen's wet nurse), 157

Mackay, George, 162, 164
Mackay, John, 24, 83
Macomb, Alexander, 62, 97, 100, 141
Mandarin, Fla., xxii, xxiv, 6, 8–9; building house in, 26; description of, 10; letters from, 9, 12, 15, 26, 28, 30, 36, 39, 41, 44, 47, 51, 53, 57, 59, 60, 66, 69, 73, 79, 90, 98, 99; sisters arrive in, 9
Marcy, Will L., 206
Mariah (slave of Edward Aldrich), 232–3
Martin, John W., 145
Marvin, [William], 230
Masi, Elizabeth Felicia ("Lizzy"). *See* Anderson, Elizabeth ("Lizzy")
Masi, Frank, 291, 297
Masi, Philip, 301
Mcbraigh, Mr. (Mr. McRea): murdered by Indians, 111
McIntosh, John M., 176
McKinstry, Mrs.: loses child, 155
McKinstry (soldier), 152
McNeil [McVeil], Mr., 111
McRae, Mr. *See* Mcbraigh, Mr.

McVeil, Mr. *See* McNeil, Mr.
Medical College of South Carolina, 51
Mexican War, 208–11, 213–227
Mexico City, 223, 24
Micanopy, 115, 135; projected as state capital, 172
Middle Florida, xxii
Mineral (Suwannee) Springs: Corinna's description of, 93; letters from, 93, 96
Monterey, Calif., 255
Monterey, Mex., 215; letter from, 213
Montgomery, Elizabeth Fanny Taylor: killed by Indians, 144–45
Mott, George S.: massacre of, 26–27, 36

Newnansville, xix, xxiv, 8, 122, 138, 162, 164, 181; description of, 102–105, 112–13; family arrives in, 104; James and Ellen's marriage in, 128; Ladies of, 104; land office in, 161; letters from, 110, 114, 118, 122, 124, 126, 142, 146, 162, 165, 167, 175, 177, 178, 200, 206, 208
New York City: sisters reside in, 281–96
Norfolk, Va., xvii, 208, 227
Nunes, Albert, 192

Ogden, Edmund Augustine, 216
Osceola, xxviii, 32, 63; capture of, 64; described by Corinna, 76–77; portrait of, 33

Page, John, 131
Palatka. *See* Pilatka
Patriot War, 45
Peachy, Dr., 230
Pearse [Pierce], Benjamin Kendrick, 41–42
Pender, W. D., 297
Penrose, Mrs. 153
Penrose (soldier), 153–54
Pensacola, 202; description of, 202–3; family settles in, 208; letters from, 203, 211, 218, 221, 225, 226

Philadelphia Saturday Chronicle, 63

phrenology, 95, 99, 109

Picolata, 3, 106; descriptions of, and stage, 46; view of, 47

Pilatka [Palatka], 166; letters from, 120, 153, 154, 168

Pillow, Gideon, 226

Pinckney, Thomas A., 230, 251

Pindarvis, James, 104

Plympton, Joseph, 154

Polk, James K., xxviii, 180, 206, 224, 226

Pomeroy (Corinna's fiancee), 7, 43, 188–89

Pope, Alexander, 61

Porcher, Peter, 132

Portsmouth, N.H., xvii, xix; view of, xx; selling house in, 11, 25, 27, 30, 62

Post No. 12, 106, 117, 118, 121; letters from, 108, 109, 118

Powell. *See* Osceola

Prairie, [Paynes], 149

Prevat, J. T., 128

Puebla, Mex., 223, 224

Reed, Rosa. *See* Rosalie Reid

Reid, Janet, 60

Reid, Mary Martha: portrait of, 56

Reid, Robert Raymond, xxvii, 57, 60, 104, 136; portrait of, 56

Reid, Rosalie, 60, 121

Richardson, Mrs., 190, 192

Rider, Emory, 84

Riley, Arabella Israel, 116, 124, 132, 135, 153–54, 190, 192; suffers loss of twins, 155

Riley, Bennet, 108, 117, 122, 132, 139, 152–56, 192, 211, 224; described, 115, 160

Rogers, Erastus, 149

Russell, [James], 258

Russell, Mrs. 192

Saltillo, Mex., 213

Sanchez, Francis R. 140

Sanchez, Joseph S., 104

San Felasco Hammock, 102

San Francisco, Calif.: letter from, 282

Santa Anna, 210, 215, 217

Savannah, 185

Scarritt, Jeremiah Mason, 212

Schoolcraft, Mrs., 188

Schureman (daguerreotypist), 223

Scott, Winfield, xviii, 26, 29, 30–32, 206, 215, 216, 217, 223, 224, 226: and Edward Willoughby Anderson's appointment to West Point, 289

Second Infantry, 108, 112, 160, 170, 224

Second Seminole War (1835–42), xvii, xxii, xxvi, 18–21, 23–42, 63, 64, 76–77, 90, 93, 102–24, 128–56, 259, 273–74

Seminole Indians, 8, 16, 258, 259; and African American allies, 8–9, 16, 20–21, 23; and rituals (green corn dance and black drink), 32. *See also* Second Seminole War

Sherwood, Walter, 145

Shippy, J. M., 218

Simmons, William Hayne, 36

Slavery, xxiv–xxv, 39–40, 119–20, 123; demographics in Florida, xxii

Slaves: and uprising, 21–22

Smith, Frances, 158

Smith, Joseph, xxvii, 158, 162

Smith, Miss (sisters' friend), 19

Smith, Persifor F. 226

Smith, Mrs. T. I., 146

Spencer, Joshua, 234

square number twelve: drawing of, 107

square system, 106–7, 118, 124

Stanley, Zilphia, 141, 207

St. Augustine, xxiv, 8, 121, 141, 181; description of, 24–25, 182–84, 186; letters from 155, 157, 182, 185, 187,

194, 196, 198; parties and society in, 55, 157; view of, 48, 159

St. Augustine Florida Herald, 27

St. Augustine News, 27

Stephen and Frances (ship), 178, 180, 195

Stevens [Stephens], Alexander, 197

Stewart, James M., 300

Stewart, Mary E., 300

Stewart, Matilda. *See* Brown, Matilda

St. Marys, Ga., xvii, 150; Ellen's thoughts on, 79; letters from, 78

Stowe, Harriet Beecher, xxiii

Sullivan, Francis P., xxix

Sullivan, Mannevillette, xxix

Tampa, 132, 139

Tampico, Mex., 214; letter from, 216

Tappen, John, xxiii

Taylor, Zachary, 84, 105, 115, 217, 264; and square system, 106

Thomasville, Ga., 168

Thompson, Wiley, 108, 149

Tiger Tail, 141, 152, 161

Traynor, Elizabeth, xiii

Treaty of Paynes Landing, 8

Trollope, Frances, 169

Twiggs, David, 110, 112, 115, 118, 138, 224, 273

Utica, N.Y., xvii, 8, 302; city plan of, 233; description of, 234–35

Valencia, Gabriel, 224

Van Buren, Martin, xxviii, 123, 126

Van Buren, William, 156, 295

Van Ness, Eugene, 217

Varon, Elizabeth, xxviii

Vera Cruz, 213, 215, 216, 221; assault on, 217, 220

Victoria, Mex., 213

Walker, Sarah, 69, 89, 95, 234, 241, 254, 255, 259, 267

Walker, Thomas, 8, 43, 89, 94, 234

Walker, William, 287

Wall, [Julia], 245, 259, 263

Wall, William H., 245

Wanderer (ship), 287

Webb, Mrs., 98

Wells, Tom Henderson, 287

Wessells, Henry, 116, 154, 255, 267; informs Ellen of James's death, 225

Wessells, Mary, 116, 137, 146; dies, 154

West Point (U.S. Military Academy), 108, 289–95

Whipple, Bishop Henry, 23–24

White, E. K., 83, 85

Wilcox, Cadmus, 297

Wilcox, De Lafayette, 106, 151

Withlacoochee, Battle of, 19

Worth, William Jenkins, xxviii, 151–53, 164, 185, 189, 190, 195, 198, 259; final campaign against Seminoles, 161; description of, 182; and Mexican War, 215, 223, 226

wreckers, 238, 243, 249, 275–76

Wright, Benjamin D., xxvii–xxviii, 211

Young, Thomas, 220

Yulee, David Levy, xxvii, xxviii, 22, 44, 104, 175, 191, 193, 287, 289; nurses Charles Brown in Charleston, 149; portrait of, 22